Systemic Financial Risk

Alexander Karminsky · Mikhail Stolbov
Editors

Systemic Financial Risk

An Emerging Market Perspective

palgrave
macmillan

Editors
Alexander Karminsky
School of Finance
National Research University Higher School of Economics
Moscow, Russia

Mikhail Stolbov
MGIMO University
Moscow, Russia

ISBN 978-3-031-54808-6 ISBN 978-3-031-54809-3 (eBook)
https://doi.org/10.1007/978-3-031-54809-3

This Palgrave Macmillan imprint is published by the registered company Springer Nature Switzerland AG
The registered company address is: Gewerbestrasse 11, 6330 Cham, Switzerland

Paper in this product is recyclable.

Preface

The book aims to comprehensively study the sources and facets of systemic financial risk, which has turned into a salient feature of international finance and risk management since the Global Financial Crisis (GFC). Initially associated with advanced economies, currently systemic financial risk is underpinned to a significant extent by the financial sectors of major emerging market economies (EMEs). Nonetheless, the peculiarities of systemic risk in the EMEs have not been studied extensively. This collective monograph seeks to partly fill this research gap.

Apart from the focus on the EMEs, the novelty of our study consists in examining emerging forms and manifestations of systemic risk. Some of them can be originated in the non-financial sector, though significantly impacting financial institutions and eventually the economy as a whole. Against this backdrop, the monograph does not only cover well-entrenched issues related to systemic risk, but also includes chapters dealing with the emerging topics, e.g. catastrophic risk modeling, ESG-related risks, the systemic impact of airlines' insolvency, etc.

In Part 1, there is a collection of chapters considering emerging research issues in risk assessment and management. Namely, new approaches to measuring financial development, trends and prospects of green finance, and cross-country financial spillovers are discussed. Also, this part contains the findings of the research highlighting the relationships between ESG and systemic risk, household income dynamics and overall financial stability.

Part 2 casts a more nuanced look at the quantitative models and methods adopted in risk assessment and risk management, putting in the spotlight such issues as measuring catastrophic risks, liquidity mismatches as well as modeling probabilities of default and the impact of macroeconomic fundamentals on capital adequacy ratios in the Russian banking sector.

Finally, Part 3 pins down a number of new regulatory challenges dealing with risk assessment and risk management. Namely, macroprudential policies which have proved efficient to mitigate systemic risk are investigated. The international experience of the banks undertaking financial resolution/recovery is presented. Last but not least, the nature of digital systemic risk in the Russian financial sector is discussed.

Since the book encapsulates diverse research questions, one can obtain a comprehensive picture of the challenges which EMEs are facing in the field of systemic financial risk assessment and management. In most cases, the challenges are discussed in the context of elaborated models and policy responses, which are based on the up-to-date theoretical contributions and empirical evidence from various fields, i.e. financial econometrics, international finance, macroeconomics, risk management, etc. Therefore, we believe this eclectic approach in terms of the themes covered and methodologies used presents a significant advantage and value added of the collective monograph.

Thanks to the innovations in the topic coverage and rigorous methodological underpinning of all the chapters, the book can be of interest for both academics and practitioners. Namely, for university professors, Ph.D. and M.A. students, it offers a novel research perspective on systemic financial risk in the EMEs, whereas policymakers, central bankers, risk managers and even private investors may be interested in testing/implementing the models and policy implications discussed in its chapters.

Moscow, Russia

Alexander Karminsky
Mikhail Stolbov

Acknowledgements

We acknowledge the efforts and dedication of many people involved in working on this collective monograph. The ideas presented in the book largely build on the fruitful discussions during the annual workshop "Systemic risks in the financial sector" hosted by the National Research University Higher School of Economics since the year 2018. We are also grateful to those who helped us design the monograph, in particular to Andrey Egorov, Ekaterina Seryakova and Ella Khromova. We are indebted to the authors of the chapters as well as to the Dean of the Faculty of Economic Sciences at NRU HSE, Sergey E. Pekarsky, who has contributed to the organization and overall success of the workshop on systemic risks since its inaugural edition. We thank immensely the Palgrave Macmillan publishing team for their assistance and expert advice. In particular, we are grateful to Tula Weis for her patience and guidance. We cannot but also mention our partners, i.e. universities, banks, financial regulators where the contributing authors and editors of the monograph work: NRU HSE, Moscow State Institute of International Relations (MGIMO University), the Bank of Russia.

Contents

Editors and Contributors

About the Editors

Prof. Alexander Karminsky is a distinguished Russian scholar in the field of banking, risk management and innovations research. He authored a number of publications in international peer-reviewed journals and monographs published by Springer. Prof. Karminsky's profile on the HSE website is https://www.hse.ru/en/org/persons/3545842. His profile on Google Scholar is https://scholar.google.ru/citations?user=8422VDgAAAAJ&hl=ru

Prof. Mikhail Stolbov majors in the research on financial stability, systemic risk as well as green finance. He has a number of publications in leading peer-reviewed journals, both domestic and international. Prof. Stolbov's profile on the MGIMO University website is https://english.mgimo.ru/people/stolbov. His profile on Google Scholar is https://scholar.google.ru/citations?user=qT4JVvEAAAAJ&hl=ru

Contributors

Artur Akhmetov is the Head of Unit in the Research and Forecasting Department at the Bank of Russia. His professional fields include equities, bonds, derivatives, FX, market risk and country risk analysis. He has Ph.D. in Economics received from a leading Russian university in 2013. He is also a holder of FRM and CFA charters, received in 2015 and 2019, respectively.

Anna Burova is the Deputy Head of Economic Research Division in the Research and Forecasting Department at the Bank of Russia. She received her Ph.D. in 2018 from the University of Tokyo. She also got ACCA (2014) and FCCA (2019) charters. Her professional interests include socio-strategic engineering and corporate finance.

Sergey Dubinin is a well-known Russian Economist, former Minister of Finance (1994), Chairman of the Supervisory Board of VTB Bank (2011–2015 and 2016–2017) and Advisor to Capital Asset JSC. Now he is Head of the Finance and Credit Department of the Faculty of Economics at Lomonosov Moscow State University. He has published numerous scientific papers on the financial problems of the USA, Italy and the European Union as a whole.

Alexandra Egorova is a Senior Lecturer in the Faculty of Economic Sciences/School of Finance at HSE University. She is also a Research Assistant in the Laboratory of Financial Innovation and Risk Management at HSE University. Her scientific interests include risk management, ratings, environmental, social, and governance (ESG) criteria, sustainability, corporate governance and finance. She has published articles on ESG factors and ESG ratings in various journals, both in Russia and internationally.

Valeriy Gamukin is a Professor at the Financial and Economic Institute at University of Tyumen. He is a recognized scholar in the research on public finance sector risk and behavioral finance. He is the author of a number of publications in international peer-reviewed journals and monographs. Since 2010, he has been a member of the New Economic Association (Russia).

Nataliya Kovaleva is an Associate Professor at a leading university in Russia and a Research Fellow at the Institute of Financial Studies of the same University. The focus of her research is banking and banks' operations in financial markets. She has authored a number of scientific and methodological publications on the functioning of banks, their activity in financial markets and investment banking in both national and international peer-reviewed journals.

Konstantin Krinichansky is a Professor in the Department of Financial Markets and Financial Engineering at a leading Russian university. He also directs the master program "Financial Mathematics and Market Analysis" at this university. He is a scholar in the field of financial sector development and finance-growth nexus research. He has authored a number of publications in international peer-reviewed journals and monographs.

Natalia Makhankova is a Senior Economist in the Research and Forecasting Department at the Bank of Russia. She is interested in financial markets and corporate finance. She has a Master's degree in Economics received at the Moscow State University in 2020.

Elizaveta Markovskaya is Associate Professor in the Finance Department of the Higher School of Economics (HSE), one of the leading Russian economic research institutions. She combines practical activities in the fields of consulting and finance with research and lecturing activities. She is an author of more than 100 publications dedicated to various aspects of the Russian and international economy development as well as corporate finance.

Vigen Minasyan is a Professor at the Higher School of Finance and Management of the Russian Academy of National Economy and Public Administration, RANEPA. He is also the Head of the Department of Corporate Finance, Investment Design and Valuation, RANEPA. He is a well-known researcher in the field of risk management, quantitative finance and portfolio investment, teaching many disciplines in these areas. He is the author of numerous publications in international peer-reviewed journals as well as monographs. He is a participant in many international conferences and also the supervisor of seminars on quantitative methods in finance at RANEPA.

Olga Miroshnichenko is a Professor in the Department of Economics and Finance at University of Tyumen. She also heads the Master's Program in Financial Economics. She is a recognized scholar in the field of banking, banking regulation and sustainable development finance. She is the author of a number of publications in international peer-reviewed journals.

Svetlana Pertseva Ph.D. (Economics), is an Associate Professor in the Department of International Finance at MGIMO University. Payment system, digital finance and green financing have been in the focus of her research expertise since 2010. Her main research interests include the digital transformation of the national and global financial system.

Oksana Petrova is an Associate Professor of English Language and Professional Communications Department at a leading university in Russia. She has been teaching financial English to the students majoring in Economics and Finance for more than 20 years. Only during the past 10 years, she coauthored 16 publications in reputable peer-reviewed journals and 6 monographs along with a number of ESP textbooks.

Herman Petrov-Nerling is a Ph.D student in the Faculty of Economic Sciences/School of Finance and research-intern at the Laboratory of Financial Innovation and Risk Management at HSE University. His main scientific fields are: spatial economics and development, socio-economic development, energy transition and ESG studies. He is an author of publications devoted to sectoral economic analysis and influence of ESG factors on the companies' performance.

Onur Polat is a Full-time Associate Professor at Bilecik University and a Research Fellow at Global Labor Organization. His expertise spans Quantitative Finance, International Finance, Financial Econometrics, Energy Economics, Computational and Statistical Modelling. With a prolific research record published in renowned journals indexed in databases like JCR, Scopus and ABS, his work contributes to these fields. His latest research and publications are available in his website https://sites.google.com/view/onurpolat/opolat.

Alexey Ponomarenko is the Head of Economic Research Division in the Research and Forecasting Department at the Bank of Russia. He took his master's degree in economics at the NRU HSE (Moscow) in 2007 and Ph.D. at the University of Strasbourg in 2016. His research interests include monetary analysis, macro-financial linkages and banking in emerging market economies.

Ekaterina Seryakova is the Head of the Market Risk Management Division of Sberbank PJSC, with more than 7 years expertise in assessing and managing ALM risks. She holds Ph.D. in Economics (Finance, Money, Credit). The academic interests include systemic risk and macroprudential policy. Namely, her Ph.D. thesis and a number of articles published in Russian scientific journals are devoted to the development of macroprudential policy instruments and systemic risk assessment.

Elena Smolina has completed her Bachelor and Master's degrees at the Higher School of Economics. She currently holds a managerial position in the field of lending at Sberbank.

Anna Vityazeva is a third year Ph.D. student in the Department of International Finance at MGIMO University. Her research focuses on green finance market in Russia. She is interested in the prospects and challenges of financing green transition. She completed her bachelor's degree in international economic relations and her master's degree in financial instruments at MGIMO.

Maria Vyshkovskaia is a Credit Risk Analyst at Citibank. She holds B.A. degree in Finance from the University of Tyumen and M.S. degree in Corporate Finance from Lund University. She has published a number of articles in peer-reviewed journals on bank management and banking regulation. She has showcased her research at several international scientific conferences, including those held at Moscow State University and HSE.

List of Figures

List of Tables

PART I

New Trends in International Financial Development and Risk Assessment

CHAPTER 1

Adapted Approaches to Measuring Financial Development

Konstantin Krinichansky

1.1 Introduction

Financial markets and financial intermediaries play an increasingly significant role in today's economy. This chapter is devoted to finding arguments supporting the importance of finance for the economy. However, this importance will actually surface when we observe politicians' actions. This can be supported by the example of the sectoral sanctions introduced against the financial sectors of such countries as Iran, Venezuela, and Russia.

Obviously, finance is used as a weapon in the case; the imposed restrictions are aimed at weakening the economies of the sanctioned countries. Unlike the above example, the economic literature that studies the relationship between finance and growth is still far from reaching a consensus on a number of issues: the nature of this relationship (Owen & Temesvary, 2014), the direction of causality (Guptha & Rao, 2018; Levine et al., 2000), the transmission channels (Cournede et al., 2015; Krinichansky &

K. Krinichansky (✉)
Moscow, Russia
e-mail: kkrin@fa.ru

A. Karminsky and M. Stolbov (eds.), *Systemic Financial Risk*,
https://doi.org/10.1007/978-3-031-54809-3_1

Sergi, 2019), etc. With all the discussion that has been held, no one questions the benefits and opportunities financial development can bring (Ang, 2008; Arestis et al., 2015; Greenwood et al., 2013; Levine, 2005). At the same time, much uncertainty and contradiction arise when scholars try to answer the following: "What circumstances matter for these benefits and opportunities to outweigh the related risks and costs?" (Hassan et al., 2011; Henderson et al., 2013; Langfield & Pagano, 2016; Matei, 2020). The modern discussion is developing around such issues as the optimal financial structure (Beck et al., 2013; Benczúr et al., 2019; Chu Khan, 2020; Xu, 2021), safeguarding financial stability (Ehigiamusoe & Samsurijan, 2021; Hodula & Ngo, 2020; Law & Singh, 2014), and monetary conditions for financial development (Andolfatto et al., 2019; Champ & Boyd, 2006; Krinichansky & Annenskaya, 2020).

One should, however, note that despite the high theoretical and methodological level of the ongoing discussions, there remains a problem. It is about operationalizing and measuring financial development. It is this issue that our paper addresses. We explore the following null hypothesis: the characteristics of the relationship between financial depth and economic growth are stable and do not depend on the method of calculation of the financial depth.

The rest of this chapter is organized as follows. In Sect. 2, we undertake an overview of approaches to measuring financial development. Section 3 provides our view of the vulnerabilities of some of the approaches available. We also outline ways to mitigate these vulnerabilities. Section 4 presents an empirical analysis of the relationship between financial development and growth, in which we show the benefits of using adapted financial depth metrics eliminating some of the vulnerabilities of existing depth indicators. Section 5 summarizes our study.

1.2 Approaches to Measuring Financial Development

Efforts to derive accurate measures of financial development have been going on for over 50 years. The starting point is Raymond Goldsmith's seminal work "Financial Structure and Development" published in 1969. Prof. Goldsmith introduced an indicator of the value of financial intermediary assets divided by GNP assuming that the size of financial intermediaries is positively correlated with the quantity of financial services provided (Goldsmith, 1969). Robert King and Ross Levine offered a more sophisticated approach to such assessment. The authors didn't adopt the asset indicator and proposed 4 alternative metrics that are more suitable for measuring the dynamics of financial development. These indicators really approximate 3 dimensions of financial development fairly well, for example, expansion of financial systems accompanied by credit growth relative to GDP and others shown in Table 1.1.

The approach of King and Levine in terms of measuring the depth of financial system is still recognized as basic and is used to measure the financial development of individual countries and in cross-country studies related to the "finance – growth" nexus.

Later papers expanded the investigated statistics and the spectrum of financial development studied. Thus, in the work of R. Levine and S. Zervos (1998), the emphasis is on the indicators of the stock market that characterize its size, liquidity, and volatility. Their list is presented in Table 1.2

The novelty of Levine and Zervos's study is as follows. The indicators ceased to be predominantly built according to the depth model. Besides depth, the researchers became equipped with indicators that lay up claim to assess the efficiency of financial systems and their stability. They are designed to detect differentiation of markets in such parameters as turnover, liquidity, pricing efficiency, and excessive stock price volatility.

In the 1990s and 2000s, the number of studies utilizing financial development metrics grew exponentially. Various systematizations of such metrics were also proposed.

One of them is the 3 × 2 matrix, implicitly presented in the World Bank working paper of 2008 (Beck et al., 2008). The indicators used are

Table 1.1 Three dimensions of financial development

Topic	*The name of financial development indicator*	*Financial development dimension*
Depth	Liquid liabilities of the financial system/GDP	Expansion of lending
Structure	Deposit money bank domestic assets/ deposit money bank domestic assets plus central bank domestic assets	The growing role of commercial banks in comparison with the role of central banks
Depth	Claims on the nonfinancial private sector/GDP	The growing role of loans to private sector

Source King and Levine (1993)

Table 1.2 Stock market development indicators

Topic	*The name of financial development indicator*
Depth	Value of listed domestic shares/GDP
Efficiency	Value of the trades of domestic shares on domestic exchanges/value of listed domestic shares (Turnover)
Depth	Value of the trades of domestic shares on domestic exchanges/GDP (Value Traded)
Stability	Volatility of stock returns (Volatility)
Efficiency	International integration measures

Source Levine and Zervos (1998)

divided into 2 categories: those related to financial institutions and those related to financial markets. It is in that paper that the classification is proposed that uses such types of indicators as depth, efficiency, and access to finance. Later, this classification laid the foundation for working out the Financial Development Index by the IMF and the corresponding set of sub-indices (Svirydzenka, 2016).

An extended classification of indicators of financial development is a 4 × 2 matrix from the work of M. Čihák and his co-authors (Čihák et al., 2012, 2013), built, in turn, on the basis of the World Bank Economic Review article (Beck et al., 2010). Here, the indicators used are also split into the categories of financial institutions and financial markets[1] and also into topics, including "stability" in addition to depth, access, and efficiency. This classification is used to label indicators in the World Bank's Global Financial Development Database (GFDD).[2] Let's look at some of the characteristics from the recent version of this database, which was published on September 22, 2022.

The database contains the indicators of depth, access, efficiency, and stability of financial systems with reference to the groups "financial institutions" or "financial markets". The total number of indicators of access is 37, depth—30, efficiency—11, stability—8, 20 indicators belong to "others" group. Compared to the previous version of the dataset (published in 2019), the following changes occurred in the new version:

[1] In fact, in both cases we deal with markets: in the first case—financial services markets; in the second one—capital markets.

[2] World Bank (2022). Global Financial Development Database. https://www.worldbank.org/en/publication/gfdr/data/global-financial-development-database.

- Six indicators were adjusted. For example, the indicator measuring the gross portfolio equity assets to GDP was replaced by a similar indicator, the numerator of which takes into account assets not only in the form of corporate shares, but also in the form of investment funds shares (Gross Portfolio Equity & Investment Fund Shares Assets/GDP);
- For 23 indicators, the calculation procedure was changed. Thus, the calculation of the depth indicators was carried out in this edition of the GFDD without using the deflation method.
- The 3 new indicators appeared (see Table 1.3), including financial depth indicator such as the volume of loans provided by fintech and big tech companies to GDP (it's measured as a flow variable).[3]

Table 1.4 provides a set of the GFDD indicators. The first two lines include two types of measures—access and depth.

Table 1.3 New concepts of Global Financial Development Database

Topic	*Indicator's name*	*Short definition*	*Sources*
Depth	Credit flows by fintech and bigtech companies to GDP (%)	New lending provided by fintech and big tech companies over a calendar year, normalized by nominal GDP	Cornelli et al. (2020)
Other	Foreign bank assets among total banks assets (%)	Percent of the banking system's assets was in banks that were foreign-controlled (i.e., where foreigners owned 50% or more equity)	World Bank Bank Regulation and Supervision Survey
Other	Government bank assets among total bank assets (%)	Percent of the banking system's assets was in banks that were government-controlled (i.e., where government owned 50% or more equity)	World Bank Regulation and Supervision Survey

Source World Bank (2022). Global Financial Development Database

[3] Available data on fintech and big tech credit volumes for a large number of countries around the world were collected by (Cornelli et al., 2020).

Table 1.4 Financial institutions and financial markets indicators balance

	Financial institutions	*Financial markets*
Access	• Bank accounts per 1,000 adults • Bank branches per 100,000 adults • Small firms with a bank loan or line of credit (%) • Saved any money in the past year (% age 15+) • Made digital payments in the past year (% age 15+) • Investments financed by banks (%)	• Value traded excluding top 10 traded companies to total value traded (%) • Market capitalization excluding top 10 companies to total market capitalization (%) • Nonfinancial corporate bonds to total bonds and notes outstanding (%)
Depth	• Private credit by deposit money banks to GDP (%) • Deposit money banks' assets to GDP (%) • Nonbank financial institutions' assets to GDP (%) • Domestic credit to private sector (% of GDP)	• Stock market capitalization to GDP (%) • Stock market total value traded to GDP (%) • Outstanding domestic private debt securities to GDP (%) • Corporate bond issuance volume to GDP (%) • Corporate bond average maturity (years)
Efficiency	• Bank net interest margin (%) • Bank lending-deposit spread • Bank noninterest income to total income (%) • Bank overhead costs to total assets (%) • Bank return on assets (%, after tax) • Bank return on equity (%, after tax)	• Stock market turnover ratio (%)
Stability	• Bank Z-score • Bank nonperforming loans to gross loans (%) • Bank capital to total assets (%) • Bank regulatory capital to risk-weighted assets (%) • Liquid assets to deposits and short-term funding (%)	• Stock price volatility

Source World Bank (2022). Global Financial Development Database

Access indicators have an important advantage over the other groups of measures, since, in fact, they directly indicate the level of financial development. Depth indicators are often misleading, as, for example, some developing countries which do not have a long history and enough experience in the development of financial markets enjoy higher depth indicators than more developed ones. Access indicators are free of such distortions.

For example, it is doubtful that China's rapidly increasing financial depth, ahead of many developed economies today, is a boon for the country's long-term economic growth. At least, the recent actions of the People's Bank of China increasingly testify to the fact that the regulator sees a threat in the overheating of some sectors and seeks to cool the market, although so far this does not lead to a decrease in its depth indicators.

Another advantage of access indicators is that they are convenient for tracking the overcoming of frictions that hinder financial development and, as a result, impede growth. In addition, access indicators are convenient for tracking the rate of adoption of financial innovations by economies. It is among the access indicators that the indicators related to the development of fintech appear for the first time.

Rows 3 and 4 of Table 1.4 contain some proxies for assessing financial systems' efficiency and stability from the GFDD. There is a kind of imbalance between pools of measures for financial institutions and financial markets, namely, when characterizing financial markets there is just one indicator of efficiency and one indicator of stability. Analyzing the literature that served as a basis for the formation of the GFDD, it can be noted that the World Bank doesn't use some of the indicators contained in the papers that appeared before the GFDD was created (in particular, one can mention [Čihák et al., 2013]). So, there were 8 efficiency indicators related to financial markets in that paper. World Bank didn't include in the GFDD the following indicators:

- Price synchronicity (co-movement)
- Private information trading
- Price impact
- Liquidity/transaction costs
- Quoted bid-ask spread for government bonds
- Turnover of bonds (private, public) on securities exchange
- Settlement efficiency.

Thus, a number of important indicators that characterize debt market as well as those that assess the efficiency of the settlement infrastructure are overlooked. Also, the indicator of stability related to financial markets is the only measure in this database. This is the stock market volatility. The other nine of the previously proposed indicators are not included in the considered database, among them volatility of sovereign bond index; two skewness coefficients applying to stock index and sovereign bond index; vulnerability to manipulation of profit when calculating the P/E ratio; duration; ratios of short-term to total bonds (domestic and international); share of short-term debt in the total amount of bonds issued; etc.

Besides, the disadvantages of approaches followed by international financial organizations to measure financial development include the fact that the set of metrics they propose does not contain the metrics tracking the state of a financial structure and the way it tends to change. We leave the issue of the development of structural measures of financial development for the next stage of our study.

1.3 Distortions of Financial Development Assessments

This section discusses some broader challenges of using indicators of financial development. An analysis of the available literature reveals the following. The first issue is that the conclusions the authors draw on the basis of theoretical models, i.e., that financial sector development has a positive impact on output growth, are not always supported by empirical studies. In particular, a large number of empirical works find a negative relationship between finance and growth. For example, Ram (1999) found that the correlation between financial development and economic growth was weakly negative or insignificant. Similar patterns are observed when regression analysis is performed for each individual country and for each sample grouped by growth rate. Garretsen et al. (2004) found that once the Levine and Zervos (1998) model is extended by adding the regressors that proxy legal and social factors, the positive relationship between stock markets and economic growth disappears. Rioja and Valev (2004) and Gründler (2021) have shown that the impact of financial development on economic growth varies for different groups of countries with different levels of financial development.

It is noteworthy that as far as the relationship between financial development and economic growth is concerned, different researchers have obtained rather controversial results, even using the same indicators. Naturally, they have also reached ambiguous conclusions using different indicators.

The above remark mainly concerns the use of indicators related to bank intermediation versus the indicators representing liquid capital markets. So, in a recent study by Cave et al. (2020), a steady negative relationship between the development of the banking sector and economic growth is found, whereas the effect of the stock market development on economic growth is positive.

Finally, problems arise when it turns out that the relationship between finance and growth is nonlinear. Nonlinearity requires explanation and interpretation. It's important to understand whether the nonlinearity is of a purely economic nature, or whether it is caused by methodological faults, or by the incorrectly calculated indicators of financial development. Beck et al. (2014) offer a number of arguments, explaining the emergence of nonlinearity in the relationship between finance and growth, which are difficult to dispute. Here are some of those arguments: the procyclical nature of credit, structural changes, and imprudent or hasty liberalization. Understanding the economic meaning of nonlinearity is good news, but it can be noted that the multiple explanations for the causes of nonlinearity only complicate the interpretation of the assessment results and the development of adequate policy measures.

Turning to criticism of individual indicators and methods of their calculation, we believe that many indicators of financial development the way they are built and used (up to the present time) do not fully meet their goals (in the sense of capturing financial development). Let's take, for instance, such depth indicators as "Stock market capitalization to GDP" and "Trading volume to GDP". How well do they reflect alterations in financial development? They will certainly be sensitive to improvements in the organization and operation of the capital market infrastructure. Reforms that include improved regulation and legislation (e.g., in terms of disclosure and countering unfair trading practices) also have a positive effect on market size or liquidity indicators. But at the same time, both size and liquidity dynamics are sensitive to a large number of other factors such as monetary policy, real interest rates, and capital account flows. These factors are not easy to control for in the panel data models. But, probably, the main drawback of individual depth indicators is that they are aimed (as intended by their developers) at capturing the effect of the size or saturation of the economy with funds streamed through the financial market channels (e.g., loans to GDP or stock market capitalization to GDP), and they suffer from the bias brought about by poor credit, bubbles, and volatility shocks that hit stock markets from time to time.

At the present time there seems to be two ways of improving the indicators, namely to perfect the methods of building certain types of FDIs and to expand the range of indicators categorized as FDIs (see Fig. 1.1).

In this paper, we focus on adjusting the financial depth metric. The formula (1.1) of the most common financial depth indicator is the following expression:

$$FD_t = \frac{0.5 \times \left({}^{PC_t}/{}_{CPI_t} + {}^{PC_{t-1}}/{}_{CPI_{t-1}} \right)}{{}^{GDP_t}/{}_{\overline{CPI_t}}} \tag{1.1}$$

FD_t—Private credit by deposit money banks in period t (the financial depth indicator); CPI_t—end of period value of the consumer price index; $\overline{CPI_t}$—annual average consumer price index in period t; GDP_t—country's economic output in period t.

Equation (1.2) demonstrates a simple approach to adjusting the taken indicator of financial development. Given the negative effect bad loans may have on growth, it is required to apply an adjustment multiplier. It is proposed to use the indicator of the share of nonperforming loans in the total credit portfolio as a component for such a multiplier:

$$FD_t^{adj} = FD_t \times (1 - NPL_t) \tag{1.2}$$

NPL_t—bank nonperforming loans to total gross loans in period t.

Further, let's review some suggestions for adjusting several of the most frequently used financial development indicators in addition to "Private credit to GDP". Domestic private debt securities indicator can be adjusted through the use of the following information:

- on corporate bond default rate;
- on speculative-grade corporate default rate;
- on foreign-currency denominated debt in total corporate debt.

Public debt to GDP ratio can be adjusted on the basis of:

- the annual average 5-year sovereign CDS spread;
- the rationed amount of "fiscal space".

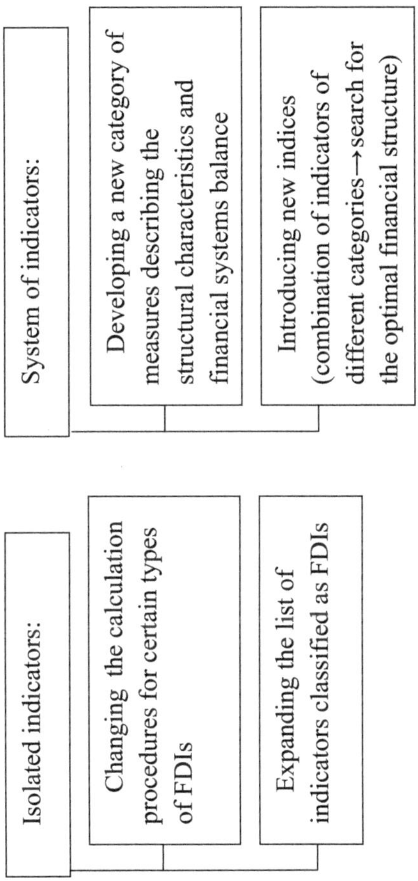

Fig. 1.1 Ways of improving the system of financial development indicators

Stock market capitalization to GDP can be adjusted using a stock return volatility-based adjustment term. Another suggested solution is an adjustment that considers the behavioral factor and the threat of collapse of an asset price bubble. For instance, new indicators related to stock market capitalization should reflect the effect of increasing share of hi-tech sector in the structure of the stock market indices or momentum effect. With regard to improving the system of indicators, the main message is as follows.

Financial development cannot be successful (bearing in mind its potential impact on long-run economic growth) if only one part of the financial system, the banking sector or the capital market, is developing well, while the other one is lagging behind in its development. Concerted efforts are required to develop both sectors. Some empiricists solved this issue by including both factors in their models. In our opinion, it is promising to add the metrics that track the structural characteristics and financial systems balance into the FDIs system. These indicators may include the following[4]:

- Securities market outstandings to broad money ratio;
- The ratio of the stock market capitalization to the private credit by deposit money banks;
- Bank credit to the sum of bank credit plus total equity and bond market capitalization ratio;
- Loans and bonds held by banks/nonbanks relative to the overall financial sector (the first four are proxies for the relative importance bank-based/market-based intermediation and the balance between the direct and the indirect financing markets);
- Ratio of assets held by the top three banks to those held by banks (a proxy for the bank asset concentration);
- Stock of foreign corporate debt to total corporate debt (a proxy for the finance opening and access to external finance);
- Gross foreign bank loans stock to GDP (the last two are the proxies for the finance opening and access to external finance); etc.

It is also appropriate to develop new metrics of this type.

[4] The indicators considered here are used by some researchers. For instance, Lynch (1996), Brei et al. (2018), Benczúr et al. (2019), and others.

Another possible solution is designing new financial development indices, which can be built on the basis of combinations of various types of indicators and serve as a basis for finding the optimal financial structure.

Gould and Melecky (2017) find that the strategy followed by developing countries in Europe and Central Asia, which consists in supporting the development of the banking sector while their capital markets remain weak, is erroneous. They propose to seek well-balanced solutions, taking into account the negative mutual influence between the increase in the access to financial services and the improvement in stability.

To comment on our proposals to enhance the system of indicators of global financial development (see Table 1.5), let us focus on two points. The first point concerns the group of indicators that are not included in the four types (from depth to stability), but are classified as "others". One of these indicators is the banking crisis dummy, which is included in the GFDD on the basis of the study "Systemic Banking Crises Revisited" by Laeven and Valencia (2018). Along with this, it is advisable to add the dummy of debt crisis. In this respect, I would like to draw attention to the methodology and results recently obtained by Mitchener and Trebesch (2021).

The authors keep a record of debt crises, in which a debt crisis is recognized as a period when sovereign bond yield spread (in relation to the benchmark) exceeds 1000 basis points in a quarter and/or when yield

Table 1.5 Expansion of the system of global financial development indicators

Indicators available in GFDD	*Suggested additional indicator*
Financial institutions	
Banking crisis dummy (1 = banking crisis, 0 = none) (GFDD.OI.19)	• Debt crisis dummy according to the concept "debt crises without default" (Mitchener & Trebesch, 2021)
Financial markets	
Domestic private debt securities to GDP (GFDD.DM.03)	• Flow Indicator for private sector debt securities
Public debt securities to GDP (GFDD.DM.04)	• Flow indicator for public sector debt securities
Stock market capitalization to GDP (GFDD.DM.01)	Flow indicator for corporate stocks

Source Author's suggestions

spreads increase too quickly, which is defined as an increase in the spread by 378 basis points or higher over the year.

In addition, a promising area of expanding the taxonomy of World Bank FDIs is the collection and publication of datasets on indicators of financial depth, in which the GDP-weighted variables will not only represent the amounts outstanding of bonds or stock market capitalization, but also amounts of new issuances in the respective years. That is, not only stock variables are of interest, but also flow variables.

1.4 Empirical Analysis of the Relationship Between Financial Development and Growth with Adjusted Depth Metrics

In this section of the chapter, the results of an empirical analysis carried out using traditional and adjusted financial depth metrics are presented. The first step is to describe the data and the model. The indicator of interest is the most commonly used financial development indicator—private credit by deposit money banks to GDP ratio.

Source data are obtained from the World Bank's World Development Indicators (WDI) and GFDD databases and the International Financial Statistics of the IMF. Our study covers the 18-year period (2000–2017). The author exploits a broad panel of countries (94). Table 1.6 provides the notations and description of the explanatory variables used.

Table 1.6 Notation and transformations of employed variables

Short notation	*Description of the series used for the econometric exercise*
FD	Logarithm of private bank credit to GDP
$(FD)^2$	Square of *FD*
inϒ	Logarithm of GDP per capita
Infl	The inverse hyperbolic sign transformation of inflation
Inv	Logarithm of investment (gross capital formation) to GDP
TO	Logarithm of trade openness (exports and imports to GDP)
GE	Logarithm of government consumption to GDP
Sch	Logarithm of gross enrollment ratio in secondary education

For starters, the data on the "Loans to GDP" indicator from the WDI[5] were borrowed and the model was estimated with the help of this measure. Then, the data on the volume of bank lending to the private sector were sampled from the IMF database.[6] The values of this indicator for all countries, included in the sample, over all the years of observations were adjusted using formula (Eq. 1.2).

Data on bank nonperforming loans to total loans ratios were taken from the GFDD database (Indicator Code: GFDD.SI.02). The properties of the dependence of economic growth on financial depth were explored using the OLS and GMM techniques.

The GMM model has been the most frequently used in the analysis of the relationship between finance and growth over the past 20 years. The dynamic panel regressions use lagged realizations of the explanatory variables as internal instruments.

Beck (2008) points out that "this method control for weak exogeneity, which means that current realizations of variables can be affected by current and past realizations of the growth rate, but must be uncorrelated with future realizations of the error term.

Thus, under the weak exogeneity assumption, future innovations of the growth rate do not affect current financial development". Thus, this method better controls for the endogeneity and overcomes the issues of omitted variables compared, for example, with cross-sectional IV regressions used in cross-country studies. In our study, we apply the system GMM estimator (Arellano & Bover, 1995; Blundell & Bond, 1998).

The system consists of the stacked regressions in differences and levels, with the moment conditions applied to the regressions in differences (Eq. 1.3) (the first part of the system) and the moment conditions applied to the regressions in levels (Eq. 1.4) (the second part).

$$
\begin{aligned}
&E\left[\Delta f(i,t-s)'(\Delta\varepsilon(i,t)+\mu(i))\right]=0,\ \text{for each } t=3,\ldots T,\ \mathrm{s}\geq 2\\
&E\left[\Delta C(i,t-s)'(\Delta\varepsilon(i,t)+\mu(i))\right]=0,\ \text{for each } t=3,\ldots T,\ \mathrm{s}\geq 2\\
&E\left[\Delta y(i,t-s)'(\Delta\varepsilon(i,t)+\mu(i))\right]=0,\ \text{for each } t=3,\ldots T,\ \mathrm{s}\geq 2,
\end{aligned}
\tag{1.3}
$$

[5] World Bank (2022). World Development Indicators Database. https://databank.worldbank.org/source/world-development-indicators.

[6] See the electronic version of the IMF's International Financial Statistics. Private credit by deposit money banks and other financial institutions (IFS line 22d and FOSAOP). https://data.imf.org/?sk=4c514d48-b6ba-49ed-8ab9-52b0c1a0179b.

where f and C—weakly exogenous explanatory variables; y—dependent variable; $\varepsilon(i,t)$ and $\mu\ (i)$—error terms; $\Delta x(t) = x(t) - x(t-1)$.

$$\begin{aligned} &E\big[f(i,t-s)'\Delta\varepsilon(i,t)\big] = 0, \text{ for each } t = 3,\ldots T,\ s \geq 2 \\ &E\big[C(i,t-s)'\Delta\varepsilon(i,t)\big] = 0, \text{ for each } t = 3,\ldots T,\ s \geq 2 \\ &E\big[y(i,t-s)'\Delta\varepsilon(i,t)\big] = 0, \text{ for each } t = 3,\ldots T,\ s \geq 2. \end{aligned} \tag{1.4}$$

The equation estimated by the system GMM in our study is written as follows:

$$\begin{aligned} \Delta GDPpc_{it} &= \alpha + \beta_1 \Delta GDPpc_{it-1} + \beta_2 \Delta GDPpc_{it-2} + \beta_3 \Delta FD_{it} \\ &+ \beta_4 (\Delta FD_{it})^2 + \beta_5 \Delta InY_i + \beta_6 \Delta Infl + \beta_7 \Delta Sch_{it} \\ &+ \beta_8 \Delta TO_{it} + \beta_9 \Delta GE_{it} + \mu_i + \Delta\varepsilon_{it}, \end{aligned} \tag{1.5}$$

where *GDPpc* is the logarithm of growth rate of real *GDP* per capita; the other variables are described in Table 1.6; i, t—indices indicating the year and the country, $i \in \{1, 2,\ldots, N\}$, $t \in \{1,2,\ldots, T\}$; β_j—the estimated coefficients; μ and ε—the regression residuals.

The model is estimated in a two-step GMM procedure.

Table 1.7 presents the results of the OLS estimations. Columns 2 and 3 contain the estimates of the regression parameters with the base indicator "Credits to GDP", and Columns 4 and 5—with the adjusted indicator. It can be seen that the values of the coefficients of the financial variable are positive in all the models. At the same time, their size and significance are higher in the models where the assessment is carried out using adjusted data for the depth variable.

Comparing the results recorded in columns 2 and 4, one can note that the coefficient of the variable of interest changes its sign from minus to plus, but remains statistically insignificant.

The analysis of the models with a quadratic term shows the following. The model run with the unadjusted credit depth variable suggests that the relationship between finance and growth may be nonlinear and it has an inverted U-shape.

However, the model using the adjusted indicator does not show this kind of nonlinearity. Both coefficients for the financial variable turn out positive, while only one of them namely the quadratic term is significant (Table 1.8).

Table 1.7 Pooled models (OLS estimation)

Variable	*Models with baseline indicator*		*Models with adjusted indicator*	
	Linear model	*Quadratic model*	*Linear model*	*Quadratic model*
1	2	3	4	5
FD	0.025^{*} (0.095)	0.014 (0.371)	0.076^{***} (0.000)	0.070^{***} (0.000)
$(FD)^2$		0.046^{***} (0.005)		0.025 (0.111)
inY	-0.109^{***} (0.000)	-0.103^{***} (0.000)	-0.108^{***} (0.000)	-0.104^{***} (0.000)
Inf	0.022 (0.589)	0.006 (0.875)	0.010 (0.804)	0.001 (0.972)
Inv	0.364^{***} (0.000)	0.378^{***} (0.000)	0.325^{***} (0.000)	0.335^{***} (0.000)
TO	0.107^{***} (0.000)	0.102^{***} (0.000)	0.112^{***} (0.000)	0.110^{***} (0.000)
GE	-0.154^{***} (0.003)	-0.146^{***} (0.004)	-0.161^{***} (0.002)	-0.159^{***} (0.002)
Sch	0.105^{*} (0.056)	0.090 (0.104)	0.119^{**} (0.028)	0.114^{**} (0.036)
const	0.102 (0.631)	0.016 (0.939)	0.167 (0.427)	0.100 (0.633)

Notes p-value in parentheses. $^{***}p < 0.01$, $^{**}p < 0.05$, $^{*}p < 0.10$

1.5 Conclusion

The existing consensus on theoretical arguments in favor of the positive impact of financial development on economic growth, given contradictory empirical results, suggests that the issue of the actual finance-growth nexus properties remains an empirical issue. In this respect, it is very important to make sure that the assessment methods used are reliable, and the data intended to characterize financial development are really suitable for this aim. In this study, we have adjusted the data on financial depth, subtracting the stock of loans that is usually called "bad loans" from the outstanding claims of financial institutions on the private sector, because, definitely, such loans do not indicate financial development, and they often signal about certain overheating in credit markets.

We obtained the following key result. After the adjustment made, the coefficients on the financial depth variable either become more economically and statistically significant (as it turned out in the pooled models), or become positive (in the models estimated using system GMM). Moreover, in the latter case, the model itself loses its properties of nonlinearity.

Table 1.8 System GMM estimation

Variable	*Models with baseline indicator*		*Models with adjusted indicator*	
	Linear model	*Quadratic model*	*Linear model*	*Quadratic model*
L1	0.166^{**} (0.026)	0.152^{**} (0.024)	0.134^{**} (0.049)	0.122^{*} (0.083)
L2	-0.158^{***} (0.000)	-0.160^{***} (0.000)	-0.173^{***} (0.000)	-0.170^{***} (0.000)
FD	−0.040 (0.325)	−0.050 (0.136)	0.039 (0.243)	0.025 (0.506)
$(FD)^2$		0.062^{**} (0.039)		0.057^{**} (0.032)
inY	−0.032 (0.806)	−0.047 (0.727)	−0.063 (0.672)	-0.070^{*} (0.540)
Inf	−0.079 (0.355)	−0.071 (0.352)	−0.083 (0.284)	−0.085 (0.243)
Inv	1.386^{***} (0.004)	1.355^{**} (0.011)	1.272^{***} (0.000)	1.260^{***} (0.001)
TO	0.582^{*} (0.095)	0.547^{*} (0.070)	0.656^{*} (0.069)	0.634 (0.108)
GE	−0.945 (0.141)	−0899 (0.174)	−1.004 (0.268)	−0.990 (0.127)
Sch	−0.648 (0.247)	−0.582 (0.261)	−0.542 (0.282)	−0.476 (0.351)
Const	−2.009 (0.440)	−1.980 (0.377)	−1.787 (0.365)	−1.826 (0.302)
AR(1) (*p*-value)	0.000	0.000	0.000	0.000
AR(2) (*p*-value)	0.248	0.346	0.438	0.528
Sargan test (*p*-value)	1.0	1.0	1.0	1.0

Notes *p*-value in parentheses (Robust Windmeijer standard errors). $^{***}p < 0.01$, $^{**}p < 0.05$, $^{*}p < 0.10$

Thus, the null hypothesis formulated in the Introduction is rejected in favor of the alternative hypothesis. We can assert that the features of the relationship between financial depth and economic growth crucially depend on the method of calculation of the financial depth. At the same time, the adjustment of the credit to GDP indicator with subtracting the nonperforming loans from gross loans allows us to provide the evidence of a positive relationship between finance and economic growth while analyzing relevant econometric models.

References

Andolfatto, D., Berentsen, A., & Martin, F. M. (2019). Money, banking and financial markets. *Review of Economic Studies*. Oxford University Press, *87*(5), 2049–2086. https://doi.org/10.20955/wp.2017.023

Ang, J. B. (2008). A survey of recent developments in the literature of finance and growth. *Journal of Economic Surveys, 22*, 536–576. https://doi.org/10.1111/j.1467-6419.2007.00542.x

Arcand, J. L., Berkes, E., & Panizza, U. (2015). Too much finance? *Journal of Economic Growth, 20*(2), 105–148. https://doi.org/10.1007/s10887-015-9115-2

Arestis, P., Chortareas, G., & Magkonis, G. (2015). The financial development and growth Nexus: A meta-analysis. *Journal of Economic Surveys, 29*(3), 549–565. https://doi.org/10.1111/joes.12086

Arellano, M., & Bover, O. (1995). Another look at the instrumental variable estimation of error-components models. *Journal of Econometrics, 68*, 29–52. https://doi.org/10.1016/0304-4076(94)01642-d

Beck, T. (2008). *The econometrics of finance and growth* (Policy Research Working Paper No. 4608). World Bank, Washington, DC. https://openknowledge.worldbank.org/handle/10986/6703

Beck, T., Demirgüç-Kunt, A., & Levine, R. (2010). Financial institutions and markets across countries and over time: The updated financial development and structure database. *The World Bank Economic Review, 24*(1), 77–92. http://www.jstor.org/stable/40647421.

Beck, T., Demirgüç-Kunt, A., & Singer, D. (2013). Is small beautiful? Financial structure, size and access to finance. *World Development, 52*, 19–33. https://doi.org/10.1016/j.worlddev.2013.05.014

Beck, T., Feyen, E., Ize, A., & Moizeszowicz, F. (2008). *Benchmarking financial development* (Policy Research Working Paper No. 4638). World Bank.

Beck, R., Georgiadis, G., & Straub, R. (2014). The finance and growth nexus revisited. *Economics Letters, 124*, 382–385.

Benczúr, P., Karagiannis, S., & Kvedaras V. (2019, December). Finance and economic growth: Financing structure and non-linear impact. *Journal of Macroeconomics, 62*, 103048. https://doi.org/10.1016/j.jmacro.2018.08.001

Blundell, R., & Bond, S. (1998). Initial conditions and moment restrictions in dynamic panel data models. *Journal of Econometrics, Elsevier, 87*(1), 115–143. https://doi.org/10.1016/s0304-4076(98)00009-8

Brei, M., Ferri, G., & Gambacorta L. (2018, November). *Financial structure and income inequality* (BIS Working Papers No. 756).

Cave, J., Chaudhuri, K., & Kumbhakar, S. C. (2020). Do banking sector and stock market development matter for economic growth? *Empirical Economics, 59*(4), 1513–1535. Springer.

Champ, B. A., & Boyd, J. H. (2006, May 15). Inflation, banking, and economic growth. *Economic Commentary*, Federal Reserve Bank of Cleveland.

Čihak, M., Demirguc-Kunt, A., & Feyen, E., Levine R. (2012). *Benchmarking financial systems around the world*(World Bank Policy Research Working Paper 6175), World Bank, 1–56. https://doi.org/10.1596/1813-9450-6175.

Čihák, M., Demirgüç-Kunt, A., Feyen, E., & Levine, R. (2013). Financial development in 205 economies, 1960 to 2010. *Journal of Financial Perspectives, 1*(2), 17–36.

Chu Khan, L. (2020, March). Financial structure and economic growth nexus revisited. *Borsa Istanbul Review, 20*(1), 24–36. https://doi.org/10.1016/j.bir.2019.08.003

Cornelli, G., Frost, J., Gambacorta, L., Rau, R., Wardrop, R., & Ziegler, T. (2020, September). *Fintech and big tech credit: A new database* (BIS Working Papers, No. 887).

Cournede, B., Denk, O., & Hoeller, P. (2015). *Finance and inclusive growth* (OECD Economic Policy Paper, No. 14). https://doi.org/10.2139/ssrn.2649801

Ehigiamusoe, K. U., & Samsurijan, M. S. (2021). What matters for finance-growth nexus? A critical survey of macroeconomic stability, institutions, financial and economic development. *International Journal of Finance & Economics, 26*(4), 5302–5320. https://doi.org/10.1002/ijfe.2066

Garretsen, H., Lensink, R., & Sterken, E. (2004). Growth, financial development, societal norms and legal institutions. *Journal of International Financial Markets, Institutions and Money, 14*, 165–183

Goldsmith, R. W. (1969). *Financial structure and development*. Yale University Press.

Gould, D. M., & Melecky, M. (2017). *Risks and returns: Managing financial trade-offs for inclusive growth in Europe and Central Asia*. World Bank, Washington, DC. https://openknowledge.worldbank.org/handle/10986/25494

Greenwood, J., Sanchez, J. M., & Wang, C. (2013). Quantifying the impact of financial development on economic development. *Review of Economic Dynamic, 16*, 194–215. https://doi.org/10.1016/j.red.2012.07.003

Gründler, K. (2021). The vanishing effect of finance on economic development. *Macroeconomic Dynamics, 25*(2), 536–578. https://doi.org/10.1017/S1365100519000312

Guptha, K. S. K., & Rao, R. P. (2018). The causal relationship between financial development and economic growth: An experience with BRICS economies. *Journal of Social and Economic Development, 20*(2), 308–326. https://doi.org/10.1007/s40847-018-0071-5

Hassan, M. K., Sanchez, B., & Yu, J. S. (2011). Financial development and economic growth. *The Quarterly Review of Economics and Finance, 51*(1), 88–104. https://doi.org/10.1016/j.qref.2010.09.001

Henderson, D. J., Papageorgiou, C., & Parmeter, C. F. (2013). Who benefits from financial development? New methods, new evidence. *European Economic Review, 63*, 47–67. https://doi.org/10.1016/j.euroecorev.2013.05.007

Hodula, M., & Ngo, N. A. (2020). *Finance, growth and (macro)prudential policy: European evidence* (Working Papers 2020/2). Czech National Bank. https://www.cnb.cz/export/sites/cnb/en/economic-research/.galleries/research_publications/cnb_wp/cnbwp_2020_02.pdf https://ideas.repec.org/p/cnb/wpaper/2020-2.html

Krinichansky, K., & Sergi, B. S. (2019). Financial development and economic growth in Russia. In Bruno S. Sergi (Eds.),*Modeling economic growth in contemporary Russia*. Emerald Publishing. https://doi.org/10.1108/978-1-78973-265-820191001

Krinichansky, K. V., & Annenskaya, N. E. (2020). Monetary conditions of financial development. *Finance and Credit, 26*(2), 349–368. https://doi.org/10.24891/fc.26.2.349

Langfield, S., & Pagano, M. (2016). Bank bias in Europe: Effects on systemic risk and growth. *Economic Policy, 31*(85), 51–106. https://doi.org/10.1093/epolic/eiv019

Law, S. H., & Singh, N. (2014). Does too much finance harm economic growth? *Journal of Banking & Finance, 41*(C), 36–44. https://doi.org/10.1016/j.jbankfin.2013.12.020

Laeven, L., & Valencia, F. (2018). *Systemic banking crises revisited, IMF WP/18/206.* https://www.imf.org/en/Publications/WP/Issues/2018/09/14/Systemic-Banking-Crises-Revisited-46232

Levine, R., Loayza, N., & Beck, T. (2000). Financial intermediation and growth: Causality and causes. *Journal of Monetary Economics, 46*(1), 31–77. https://doi.org/10.1016/S0304-3932(00)00017-9

Levine, R. (2005). Finance and growth: Theory and evidence. In P. Aghion and Steven N. Durlauf (Eds.), *Handbook of economic growth* (pp. 865–934). Elsevier. https://doi.org/10.1016/S1574-0684(05)01012-9

Lynch, D. (1996). Measuring financial sector development: A study of selected Asia-Pacific countries. *The Developing Economies, 34*(1), 1–27. https://doi.org/10.1111/j.1746-1049.1996.tb00727.x

Matei, I. (2020). Is financial development good for economic growth? Empirical insights from emerging European countries. *Quantitative Finance and Economics, 4*(4), 653–678. https://doi.org/10.3934/QFE.2020030

Mitchener, K. J., & Trebesch, C. (2021). *Sovereign debt in the 21st century: Looking backward, looking forward* (CESifo Working Paper No. 8959), CESifo, Munich. https://www.cesifo.org/en/publikationen/2021/working-paper/sovereign-debt-21st-century-looking-backward-looking-forward

Owen, A. L., & Temesvary, J. (2014). Heterogeneity in the growth and finance relationship: How does the impact of bank finance vary by country and type of lending? *International Review of Economics and Finance, 31*, 275–288. https://doi.org/10.1016/j.iref.2014.02.007

Ram, R. (1999). Financial development and economic growth: additional evidence. *Journal of Development Studies, 35*, 164–174.

Svirydzenka, K. (2016). *Introducing a new broad-based index of financial development* (IMF Working Paper WP/16/5), International Monetary Fund. https://doi.org/10.5089/9781513583709001

World Bank. (2022). *Global financial development database*. https://www.worldbank.org/en/publication/gfdr/data/global-financial-development-database.

Xu, G. (2021). Reassessing the literature on the relationship between financial structure and economic growth. *Review of Economics, 72*(2), 149–182. https://doi.org/10.1515/roe-2021-0016

CHAPTER 2

Green Finance: Trends, Risks and Regulation

Svetlana Pertseva and Anna Vityazeva

2.1 Introduction

The issues of sustainable development and green financing are an urgent agenda today. The key mechanism for solving these issues is placing green securities on the financial market. Green instruments are an innovative method of financing targeted environmental projects. The theoretical basis of sustainable development is the concept of a green economy, which explains the correlation between economic growth and the state of the environment.

The green economy concept was first coined in the late 1980s by Pearce et al. (1989) in their widely known report "Blueprint for a Green Economy" and the first attempt to conceptualize the green economy

S. Pertseva (✉)
Department of International Finance, MGIMO University, Moscow, Russia
e-mail: sup.05@mail.ru

A. Vityazeva
MGIMO University, Moscow, Russia
e-mail: annavityazeva@inbox.ru

A. Karminsky and M. Stolbov (eds.), *Systemic Financial Risk*,
https://doi.org/10.1007/978-3-031-54809-3_2

occurred two years later by Jacobs (1991) in his book “The Green Economy”. In recent years, research on green finance and energy policy has attracted more and more attention from scholars.

Some scholars have set up a framework for green finance and defined green finance (Zadek & Flynn, 2013; Lindenberg, 2014; Taghizadeh-Hesary & Yoshino, 2019; Wang & Zhi, 2016; Zhang et al., 2019; Hafner et al., 2020). At the same time, creating a green economic system is impossible without a stable system of green financing, where one of the most effective tools is the issuance of green bonds.

Green finance will solve both the current problems associated with the coronavirus pandemic and the global challenges of sustainable development and environmental protection. The capacity of the international market of green financing is still relatively small, but, according to experts, it is very promising. At the same time, the analysis of further prospects for its development requires a more detailed study including analyzing current trends and risks shaping the sustainable finance market given the current geopolitical situation.

For the research, the authors used methods of classification and comparison and analysis of statistical data.

2.2 Material and Method

The main trend shaping sustainable finance market in general and green finance in particular is steady growth. Interest in sustainable finance is growing globally as more companies and governments use green capital markets to meet their environmental, social and governance (ESG) goals and growing investor expectations. Environmental sustainability is fast becoming a priority for consumers, businesses and governments, as climate change is accelerating with recognizable impacts. In response, leading financial services firms across banking, investment and insurance have launched a wide array of green finance products and experiences to contribute to climate change goals. For example, green finance has grown rapidly from a low base, rising from \$5.2bn in 2012 to \$540.6bn in 2021. However, the share of green finance in the overall financial market sits at just above 4% globally. Green finance includes green bonds; green loans; venture capital (VC) and private equity (PE) funding for green tech; green IPOs; and green acquisitions, which use funds to buy companies that bring environmental benefits, and alternative investment (crowdfunding).

According to the Climate Bonds Initiative, green bonds hit $522.7bn in 2021; this accounts for more than half of all green finance. Green loans exceeded $135bn; increased consumer and business demand enabled some financial services firms to book double-digit growth in those loans. Data from Venture Scanner indicate that VC funding, PE funding, green tech acquisitions and green tech IPOs made up the remaining US$63.2bn. While Q1 saw the lowest volumes since Q4 2020, green issuance picked up in Q2, with $121.3bn, a 25% increase on the quarter. June was the busiest month of the year, closing the first half at almost $47bn, or 22% of the H1 green-themed volume. This brings cumulative green labeled issuance closer to the $2tn milestone, at just under $1.9tn (Fig. 2.1).

The growing popularity of green and climate bonds, which has also led to a greater issue of social and other sustainable bonds, as well as the development of other green financial instruments, indicates that both public and private sectors are aimed at mobilizing the capital needed to achieve sustainable development goals. Green bonds continue to dominate green finance, with global green bond annual issuance increasing from $2.3bn in 2012 to $511.5bn in 2021. Cumulatively, green bond issuance totaled $1.4tn over 2012–21, representing 93.1% of green finance across the decade. The year 2021 was a record year for the green bond market, as the annual issuance exceeded the important half-trillion dollar mark for the first time, with total issuance of $1.6tn, indicating that the green bond market was experiencing a tremendous boom. The reasons are the following investors, managers, shareholders, clients and society at large have started taking into consideration environment, social

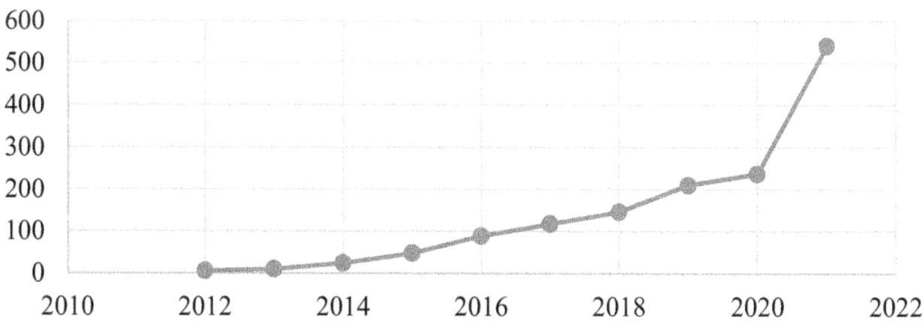

Fig. 2.1 Green finance market size ($bn) (*Source* Climate Bonds Initiative https://www.climatebonds.net/)

and governance issues; tapping green and social finance helps companies and investors hedge and mitigate risks associated with sustainability issues such as climate-related risks; furthermore, QE and negative real interest rates affect the growth of sustainable finance. Developed markets continued to dominate issuance, accounting for 73% of green bond volume in 2021. The USA and Germany topped green bond issuance in 2020 and 2021, issuing more than $80bn and $60bn, respectively, in 2021. Renewable energy attracted the largest share of green investment across sectors and issuer types in 2021, followed by low-carbon buildings and transportation (Fig. 2.2).

With the global economy recovering from the devastating effects of the COVID-19 pandemic, interest in government green bonds has also surged, with sovereign green bond issuance reaching totally $161bn, of which $72.8bn was for 2021 alone, with the UK providing 30% of the supply as it supported its COP26 obligations with a $21bn issue of two types of green bonds. Among developed countries, the largest issuers of sovereign green bonds are: Belgium, France, Germany, Ireland, Italy, Korea, Lithuania, the Netherlands and Sweden; among developing countries: Chile, Egypt, Fiji, Hungary, Indonesia, Nigeria, Poland, Seychelles and Thailand. Notably, in 2018, Indonesia became the first country in the world to issue a sukuk, an Islamic financial certificate that is the equivalent of a bond in the Western financial system. In 2019, the first issue of sub-federal green bonds took place—they were issued by the state of Victoria in Australia.

In the first half of the year 2022, volumes of $27.4bn in new sovereign bonds or taps were added to the Climate Bonds GBDB. Germany made

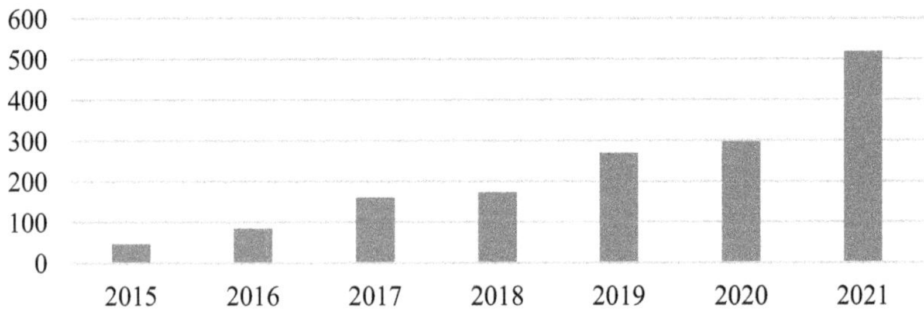

Fig. 2.2 Green bonds market size ($bn) (*Source* Climate Bonds Initiative https://www.climatebonds.net/)

the largest contribution with $7.8bn, reopening its 2030 (EUR1.5bn/ USD1.7bn), 2031 (EUR1.5bn/ USD1.6bn) and 2050 (EUR4.0bn/ USD4.5bn) deals. By the end of H1 2022, Germany had raised over EUR30bn (USD36.3bn) since its green bond program was launched in 2020. The German government is planning to issue a new green federal bond in Q3 as part of its strategy to give investors worldwide access to green benchmark bonds and set up a green yield curve. France followed closely, with its new 2040 inflation linked deal (EUR4.0bn/ USD4.2bn) and reopening of its 2039 bullet bond (EUR2.8bn/ USD3.2bn). Denmark priced its debut green bond in January (DKK5bn/ USD20m), a 2031 maturity. Hong Kong, the Netherlands, Indonesia and Hungary returned to the market, too.

Another current trend in the global financial system is the continuing development of national taxonomies, as well as deepening and tightening of relevant standards, and the increasing integration of sustainable finance regulation into national development strategies and agendas. Green taxonomies will continue to shape the future of the sustainable finance market as they evolve around the globe. In addition to existing taxonomy regulations or guidance in China, the European Union, Japan, Malaysia and Mongolia, taxonomy regulations have been launched in the ASEAN, Colombia, Indonesia, Russia, South Africa, South Korea, Sri Lanka and Vietnam. High-level guidance has also been published in Bangladesh. Some 20 countries have now developed or are developing such national taxonomies.

The role of the financial sector in the global energy transition and the achievement of «net zero» is constantly growing. Since 2019, the world's largest financial companies have begun to actively join the global movement to achieve zero emissions by 2050. Many financial institutions around the world have announced that they will stop financing coal-fired power plants. In 2021, many more of the world's largest financial companies (defined as financial companies with more than $500bn in assets) have committed to net-zero emissions by 2050. It is worth noting that the first such commitment among the largest financial companies was made relatively recently in 2019. The year 2021 was proclaimed the year of "net zero" in banking: as of June 2021, 45 of the 60 largest financial institutions (LFIs) have committed to net-zero emissions, totaling $70tn in assets.

Another trend is the increasing pressure on company management from investors to be more proactive and aware of ESG issues. The growing momentum of ESG is fueled by customer demand and external pressure. Investors are beginning to play an increasing role in incorporating the ESG agenda into a company's long-term development strategy. For example, in December 2021, the Coalition for a Responsible Exxon (CURE), one of the world's largest oil companies, Exxon Mobil, demanded that the company change its CEO and take more action to reduce greenhouse gas emissions, claiming that recently appointed board members and management are not doing enough to reduce greenhouse gas emissions and transition to clean energy.

Given the current geopolitical situation and sanctions on Russian oil supplies, it is very likely that this will also encourage markets to pay more attention to alternative energy sources and «green» investments. A series of global disruptions have made it clear that investing in renewable energy necessary to avoid future energy crises and to prevent climate change. Renewables have gained further momentum amid the energy crisis. In its recent World Energy Outlook, the International Energy Agency (IEA) said that the energy crisis has the potential to speed up the global energy transition. The IEA expects global investment in clean energies to rise to about $2tn per year by the end of the decade—that's an increase of 50 percent compared to today. At the UN Climate Change Conference COP27, the European Investment Fund, Europe's largest provider of risk finance, committed nearly 250 million euro with five equity funds to back up to 2.5 billion euro of climate action in Europe. This is an important contribution to the EU's efforts to reach net zero.

As for the risks to the global green finance, greenwashing remains one of the main problems. Despite the impressive steady growth of the global sustainable finance market, the lack of transparency in the labeling of financial instruments and mandatory disclosure raises the question how much these indicators are affected by greenwashing. "We must have zero tolerance for net-zero greenwashing", António Guterres said at the launch at COP27 in Sharm el-Sheikh, Egypt.

Despite the recent surge of global sustainable finance market, the financing gap for the sustainable development goals (SDGs) has actually widened, primarily in developing countries which may lead to unintended consequences. However, a number of additional challenges remain—many of which are exacerbated in developing countries. The absence of reliable data, a lack of transparency in the unlisted sector, limited flexibility, credit risk, regulatory hurdles and currency issues all represent obstacles to investment.

Global central banks are currently in tightening mode which means that the decline in market liquidity could lead to a shift in government priorities from climate issues to the energy crisis and rising costs of living. As a result, some «green» projects may be put on hold.

The rapid growth in green finance is part of a broader wave of sustainable finance. But the lack of standardized definitions, taxonomies or reliable data makes it difficult to size the green finance market. "Green finance" and "sustainable finance" are sometimes used interchangeably but are not the same. Sustainability-linked bonds should not be considered part of green finance because, although they're linked to firms' overall sustainability targets, they could be used for general corporate purposes and not strictly for projects that have positive environmental or climate benefits.

As for the regulatory aspects of the green transition, it is worth emphasizing that the impact of climate change on the financial sector has long been a contentious issue. Only now financial authorities are starting to examine potential risks which supervised entities are likely to face in the near future. Those risks are usually divided into two broad categories:

- Physical risks refer to the risks of financial losses due to a physical damage of property and infrastructure and ensuing disruptions in business activities caused by extreme climate-related hazards;
- Transition risks, in their turn, are connected with the financial implications of a disorderly transition to a low-carbon economy, including policy changes (for instance, unilateral cross-border carbon taxes), reputational impact, technological limitations as well as shifts in market preferences.

Such risks are roughly estimated to wipe off up to 18% of the world GDP by 2050. Nevertheless, there is still no broad consensus on a coordinated approach to mitigating climate-related risks, as the scope and impact of possible measures are difficult to gauge. Meanwhile, without a top-down communication, financial institutions' role in fostering a smooth transition to a low-carbon economy could be undermined.

All regions see sustainable finance regulation as critical to increasing market transparency and reducing risks of greenwashing.

European Union countries continue to lead in depth and breadth of regulatory initiatives, while Asia has accelerated the pace of new initiatives, and North America and Australia have significantly increased regulatory activity. The UK "has the most expansive regulatory framework of any country outside the EU". The key topics in sustainable finance regulation are taxonomies; product standards, disclosures and labeling; management and disclosure of climate risks; management and disclosure of ESG risks; ESG in stewardship; and green bond guidelines. Regulators are prioritizing management of climate-related financial risk and prevention of greenwashing, but nature-related risks and social issues are beginning to get more attention as well. Moving on to the regulatory response to climate-related risks worldwide, we would like to dwell specifically on prudential regulation, which, in our opinion, is quite an adequate option, given uncertain and non-linear character of climate-related risks manifestation which make climate events tantamount to tail-risk events referred to as a "black swan". In 2020, experts of the Bank for International Settlements compared climate-related risks with "green swans" suggesting that the odds of their realization are anything but reflected in historical statistical data.

The scheme presented illustrates how climate-related changes can transmit and translate into banks' financial risks through the following key components:

- Climate risk drivers: these represent climate-related changes that could give rise to financial risks. They are classified into either physical or transition risks.
- Transmission channels: refer to the causal chains that explain how climate risk drivers impact banks directly and indirectly through their counterparties, assets and the economy in which they operate.
- Sources of variability: the likelihood and size of the impact of climate risk drivers can be affected by a number of additional variables. These include: the geographic location of the bank, asset or exposure, interactions and interdependencies between transmission channels and climate risk drivers that can amplify impacts, and mitigants that reduce or offset impacts.
- Financial risks: climate-related risks seem to be captured within the existing microprudential framework since they manifest themselves through traditional channels like credit, market, liquidity risks, etc. However, it is pivotal to remember that the unique features of climate-related risks may hamper the proper use of the existing

framework, which is largely backward-looking and based on historical loss experience. Besides, capital requirements in particular focus on risks that will materialize over a relatively short-term horizon whereas climate risks will take time to demonstrate their impact.

After studying the approaches of a number of the most climate-active regulators, we have come to the conclusion that their activities are primarily focused on risk assessment exercises (scenario analyses and stress tests) as well as integration of risks into their operational framework (long-term strategy, management of own portfolio, internal control) whereas detailed requirements are still under development. In some jurisdictions, relevant authorities have already issued recommendations for banks and insurers (ECB, PRA, BaFin, APRA). Besides, some central banks are seeking to enhance their own credibility by disclosing climate-related information in compliance with TCFD Recommendations.

Likewise, foreign regulators have devised special recommendations covering such aspects as the consideration of climate risks in financial institutions' business strategy, risk appetite, corporate governance and risk management. In the European Union, banks and insurance companies should also define their own quantitative and qualitative climate risk metrics, limits and thresholds.

During the last two years, the Bank of Russia accelerated the integration of climate considerations into its activities, having joined NGFS and established a special Working Group on Financing for Sustainable Development. Underway is also the work on conducting a long-term stress test, issuing consultation papers on the consideration of both transition and physical risks by banks and insurance companies.

2.3 Conclusion

The global green finance market has grown by more than a 100-fold over the last decade, but still only accounts for 4% of the global financial market, so there is still much space to grow. Green bonds account for the largest share of the green finance market, with issuance increasing from \$2.3bn in 2012 to \$511.5bn in 2021. Cumulative green bond issuance totaled \$1.4trn over 2012–21, representing 93.1% of green finance across the decade which indicates that the issuance of green bonds is gaining momentum and is likely to continue. Green taxonomies will continue to shape the future of the sustainable finance market as they evolve around the globe. Some 20 countries have now developed or are developing such national taxonomies. As for the risks of green transition, the main of them include greenwashing, the financing gap for the sustainable development goals (SDGs) primarily in developing countries, lack of standardized definitions, taxonomies or reliable data. The key topics in sustainable finance regulation are taxonomies; product standards, disclosures and labeling; management and disclosure of climate risks; management and disclosure of ESG risks; ESG in stewardship; and green bond guidelines. Regulators are prioritizing management of climate-related financial risk and prevention of greenwashing, but nature-related risks and social issues are beginning to get more attention as well.

References

Taghizadeh-Hesary and Yoshino (2019), Hafner et al. (2020)

Climate Bonds Initiative https://www.climatebonds.net/

Jacobs, M. (1991). *The green economy: Environment, sustainable development, and the politics of the future*. Pluto Press.

Lindenberg, N. (2014, April 15). *Definition of green finance*. DIE mimeo.

Pearce, D., Markandya, A., & Barbier, E. B. (1989). *Blue print for a green economy*. Earthscan.

The Central Banks and Supervisors Network for Greening the Financial System (NGFS), official website. https://www.ngfs.net/en/about-us/governance/origin-and-purpose

The green swan. Central banking and financial stability in the age of climate change, BIS, January 2020

Wang, Y., & Zhi, Q. (2016). The role of green finance in environmental protection: Two aspects of market mechanism and policies. *Energy Procedia, 104*, 311–316. https://doi.org/10.1016/j.egypro.2016.12.053

Zadek, S., & Flynn, C. (2013). *South-originating green finance: Exploring the potential*. Geneva International Finance Dialogues. Geneva: UNEPFI, 22 p. https://www.iisd.org/system/files/publications/south-originated_green_finance_en.pdf

Zhang, D., Zhang, Z., & Managi, S. (2019). A bibliometric analysis on green finance: Current status, development, and future directions. *Finance Research Letters, 29*, 425–430. https://doi.org/10.1016/j.frl.2019.02.003

CHAPTER 3

Dynamic BRICS Stock Market Linkages as a Channel of Systemic Risk Transmission: Evidence from the Asymmetric Connectedness Approach

Onur Polat

3.1 Introduction and Literature Review

The COVID-19 health crisis and the Russian-Ukrainian conflict broken out on February 24, 2022, propelled a prominent surge in geopolitical risk (GPR) confronted by global financial markets. Geopolitical risk is an essential indicator shaping investment decisions and has a vital role in the soundness of financial markets (Elsayed & Helmi, 2021).

GPR unravels various facets signifying political soundness at the global or national level. The GPR emerges from a diverse set of events ranging from terrorist attacks to climate change (Caldara & Iacoviello, 2022). The GPR sharply amplifies around political/financial upheavals such as the

O. Polat (✉)
Department of Public Finance, Associate Professor, Bilecik Seyh Edebali University, Bilecik, Turkey
e-mail: onur.polat@bilecik.edu.tr

A. Karminsky and M. Stolbov (eds.), *Systemic Financial Risk*,
https://doi.org/10.1007/978-3-031-54809-3_3

global recession of 2008, the Arab Spring, the 2014 Crimean crisis, the Brexit referendum, the COVID-19, and the Russian-Ukrainian conflict. During these burst episodes, the soundness of local/global financial markets tends to deteriorate and financial contagion markedly escalates (Hedström et al., 2021; Zorgati & Garfatta, 2021). The contagion mechanism is an important manifestation of materializing systemic risk.

Although it is hard to quantify the financial contagion, researchers have employed various econometric approaches to measuring it such as the correlation analysis (Chiang et al., 2007; Syllignakis, 2011), co-movements (Kallberg & Pasquariello, 2008; Phylaktis & Xia, 2009), and the wavelet decompositions (Gallegati, 2012). In this vein, Diebold and Yilmaz (2009, 2012) introduced a new methodology, known as the DY, which relied on the Cholesky factor identification of a VAR model. This approach has been extensively employed by researchers to determine financial connectedness/contagion in various financial markets (Demirer et al., 2018; Liu & Gong, 2020).

More recently, studies have focused on the dynamic nature of the connectedness of financial markets by employing TVP-VAR-based connectedness methodology of Antonakakis and Gabauer (2017). Distinctive from the DY, this approach doesn't estimate connectedness in a particular window size and is sensitive to outliers. This methodology has raised overwhelming attention by scholars, and studies have implemented this approach to compute the dynamic connectedness among financial indicators (Adekoya & Oliyide, 2021; Balcilar et al., 2021; Gabauer & Gupta, 2018; Umar et al., 2022a, 2022b).

The BRICS countries constitute 16% of the world market capitalization, where China and India contribute 10% and 3%, respectively. Besides, total GDP of BRICS countries accounts for approximately 22% of the world GDP with tight trade relationships with the rest of the world (Panda et al., 2021). Moreover, the recent geopolitical distress incidents such as the COVID-19 pandemic and the Russian-Ukrainian conflict originated in the members of BRICS.

Therefore, a strand of recent literature has delved into the linkages of BRICS financial markets (Ahmad et al., 2018; Bagheri et al., 2022; Dahir et al., 2020; Li et al., 2021).

Our contribution to the extant literature is two folds. First, we estimate the asymmetric returns connectedness of BRICS stock markets by employing a newly engineered methodology. Second, we focus on the dynamic asymmetric linkages among the BRICS MSCI ETFs in the wake of geopolitical stress incidents such as the COVID-19 pandemic and the Russian-Ukrainian conflict. In doing so, we describe an important transmission mechanism of materializing systemic risk across key EMEs.

We proceed with the study as follows. Sections 3.2 and 3.3 present the data and the methodology of the study, respectively. Section 3.4 provides the empirical results of the work. Section 3.5 draws the main findings of the study and concludes it.

3.2 Data

The dataset of this study includes BRICS MSCI ETFs, namely iShares MSCI ETFs for Brazil, Russia, India, China, and South Africa. We collected the data from the investing database and the sample period spans from January 2, 2019, to March 3, 2022, period. Following Adekoya et al. (2022), the returns are split into their positive and negative components as follows:

$$S_t = \{0, ify_t < 01, ify_t \geq 0 \tag{3.1}$$

$$y_t^+ = S_t.y_t \tag{3.2}$$

$$y_t^- = (1 - S_t).y_t \tag{3.3}$$

where y_t^+ and y_t^- represent the positive and negative returns.

We utilize the log daily returns of the MSCI ETFs in the analysis. The summary stats for returns and their plots are presented in Table 3.1 and Fig. 3.1, respectively.

Table 3.1 indicates that the highest return is provided by the India MSCI ETF and followed by the South Africa MSCI ETF. Particularly, the Russia MSCI ETF provides negative returns due to the heightened geopolitical risk that was propelled by the Russian-Ukrainian conflict. Unsurprisingly, the Russia MSCI ETF has the highest volatility among all returns. Contrariwise, China has the lowest variance among BRICS countries. All returns are tailed to the left and are featured by excess kurtosis, signifying their leptokurtic characteristics. Based on the correlation table, returns are positively correlated and economically meaningful.

Figure 3.1 shows that all return series have substantial spikes around the second week of March 2020, which corresponds to the official declaration of the COVID-19 pandemic by the World Health Organization

Table 3.1 Summary statistics for the RVs

	Brazil	*Russia*	*India*	*China*	*South Africa*
Mean	0.01	−0.11	0.04	0.02	0.04
Variance	7.26***	9.26***	3.35***	2.76***	4.59***
Skewness	−1.03***	−4.09***	−1.05***	−0.26***	−0.92***
Excess Kurtosis	13.90***	39.97***	17.58***	2.89***	8.57***
JB	6590.60***	55,488.26***	10,449.70***	289.45***	2563.28***
Kendall	Brazil	Russia	India	China	South Africa
Brazil	1.00***	0.36***	0.33***	0.30***	0.42***
Russia	0.36***	1.00***	0.37***	0.34***	0.43***
India	0.33***	0.37***	1.00***	0.34***	0.39***
China	0.30***	0.34***	0.34***	1.00***	0.42***
South Africa	0.42***	0.43***	0.39***	0.42***	1.00***

Note ***, **, * represent 1%, 5%, and 10% represent statistical significance levels, respectively

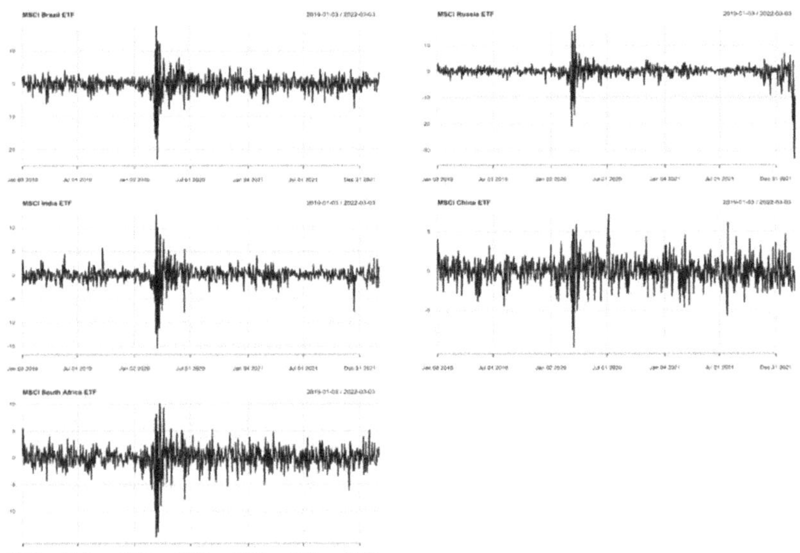

Fig. 3.1 BRICS MSCI ETFs Returns

(WHO). Furthermore, the Russia MSCI ETF exhibited a significant spike on February 24, 2022, on which Russia's military operation began.

3.3 Methodology

Asymmetric Connectedness

Adekoya et al. (2022) proposed the TVP-VAR-based asymmetric connectedness methodology which uses positive and negative absolute returns. This approach is based on the TVP-VAR connectedness approach of Antonokakis et al. (2020) which is an extension of the approach of Diebold and Yilmaz (2014). In this approach, the variance–covariance matrix varies via a Kalman filter estimation with forgetting factors in the spirit of Koop and Korobilis (2013).

The $TVP - VAR(p)$ model is introduced as follows:

$$z_t = B_t y_{t-1} + \varepsilon_t \varepsilon_t | \Omega_{t-1} \sim N(0, \Sigma_t) \tag{3.4}$$

$$vec(B_t) = vec(B_{t-1}) + \gamma_t \qquad \gamma_t | \ \Omega_{t-1} \sim N(0, \Xi_t) \tag{3.5}$$

With

$$z_{t-1} = \left(z_{t-1} z_{t-2} \vdots z_{t-p} \right) B_t\prime = \left(B_{1t} B_{2t} \vdots B_{pt} \right) \tag{3.6}$$

here Ω_{t-1} represent all information available until $t - 1$; y_t and z_t denote $n \times 1$ and $np \times 1$ vectors. B_t and B_{it} are $n \times np$ and $np \times 1$ dimensional matrices, respectively. ε_t and γ_t are $n \times 1$ and $n^2 p \times 1$ dimensional vectors, respectively. Σ_t and Ξ_t are $n \times n$ and $np \times n^2 p$ dimensional matrices, respectively.

The VMA representation of z_t is defined as $\sum_{j=0}^{\infty} A_{jt} \mu_{t-j}$, where A_{jt} is the $n \times n$ dimensional matrix. $GIRF\left(\Psi_{ij,t}(H)\right)$ is introduced as follows:

$$GIRF\left(H, \rho_{j,t}, \ \Omega_{t-1}\right) = E\left(z_t + H | e_j = \rho_{j,t}, \Omega_{t-1}\right) - E\left(z_{t+j} | \Omega_{t-1}\right) \tag{3.7}$$

$$\psi_{j,t}(H) = \frac{A_{H,t} \sum_t e_j}{\sqrt{\sum_{j\,j,t}}} \frac{\rho_{j,t}}{\sqrt{\sum_{j\,j,t}}} \quad \beta_{j,t} = \sqrt{\sum_{j\,j,t}} \tag{3.8}$$

$$\Psi_{j,t}(H) = \Sigma_{jj,t}^{-1/2} A_{H,t} \Sigma_t e_j \tag{3.9}$$

here e_j is an $n \times 1$ selection vector. The $GFEVD\big(\tilde{\Phi}_{ij,t}(H)\big)$ was computed, based on $\tilde{\Phi}_{ij,t}(H)$ as follows:

$$\tilde{\Phi}_{ij,t}(H) = \frac{\sum_{t=1}^{H-1} \Psi_{ij,t}^2}{\sum_{j=1}^{n} \sum_{t=1}^{H-1} \Psi_{ij,t}^2} \tag{3.10}$$

with $\sum\limits_{j=1}^{n} \tilde{\Phi}_{ij,t}(H) = 1$, and $\sum\limits_{i,j=1}^{n} \tilde{\Phi}_{ij,t}(H) = n$.

The total connectedness index (TCI):

$$C_t(H) = \frac{\sum_{i,j=1,i \neq j}^{n} \tilde{\Phi}_{ij,t}(H)}{\sum_{i,j=1}^{n} \tilde{\Phi}_{ij,t}(H)} * 100 = \frac{\sum_{i,j=1,i \neq j}^{n} \tilde{\Phi}_{ij,t}(H)}{n} * 100 \tag{3.11}$$

Overall directional connectedness to others:

$$C_{i \to j,t}(H) = \frac{\sum_{j=1,i \neq j}^{n} \tilde{\Phi}_{ji,t}(H)}{\sum_{j=1}^{n} \tilde{\Phi}_{ji,t}(H)} * 100 \tag{3.12}$$

Overall directional connectedness from others:

$$C_{i \leftarrow j,t}(H) = \frac{\sum_{j=1,i \neq j}^{n} \tilde{\Phi}_{ij,t}(H)}{\sum_{j=1}^{n} \tilde{\Phi}_{ij,t}(H)} * 100 \tag{3.13}$$

Net total directional connectedness:

$$C_{i,t}(H) = C_{i \to j,t}(H) - C_{i \leftarrow j,t}(H) \tag{3.14}$$

To improve this connectedness measure, Chatziantoniou and Gabauer (2021) adjusted the TCI as follows:

$$C_t(H) = \left(\frac{n}{n-1}\right) \frac{\sum_{i,j=1,i \neq j}^{n} \tilde{\Phi}_{ij,t}(H)}{n} = \frac{\sum_{i,j=1,i \neq j}^{n} \tilde{\Phi}_{ij,t}(H)}{n-1} \tag{3.15}$$

3.4 Empirical Findings

Average Connectedness Results

First, we present average connectedness measures in Table 3.2.

In Table 3.2, the off-diagonal values represent the shocks from the i-th element to the j-th element in the network. The overall connectedness results imply that the BRICS MSCI EFTs have an interconnectedness

Table 3.2 Average Connectedness Results for BRICS MSCI ETFs

Overall						
	Brazil	*Russia*	*India*	*China*	*South Africa*	*FROM*
Brazil	48.36	13.05	11.95	10.64	16.01	51.64
Russia	12.91	46.96	12.8	10.84	16.5	53.04
India	12.34	12.66	49.49	11.14	14.37	50.51
China	11.14	10.91	11.26	48.92	17.77	51.08
South Africa	14.38	14.89	12.91	15.59	42.22	57.78
TO	50.77	51.52	48.92	48.2	64.65	264.06
NET	−0.88	−1.52	−1.59	−2.88	6.87	TCI = 52.81%
Positive						
	Brazil	Russia	India	China	South Africa	FROM
Brazil	55.68	12.02	10.12	8.2	13.98	44.32
Russia	11.94	53.4	11.13	9.49	14.05	46.6
India	9.9	10.94	56.99	10.11	12.06	43.01
China	8.69	9.4	10.15	56.61	15.15	43.39
South Africa	12.67	12.8	11.13	14.09	49.31	50.69
TO	43.19	45.16	42.53	41.9	55.23	228.01
NET	−1.13	−1.45	−0.48	−1.49	4.54	TCI = 45.60%
Negative						
	Brazil	Russia	India	China	South Africa	FROM
Brazil	47.67	12.97	13.49	10.53	15.35	52.33
Russia	12.37 lePara>	47.38	14.31	9.78	16.17	52.62
India	13.38	15.01	46.53	10.77	14.31	53.47
China	11.54	10.19	11.21	51.21	15.85	48.79
South Africa	13.94	15.37	13.33	13.6	43.76	56.24
TO	51.23	53.53	52.34	44.67	61.67	263.45
NET	−1.1	0.92	−1.13	−4.12	5.43	TCI = 52.69%

Notes Results are obtained by application with lag 1 (BIC) and a 10-step ahead forecast error variance decomposition (FEVD)

level of an average of around 53%. Furthermore, except for the South Africa MSCI EFT, all other BRICS MSCI EFTs are the net receiver of the return shocks.

The rest of Table 3 shows the average connectedness results for positive/negative returns. Several results are worth noting: First, the total connectedness index (TCI) for the negative returns (52.69%) is higher than the TCI for the positive returns (45.60%). Second, likewise, the results for the overall connectedness of all MSCI EFTs except for South Africa are the net receiver of return shocks. As for the results of the negative returns, Russia becomes the net transmitter of shocks along with South Africa. This finding is not surprising and highlights the negative shocks stemming from Russia due to the strengthening geopolitical risk. However, the average results for the connectedness are static and don't provide a complete picture of the time-varying nature of asymmetric connectedness. Consequently, we proceed with our analysis by focusing on dynamic connectedness.

Time-Varying Connectedness

We estimate the overall dynamic connectedness of BRICS MSCI ETFs and depict them in Fig. 3.2.[1]

Overall dynamic connectedness results illustrated in Fig. 3.2 demonstrate that the connectedness of the system fluctuates between 32 and 80%, and peaks on 18 March 2020 at 76.66% (5 days after the official announcement of COVID-19 as a pandemic). Likewise, the total connectedness based on the positive and negative returns exhibits similar patterns and hits their apexes on 18 March 2020 (75.61% and 77.18%, respectively). Nonetheless, there exist disparities between positive and negative returns, and the TCI relied on the negative returns to dominate the study episode except for the period between May and October 2021. This finding is unsurprising since investors and stakeholders react more to negative shocks to hedge against unfavorable developments in financial markets (Adekoya et al., 2022).

[1] The black-shaded area indicates the dynamics of the TCI when both positive and negative returns are considered; the green/ red line exhibits the dynamic TCI when only positive/negative returns are considered.

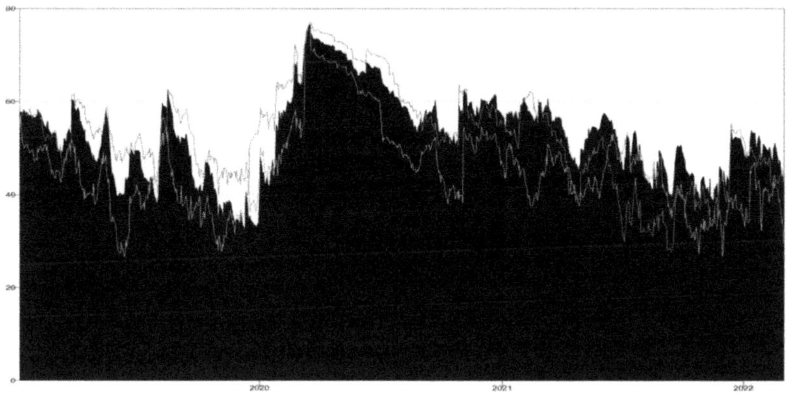

Fig. 3.2 Dynamic overall connectedness (*Notes* Results are obtained by applying a VAR model with lag 1 (BIC) and 10-step ahead FEVD)

Dynamic Net Directional Connectedness

We focus on the net directional connectedness to determine the transmitting or receiving role of the BRICS MSCI ETFs throughout the observation period. Figure 3.3 displays the findings of the net directional connectedness of countries.[2]

Several results are worth noting based on Fig. 3.3. First, among all indices only the MSCI ETF for South Africa return persists in its transmitting role over most of the time of the observation period. This finding is rather surprising yet in line with the results of previous studies (Akhtaruzzaman et al., 2022; Ji et al., 2017). Second, the negative return spillovers are higher than the positive spillovers in size for all indices most of the time, signifying that the BRICS MSCI ETF market is more sensitive to negative news. Manifestly, except for Brazil, China, and South Africa, the spillovers for the negative returns dominate the period between the second half of 2021 and the first quarter of 2022 due to the Russian-Ukrainian conflict. Third, China flips to the net receiver of shock starting in March 2020. This result is consistent with the study of Liu et al. (2022) that detected a net receiving role of risk transmission for China following the first wave of the COVID-19 pandemic. Finally, except for India, all

[2] Positive/negative values indicate the transmitters/receivers in the system.

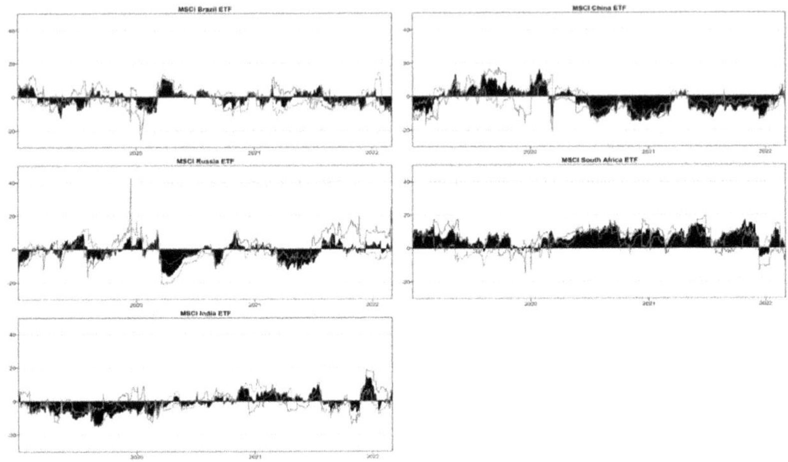

Fig. 3.3 Time-varying net directional connectedness (*Notes* Results are obtained by application with lag 1 (BIC) and a 10-step ahead FEVD)

net spillovers prominently amplify in the first quarter of 2020 triggered by the first wave of the pandemic.

3.5 Conclusion

This study examines the asymmetric time-varying connectedness for the returns of BRICS MSCI ETFs in the wake of geopolitical stress triggered by the COVID-19 pandemic and the Russian-Ukrainian conflict. To this end, we implemented a newly elaborated approach by Adekoya et al. (2022).

Results of the asymmetric connectedness approach based on the TVP-VAR model indicate that the TCI for the negative returns is larger relative to the overall connectedness index. This finding suggests that the BRICS MSCI ETF market is more sensitive to negative shocks than to positive shocks and investors benefit from hedging opportunities during turmoil times. Moreover, particularly for Russia, the negative return spillovers dominate the period between the second half of 2021 and the first quarter of 2022. Additionally, China changes its role to become a net transmitter of return spillovers following the emergence of the COVID-19 pandemic.

Our study implies the following policy recommendation and insights on the market participants. Investors and portfolio managers can benefit by structuring efficient hedging strategies in times of financial/ geopolitical turbulence. Policymakers should construct an efficient risk monitoring mechanism to alleviate the adverse impacts of geopolitical distress on financial markets.

References

Adekoya, O. B., & Oliyide, J. A. (2021). How COVID-19 drives connectedness among commodity and financial markets: Evidence from TVP-VAR and causality-in-quantiles techniques. *Resources Policy, 70*, 101898.

Adekoya, O. B., Akinseye, A. B., Antonakakis, N., Chatziantoniou, I., Gabauer, D., & Oliyide, J. (2022). Crude oil and Islamic sectoral stocks: Asymmetric TVP-VAR connectedness and investment strategies. *Resources Policy, 78*, 102877.

Akhtaruzzaman, M., Benkraiem, R., Boubaker, S., & Zopounidis, C. (2022). COVID-19 crisis and risk spillovers to developing economies: Evidence from Africa. *Journal of International Development, 34*(4), 898–918.

Ahmad, W., Mishra, A. V., & Daly, K. J. (2018). Financial connectedness of BRICS and global sovereign bond markets. *Emerging Markets Review, 37*, 1–16.

Antonakakis, N., & Gabauer, D. (2017). *Refined Measures of Dynamic Connectedness based on TVP-VAR (No. 78282)*. University Library of Munich, Germany.

Antonakakis, N., Chatziantoniou, I., & Gabauer, D. (2020). Refined measures of dynamic connectedness based on time-varying parameter vector autoregressions. *Journal of Risk and Financial Management, 13*(4), 84.

Alola, A. A., & Bekun, F. V. (2021). Pandemic outbreaks (COVID-19) and sectoral carbon emissions in the United States: A spillover effect evidence from Diebold and Yilmaz index. *Energy & Environment, 32*(5), 945–955.

Bagheri, E., Ebrahimi, S. B., Mohammadi, A., Miri, M., & Bekiros, S. (2022). The dynamic volatility connectedness structure of energy futures and global financial markets: Evidence from a novel time-frequency domain approach. *Computational Economics, 59*(3), 1087–1111.

Balcilar, M., Gabauer, D., & Umar, Z. (2021). Crude Oil futures contracts and commodity markets: New evidence from a TVP-VAR extended joint connectedness approach. *Resources Policy, 73*, 102219.

Caldara, D., & Iacoviello, M. (2022). Measuring geopolitical risk. *American Economic Review, 112*(4), 1194–1225.

Caloia, F. G., Cipollini, A., & Muzzioli, S. (2019). How do normalization schemes affect net spillovers? A replication of the Diebold and Yilmaz (2012) study. *Energy Economics, 84*, 104536.

Chatziantoniou, I., & Gabauer, D. (2021). EMU risk-synchronisation and financial fragility through the prism of dynamic connectedness. *The Quarterly Review of Economics and Finance, 79*, 1–14.

Chiang, T. C., Jeon, B. N., & Li, H. (2007). Dynamic correlation analysis of financial contagion: Evidence from Asian markets. *Journal of International Money and Finance, 26*(7), 1206–1228.

Cui, T., Suleman, M. T., & Zhang, H. (2022). Do the green bonds overreact to the COVID-19 Pandemic? *Finance Research Letters, 49*, 103095.

Dahir, A. M., Mahat, F., Noordin, B. A. A., & Ab Razak, N. H. (2020). Dynamic connectedness between Bitcoin and equity market information across BRICS countries: Evidence from TVP-VAR connectedness approach. *International Journal of Managerial Finance 16*(3), 357–371.

Demirer, M., Diebold, F. X., Liu, L., & Yilmaz, K. (2018). Estimating global bank network connectedness. *Journal of Applied Econometrics, 33*(1), 1–15.

Diebold, F. X., & Yilmaz, K. (2009). Measuring financial asset return and volatility spillovers, with application to global equity markets. *The Economic Journal, 119*(534), 158–171.

Diebold, F. X., & Yilmaz, K. (2012). Better to give than to receive: Predictive directional measurement of volatility spillovers. *International Journal of Forecasting, 28*(1), 57–66.

Diebold, F. X., & Yılmaz, K. (2014). On the network topology of variance decompositions: Measuring the connectedness of financial firms. *Journal of Econometrics, 182*(1), 119–134.

Elsayed, A. H., & Helmi, M. H. (2021). Volatility transmission and spillover dynamics across financial markets: The role of geopolitical risk. *Annals Operations Research, 305*(1), 1–22.

Gabauer, D., & Gupta, R. (2018). On the transmission mechanism of country-specific and international economic uncertainty spillovers: Evidence from a TVP-VAR connectedness decomposition approach. *Economics Letters, 171*, 63–71.

Gallegati, M. (2012). A wavelet-based approach to test for financial market contagion. *Computational Statistics & Data Analysis, 56*(11), 3491–3497.

Hedström, A., Zelander, N., Junttila, J., & Uddin, G. S. (2020). Emerging market contagion under geopolitical uncertainty. *Emerging Markets Finance and Trade, 56*(6), 1377–1401.

Ji, Q., Liu, B. Y., Zhao, W. L., & Fan, Y. (2020). Modelling dynamic dependence and risk spillover between all oil price shocks and stock market returns in the BRICS. *International Review of Financial Analysis, 68*, 101238.

Kallberg, J., & Pasquariello, P. (2008). Time-series and cross-sectional excess comovement in stock indexes. *Journal of Empirical Finance, 15*(3), 481–502.

Koop, G., & Korobilis, D. (2013). Large time-varying parameter VARs. *Journal of Econometrics, 177*(2), 185–198.

Li, Y., Huang, J., Gao, W., & Zhang, H. (2021). Analyzing the time-frequency connectedness among oil, gold prices and BRICS geopolitical risks. *Resources Policy, 73*, 102134.

Liu, T., & Gong, X. (2020). Analyzing time-varying volatility spillovers between the crude oil markets using a new method. *Energy Economics, 87*, 104711.

Liu, Y., Wei, Y., Wang, Q., & Liu, Y. (2022). International stock market risk contagion during the COVID-19 pandemic. *Finance Research Letters, 45*, 102145.

Panda, P., Vasudevan, S., & Panda, B. (2021). Dynamic connectedness among BRICS and major countries stock markets. *Journal of Public Affairs, 21*(3), e2265.

Phylaktis, K., & Xia, L. (2009). Equity market comovement and contagion: A sectoral perspective. *Financial Management, 38*(2), 381–409.

Syllignakis, M. N., & Kouretas, G. P. (2011). Dynamic correlation analysis of financial contagion: Evidence from the Central and Eastern European markets. *International Review of Economics & Finance, 20*(4), 717–732.

Umar, Z., Polat, O., Choi, S. Y., & Teplova, T. (2022a). The impact of the Russia-Ukraine conflict on the connectedness of financial markets. *Finance Research Letters, 48*, 102976.

Umar, Z., Polat, O., Choi, S. Y., & Teplova, T. (2022b). Dynamic connectedness between non-fungible tokens, decentralized finance, and conventional financial assets in a time-frequency framework. *Pacific-Basin Finance Journal, 76*, 101876.

Zorgati, I., & Garfatta, R. (2021). Spatial financial contagion during the COVID-19 outbreak: Local correlation approach. *The Journal of Economic Asymmetries, 24*, e00223.

CHAPTER 4

Household Income and Financial Stability of the Banking Sector: Data from Russia

Olga Miroshnichenko, Maria Vyshkovskaia, and Valeriy Gamukin

4.1 Introduction

The development of the financial sector contributes to economic growth through the accumulation and optimization of capital allocation, increased welfare, information transparency, and absorption of the adverse consequences of financial crises (Allen & Wood, 2006; Berger et al., 2020; Čihák et al., 2012; Destek et al., 2020; Financial Development, IMF; Levine, 2005; Schinasi, 2004). The financial sector development is largely reliant on the stability of its segments, including the banking sector (Rahman et al., 2022). The proportions between the sectors of the

O. Miroshnichenko (✉) · V. Gamukin
Tyumen State University, Tyumen, Russia
e-mail: o.s.miroshnichenko@utmn.ru

V. Gamukin
e-mail: v.v.gamukin@utmn.ru

M. Vyshkovskaia
Citibank, Moscow, Russia

A. Karminsky and M. Stolbov (eds.), *Systemic Financial Risk*,
https://doi.org/10.1007/978-3-031-54809-3_4

financial system differ from country to country. In this regard, the effects of fragility of an underdeveloped sector or a few underdeveloped financial sectors cannot be compared with the consequences of fragility in the dominant sector.

Historically, it was believed that with sustainability at the micro-level, the banking sector as a whole was also sustainable. Later, there comes an understanding of the shortcomings of this approach. Additional risks that do not appear at the level of each specific bank could still manifest themselves at the macro-level and the consequences of them affect all financial intermediaries as well as economic agents in other sectors (Borio et al., 2020; Schinasi, 2004). As a result of understanding the causes of financial crises, the regulators aiming to safeguard financial stability realize the inextricable link between the banking sector and the economy as a whole, its individual sectors, including the household sector (IMF; Borio et al., 2020; Contreras et al., 2021).

In this regard, much attention from the scientific community and regulators is focused on identifying specific macroeconomic indicators that not only correlate with the level of financial sector stability, but also possess certain predictive power. Considerable attention is paid to the definition of early warning indicators of crises in the financial system as a whole or its individual elements (Alessi & Detken, 2018; Dawood et al., 2017; Gryzunova et all, 2019; Ivanov et al., 2018; Manuylenko et al., 2020; Vašíček et al., 2017), while assessing and forecasting the state of the banking sector has received limited attention so far (Drehmann & Juselius, 2014; Hanschel & Monnin, 2005; Gehrig & Iannino, 2021). Researchers are trying to identify the causes of crises that have already occurred, but they do not pay enough attention to factors that can predict a crisis (Kauko, 2014).

A stable banking system in the economies where it dominates among financial sectors can absorb fragility in other, less developed sectors, and reduce possible negative consequences by mitigating systemic risks. At the same time, by analogy with systemically important banks, that could reduce fragility of small banks and, under certain conditions, ensure the stability of the banking sector as a whole but also act as a source of systemic risks and require separate assessment and special regulation, the dominant banking sector and its stability also requires a separate assessment.

The methodology of many studies of financial (in)stability is to construct an index of financial stress using indicators that are recognized as symptoms of stress (Aldasoro et al., 2018; Drehmann & Juselius, 2014; Flori, 2021). It was found that indicators of one crisis do not always allow to predict other types of crises (Frankel & Saravelos, 2012). The research is most often based on the data from the OECD countries and the United States (Berger et al., 2020; Gehrig & Iannino, 2021), as well as the Asian countries (Truong et al., 2021). Fewer studies focus on the data from developing countries with unique features of the economic system (Cevik et al., 2013; Lepers & Serrano, 2020).

The early warning indicators may differ for different countries and groups of countries (Beck et al., 2013; Frankel & Saravelos, 2012). In this regard, the set of indicators that can be effective as a benchmark for regulators around the world as well as the values of these indicators that allow assessing the stability of the banking sector requires a study of national characteristics. Thus, there is a need to expand the coverage of studies using data from other countries. Countries that are major oil suppliers to global markets and have additional features of economic relations determined by the dynamics of world oil prices deserve special attention (Alsamara et al., 2019; Flori et al., 2021; Lepers & Serrano, 2020; Polbin et al., 2020).

This study aims to fill the described gaps in empirically grounded knowledge in the field of identifying indicators that have the potential to predict the sustainability of the banking sector in an emerging economy with a significant share of oil exports, and which can serve as a reference point for the national regulator in determining the regulatory strategy.

A distinctive feature of this study is that it uses the financial stability index as an indicator of the banking sector resilience. It consists of a number of indicators of the financial stability of the Russian banking system, data on which are published by the Bank of Russia. The construction of the financial stability index allows to derive a single indicator reflecting the aggregate characteristics of the banking sector sustainability. At this stage, the financial stability index could be considered as an indicator mirroring more common financial stress indices. However, in the following studies, in connection with actively developing approaches to determining the stability of the banking system, indicators of stability may go beyond the identification of stress, which can determine its advantage over the financial stress index. In addition, the predictive power of the financial stress index decreases when an unpredictable event with large-scale consequences occurs, such as the COVID-19 pandemic, which has increased systemic risk in all countries (Berger et al., 2021). The purpose of the financial stress index is to predict the crisis and prevent possible adverse consequences from its implementation; the purpose of the financial stability index is, on the contrary, to ensure the strengthening of stability, even when there are no negative trends in indicators or negative trends are not significant, which corresponds to the basic idea of the Basel Accords.

Since the stability of the banking sector is influenced by economic and political conditions (Gehrig & Iannino, 2021), we proceed from the assumption that the change in the value of the financial stability index as a result of changes in the values of macroeconomic indicators determines the change in the state of the banking sector. The construction of the financial stability index solves the problem of subjectivity in assessing individual indicators of banking stability and also provides an opportunity to assess the impact of certain macroeconomic factors on the stability of the banking sector as a whole. One of the most important macroeconomic indicators that determine the capacity and riskiness of the banking sector's operations with households as bank counterparties is the household income. Thus, we test if there is any effect of household income on the stability of the banking sector. This research question is important for making appropriate regulatory decisions. Moreover, such decisions may go beyond macroprudential regulation. Our research allows to understand what socio-economic processes require further understanding and careful study. Namely, this study aims to develop the index of financial stability of the banking sector based on the data from Russia for the period 2002–2019 and to assess the impact of household income on the stability of the banking sector, measured using the constructed index of financial stability.

The chapter is structured as follows: Sect. 4.2 sets out the main theoretical background, Sect. 4.3 contains a description of the research methodology, Sect. 4.4 presents a discussion of the research results, and Sect. 4.5 concludes.

4.2 Theoretical Background

The stability of the banking sector constitutes an element of financial stability and is a kind of continuum corresponding to a variety of combinations of interactions between the banking sector and individual banks with other sectors and among themselves (Allen & Wood, 2006; Schinasi, 2004). A number of authors define financial sustainability as the absence of a crisis (Aspachs et al., 2009). This opinion is shared by the World Bank in determining financial sustainability (World Bank, 2020). While there are many definitions of the concept, most of them concur that financial stability is the absence of situations (crises) in which the financial system loses its ability to perform its functions. The theoretical literature proceeds from the fact that, in an effort to increase profits in the face of an upturn, banks tend to expand the volume of investments, including lending, and extend their maturities. Further, with a decrease in effective demand for bank loans, the requirements for borrowers are reduced, which, in turn, acts as a reason for the growth of overdue debt (Drehmann & Juselius, 2014; Miroshnichenko et al., 2020). An unfavorable consequence of the presence of overdue debt is the emergence of non-performing loans on the bank balance sheet. Non-performing loans create the need to fill additional liquidity gaps. Increased credit risks put additional pressure on capital, resulting in an uplift in the denominator of the capital adequacy ratio. On the one hand, the growth of arrears increases the need to create a provision for possible loan losses, thereby increasing costs and reducing profits. On the other hand, the growth of non-performing loans reduces the income received. Lack of income for the formation of the required amount of reserve potentially contributes to the formation of a loss, which, in turn, reduces the amount of capital. This exacerbates the difficulties with maintaining capital adequacy. At some point, accumulated imbalances lead to a loss of stability. Central banks and supervisory authorities regularly assess the situation in the banking sector, which is a vital element of the financial system. These assessments are centered on two main questions: what the current state of the banking sector is and how it will develop in the medium term. To assess and predict imbalances, the corresponding indicators are used, the composition and calculation method of which is changing. The scientific community takes an active part in the search for informative indicators.

Earlier studies (Demirgüç-Kunt et al., 2008; Goldstein et al., 2000; González-Hermosillo, 1999) use binary variables, gauging only two states of the banking sector: the presence of a crisis and its absence. However, later, such an approach was recognized as deficient, since the absence of a full-scale crisis does not always indicate that the banking system is fully stable. Researchers are unanimous on the fact that periods of stability and crisis manifest themselves in different ways and that their identification requires a certain degree of subjectivity. This statement suggests that a single variable cannot capture all the complexity of these states.

The problem of banking sector financial stability, its assessment, identification of possible accumulated imbalances and their regulation has led to increased attention of international institutions to the development of relevant regulatory approaches. After the world financial crisis of 1997–1998, the International Monetary Fund developed the Financial Soundness Indicators (FSIs) system. FSIs for banks are combined into main and additional. The main indicators include the ones that assess capital and its adequacy, asset quality, income and profitability, liquidity, and sensitivity to market risk (IMF, FSIs, 2022). FSIs are adopted by national regulators taking into account country-specific factors. The published FSIs also serve as an empirical basis for scientific research on the stability of the banking sector and crises.

At the same time, financial sustainability is a notion which is not easy to measure. The scientific and professional community has not come to a consensus regarding a specific indicator that would allow to assess it. In order to obtain a single indicator, researchers and national supervisory authorities develop index indicators that combine a set of variables which proxy financial stability in a particular aspect of banking activities. The advantage of the index indicator is that it allows to assess the change in the level of financial stability of the banking sector over time and to identify the presence of negative dynamics at an earlier stage. In addition to direct assessment of the current level of financial stability, an important scientific issue is to forecast the financial stability of the banking system. An assessment of the future level of financial stability in the medium term can serve a useful input to the analysis of the state of the banking sector. With the ability to predict the level of resilience, supervisors will be able to take proactive measures to prevent major problems in the banking system, including the regulation of mandatory capital requirements.

The indicators that are used to assess the stability of the banking sector are a projection of a different sets of interactions of the banking sector with non-financial and other financial sectors of the economy. Recently, a large amount of research has been devoted to the so-called early warning indicators systems (Berger et al., 2020; Dawood et al., 2017; Hanschel & Monnin, 2005; Kauko, 2014; Truong et al., 2021). Their main purpose is to forecast crisis situations in the financial sector. The causes of the crisis in the banking sector in different countries were the rapid growth of domestic credit, the growth of international borrowing, the real estate market bubble, and a sharp rise in asset prices (Kauko, 2014). The main signals of an impending crisis in the banking sector were the growth in the share of non-performing loans, increased borrowing in the interbank markets, a decrease in capital adequacy ratio, and an increase in the share of subprime mortgage loans in bank balance sheets (Cox & Wang, 2014; Gehrig & Iannino, 2021). The increased need for liquidity negatively affected the return on assets and net interest margins, and also increased the costs of banks for loan provisions (Chen et al., 2021).

Researchers and national regulators have empirically shown the nexus between the financial stability of the banking sector and a number of other indicators, as well as the predictive capabilities of these indicators. These include indicators of GDP, the volume of investments in the economy, stock market indices, and prices for residential real estate. In the studies on the topic, two important findings were documented. First, there is empirical evidence of the relationship between the economic performance of the real sector and the main indicators of the banking sector's financial health. Second, the possibility of using indicators of non-financial sectors of the economy to predict the state of the banking sector was confirmed. At the same time, it is stated that one of the most important counterparties of the banking sector is the household sector. The financial decisions of households, including decisions on interaction with banks, are influenced by their income, its size, and other characteristics. (Aller & Grant, 2018; Bell & Pain, 2000; Bellettini et al., 2019; Goldstein et al., 2000).

Theoretical predictions suggest that an increase in household income and a rise in stock markets have a positive impact on the stability of the banking system. However, the results of empirical studies do not appear to support these hypotheses. According to a number of studies (Alessi & Detken, 2018; Dawood et al., 2017; Hanschel & Monnin, 2005; Vašíček et al., 2017), historical data show that in the past, positive dynamics of macroeconomic indicators led to recession and debt crises, and correspondingly to an increase in the level of stress in the banking sector, reducing its resilience. It was found that household debt as well as dislocated housing prices is a potential source of banking sector vulnerability (Aldasoro et al., 2018). When studying the relationship between banking stability and the household sector, increased attention is paid to the indicators capturing the well-being of the population, such as household income, income volatility, income inequality, unemployment, and others (Aller & Grant, 2018; Bell & Pain, 2000; Contreras et al., 2021; Destek et al., 2020), as well as to the indicators of the intensity of household demand for banking services and the volume of interaction between the households and banks, such as the volume of loans, the volume of deposits, and the average volume of loans and deposits per capita (Andersson & Mayock, 2014; Cox & Wang, 2014; Kauko, 2014; Kelly & McCann, 2016; Koniagina, 2017; Maslennikov & Larionov, 2020; Voronova et al., 2018).

Another important group of indicators that influence banking stability is indicators of the general market situation and the state of the country's economy as a whole (Nazlioglu et al., 2015). These indicators include the main stock market indices, the exchange rate of the national currency, and the key interest rate (Frankel & Saravelos, 2012; Lepers & Serrano, 2020). For the Russian economy, which has a significant degree of reliance on raw materials, an important indicator is the world prices for fuel and energy resources. Based on the above, this study tests the hypothesis about the importance of household income in determining the stability of the Russian banking sector measured using the constructed financial stability index.

4.3 Methodology

The research consists of two main stages:

1. Construction of the financial stability index of the Russian banking sector;
2. Estimating a regression model of the relationship between the financial stability of the banking sector and macroeconomic indicators of the non-financial sector, including household income.

For developing economies, it is not always possible to conduct assessments over long periods of time, due to the lack of relevant data, which is, among other things, conditioned by the relatively recent transition from socialism to a market economy. In Russia, which made such a transition in the 1990s of the twentieth century, data have been accumulated since the economic recovery after the crisis of 1997–1998, which makes it possible to study the influence of household income on the stability of the banking sector over this period of time. The study uses quarterly data for seven indicators included in the financial stability index of the Russian banking system and 15 macroeconomic indicators describing the state of the Russian economy, which are tested as independent variables in the model. The sample time period is from 2002 to 2019

(Miroshnichenko & Vyshkovskaia, 2021). Nominal variables are used as they demonstrate statistical significance (Gambera, 2000; Hanschel & Monnin, 2005). Descriptive statistics of the sample variables are provided in Appendix A.

Financial Stability Index

This section describes the process of developing a financial stability index that summarizes the current state of the Russian banking sector in one dimension.

The most common method for assessing the state of the financial system in general, or the banking sector in particular, is the calculation of the stress index. However, this study aims to construct the financial stability index, which is an essential component of sustainable development of the financial system. There are two main reasons for this: (i) the specifics of the sample represented by data on financial soundness indicators and (ii) justified by the authors' potential superiority of empirical research based on the theory of sustainable development of the banking system. There are several ways to construct an index, that is, to aggregate separate indicators of the stability of individual segments into a composite indicator of the financial stability of the banking sector. In this study, we used the variance-equal weighting method, which is the most widespread in the literature. This method is assuming the equal importance (weight) of each variable in the final index. It consists of the two steps. The first of them is standardizing the variables by subtracting the mean from each variable and then dividing by the standard deviation in order to express them with the same units, and the second is aggregating them using identical weights. The index formula is the following:

$$I_t = \sum_{i=1}^{k} \frac{X_{i,t} - \overline{X}_i}{\sigma_i} \tag{4.1}$$

$\Sigma_{i=1}^{k}$—the number of variables in the index,
$X_{i,t}$—variable i in period t,
$\overline{X}_i$—the mean of the variable X_i,
σ_i—standard deviation of the variable X_i.

Macroprudential indicators published by the Bank of Russia and recommended by the IMF as Financial Soundness Indicators for depository institutions were chosen as the variables for calculating the financial soundness index of the Russian banking sector:

- capital adequacy ratio;
- credit risk as an indicator of asset quality;
- liquidity;
- market risk;
- efficiency (ROA, ROE).

The first group of indicators in the index is represented by the indicator of Tier 1 capital adequacy, which is most often the case in the literature (Lepers & Serrano, 2020). It is used because it includes higher quality sources that have a better ability to cover unforeseen costs, and therefore more reliably demonstrates the level of sustainability. The Tier 1 capital adequacy indicator best reflects the ability of the banking sector to generate capital and overcomes distortions that may be caused by additional injections of state support for the banking system in the form of subordinated liabilities during crises. In addition, in the analyzed period, the regulatory methodology for calculating capital was changed. However, it did not affect the sources included in the composition of tier 1 capital. The indicators of the share of bad loans in the total volume of loans and the volume of provisions for possible loan losses as a percentage of the total issued loans volume, the most commonly used in the scientific literature, were selected as indicators of credit risk (Mocetti & Viviano, 2017). When using the indicators to compute the index, it is necessary to subtract one from the indicated coefficients in order to bring them into direct relationship with financial stability.

Liquidity in the index is represented by the ratio of customer funds to total loans. This indicator best demonstrates the ability of banks to meet their obligations before customers in a timely manner (Lepers & Serrano, 2020). The efficiency is captured by the indicators of profitability, namely the return on assets and return on equity of banks, the use of which is also found in the literature (Bongini et al., 2019; Elekdag et al., 2020). Assessing the plausibility of an index is the most difficult task, since the real sequence of events in the banking sector is not known with sufficient accuracy. Many researchers propose to compare the values of the computed index with expert estimates of the historical level of financial stability (Bordo & Eichengreen, 1999; Illing & Liu, 2003). Despite the fact that among experts there is also no common opinion on the intensity and chronology of crises, expert assessments can be used to evaluate the reliability of the obtained results. In this study, after a visual assessment of the constructed financial stability index, it is decomposed to determine the contribution of each factor to the overall stability of the Russian banking sector.

Regression Model

The construction of the model involves the investigation and identification of factors influencing the state of the Russian economy and affecting the stability of the banking sector, measured with the aid of the proposed financial stability index, which is the dependent variable. The hypothesis of this study is that it is the indicator related to household income appear one of the most significant for predicting stability in the banking sector. When studying the relationship between household income and the state of the banking sector, indicators such as the dynamics of total income, average income per capita, income inequality, including the Gini coefficient, the ratio of bank debt to income, and the unemployment rate are used. Based on the previous studies, as well as taking into account the availability of statistical data on macroeconomic indicators, a database of 15 variables describing the state of the Russian economy was compiled.

The variables were selected for the final model using a two-stage algorithm. At the first step, the relationships between macroeconomic indicators, which serve as explanatory variables in the model, were tested. This step is necessary to avoid multicollinearity in the final model.

While testing the data set, strong correlations between the available explanatory variables were revealed. Thus, indicators with a correlation of more than 90% were combined into separate groups. In total, six groups of indicators were formed. Explanatory variable groups are presented in Appendix B.

The first group includes indicators of household income as well as the volumes of loans and deposits. All of them are significantly correlated with each other. This suggests that indicators of the banking services demand volume also indirectly reflect the size of the household income. The indicator of the household debt growth, which is close to the indicators from the first group, has a weaker correlation with other indicators of the banking services demand volume, and for this reason it is singled out into a separate group. According to relevant studies (Kelly & McCann, 2016), the unemployment rate can become as important a determinant of financial soundness as household income. At the same time, despite the conceptual connectivity of these indicators, the correlation between them is rather weak and, when used together in a model, they can improve its explanatory power.

The indicators of arrears follow a distinctive pattern. They form another group and can enter the final model. The fifth group is represented by the indicators of oil price as one of the main factors affecting economic growth in Russia (Polbin et al., 2020) and the Russian stock market index. Finally, income inequality as measured by the Gini coefficient has proven to be effective in determining the probability of banking crises in the previous studies (Bellettini et al., 2019). Since it turned out to be relatively unrelated to household income and other explanatory variables, it has a potential, if significantly related to the dependent variable, to be included in the final model. At the second stage, one indicator that has the greatest correlation with the dependent variable was selected from each group. Thus, by identifying the strongest relationships between the explanatory variables and the financial stability index, five regressors were introduced into the final model: household income, an increase in the average volume of household loans per capita, the share of overdue debt on loans to individuals and non-financial organizations, the price of Brent oil, and the unemployment rate in the country.

4.4 Results

Considering the Russian banking sector, there are two crisis periods: 2009–2010 and 2015–2017 that are usually recognized over the 2002–2019 horizon. The first crisis period was a consequence of the US mortgage crisis caused by a significant rise of risky mortgage loans and then escalated into the global financial crisis. The crisis in Russia was caused by a sharp decline in oil prices and the collapse of the national stock market, while the situation was aggravated by the presence of a large volume of external borrowing by banks and private non-financial firms. The banking crisis, in particular, was caused by the aggressive lending policy of banks, a high share of overdue loans in the loan portfolio, and the inadequacy of the amount of equity capital to the accepted risks. This crisis is considered the largest over the period under study.

The 2015–2017 crisis was marked by a sharp depreciation of the Russian currency caused by a rapid decline in world oil prices, a shift in the exchange rate regime of the national currency, as well as the introduction of economic sanctions against Russia. The main consequences were an increase in inflation and a decrease in real household income.

Figure 4.1 shows the results obtained when calculating the financial stability index for the Russian banking sector. The diagram indicates that the values of the obtained index correlate with the chronology of crisis periods and the corresponding levels of financial stability. It can be observed that before the crisis, namely, in 2008, the level of financial stability was much higher than the average for the period. After a sharp decline in stability by 10 points caused by the 2009 crisis, the banking sector failed to return to its initial level, as already at the end of 2014 it faced a new fall by 5 points. In recent years, there has been a positive trend. However, the 2020 adverse conditions due to the pandemic adversely affected the recovery of the banking sector (Berger et al., 2021).

It possible to decompose the financial stability index into its constituent indicators and determine the contribution of each factor to the financial stability of the banking sector. Figure 4.2 shows the decomposition of the index. A positive (negative) value indicates that the variable is higher (lower) than the average value for the sample and indicates a greater (lower) level of stability in the system than the average for the period. The decomposition of the index shows that during the crisis period from 2015 to 2017, six out of seven indicators were below their historical average. The largest negative values were for capital adequacy and profitability indicators. Capital adequacy is also the only indicator

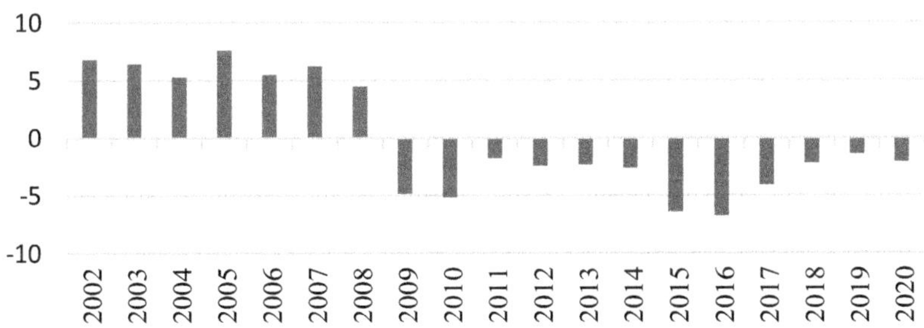

Fig. 4.1 Financial stability index of the Russian banking sector dynamics 2002–2020 (*Source* Bank of Russia, Authors' calculations)

that has been consistently below average over the past nine years. The most significant decrease was observed in 2016, and then the value of the capital adequacy ratio was getting closer to the average annually, corresponding to the stabilization of the general situation in the sector. Strengthening the level of financial stability was also achieved thanks to the improved profitability, liquidity, and reduced market risk.

Thus, the developed index is an attempt to identify fluctuations in the level of banks' financial soundness. The index is a set of conditions in the banking sector, ranging from a high level of stability when the banking sector is sound and balanced, to a low level of stability when the banking sector is in a state of distress. A correct assessment of the current state of the banking sector is a primary and very important step in ensuring the sustainable development of the financial system in the future.

According to the index, the highest level of financial stability was detected in 2008, 2011, and 2019. The peaks of the crisis periods were in 2009–2010 and 2016. The decomposition of the index showed that the

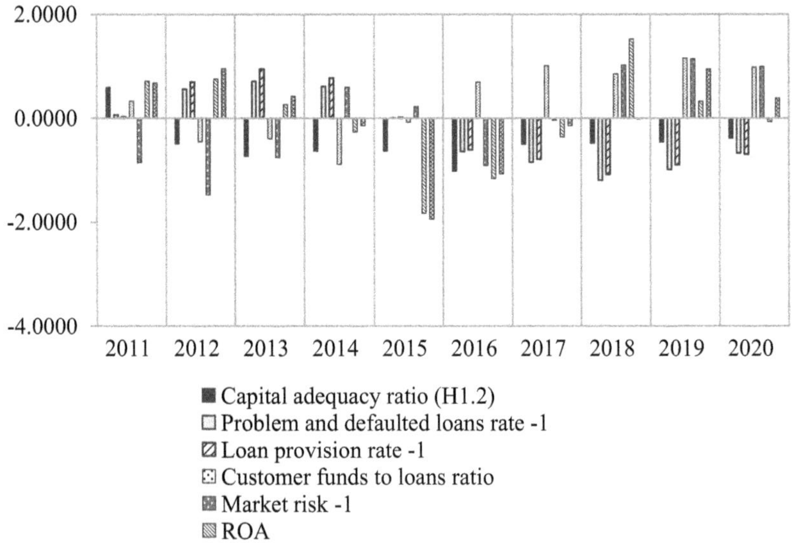

Fig. 4.2 Financial stability index decomposition 2011–2019 (*Source* Bank of Russia, Authors' calculations)

indicators of capital adequacy as well as the ratio of the financial result to total assets and capital react most sharply to systemic stress.

The constructed index was used as the dependent variable in the regression model. The main characteristics of the model are presented in Table 4.1. Three ratios have a 1% significance level. The coefficients of the oil price and increase in average per capita loans variables are significant at the 5% and 10% levels, respectively. An R-square of 0.86 is relatively high. The model estimation showed the absence of multicollinearity, which confirms the reliability of the coefficients in the model. The lags of the variables range from three quarters for the household income to 8 quarters for the oil price. The model shows a significant negative effect of indicators of household income, oil price, the share of overdue loans to individuals and non-financial organizations, as well as unemployment rate on the financial stability index. At the same time, an increase in the average per capita loan volume has a positive effect on the level of financial stability of the banking sector.

Despite the fact that a classical theoretical approach suggests a direct relationship between the dynamics of household income and the development of the country's economy, the global financial crisis, one of the reasons for which was the growth of subprime debt in the absence of a decrease in household income, questioned this classical approach. A number of empirical studies show an inverse relationship between credit expansion and financial sustainability. This is due to the cyclical nature of lending (Demirgüç-Kunt et al., 2008; Lowe & Borio, 2002). Increased lending precedes a credit boom and subsequent recession. At the same time, a number of studies also indicate the presence of cyclicality in household income (Büyükkarabacak & Valev, 2010). Therefore, this indicator can also be considered as a predictor of the state of the banking sector. It was found that in times of financial stability, households do not expect adverse crisis manifestations, which is revealed in their relations with banks (Allen & Wood, 2006) and is reflected in bank balance sheets. And due to the fact that, presumably, it takes some time for the positive dynamics in the household income to instill confidence in households' financial position and be reflected in the expansion of interaction with credit institutions through making deposits and obtaining loans, indicators of household income may have the ability to give earlier warning than indicators of the credit cycle. The assumptions expressed above are confirmed by the results of the obtained model. The variable of non-performing loans rate on the loans to individuals and non-financial organizations has

Table 4.1 Macroeconomic factors and the financial stability index of the banking sector regression model

	FSI
Log household income (−3)	−2.873***
	(0.754)
Log Brent oil price (−8)	−1.249**
	(0.612)
NPL rate	−0.429***
	(0.108)
Increase in per capita household loan volume	5.987*
	(3.286)
Unemployment rate	−1.221***
	(0.290)
Constant	39.830***
	(6.841)
Observations	71
R-squared	0.863

This table presents a regression model based on time series of quarterly data for the period 2002–2019. The dependent variable is represented by the banking sector financial stability index (FSI). The two independent variables are lagged. For the household income variable, the lag is 3 quarters. The oil price variable has a lag of 8 quarters. The robust standard errors of the variables are in parentheses. *, **, and *** denote the 10%, 5%, and 1% significance levels, respectively

a negative coefficient. This suggests that a commensurate decrease in the level of financial stability occurs simultaneously with an increase in the non-performing loans rate.

The hypothesis that the indicator of the volume of loans will become one of the predictors of financial stability has not been confirmed. There is no lag for the increase in loan volume per capita. Moreover, there is a significant positive relationship between the indicator and the dependent variable. Therefore, an increase in the loan volume per capita has a positive effect on the financial stability of the banking sector, which is consistent with the classical approach. This is due to the fact that the average volume of loans per capita is growing by new unimpaired debt with regular interest payments. This contributes to the growth of bank income and has a positive effect on the profitability of the banking sector as an indicator of its financial soundness. According to the model, the time interval between an increase in household income and a decrease in the level of financial stability of the banking system is three quarters. We can also conclude that the increase in household income anticipates an increase in the non-performing loans rate by three quarters. The explanatory variable represented by the indicator of household income has a negative coefficient, which indicates a negative effect of increase in household income on the level of financial stability of the banking sector. The coefficient of the oil price variable indicates a negative effect of the change in the oil price and the level of financial stability of the banking system. At the same time, the oil price variable has the capability to provide the earliest warning. The lag of this indicator is eight quarters or two years. Thus, it can be assumed that the positive dynamics in the oil market does not immediately affect the households' financial position. A corresponding increase in household income occurs in more than a year.

Finally, according to the model, the unemployment rate has a negative relationship with the banking sector financial stability index. However, since there is no lag for this variable, the unemployment rate could not be considered an early warning indicator. Therefore, the negative dynamics of the unemployment rate coincides with the appearance of negative trends in the banking sector.

It should be noted that the final model has limitations. First, the explanatory variables included in the model largely, but not fully, explain the dynamics of the stability indicator of the banking system. They are not the only factors behind the state of the banking sector. Other factors can also affect the change in the level of financial stability, but they are not included in the model. This includes, for example, political frictions or legal system deficiencies that are difficult to measure. Second, the uncertainty was associated not only with the choice of explanatory variables, but also with the imperfect reliability of the banking sector financial stability assessment of the dependent index variable. In this regard, the results of the model are able to only approximately capture the actual situation. Despite this, the model made it possible to draw an important conclusion for the research question. Based on the results obtained from the model, an increase in oil price and a subsequent increase in household income lead to an increase in the non-performing loans rate and the unemployment rate and determine a decrease in the level of financial stability of the banking sector. Certainly, the negative relationship between the indicators of oil price, household income and the level of financial stability contradicts the classical approach. However, modern studies (Alsamara et al., 2019; Cevik et al., 2013) draw similar conclusions. The negative relationship between the positive dynamics of macroeconomic indicators and the financial stability of the banking sector is explained by the fact that the economic upturn in the real sector provokes banks to increase the volume of services provided and, first of all, the volume of lending by taking greater risks in order to obtain greater profits. This aggressive policy results in an increase in the share of arrears in banks' loan portfolios, which leads to a decrease in the level of financial stability in the banking sector. This was the reason for the largest global financial crisis of 2008–2009. The results of the empirical analysis confirm a similar development of the situation in the Russian banking sector.

Thus, the resultant model confirmed the existence of a serious problem in the Russian banking sector, which is also typical for the financial systems of other countries. The problem is that banks take on an excessive amount of risk during periods of favorable macroeconomic conditions in the real sector. The solution to the problem and the main task of the regulator at the current stage is the implementation of a proper macroprudential policy, including the mechanism of countercyclical surcharges to the capital adequacy ratios of banks, as well as the development of debt level caps depending on the borrower's income. Macroeconomic indicators that can serve as a benchmark for introducing capital buffers are identified in many studies.

The results of the model developed in the study showed that the main predictors that supervisors can focus on for taking proactive anti-crisis measures are oil price, household income, as well as the indicators of the banks' loan portfolio.

4.5 Conclusions

In this study, a financial stability index of the Russian banking system was constructed, which makes it possible to assess the sector's current state. The assessment of the historical values of the index has confirmed its reliability. The main conclusion of the study was made on the basis of the regression model describing the relationship between the developed financial stability index and macroeconomic indicators. The model revealed a statistically significant negative effect of changes in the indicators of household income, oil price, as well as non-performing loans rate and unemployment rate on the financial stability index of the Russian banking system. The relationship between the variables suggests the presence of lags of 3 and 8 quarters for household income and oil prices, respectively. Thus, these indicators are able to predict changes in the level of financial stability of the Russian banking sector.

Further research could be devoted to assessing the influence of the identified significant factors on the stability of other financial sectors, in addition to the banking sector, and testing hypotheses about the direction of such influence. Our results can be useful for regulators in the implementation of macroprudential policy, as well as in the selection of tools to regulate socio-economic processes related to household income indicators.

Acknowledgements The reported study was funded by RFBR, project № 19-010-00801.

Appendix A

Descriptive statistics.

	Obs	*Mean*	*Median*	*Standard deviation*	*Min*	*Max*
Financial stability index	73	3.69	−1.24	4.24	−6.60	9.05
Household income	73	8002.93	8008.70	4888.41	1024.11	17,117.90
Household income per capita	73	19,173.71	18,690.00	10,235.82	3504.50	37,492.67
Loans to households	73	168.88	126.07	146.86	1.34	478.24
Increase in household loans	73	8.29	6.02	9.04	−6.11	34.46
Loans to households per capita	73	1162.62	882.92	1001.71	9.21	3258.56
Increase in per capita household loans	73	0.08	0.06	0.09	−0.06	0.35
Household deposits	73	11.94	12.18	1.25	9.34	13.47
Household deposits per capita	73	7.13	7.49	1.16	4.56	8.51
Unemployment	73	1.94	1.96	0.22	1.59	2.52
Gini coefficient	73	0.41	0.41	0.01	0.40	0.42

(continued)

(continued)

	Obs	*Mean*	*Median*	*Standard deviation*	*Min*	*Max*
Household NPL rate	73	7.03	6.52	2.12	1.12	17.52
Corporate NPL rate	73	4.74	5.41	2.48	0.98	9.21
Corporate and household NPL rate	73	6.06	6.29	3.94	1.29	13.11
RTSI	73	6.64	6.88	0.87	4.23	7.74
Brent oil price	73	65.06	61.87	31.18	19.80	126.32

Appendix B

Explanatory variables and their correlation with the dependent variable.

Explanatory variables	*Correlation with the dependent variable*
Group 1[a]	
Household income	−0.7759
Household income per capita	−0.7654
Loans to households per capita	−0.7181
Loans to households	−0.7136
Household deposits	−0.7005
Household deposits per capita	0.7042
Group 2	
Increase in per capita household loans	0.7308
Increase in household loans	0.7273
Group 3	
Unemployment rate	0.4397
Group 4[a]	
Corporate and household NPL rate	−0.8634
Household NPL rate	−0.8437
Corporate NPL rate	−0.8371
Group 5[b]	
Oil price	−0.6780
RTSI	−0.6130
Group 6	
Gini coefficient	−0.3700

[a]The correlation between the variables in the group exceeds 0.9

[b]Despite the fact that the correlation between the variables is 0.79, they are grouped according to economic sense

References

Aldasoro, I., Borio, C. E. V., & Drehmann, M. (2018, March 11). Early warning indicators of banking crises: Expanding the family. *BIS Quarterly Review*. Available at SSRN: https://ssrn.com/abstract=3139160

Alessi, L., & Detken, C. (2018). Identifying excessive credit growth and leverage. *Journal of Financial Stability, 36*, 39–52. https://doi.org/10.1016/j.jfs.2017.06.005

Allen, W. A., & Wood, G. (2006). Defining and achieving financial stability. *Journal of Financial Stability, 2*(2), 152–172. https://doi.org/10.1016/j.jfs.2005.10.001

Aller, C., & Grant C. (2018). The effect of the financial crisis on default by Spanish households. *Journal of Financial Stability, 36*, 39–52. https://doi.org/10.1016/j.jfs.2018.02.006

Alsamara, M., Mrabet, Z., Jarallah, S., & Barkat, K. (2019, August). The switching impact of financial stability and economic growth in Qatar: Evidence from an oil-rich country. *The Quarterly Review of Economics and Finance, 73*, 205–216. https://doi.org/10.1016/j.qref.2018.05.008

Andersson, F., & Mayock, T. (2014). Loss severities on residential real estate debt during the Great Recession. *Journal of Banking & Finance, 46*, 266–284. https://doi.org/10.1016/j.jbankfin.2014.05.010

Aspachs, O., Goodhart, C., & Segoviano, M. (2009). *Searching for a metric for financial stability* (LSE Financial Markets Group Special Paper Series. No 167, pp. 1–65). https://www.fmg.ac.uk/publications/special-papers/searching-metric-financial-stability

Beck, T., De Jonghe, O., & Schepens, G. (2013). Bank competition and stability: Cross-country heterogeneity. *Journal of Financial Intermediation, 22*(2), 218–244. https://doi.org/10.1016/j.jfi.2012.07.001

Bell, J., & Pain, D. (2000, December). Leading indicator models of banking crises—A critical review. Financial Stability Review, Bank of England, 1–37. https://www.bankofengland.co.uk/-/media/boe/files/financial-stability-report/2000/december-2000.pdf

Bellettini, G., Delbono, F., Karlström, P., & Pastorello, S. (2019). Income inequality and banking crises: Testing the level hypothesis directly. *Journal of Macroeconomics, 62*, 36–57. https://doi.org/10.1016/j.jmacro.2018.08.007

Berger, A. N., Demirgüç-Kunt, A., Moshirian, F., & Saunders, A. (2021). The way forward for banks during the COVID-19 crisis and beyond: Government and central bank responses, threats to the global banking industry. *Journal of Banking & Finance*, 106303. Available online 23 August 2021. https://doi.org/10.1016/j.jbankfin.2021.106303

Berger, A. N., & Molyneux, P., & Wilson, J. O. S. (2020, June). Banks and the real economy: An assessment of the research. *Journal of Corporate Finance, 62*, 101513. https://doi.org/10.1016/j.jcorpfin.2019.101513

Bongini, P., Cucinelli, D., Di Battista, M. L., & Nieri, L. (2019, September). Profitability shocks and recovery in time of crisis evidence from European banks. *Finance Research Letters, 30*, 233–239.https://doi.org/10.1016/j.frl.2018.10.003

Bordo, M., & Eichengreen, B. (1999). Is our Current International Economic Environment Unusually Crisis Prone? *RBA Annual Conference*. Reserve Bank of Australia. https://ideas.repec.org/h/rba/rbaacv/acv1999-03.html

Borio, C., Drehmann, M., & Xia, F. D. (2020, December). Forecasting recessions: The importance of the financial cycle. *Journal of Macroeconomics, 66*. https://doi.org/10.1016/j.jmacro.2020.103258

Lowe, P., & Borio, C. (2002). *Asset prices, financial and monetary stability: Exploring the nexus* (BIS Working Papers, No 114). Bank for International Settlements.

Büyükkarabacak, B., & Valev, N. T. (2010). The role of household and business credit in banking crises. *Journal of Banking & Finance, 34*(6), 1247–1256. https://doi.org/10.1016/j.jbankfin.2009.11.022

Cevik, E., Dibooglu, S., & Kutan, A. (2013). Measuring financial stress in transition economies. *Journal of Financial Stability, 9*, 597–611. https://doi.org/10.1016/j.jfs.2012.10.001

Chen, W.-D., Chen, Y., & Huang, S.-C. (2021, October). Liquidity risk and bank performance during financial crises. *Journal of Financial Stability, 56*, 100906. https://doi.org/10.1016/j.jfs.2021.100906

Čihák, M., Demirgüç-Kunt, A. Feyen, E., & Levine, R. (2012). *Benchmarking financial systems around the world* (Policy Research Working Paper, No 6175, p. 1–46). http://hdl.handle.net/10986/12031

Contreras, S., Ghosh, A., & Hasan, I. (2021, February). Income inequality and minority labor market dynamics: Medium term effects from the Great Recession. *Economics Letters, 199*, 109717. https://doi.org/10.1016/j.econlet.2020.109717

Cox, R. A. K., & Wang, G. W.-Y. (2014, July). Predicting the US bank failure: A discriminant analysis. *Economic Analysis and Policy, 44*(2), 202–211. https://doi.org/10.1016/j.eap.2014.06.002

Dawood, M., Horsewood, N., & Strobel, F. (2017). Predicting sovereign debt crises: An Early Warning System approach. *Journal of Financial Stability, 28*, 16–28. https://doi.org/10.1016/j.jfs.2016.11.008

Demirgüç-Kunt, A., Detragiache E., & Tressel, T. (2008). Banking on the Principles: Compliance with Basel core principles and bank soundness. *Journal of Financial Intermediation, 17*(4), 511–542. https://doi.org/10.1016/j.jfi.2007.10.003

Destek, M. A., Sinha, A., & Sarkodie, S. A. (2020). The relationship between financial development and income inequality in Turkey. *Journal of Economic*

Structures, 9, Article number: 11. https://doi.org/10.1186/s40008-020-0187-6

Drehmann, M., & Juselius M. (2014, July–September). Evaluating early warning indicators of banking crises: Satisfying policy requirements. *International Journal of Forecasting, 30*(3), 759–780. https://doi.org/10.1016/j.ijforecast.2013.10.002

Elekdag, S., Malik, S., & Mitra, S. (2020, November). Breaking the bank? A probabilistic assessment of Euro Area Bank profitability. *Journal of Banking & Finance, 120*, 105949. https://doi.org/10.1016/j.jbankfin.2020.105949

IMF. (2020). *Financial development index*. https://data.imf.org/?sk=F8032E80-B36C-43B1-AC26-493C5B1CD33B

IMF. (2022). *Financial Soundness Indicators (FSIs)*. https://data.imf.org/?sk=51B096FA-2CD2-40C2-8D09-0699CC1764DA

Flori, A., Pammolli, F., & Spelta, A. (2021, June). Commodity prices co-movements and financial stability: A multidimensional visibility nexus with climate conditions. *Journal of Financial Stability, 54*, 100876.

Frankel, J., & Saravelos, G. (2012, July). Can leading indicators assess country vulnerability? Evidence from the 2008–09 global financial crisis. *Journal of International Economics, 87*(2), 216–231. https://doi.org/10.1016/j.jinteco.2011.12.009

Gambera, M. (2000). Simple forecasts of bank loan quality in the business cycle. Federal Reserve Bank of Chicago. Emerging Issues. https://www.chicagofed.org/sr-2000-3-pdf

Gehrig, T., & Iannino, M. C. (2021, August). Did the Basel Process of capital regulation enhance the resiliency of European banks? *Journal of Financial Stability, 55*, 100904 https://doi.org/10.1016/j.jfs.2021.100904

Goldstein, M., Kaminsky, G. L., & Reinhart, C. M. (2000). *Assessing financial vulnerability: An early warning system for emerging markets* (pp. 1–56). Institute for Financial Economics.

González-Hermosillo, B. (1999). *Determinants of ex-ante banking system stress: A macro-micro empirical exploration of some recent episodes* (IMF Working Paper, No 99/33, pp. 1–114). https://www.elibrary.imf.org/view/journals/001/1999/033/001.1999.issue-033-en.xml

Gryzunova, N. V., Pyatanova, V. I., Manuylenko, V. V., & Ordov, K. V. (2019). Models of credit limit-setting for companies as means of encouraging competitiveness. *Entrepreneurship and Sustainability Issues, 7*(1), 615–625. https://doi.org/10.9770/jesi.2019.7.1(43)

Hanschel, E., & Monnin, P. (2005). *Measuring and forecasting stress in the banking sector: Evidence from Switzerland* (BIS Working Papers, No 22, pp. 431–449). Bank for International Settlements. https://econpapers.repec.org/bookchap/bisbisbpc/22-22.htm

Illing, M., & Liu, J. (2003). *An index of financial stress for Canada* (Bank of Canada Working Papers, No 14, pp. 1–63). Bank of Canada. https://www.bankofcanada.ca/2003/06/working-paper-2003-14/

Ivanov, V. V., Lvova, N. A., Pokrovskaia, N. V., & Naumenkova, S. V. (2018). Determinants of tax incentives for investment activity of enterprises. *Journal of Tax Reform, 4*(2), 125–141. https://doi.org/10.15826/jtr.2018.4.2.048

Kauko, K. (2014, September). How to foresee banking crises? A survey of the empirical literature. *Economic Systems, 38*(3), 289–308.https://doi.org/10.1016/j.ecosys.2014.01.001

Kelly, R., & McCann, F. (2016). Some defaults are deeper than others: Understanding long-term mortgage arrears. *Journal of Banking & Finance, 72*, 15–27. https://doi.org/10.1016/j.jbankfin.2016.07.006

Koniagina, M. N. (2014). Dynamics of bank deposits in 2014–2015 under conditions of fluctuations in the Russian ruble exchange rate: Analysis and interpretation. *St Petersburg University Journal of Economic Studies, 33*(4), 593–601. https://doi.org/10.21638/11701/spbu05.2017.404

Lepers, E., & Serrano, A. S. (2020, January). Decomposing financial (in)stability in emerging economies. *Research in International Business and Finance, 51*, 101068. https://doi.org/10.1016/j.ribaf.2019.101068

Levine, R. (2005). *Finance and growth: Theory and evidence* (Handbook of economic growth, No. 1, pp. 865–934). https://doi.org/10.1016/S1574-0684(05)01012-9

Manuylenko, V., et al. (2020). Development and implementation of alternative concept for expected and unexpected losses in corporations. *TEM Journal, 9*(3), 1116–1125. https://doi.org/10.18421/TEM93-37

Maslennikov, V. V., & Larionov, A. V. (2020). Impact of the behavioral cycle on cash flow formation. *Finance: Theory and Practice, 24*(5), 100–111. https://doi.org/10.26794/2587-5671-2020-24-5-100-111

Miroshnichenko, O. S., Voronova, N. S., & Gamukin, V. V. (2020). The development of macroprudential regulation of bank household lending in Russia. *Finance: Theory and Practice, 24*(4), 75–87. https://doi.org/10.26794/2587-5671-2020-24-4-75-87

Miroshnichenko, O., & Vyshkovskaia, M. (2021). FSI, Household income, deposits, loans, unemployment of Russia 2002–2019. *Mendeley Data, V1*.https://doi.org/10.17632/86w7m526c6.1

Mocetti, S., & Viviano, E. (2017). Looking behind mortgage delinquencies. *Journal of Banking & Finance, 75*, 53–63. https://doi.org/10.1016/j.jbankfin.2016.11.002

Nazlioglu, S., Soytas, U., & Gupta, R. (2015). Oil prices and financial stress: A volatility spillover analysis. *Energy Policy, 82*, 278–288.

Polbin, A., Skrobotov, A., & Zubarev, A. (2020). How the oil price and other factors of real exchange rate dynamics affect real GDP in Russia. *Emerging*

Markets Finance and Trade, 56(15), 3732–3745. https://doi.org/10.1080/1540496X.2019.1573667

Rahman, M. L., Troster, V., & Uddin, G. S., & Yahya, M. (2022, January). Systemic risk contribution of banks and non-bank financial institutions across frequencies: The Australian experience. *International Review of Financial Analysis, 79*, 101992. https://doi.org/10.1016/j.irfa.2021.101992

Schinasi, G. J. (2004, October). *Defining financial stability* (IMF Working Paper No. 04/187). Available at SSRN: https://ssrn.com/abstract=879012

Truong, C., Sheen, J., Trück, S., & Villafuerte, J. (2021). Early warning systems using dynamic factor models: An application to Asian economies. *Journal of Financial Stability*, 100885. Available online 19 May 2021. https://doi.org/10.1016/j.jfs.2021.100885

Vašíček, B., Žigraiová, D., Hoeberichts, M., Vermeulen, R., Šmídková, K., & Haan, J. (2017). Leading indicators of financial stress: New evidence. *Journal of Financial Stability, 28*, 240–257. https://doi.org/10.1016/j.jfs.2016.05.005

Voronova, N. S., & Miroshnichenko, O. S. (2018). People's incomes as a potential for development of bank lending: Comparative analysis of Russian regions. *Economic and Social Changes: Facts, Trends, Forecast, 11*(4), 144–159. https://doi.org/10.15838/esc.2018.4.58.9

World Bank. (2020). *Key terms explained*. https://www.worldbank.org/en/publication/gfdr/gfdr-2016/background/key-terms-explained

CHAPTER 5

The Impact of ESG Rating on Companies' Resilience to Systemic Risks

Alexandra Egorova and Herman Petrov-Nerling

5.1 Introduction

An increasing number of emerging threats every year contributes to the buildup of systemic risks and at the same time accentuates the importance of maintaining sustainability of financial institutions and non-financial entities. While it is not possible to develop a universal approach for any crisis event, companies develop a wide range of preventive and reactive anti-crisis measures to maintain business continuity. Among the basic principles of such anti-crisis measures, one should emphasize the sustainability components included in the ESG rating.

ESG ratings can provide valuable insights into a company's long-term sustainability and resilience, which can be critical in today's complex and rapidly changing business environment. By considering ESG factors,

The research was supported by RNF (proj. #23-18-00756).

A. Egorova (✉) · H. Petrov-Nerling
NRU HSE, Moscow, Russia
e-mail: a.egorova@hse.ru

A. Karminsky and M. Stolbov (eds.), *Systemic Financial Risk*,
https://doi.org/10.1007/978-3-031-54809-3_5

investors and other stakeholders can make more informed decisions that not only benefit their own interests but also contribute to a more sustainable and equitable future for all.

ESG ratings can be connected with systemic risks in several ways. For example:

1. Environmental risks: Companies that are highly dependent on natural resources or operate in the industries with a high environmental impact (such as oil and gas or mining) may be more exposed to environmental risks such as climate change, natural disasters or regulatory changes. ESG ratings can help investors identify which companies are better prepared to manage these risks and mitigate their impact.
2. Social risks: Companies that have a poor track record on issues such as labor rights, human rights or community engagement may face social risks such as boycotts, protests or reputational damage. ESG ratings can help investors identify which companies are more socially responsible and better positioned to avoid these risks.
3. Governance risks: Companies with weak governance structures or a history of ethical lapses may be more vulnerable to governance risks such as fraud, corruption, or legal liability. ESG ratings can help investors identify which companies have strong governance practices and are less likely to face these risks.

This study that should highlight such cases and improve understanding of the impact of ESG principles on companies' resilience to systemic risks and their ability to cope with crises. To do this, we have identified the main systemic risks and crises that a company may face. For now, we prepare a comparison of companies' position in ESG ratings and its financial performance in the context of the type and scale of the crisis situation it faced during the observed period. The purpose of our study is defined as "assessing the impact of the ESG rating of companies on their stability in the face of crisis situations and the possibility of reducing the consequences of systemic risks".

An object of the research is companies operating in IT, energy, chemical industry, retail, oil and gas, and mining industry. **The subject of the research is** environmental, social and corporate factors and the systemic risks they may cause, as well as the financial performance of firms. **Main**

target is the identification of the most significant systemic risks caused by ESG practices that affect the financial performance of organizations.

This study aims to answer the following questions:

- How successful will companies be in overcoming systemic risks depending on their ESG rating? Which ESG criteria have the greatest impact on a company's ability to successfully overcome crises and manage systemic risks?
- Are companies with high positions in ESG ratings generally more resistant to crises?
- To what extent will the company's compliance with the ESG criteria be in demand after overcoming the crisis? If there are no crisis situations in the industry, country or world for a long period, will the company's compliance with the principles of sustainable development retain its expediency?

The answers to these questions can be obtained by testing the following hypotheses:

H1. Company's high ESG performance increases its resistance to systemic risks.

H1a. High E (ecology) component score has a positive impact on the company's financial performance and its resilience to systemic risks.
$FI_i = \beta 0 + \beta 1 * E_i + \beta 2 * EBITDAmargin_i + \beta 3 * Leverage_i + \beta 4 * \ln assets_i + \varepsilon_i.$

H1b. High S (social) component score has a positive impact on the company's financial performance and its resilience to systemic risks.
$FI_i = \beta 0 + \beta 1 * S_i + \beta 2 * EBITDAmargin_i + \beta 3 * Leverage_i + \beta 4 * \ln assets_i + \varepsilon_i.$

H1c. High G (governance) component score has a positive impact on the company's financial performance and its resilience to systemic risks.
$FI_i = \beta 0 + \beta 1 * G_i + \beta 2 * EBITDAmargin_i + \beta 3 * Leverage_i + \beta 4 * \ln assets_i + \varepsilon_i.$

For further work, it is also necessary to present the selected variables for the model. Separate explanations are required for the ESG rating.

- Variable ESG denotes the company's overall rating, which is expressed in a letter form, starting with the lowest score of D and ending with the best result of A+.
- Variable E is the assessment of the company's attitude toward the environment. The following factors can be singled out: the presence of a special environmental policy of the company, the impact on the atmosphere and the aquatic environment, the presence of green projects, as well as the quality of waste collection and processing. The E variable has been converted from alpha to numeric in the same way as ESG.
- Variable S assesses the company's social responsibility: attitude toward employees and their labor protection, the presence of a policy to improve socially significant indicators, timely and decent wages to employees. The S variable was converted from letter to categorical in a similar way to ESG.
- Variable G is the company's assessment of the quality of management. This category can include the business reputation of the company, performance indicators of the board of directors, high diversification of managers, the presence of a policy to manage and reduce the risks of the company, the protection and priority of the interests of owners, as well as the transparency of business processes. The G variable was converted from letter to categorical in a similar way to ESG.

5.2 Literature Review

When conducting our study, we considered 35 research papers on the relationship between the ESG indicators and the financial performance of the companies. Results are summarized in Table 5.1.

5.3 Data

For further research, a database was assembled based on the information provided by the Refinitiv. This source was chosen for several reasons: firstly, ESG indicators are presented on average over 10 years, which is a

Table 5.1 Literature review

Name, year, author	*Period*	*Financial indicators*	*Geography*	*Industry*	*E*	*S*	*G*
Raisa Almeyda and Darmansyah (2019). The Influence of Environmental, Social and Governance (ESG) Disclosure on Firm Financial Performance	2014–2018	ROA, ROC, share price and P/E	USA, Canada, Japan, Germany, Italy, France, UK	Real estate	Positive	No connection	No connection
ABM Fazle Rahi, Ruzlin Akter, Jeaneth Johansson (2021). Do sustainability practices influence financial performance? Evidence from the Nordic financial industry	2015–2019	ROIC, ROE, ROA, EPS	Sweden, Denmark, Finland and Norway	Financial sector	Negative	Negative	Mixed

(continued)

Table 5.1 (continued)

Name, year, author	*Period*	*Financial indicators*	*Geography*	*Industry*	*E*	*S*	*G*
Alberto A. Lopez-Toro, Eva Maria Sanchez-Teba, Maria Dolores Benítez-Márquez, Mercedes Rodriguez-Fernández (2021). Influence of ESGC Indicators on Financial Performance of Listed Pharmaceutical Companies	2018–2019	ROE, ROA, Q-Tobin	USA, Europe	Pharmaceuticals	Positive	Positive	Positive
Ebru Saygilia, Serafettin Arslanb, Ayse Ozden Birkanc (2021). ESG practices and corporate financial performance: Evidence from Borsa Istanbul	2007–2017	ROA, Q-Tobin	Turkey	Non-financial companies included in XKURY (an index of the largest companies in Turkey)	Negative	Positive	Positive

Name, year, author	*Period*	*Financial indicators*	*Geography*	*Industry*	*E*	*S*	*G*
Rim El Khoury, Viviane Naimy, Sahar Iskandar (2021). ESG Versus Corporate Financial Performance: Evidence from East Asian Firms in the Industrials Sector (2021)	2011–2017	ROA, ROE, Stock return (RET), Price-to-book ratio (PB)	East Asia	Industrial sector (transportation and capital goods industry)	Negative	Positive in SR, Negative in LR (except RET, PB)	No connection (ROA, ROE), Positive (RET, PB)
Mercedes Rodríguez-Fernández, Eva M. Sánchez-Teba, Alberto A. López-Toro, Susana Borrego-Domínguez (2019). Influence of ESGC Indicators on Financial Performance of Listed Travel and Leisure Companies	2017	ROE, ROA, Q-Tobin	USA, Europe, Asia	Tourism	No connection	No connection	Positive (ROA, ROE), Negative (Q-Tobin)

(continued)

Table 5.1 (continued)

Name, year, author	*Period*	*Financial indicators*	*Geography*	*Industry*	*E*	*S*	*G*
Mita Kurnia Yawika, Susi Handayani (2018). The Effect of ESG Performance on Economic Performance in the High Profile Industry in Indonesia	2015–2017	EBITDA margin, ROA, MBV	Indonesia	All	Negative (MBV)	No connection	Positive (EBITDA margin, ROA), Negative (MBV)
R. El Khoury, N. Nasrallah, B. Alareeni (2021). ESG and financial performance of banks in the MENAT region: Concavity—convexity patterns	2007–2019	ROE, ROA, Q-Tobin	Middle East, North Africa, Turkey	Banks	Convex relationship with market returns (Q-Tobin)	Non-linear	Concave relationship with accounting indicators (ROE, ROA)

Name, year, author	*Period*	*Financial indicators*	*Geography*	*Industry*	*E*	*S*	*G*
Mohammad Hassan Shakil, Nihal Mahmood, Mashiyat Tasnia, Ziaul Haque Munim (2019). Do environmental, social and governance performance affect the financial performance of banks? A cross-country study of emerging market banks	2015–2018	ROE, ROA	Developing countries (India, China, Taiwan, Russia, etc.)	Banks	Positive	Positive	No connection
Patrick Velte (2017). Does ESG performance have an impact on financial performance? Evidence from Germany	2010–2014	ROA, Q-Tobin	Germany	Companies listed on the German Prime Standard (DAX30, TecDAX, MDAX)	Positive	Positive	Positive
Karishma K Dalal, Nimit Thacker (2019). ESG and Corporate Financial Performance: A Panel Study of Indian Companies	2015–2017	ROA, Q-Tobin	India	Indian firms included in NSE 100 ESG Index database	Positive	Positive	Positive

(continued)

Table 5.1 (continued)

Name, year, author	*Period*	*Financial indicators*	*Geography*	*Industry*	*E*	*S*	*G*
Haris Ramić (2019). Relationship between ESG performance and financial performance of companies: an overview of the issue	2005–2015	ROE, ROA, Q-Tobin	The whole world	Everything except the financial sector	Positive	Positive	Positive (ROA, ROE), Negative (Q-Tobin)
Changhong Zhao, Yu Guo, Jiahai Yuan, ID, Mengya Wu, Daiyu Li, Yiou Zhou and Jiangang Kang (2018). ESG and Corporate Financial Performance: Empirical Evidence from China's Listed Power	2016	ROE, ROA, ROIC	China	Energy	Positive	Positive	Positive

Name, year, author	*Period*	*Financial indicators*	*Geography*	*Industry*	*E*	*S*	*G*
Mercedes Rodríguez-Fernández, Eva M. Sánchez- Teba, Alberto A. López-Toro and Susana Borrego-Domínguez (2019). Influence of ESGC Indicators on Financial Performance of Listed Travel and Leisure Companies	2017–2019	ROE, ROA, Q-Tobin	The whole world	Tourism	No connection	No connection	Positive (ROA, ROE), Negative (Q-Tobin)
Renard Siew (2012). ESG scores and its influence on firm performance: Australian evidence	2008–2010	ROA, ROE, ROIC, EBITDA margin, EPS, DPS, DY, EV, MC/TR, P/BV	Australia	All	No connection	No connection	No connection

(continued)

Table 5.1 (continued)

Name, year, author	*Period*	*Financial indicators*	*Geography*	*Industry*	*E*	*S*	*G*
Yaghoub Abdi, Xiaoni Li, Xavier Càmara -Turull (2021). Exploring the impact of sustainability (ESG) disclosure on firm value and financial performance (FP) in airline industry: the moderating role of size and age	2009–2019	market-to-book ratio, Q-Tobin	The whole world	Aviation industry	Positive (Tobin's Q)	Positive (Tobin's Q)	Positive (Tobin's Q)
Indarawati Tarmuji, Ruhanita Maelah and Nor Habibah Tarmuji (2016). The Impact of Environmental, Social and Governance Practices (ESG) on Economic Performance: Evidence from ESG Score	2010–2014	ROA, Q-Tobin	Malaysia, Singapore	All	Positive	Positive (Singapore)	Positive (Malaysia)

Name, year, author	*Period*	*Financial indicators*	*Geography*	*Industry*	*E*	*S*	*G*
Marcel C. Minutolo, Werner D. Kristjanpoller, John Stakeley (2019). Exploring environmental, social and governance disclosure effects on the S&P 500 financial performance	2009–2015	ROA, Q-Tobin	The whole world	All	Positive Tobin's Q (for large companies) Negative ROA Tobin's Q (for small companies)	Positive Tobin's Q (for large companies) Negative ROA Tobin's Q (for small companies)	Positive Tobin's Q (for large companies) Negative ROA Tobin's Q (for small companies)
Caterina De Lucia, Pasquale Pazienza, Mark Bartlett (2020). Does Good ESG Lead to Better Financial performances by firms? Machine Learning and Logistic Regression Models of Public Enterprises in Europe	2018–2019	ROA, ROE	Europe	All	Positive	Positive	Positive

(continued)

Table 5.1 (continued)

Name, year, author	*Period*	*Financial indicators*	*Geography*	*Industry*	*E*	*S*	*G*
Jun Xie and Wataru Nozawa and Michiyuki Yagi and Hidemichi Fujii and Shunsuke Managi. Do environmental, social and governance activities improve corporate financial performance?	2015	ROA, Q-Tobin, Asset, COGS	The whole world	All	Positive	Positive	Positive (with a moderate level of information disclosure)
George H. IONESCU, Daniela FIROIU, Ramona PIRVU, Ruxandra Dana VILAG (2019). The impact of ESG factors on market value of companies from travel and tourism industry	2010–2015	ROA, Q-Tobin	The whole world	Travel and tourism	Positive (US Negative)	Negative	Positive (US) Negative (Europe, Asia)

Name, year, author	*Period*	*Financial indicators*	*Geography*	*Industry*	*E*	*S*	*G*
Kamal Hassan Halbouni (2013). Corporate governance, economic turbulence and financial performance of UAE-listed firms	2008	ROE, ROA, Q-Tobin	UAE	All			Positive (ROE, ROA), Negative (Q -Tobin)
Nuria Reguera - Alvarado, Pilar de Fuentes, Joaquina Laffarga (2015). Does Board Gender Diversity Influence Financial Performance? Evidence from Spain	2005–2009	Q-Tobin	Spain	Non-financial companies			Positive
Martin Kyere, Marcel Ausloos (2019). corporate governance and financial performance in the UK	2014	ROA, Q-Tobin	Great Britain	Non-financial companies			Positive (ROA), Negative (Q-Tobin)
Janka Grofcikova (2020). Impact of selected determinants of corporate governance on financial	2017	ROA, ROE, ROS, EQ, DPS	Slovakia	Non-financial companies, insurance companies, banks			Mixed

(continued)

Table 5.1 (continued)

Name, year, author	*Period*	*Financial indicators*	*Geography*	*Industry*	*E*	*S*	*G*
Patrick Velte (2019). Does CEO power moderate the link between ESG performance and financial performance? A focus on the German two-tier system	2010–2018	ROA	Germany	All			Positive
Harjoto, M., Laksmana, I., & Lee, R. (2015). Board Diversity and Corporate Social Responsibility	1999–2011	ROA, Leverage, CAPEX	USA	All			Positive
Terjesen S, Couto EB, Francisco PM (2016). Does the presence of independent and female directors impact firm performance? A multi-country study of board diversity	2010	ROA, Q-Tobin	All	All			Positive

Name, year, author	*Period*	*Financial indicators*	*Geography*	*Industry*	*E*	*S*	*G*
Puni, A. and Anlesinya, A. (2020). Corporate governance mechanisms and firm performance in a developing country	2006–2018	ROA, ROE, EPS, Q-Tobin	Ghana	All			Positive
Goel, P. (2018). Implications of corporate governance on financial performance: an analytical review of governance and social reporting reforms in India	2012–2016	ROS, ROA, ROE, Q-Tobin, Market capitalization, PE	India	All			Positive (2012, 2013), No (2015, 2016)
Eklof, J., Podkorytova, O., & Malova, A. (2018). Linking customer satisfaction with financial performance: an empirical study of Scandinavian banks	2004–2014	ROA, ROE, profit margin and operating income	Scandinavia	Banks		Positive	

(continued)

Table 5.1 (continued)

Name, year, author	*Period*	*Financial indicators*	*Geography*	*Industry*	*E*	*S*	*G*
N.Yu. _ Zhukova, A.E. Melikova (2021). Corporate Social Responsibility: Strengthening Brand Value and Affecting Company's Financial Performance	2009–2019	ROA, ROE, market capitalization	USA	Retail, other		Positive	
Peng, C.W. and Yang, M.L. (2014). The Effect of Corporate Social Performance on Financial Performance: The Moderating Effect of Ownership Concentration	1996–2006	ROA, ROE, ROIC	Asia	All		Negative	

Name, year, author	*Period*	*Financial indicators*	*Geography*	*Industry*	*E*	*S*	*G*
E. Adegbite, Y. Guney, F. Kwabi, S. Tahir (2019). Financial and corporate social performance in the UK listed firms: The relevance of non-linearity and lag effects	2002–2015	ROA, Q-Tobin	Great Britain	All		Mixed	
F. H. Verbeeten, R. Gamerschlag, K. Möller (2016). Are CSR disclosures relevant to investors? Empirical evidence from Germany	2010–2014	Market capitalization, EBITDA margin	Germany	All	Negative	Positive	

fairly long and representative time period for the study; secondly, information about the ESG rating is presented from the MSCI source, which is currently the most popular among ESG sources.

The selection of companies was made on the basis of their ratings in the selected sectors by the rating agency *Sustainalytics*. The selected companies constituted a highly diversified sample, which covers the whole spectrum of ESG score, ranging from A+ to D−. Due to such sample diversity, the results should be quite representative, capturing the real picture of the market. It was also decided to include the top 10 large companies in each of the industries in the sample, since they have a strong impact on the entire market.

The sample includes companies from around the world: there are companies representing 22 developed countries (including the USA, Canada, Norway, Italy, Great Britain, Japan and others) and 13 developing countries (China, Russia, South Africa, Mexico and others). The data in the sample have a panel structure, since this approach provides several important advantages. It allows to take into account the individual characteristics of each company, presents a greater variability of information and reduces multicollinearity, and also increases the efficiency of econometric estimation. In addition, the choice in favor of panel data analysis was made based on the premise that the ESG rating has a time dependence (if a company starts implementing ESG innovations, then its rating in the current period will depend on the previous one).

5.4 Results

The results of the impact of the ESG components on financial performance and resistance to systemic risks are summarized in Table 5.2.

In an empirical study of the influence of the E component on all the companies under study, it was found that the environmental factor has a positive effect on the financial performance of the company, and this influence is associated exclusively with industrial sectors (no influence is observed in industries with low sensitivity). The explanation is that investors overvalue companies that care about the environment and meet E requirements.

This assessment by investors is based on the premise that despite falling sales and increasing debt in the future, the company will be able to gain market credibility and generate higher returns. In industries with low sensitivity, there is no relationship, since these industries are less exposed to environmental risks, so it is more difficult for investors to assess the result of meeting environmental requirements.

Table 5.2 Results of analysis

		Hla High E (ecology) component score has a positive impact on the company's financial performance and it's resilience to systemic risks		*Hlb. High S (social) component score has a positive impact on the company's financial performance and its resilience to systemic risks*		*Hlc High G (governance) component score has a positive impact on the company's financial performance and its resilience to systemic risks*	
		Hypothesis	*Results*	*Hypothesis*	*Results*	*Hypothesis*	*Results*
Q-Tobin	A	Positive	Positive	Positive	Independent	Positive	Positive
P/S	b	Positive	Positive	Positive	Independent	Positive	Positive
EV/ EBITDA	c	Positive	Positive	Positive	Independent	Positive	Independent

5.5 Conclusion

When studying the social factor on companies both in the general sample and in the industry, it was found that there is practically no influence. Despite the fact that social initiatives can improve the image, recognition and brand of the company, this effect is minimal. Social initiatives have less impact on the company's financial efficiency (profit, revenue, margin), so the market is not inclined to overestimate these initiatives.

The corporate governance factor has a positive impact both on all companies and in industry samples separately. As expected in the literature review, the quality, diversity of management, their control by the board of directors, as well as an increase in the transparency of information can mitigate the principal-agent problem and increase investor confidence, which increases the market value of the company and also allows you to increase the company's profit due to the fact that quality management takes into account the interests of all stakeholders. It should be noted that the strongest revaluation of this factor is observed in the industrial sector, which may be due to the fact that these industries are more conservative, changes in the management of companies occur quite rarely, so investors tend to overestimate such rare events.

References

Abdi, Y., Li, X., & Càmara-Turull, X. (2021). Exploring the impact of sustainability (ESG) disclosure on firm value and financial performance (FP) in the airline industry: The moderating role of size and age. *Environment, Development and Sustainability, 24*(4), 5052–5079.

Adegbite, E., Guney, Y., Kwabi, F., & Tahir, S. (2019). Financial and corporate social performance in the UK listed firms: The relevance of non-linearity and lag effects. *Review of Quantitative Finance and Accounting, 52*, 105–158.

Almeyda, R., & Darmansyah. (2019). The influence of Environmental, Social, and Governance (ESG) disclosure on firm financial performance. *IPTEK Journal of Proceedings Series*, (5), 278–290.

Anlesinya, A., & Puni, A. (2020). Corporate governance mechanisms and firm performance in a developing country. *International Journal of Law and Management, 62*(2), 147–169.

Ausloos, M., & Kyere, M. (2019). Corporate governance and financial performance in the United Kingdom. *International Journal of Finance & Economics, 26*(2), 1871–1885.

Bartlett, M., De Lucia, C., & Pazienza, P. (2020). Does good ESG lead to better financial performances by firms? Machine learning and logistic regression models of public enterprises in Europe. *Sustainability, 12*(13), 5317.

Battiston, S., Mandel, A., Monasterolo, I., Schütze, F., & Visentin, G. (2017). A climate stress-test of the financial system. *Nature Climate Change, 7*(4), 283–288.

El Khoury, R., Nasrallah, N., & Alareeni, B. (2021). ESG and financial performance of banks in the MENAT region: Concavity—convexity patterns. *Journal of Sustainable Finance & Investment, 13*(1), 406–430.

El Khoury, R., Naimy, V., & Iskandar, S. (2021). ESG versus Corporate financial performance: Evidence from East Asian Firms in the industrials sector. *Studies of Applied Economics, 39*(3).

Eklof, J., Podkorytova, O., & Malova, A. (2018). Linking customer satisfaction with financial performance: An empirical study of Scandinavian banks. *Total Quality Management & Business Excellence, 31*(15–16), 1684–1702.

Fazle Rahi, A. B. M., Akter, R., & Johansson, J. (2021). Do sustainability practices influence financial performance? Evidence from the Nordic financial industry. *Accounting Research Journal, 35*(2), 292–314.

Goel, P. (2018). Implications of corporate governance on financial performance: An analytical review of governance and social reporting reforms in India. *Asian Journal of Sustainability and Social Responsibility, 3*(1), 1–21.

Grofcikova, J. (2020). Impact of selected determinants of corporate governance on financial performance. *Ekonomicko-manazerske spektrum, 14*(2), 12–23.

Guo, Y., Zhao, C., Yuan, J., Wu, M., Li, D., Zhou, Y., & Kang, J. (2018). ESG and corporate financial performance: Empirical evidence from China's listed power. *Sustainability, 10*(8), 2607.

Halbouni, K.H. (2013). Corporate governance, economic turbulence and financial performance of UAE-listed firms. *Studies in Economics and Finance, 30*(2), 118–138.

Harjoto, M., Laksmana, I., & Lee, R. (2015). Board diversity and corporate social responsibility. *Journal of Business Ethics, 132*, 641–660.

Hassan Shakil, M., Mahmood, N., Tasnia, M., & Munim, Z. H. (2019). Do environmental, social and governance performance affect the financial performance of banks? A cross-country study of emerging market banks. *Management of Environmental Quality: An International Journal, 30*(6), 1331–1344.

Ionescu, G., Firoiu, D., Pirvu, R., & Vilag, R (2019). The impact of esg factors on market value of companies from travel and tourism industry. *Technological and Economic Development of Economy, 25*(5), 820–849.

Krüger, P. (2015). Corporate goodness and shareholder wealth. *Journal of Financial Economics, 115*(2), 304–329.

Kurnia Yawika, M., & Handayani, S. (2018). The effect of ESG performance on economic performance in the high profile industry in Indonesia. *Journal of International Business Economics, 7*(2), 112–121.

López-Toro, A. A., Sánchez-Teba, E. M., Benítez-Márquez, M. D., & Rodríguez-Fernández, M. (2021). Influence of ESGC indicators on financial performance of listed pharmaceutical companies. *International Journal of Environmental Research and Public Health, 18*(9), 4556.

Minutolo, M. C., Kristjanpoller, W. D., & Stakeley, J. (2019). Exploring environmental, social, and governance disclosure effects on the S&P 500 financial performance. *Business Strategy and the Environment, 28*(6), 1083–1095.

Peng, C. W., & Yang, M. L. (2014). The effect of corporate social performance on financial performance: The moderating effect of ownership concentration. *Journal of Business Ethics, 123*, 171–182.

Reguera-Alvarado, N., de Fuentes, P., & Laffarga, J. (2015). Does board gender diversity influence financial performance? Evidence from Spain. *Journal of Business Ethics, 141*, 337–350.

Ramić, H. (2019). *Relationship between ESG performance and financial performance of companies: An overview of the issue*. University of Lausanne.

Saygilia, E., Arslanb, S., & Birkanc, A. O. (2021). ESG practices and corporate financial performance: Evidence from Borsa Istanbul. *Borsa Istanbul Review, 22*(3), 525–533.

Schoenmaker, D., & Wierts, P. (2015). Regulating the financial cycle: An integrated approach with a macroprudential filter for the European Union. *Environment and Planning C: Government and Policy, 33*(5), 1087–1106.

Siew, R. (2012). ESG scores and its influence on firm performance: Australian evidence. In *Australian school of business school of accounting, school of accounting seminar series semester* (Vol. 2, pp. 1–30). University of New South Wales.

Terjesen, S., Couto, E. B., & Francisco, P. M. (2016). Does the presence of independent and female directors impact firm performance? A multi-country study of board diversity. *Journal of Management & Governance, 20*, 447–483.

Thoma, J., & Chen, D. (2019). ESG integration and portfolio risk: An empirical analysis on the impact of ESG on systematic risk. *The Journal of Investing, 28*(5), 115–128.

Tarmuji, I., Maelah, R., & Tarmuji, N. H. (2016). The impact of Environmental, Social and Governance Practices (ESG) on economic performance: Evidence from ESG Score. *International Journal of Trade, Economics and Finance, 7*(3), 67.

Velte, P. (2017). Does ESG performance have an impact on financial performance? Evidence from Germany. *Journal of Global Responsibility, 8*(2), 169–178.

Velte, P. (2019). Does CEO power moderate the link between ESG performance and financial performance? A focus on the German two-tier system. *Management Research Review, 43*(5), 497–520.

Verbeeten, F. H., Gamerschlag, R., & Möller, K. (2016). Are CSR disclosures relevant to investors? Empirical evidence from Germany. *Management Decision, 54*(6), 1359–1382.

Xie, J., Nozawa, W., Yagi, M., Fujii, H., & Managi, S. (2019). Do environmental, social, and governance activities improve corporate financial performance? *Business Strategy and the Environment, 28*(2), 286–300.

Zhukova, N. Y., & Melikova, A. E. (2021). *Corporate social responsibility: Strengthening brand value and affecting company*. Deputy Editors-in-Chief, 84.

PART II

Quantitative Methods and Models in Emerging Markets' Risk Management

CHAPTER 6

New Ways of Measuring Catastrophic Risk

Vigen Minasyan

6.1 Introduction

The risk measure is a mapping ρ of a set of random variables X associated with risk portfolios of assets and/or liabilities (the result variables of these portfolios) into a real line R. In the following discussion, X will be represented as the value of the corresponding losses, i.e. positive values of the X variables will represent losses, while negative values will represent gains. Distortion risk measures represent a special and important group of risk measures widely used in finance and insurance as a calculation of capital requirements and the principles of calculating indicators related to risk appetite for the regulator and company executive. Several popular risk measures have proven to belong to distortion risk measures—for example, value at risk (VaR), tail value at risk, expected shortfall (ES) (Crouhy et al., 2006; Hull, 2007; Jorion, 2007), or Wang's distortion

V. Minasyan (✉)
Russian Presidential Academy of National Economy and Public Administration, Moscow, Russia
e-mail: minasyanvb@ranepa.ru

Department of Corporate Finance SHFM, Moscow, Russia

A. Karminsky and M. Stolbov (eds.), *Systemic Financial Risk*,
https://doi.org/10.1007/978-3-031-54809-3_6

measure (Wang, 2000). Distortion risk measures satisfy the most important properties that a "good" risk measure should have, including positive homogeneity, translation invariance, and monotonicity (Risk measures for the 21st century., 2004). In our previous works, we introduced a family of risk measure called "VaR to the power of t" ($\text{VaR}_p^{(t)}[X]$) for any confidence probability p and any real $t \geq 1$ (Minasyan, 2019, 2020). In these works, computational formulas for risk measure $\text{VaR}_p^{(t)}[X]$ were obtained. Also, the relationships between these measures and the measures such as $\text{ES}_p[X]$ for some specific loss distribution laws were investigated. We revealed that the relative persistence level for each measure can depend both on the loss distribution law and on the confidence probability with which these measures are calculated. However, for almost all loss distribution laws and for all confidence probabilities of practical interest, risk measure $\text{VaR}_p^{(t)}[X]$ for any real $t \geq 2$ turns out to be more persistent, providing a more "careful" risk assessment than, for example, risk measure $\text{ES}_p[X]$.D. Denneberg, S. Wang, and J. Dhaene (Denneberg, 1994; Minasyan, 2020a, 2020b) proved that when the corresponding distortion function is concave, the distortion risk measure is also sub-additive. VaR is one of the most popular risk measures used in risk management and banking supervision because of its computational simplicity and for some regulatory reasons, regardless of its shortcomings as a risk measure. For example, VaR is not a sub-additive risk measure (Artzner et al., 1999; Wang et al., 2000). Being coherent (Hull, 2007; Jorion, 2007), ES risk measure is only interested in losses in excess of VaR and ignores useful information about the distribution of losses below VaR. L. Zhu and H. Li (Denuit et al., 2005) presented and studied the tail distortion risk measure reformulated by F. Yang (Zhu & Li, 2012) as follows.

C. Yin and D. Zhu (Yang, 2015) described three methods for building distortion risk measures: the composite method, the mixing method, and the copula-based approach. We will use the results of this work. Many researchers have proposed new classes of distortion measures. For example, J. Belles-Sampera, M. Guillén, and M. Santolino (Yin & Zhu, 2018) proposed a new class of distortion risk measures called GlueVaR risk measures to extend VaR and ES. They can be expressed as a combination of VaR and ES indicators at different levels of confidence probabilities. They obtained closed-form analytical expressions for the most commonly used distribution functions in finance and insurance.

The subfamily of these risk measures satisfies the tail sub-additivity property, which means that diversification benefits can persist, at least in certain cases. The application of GlueVaR risk measures related to capital allocation was discussed by J. Belles-Sampera, M. Guillén, and M. Santolino (Belles-Sampera et al., 2014). U. Cherubini and S. Mulinacci (Belles-Sampera et al., 2014) proposed a class of distortion measures based on contamination from an external "scenario" variable. For a scenario-dependent variable whose risk is modeled by a copula function with horizontally concave portions, they give conditions for the coherence axiom and offer examples of these class measures based on the copula function.

It would be interesting to investigate the relationship between two classes of risk measures: distortion risk measures and VaR to the power of t. We introduce a family of new risk measure "ES to the power of t" ($\mathrm{ES}_p^{(t)}[X]$) at any confidence probability p and any real $t \geq 1$. We investigated the relationship of two classes of risk measures: distortion and ES to the power of t It is proved that risk measure "ES to the power of t" is a subset of distortion risk measures. Thus, for any $t \geq 1$, any risk measure "ES to the power of t is a distortion risk measure with a certain distortion function. In this case, this distortion function will be presented.

It is hard to believe in a unique risk measure that can encompass all of its characteristics. It does not exist. Moreover, since a single number is associated with each risk measure, it cannot exhaust all information about the risk. According to Minasyan 2020, risk measure "VaR to the power of t" allows by changing the value of t, to study the right tail of the loss distribution with any accuracy required for the given case, i.e. investigate the tail of the distribution as carefully as it is necessary in the given circumstances. It is prudent to look for risk measures ideal for a particular problem. Since all the proposed risk measures are flawed and limited in application, selecting the appropriate risk measure is still relevant in risk management.

6.2 Distortion Risk Measures

Distortion Functions

A distortion function g: $[0, 1] \to [0, 1]$ is a non-decreasing function such that $g(0) = 0$, $g(1) = 1$. Many distortion functions g have already been proposed in the literature. Some commonly used distortion functions are listed here. The work by M. Denuit, J. Dhaene, M. Goovaerts, and R. Kaas (Artzner et al., 1999) presents the summary of other distortion functions.

- Function $g(x) = 1_{\{x>1-p\}}$, where 1_A is the indicator function and equals 1 at event A, and equals 0 otherwise, is a concave distortion function. Here, in applications, p will represent the preselected confidence level with which the corresponding risk measure is intended to be calculated.
- Incomplete beta-function $g(x) = \frac{1}{\beta(a,b)} \int_0^x t^{a-1}(1-t)^{b-1}dt$, where

  $a > 0$ and $b > 0$ are the parameters and $\beta(a,b) = \int_0^1 t^{a-1}(1-t)^{b-1}dt$.

  In particular, if $b = 1$, we obtain the power distortion function $g(x) = x^a$, and if $a = 1$, we obtain the dual-power distortion function $g(x) = 1 - (1-x)^b$.

- Power distortion $g(x) = x^\alpha$ is a concave distortion function if $0 < \alpha < 1$ and a convex distortion function if $\alpha > 1$.
- Exponential distortion $g(x) = \frac{e^x - 1}{e - 1}$ is a convex distortion function.
- Sinusoidal distortion $g(x) = \sin \frac{\pi}{2} x$ is a concave distortion function.
- Function $g(x) = xe^{1-x}$ 1 is a concave distortion function.
- Logarithmic distortion $g(x) = \frac{\ln(x+1)}{\ln 2}$ is a concave distortion function.
- Distortion Wang $g(x) = \Phi(\Phi^{-1}(x) + \Phi^{-1}(p))$, , $0 < p < 1$, where Φ is the standard normal distribution function. Obviously, this is an increasing function (since these are functions $\Phi(x)$ and $\Phi^{-1}(x)$) and $g(0) = \Phi(\Phi^{-1}(0) + \Phi^{-1}(p)) = \Phi(-\infty) = 0$ and $g(1) = \Phi(\Phi^{-1}(1) + \Phi^{-1}(p)) = \Phi(+\infty) = 1$, and $g(\frac{1}{2}) = \Phi(\Phi^{-1}(\frac{1}{2}) + \Phi^{-1}(p)) = \Phi(\Phi^{-1}(p)) = p$.
- Lookback distortion $g(x) = x^p(1 - p\ln x)$, $p \in (0, 1]$. Obviously, this is an increasing function, which is easy to check: $g'(x) = -p^2 x^{p-1} \ln x > 0$ if $x \in [0,1]$, and $g(0) = \lim_{x \to +0} g(x) = 0$ and $g(1) = 1$.
- Identity function $g(x) = x$ is the smallest concave distortion function and also the largest convex distortion function.

- $g_0(x) = 1_{\{x>0\}}$ is concave on [0,1] and is the largest of all non-identical concave distortion functions. $g^0(x) = 1_{\{x=1\}}$ 0 is convex on [0,1] and is the smallest of all non-identical convex distortion functions.
- For $0 < p < 1$, $g(x) = \min\{\frac{x}{1-p}, 1\}$ is smallest concave distortion function, such that $g(x) \geq 1_{\{x>1-p\}}$.

Distortion Risk Measures

If (Ω, F, P) is a common probability space where all random variables that represent the risks are defined. If F_X is an integral distribution function of random variable X, we denote the dual distribution function as $\overline{F}_X$, i.e. $\overline{F}_X = 1 - F(x) = P\{X > x\}$. Let g be the distortion function. *Distorted expectation of random variable* X is $\rho_g[X]$ [ ] and is defined as

$$\rho_g[X] = \int_0^{+\infty} G\left(\overline{F}_X(x)\right)dx + \int_{-\infty}^{0} \left[g\left(\overline{F}_X(x)\right) - 1\right]dx, \qquad (6.1)$$

provided that at least one of the two integrals above is finite. If X is a non-negative random variable, then ρ_g is simplified to

$$\rho_g[X] = \int_0^{+\infty} g(\overline{F}_X(x))dx.$$

This definition implies that if the distortion function is an identical function, $g(x) = x$, then the distorted expectation coincides with the usual expectation: $\rho_g[X] = E[X].\rho_g[X] = E[X]$.

Due to the fact that the expected value of a random variable is considered the most important way to assess the future value of random variable X, we assume that since risks arise due to some value deviation of a random variable from its expected value, then risk measures can be modeled as a "distortion" of the expected value using the appropriate distortion function.

Distorted expectation $\rho_g[X]$ is called the *distortion risk measure with distortion function g* (Cherubini & Mulinacci, 2014). We can prove that, as was first observed by M. Denuit, J. Dhaene, M. Goovaerts, and R. Kaas (Artzner et al., 1999), the known risk measure VaR (Crouhy et al., 2006;

Hull, 2007; Jorion, 2007) is a distorted risk measure corresponding to distortion function $g(x) = 1_{\{x>1-p\}}$, $p \in (0, 1)$, i.e. the following proposition is true.

Proposition 1

(Cherubini & Mulinacci, 2014)

For the distortion function $g(x) = 1_{\{x>1-p\}}$, $p \in (0, 1)$ if distribution function F_X is continuous, the corresponding risk measure is $\rho_g[X] = VaR_p[X]$

J. Dhaene et al. (Cherubini & Mulinacci, 2014) also proved two important facts that describe the relationship of all distortion risk measures obtained by distortion functions that are continuous on the right on [0,1) or left on (0,1] with the risk measure VaR.

Theorem 1 When g is a continuous distortion function on the right on [0,1), the distorted expectation $\rho_g[X]$ has the following representation:

$$\rho_g[X] = \int_{[0,1]} VaR^{+}_{1-q}[X]dg(q),$$

where $\mathrm{VaR}^{+}_{p}[X] = \sup\{x|F_X(x) \leq p\}$.

Theorem 2 When g is a continuous distortion function on the left on [0,1), the distorted expectation $\rho_g[X]$has the following representation:

$$\rho_g[X] = \int_{[0,1]} VaR_{1-q}[X]dg(q) = \int_{[0,1]} VaR_q[X]d\overline{g}(q),$$

where $\mathrm{VaR_p}[X] = \inf\{x|F_X(x) \geq p\}$ and $\overline{g}(q) = 1 - g(1-q)$ are the dual distortion to g.

Obviously, $\overline{\overline{g}} = g$, and g is continuous on the left if and only if $\overline{g}$ is continuous on the right; g is concave if and only if $\overline{g}$ is convex. Distortion risk measures are a special class of risk measures introduced by D. Denneberg (Minasyan, 2020b) and modified by S.S. Wang (Dhaene et al., 2012; Wang, 2000). Distortion risk measures satisfy many properties, including positive homogeneity, translation invariance, and monotonicity.

A risk measure is coherent if it satisfies the following set of four properties (Artzner et al., 1996; Wang et al., 1998):

(M) monotonicity: $\rho(X) \leq \rho(Y)$ if $P\,(X \leq \ Y) = 1$;
(P) positive homogeneity: for any positive constant c > 0 and loss X, $\rho\,(cX) = c\rho\,(X)$;
(S) sub-additivity: for any losses X, Y, then $\rho(X+Y) \leq \rho(X)+\rho(Y)$;
(T) translation invariance: if c is constant, then $\rho\,(X+c) = \rho\,(X)-c$.

Risk measure ρ is called a convex risk measure if it satisfies the properties of monotonicity, translation invariance, and the following convexity property: (C) convexity:

$$\rho(\lambda X + (1-\lambda)\,Y) \leq \lambda\rho\,(X) + (1-\lambda)\,\rho\,(Y),\ 0 \leq \lambda \leq 1.$$

Obviously, under the assumption of positive homogeneity, monotonicity, and translation invariance, the convexity of the risk measure is equivalent to sub-additivity. Another distortion risk measure (Cherubini & Mulinacci, 2014), besides VaR, is the well-known measure ES (expected shortfall), conditional VaR (Crouhy et al., 2006; Hull, 2007; Jorion, 2007).

Proposition 2

(Cherubini & Mulinacci, 2014)

For distortion function $g(x) = \min\{\frac{x}{1-p}, 1\}$, p $\in$ [0, 1] under the assumption that the distribution function F_X is continuous, the corresponding distorted risk measure is $\rho_g[X] = \mathrm{ES}_p[X]$

The following theorem (Belles-Sampera et al., 2014) is useful and can be used to order distortion risk measures in terms of their distortion functions.

Theorem 3 (Belles-Sampera et al., 2014)

If $g\,(x) \leq g^*\,(x)$ for $x \in [0,1]$, then $\rho_g[X] \leq \rho_{g^*}[X]$ for any random variable X.

Distortion Risk Measures VaR to the Power of t, $t \geq 1$, ($VaR_p^{(t)}$)

Today, risk measure VaR is probably the second most commonly used risk measure, both in theory and in practice, after volatility (standard deviation). Since the end of the twentieth century, ES (Expected

Shortfall) measure, conditional VaR, the measure of expected tail losses exceeding VaR, has found sufficient application in risk management. ES is perceived as a risk measure that specifies VaR measure, more conservative, considering tail losses, unlikely but large ("black swan").

The concept of a new measure "VaR squared" $VaR^{(2)}$ (Minasyan, 2019a, 2019b) estimates risks more conservatively than VaR and is often more conservative than ES, assessing risk as a certain threshold value that is not overcome with a given probability (as VaR), and not as some average value from the set of "bad", tail loss values, like ES.

Following the ideas in Minasyan, 2019a, 2019b in Minasyan 2020a we introduced the concept of risk measure VaR to any power $t \geq 1$ and derived formulas that allow to calculate $VaR^{(t)}$ as usual measure VaR with a certain modified confidence probability.

The Concept of VaR to Any Natural Power $VaR^{(n)}$

In papers (Minasyan, 2019a, 2019b), we introduced a new risk measure to supplement VaR, tracking rare tail events associated with great financial losses.

Risk measure "*VaR squared*" $VaR_p^{(2)}$ *with a confidence level* p is the value that will not be exceeded by the loss if its threshold value VaR_p is exceeded with a confidence level p during a given time.

Paper (Minasyan, 2019b) presents the following formula:

$$VaR_p^{(2)}[X] = VaR_{1-(1-p)^2}[X]. \tag{6.2}$$

Thus, to calculate new catastrophic risk measure "VaR squared", a general formula has been obtained. We should just calculate risk measure VaR with confidence level $1 - (1 - p)^2$.

The concept of $VaR^{(2)}$ in Minasyan, 2020 was generalized considering the fact that the confidence probability p' when determining $VaR^{(2)}$, i.e. the threshold value that the profit will not exceed (the loss will exceed), provided that it is not exceeded (exceeded) by VaR_p with probability p', may differ from p. This risk measure, which can be called "bi-VaR", was designated as $VaR_{p,p'}^{(2)}$ and the following formula was obtained:

$$VaR_{p,p'}^{(2)}[X] = VaR_{1-(1-p)(1-p')}[X] \tag{6.3}$$

We will introduce the concept of risk measure VaR to the power of *n*, where *n* is any natural number, and will give formulas to calculate risk measure VaR to the power of *n*, $VaR^{(n)}$ (Minasyan, 2020a).

We represent usual risk measure VaR as:

$VaR_p^{(1)}[X] = VaR_p[X] = VaR_{p_1}[X]$, where $p_1 = 1 - (1 - p)$.

According to the formula, $VaR_p^{(2)}[X] = VaR_{p_2}[X]$, where $p_2 = 1 - (1 - p_1)^2$.

Naturally, according to the definition, we can assume that "VaR to the third power" is just $VaR_{p2,p}^{(2)}[X]$. Thus, we get that

$VaR_p^{(3)}[X] = VaR_{p2,p}^{(2)}[X] = VaR_{p_3}[X]$, where according to (6.3) $p_3 = 1 - (1 - p_2)(1 - p)$. Following this way, we introduce risk measure "VaR to the power of *n*" for any natural number *n* as $VaR_{p_{n-1},p}^{(2)}[X]$, where $p_{n-1} = 1 - (1 - p)^{n-1}$ and we obtain that

$VaR_p^{(n)}[X] = VaR_{p_{n-1},p}^{(2)}[X] = VaR_{p_n}[X]$, where according to (6.3).

$p_n = 1 - (1 - p_{n-1})(1 - p)$.

The concept of risk measure "VaR to the power of *n*" was introduced (Minasyan, 2020) for any natural number n and the formula was obtained that reduces their calculations to the calculation of usual risk measure VaR with a confidence level changed in a certain way.

$$VaR_p^{(n)}[X] = VaR_{1-(1-p)^n}[X]. \tag{6.4}$$

Thus, to calculate risk measure $VaR_p^{(n)}$, we should just calculate risk measure VaR with confidence level $1 - (1 - p)^n$.

Risk Measures "Poly-VaR"

We will introduce (like we did in Minasyan, 2020) a family of measures that generalize measures $VaR_p^{(n)}[X]$ and allow the confidence probabilities used for various powers of VaR to be different.

We will represent usual risk measure $\mathrm{VaR}_p[X] = \mathrm{VaR}_{\tilde{p}1}$, where $\tilde{p}_1 = p_1 = p = 1 - (1 - p)$.

By formula (6.7), we introduce the concept of risk measure "poly-VaR to the second power", "bi-VaR":

$$\mathrm{VaR}_{p1,p2}^{(2)}[X] = \mathrm{VaR}_{\tilde{p}2}[X], \text{ where } \tilde{p}_2 = 1 - (1 - p_1)(1 - p_2).$$

Accordingly, risk measure "poly-VaR to the third power" is as follows:

$$VaR^{(3)}_{p_1,p_2,p_3}[X] = VaR^{(2)}_{\tilde{p}_2,p_3}[X] = VaR_{\tilde{p}_3}[X],$$

where $\tilde{p}_3 = 1 - (1 - \tilde{p}_2)(1 - p_3)$.

Thus, risk measure "poly-VaR to the power of n" is defined as follows:

$$VaR^{(n)}_{p_1,p_2,\ldots,p_n}[X] = VaR^{(2)}_{\tilde{p}_{n-1},p_n}[X] = VaR_{\tilde{p}_n}[X],$$

where $\tilde{p}_n = 1 - (1 - \tilde{p}_{n-1})$.

Work (Minasyan, 2020) provides the following formula to calculate the poly-VaR to the power of n":

$$VaR^{(n)}_{p_1,p_2,\ldots,p_n}[X] = VaR_{1-(1-p_1)(1-p_2)\ldots(1-p_n)}[X], \tag{6.5}$$

that expresses it in terms of usual risk measure VaR with the confidence probability recalculated in a certain way.

Risk Measure VaR to Any Real Power $t \geq 1$, $VaR^{(t)}_p[X]$

Any real number $t \geq 1$ can be unambiguously represented as: $t = k + \alpha$, where k is a natural number, and α is a real number, and $0 \leq \alpha < 1$. Obviously, k is the integer part of t, and α is its fractional part. Naturally, risk measure VaR to any real power $t \geq 1$, $VaR^{(t)}_p[X]$ is as follows (Minasyan, 2020a):

$$VaR^{(t)}_p[X] = VaR^{(k+1)}_{\underbrace{p,\,p,\,\ldots,\,p}_{k},\alpha p}[X] \tag{6.6}$$

In particular, using formulas (6.5) and (6.6), we have:

$$VaR^{(1+\alpha)}_p[X] = VaR^{(2)}_{p,\alpha p}[X] = VaR_{1-(1-p)(1-\alpha p)}[X] \tag{6.7}$$

and

$$VaR^{(2+\alpha)}_p[X] = VaR^{(3)}_{p,p,\alpha p}[X] = VaR_{1-(1-p)^2(1-\alpha p)}[X] \tag{6.8}$$

etc.,

$$VaR^{(t)}_p[X] = VaR^{(k+\alpha)}_p[X] = VaR_{1-(1-p)^k(1-\alpha p)}[X] \tag{6.9}$$

By means of risk measure $VaR_p^{(t)}[X]$, a risk manager can research the left tail of the profit distribution law for confidence probabilities that are multiples of the initial confidence probability p, as well as the fraction of this probability, to obtain very detailed information about less probable but more catastrophic risks.

New Risk Measures ES to Any Power of t, $t \geq 1, ES_p^{(t)}[X]$

We have already discussed an important risk measure, $ES_p[X]$ (Expected Shortfall) risk measure (conditional VaR), the measure of expected tail losses exceeding $VaR_p[X]$. It is used as a risk measure, specifying VaR measure, more conservative, considering tail losses, unlikely, but great. In the second section, we described risk measure $VaR_p^{(t)}[X]$, which at $t \geq 2$ often gives a more conservative risk assessment than $ES_p[X]$.

Now, we introduce a new family of risk measure "ES to the power of t" for any $t \geq 1$.

First, we will introduce the concept of new risk measure—"ES squared" (Minasyan, 2020b).

Risk measure "ES squared" denoted as $ES_p^{(2)}[X]$ is the value of the expected tail losses exceeding $VaR_p^{(2)}[X]$, i.e. by definition $ES_p^{(2)}[X] = E[X|X > VaR_p^{(2)}[X]$ (symbol E[X|A] denotes the conditional mathematical expectation of the random variable X if event A takes place).

Note that since $VaR_p^{(2)}[X] = VaR_{1-(1-p)^2}[X]$, the value of $ES_p^{(2)}[X]$ can be obtained by averaging the values of corresponding $\mathrm{VaR_q}[X]$ to variable q on segment $[1\text{-}(1-p)^2, 1]$.

If the loss distribution continues, we obtain the following useful representation for $ES_p^{(2)}[X]$:

$$ES_p^{(2)}[X] = \frac{1}{(1-p)^2} \int\limits_{[1-(1-p)^2,1]} VaR_q[X]dq \tag{6.10}$$

By analogy with ES squared, we introduce the concept of new risk measure ES to the power of n, where n is any natural number. *Risk measure "ES to the power of n"* (Minasyan, 2020), which we will designate as $ES_p^{(n)}[X]$, is the value of the expected tail losses exceeding $VaR_p^{(n)}[X]$, i.e. by definition $ES_p^{(n)}[X] = E[X|X > VaR_p^{(n)}[X]$.

Note that since $VaR_p^{(n)}[X] = VaR_{1-(1-p)^n}[X]$, the value of $ES_p^{(n)}[X]$ can be obtained by averaging the values of corresponding $\mathrm{VaR_q}[X]$ to variable q on segment $[1\text{-}(1-p)^n, 1]$.

If the loss distribution continues, we obtain the following useful representation for $ES_p^{(n)}[X]$:

$$ES_p^{(n)}[X] = \frac{1}{(1-p)^n} \int\limits_{[1-(1-p)^n,1]} VaR_q[X]dq \tag{6.11}$$

Note that a useful formula is obtained from formula (6.11), which allows expressing $ES_p^{(n)}[X]$ by usual risk measure ES with the confidence probability changed in a certain way:

$$ES_p^{(n)}[X] = ES_{1-(1-p)^n}[X] \tag{6.12}$$

Now we will introduce new concept "ES to the power of t", where t is any real number, $t \geq 1$. We represent tt as: $\mathrm{t} = \mathrm{k} + \alpha$, where k is a natural number, and α is a real number $0 \leq \alpha < 1$.

We will call *risk measure "ES to the power of t"* (Minasyan, 2020), denoted as $ES_p^{(t)}[X]$, the value of the expected tail losses exceeding $VaR_p^{(t)}[X]$, i.e. by definition $ES_p^{(t)}[X] = E[X|X > VaR_p^{(t)}[X]$.

Note that since $VaR_p^{(t)}[X] = VaR_{1-(1-p)^k(1-\alpha p)}[X]$, the value of $ES_p^{(t)}[X]$ can be obtained by averaging the values of corresponding $\mathrm{VaR_q}[X]$ to variable q on segment $[1\text{-}(1-p)^k(1-\alpha p), 1]$.

If the loss distribution continues, we obtain the following useful representation for $ES_p^{(t)}[X]$:

$$ES_p^{(t)}[X] = \frac{1}{(1-p)^k(1-\alpha p)} \int\limits_{[1-(1-p)^k(1-\alpha p),1]} VaR_q[X]dq \tag{6.13}$$

Note that a useful formula is obtained from formula (6.13), which allows expressing $ES_p^{(t)}[X]$ by usual risk measure ES with the confidence probability changed in a certain way (Minasyan, 2020b).

$$ES_p^{(t)}[X] = ES_{1-(1-p)^k(1-\alpha p)}[X] \tag{6.14}$$

The following relations are valid between all the introduced risk measures:$VaR_p[X] \leq ES_p[X], VaR_p^{(2)}[X] \leq ES_p^{(2)}[X], \ldots, VaR_p^{(n)}[X] \leq$

$ES_p^{(n)}[X], \ldots$

$$VaR_p[X] \le VaR_p^{(2)}[X] \le \ldots \le VaR_p^{(n)}[X] \le \ldots$$

However, the ratio between risk measures $ES_p^{(n)}[X]$ and $VaR_p^{(n+1)}[X]$ may depend on the distribution law X and even on the confidence level p (Minasyan, 2019b).

6.3 Methods for Creating New Distortion Functions and Distortion Risk Measures

Distortion functions can be viewed as a starting point for a family of distortion risk measures. Thus, building and selecting distortion functions play an important role in developing families of risk measures with different properties. C. Yin and D. Zhu (Yin & Zhu, 2018) consider three methods: the composite method, mixing methods, and copula-based method, which allow building new classes of distortion functions and measures using the available ones. In this work, we will discuss only the composite method.

Composite Method

The first approach to building distortion functions is the composite method that uses a composition of distortion functions. If $h_1, h_2, \ldots$ are distortion functions, we will define $f_1(x) = h_1(x)$ and complex functions $f_n(x) = f_{n-1}(h_n(x))$, $n = 1, 2, \ldots$ It is easy to check $f_n(x)$,

$n = 1, 2, \ldots$ are also distortion functions. If $h_1, h_2, \ldots$ are concave distortion functions, then each $f_n(x)$ is concave, and they satisfy the conditions:

$$f_1 \le f_2 \le f_3 \le \ldots$$

and the corresponding risk measures satisfy (by Theorem 3)

$$\rho_{f_1}[X] \le \rho_{f_2}[X] \le \rho_{f_3}[X] \le \ldots$$

We will consider two distortion functions g_1 and g_2. If

$$g_2(x) = \begin{cases} \frac{x}{1-p}, \text{if } 0 \le x \le 1-p \\ 1, \text{if } 1-p < x \le 1, \end{cases}$$

then

$$g_p(x) = g_1(g_2(x)) = \begin{cases} g_1(\frac{x}{1-p}), \text{ if } 0 \le x \le 1-p \\ 1, \text{ if } 1-p < x \le 1, \end{cases}$$

Corresponding risk measure $\rho_{g_p}[X]$ is a tail distortion risk measure first presented by L. Zhu and H. Li (Zhu & Li, 2012) and reformulated by F. Yang (Yang, 2015). In particular, in the space of continuous random variable losses.

$$\rho_{g_p}[X] = \int_0^\infty g_p(1 - P(X \le x | X > VaR_p[X]))dx$$

If $g_1(x) = x^r, 0 < r < 1$ and

$$g_2(x) = \begin{cases} \frac{x}{1-p}, if\ 0 \le x \le 1-p \\ 1,\ if\ 1-p < x \le 1, \end{cases}$$

then

$$g_{12}(x) = g_1(g_2(x)) = \begin{cases} (\frac{x}{1-p})^r,\ if\ 0 \le x \le 1-p \\ 1,\ if\ 1-p < x \le 1, \end{cases}$$

and

$$g_{21}(x) = g_2(g_1(x)) = \begin{cases} \frac{x^r}{1-p}, if\ 0 \le x \le (1-p)^{\frac{1}{r}} \\ 1,\ if\ (1-p)^{\frac{1}{r}} < x \le 1, \end{cases}$$

Obviously, $g_1 < g_{21}$ and $g_2 < g_{12}$, so by Theorem $\rho_{g_1}[X] < \rho_{g_{21}}[X]$ and $\rho_{g_2}[X] < \rho_{g_{21}}[X]$.

In essence, it is sometimes necessary to distort the initial distribution more than once. We will consider a few more examples of distortion functions obtained by the composite method as a composition of known distortion functions and will study the corresponding distortion measures risks.

Example 1

We will study exponential distortion function $g(x) = \frac{e^x-1}{e-1}$ is a convex distortion function and indicator concave distortion function $1_{\{x>1-p\}}$.

It is easy to check that the composition of any distortion function $g(x)$ (in particular, this one) with $1_{\{x>1-p\}}$ in the following order $g(1_{\{x>1-p\}}) = 1_{\{x>1-p\}}$, i.e. it does not create a new distortion function. If we change the order of creating the superposition, i.e. consider distortion function $1_{\{x>1-p\}}(g(x))$.

However, since $h(x) = 1_{\{x>1-p\}}(g(x)) = 1_{\{g(x)>1-p\}}(x)$ and inequality $\frac{e^x-1}{e-1} > 1 - p$ equivalent to inequality $x > \ln(1 + (e-1)(1-p))$, then $h(x) = 1_{\{x>1-p\}}(g(x)) = 1_{\{x>\ln(1+(e-1)(1-p))\}}(x) = 1_{\{x>1-[1-\ln(1+(e-1)(1-p))]\}}(x)$.

According to Proposition 1, $\rho_h[X] = VaR_{1-\ln(1+(e-1)(1-p))}[X]$ is distortion risk measure corresponding to the given distortion function, i.e. known risk measure VaR with the confidence level changed in such a way. This risk measure grows very slowly with an increase in confidence. For example, if the initial confidence level is $p = 0.95$, then $\rho_h[X] \approx VaR_{0.032}[X]$.

Example 2

We will look at logarithmic distortion function $g(x) = \frac{\ln(x+1)}{\ln 2}$, a concave distortion function, as well as at indicative concave distortion function $1_{\{x>1-p\}}$.

Let's consider a distortion function built with this superposition: $1_{\{x>1-p\}}(g(x))$.

However, since $h(x) = 1_{\{x>1-p\}}(g(x)) = 1_{\{g(x)>1-p\}}(x)$ and inequality $\frac{\ln(x+1)}{\ln 2} > 1 - p$ is equivalent to inequality $x > 2^{1-p} - 1$, then $h(x) = 1_{\{x>1-p\}}(g(x)) = 1_{\{x>2^{1-p}-1\}}(x) = 1_{\{x>1-[1-(2^{1-p}-1)]\}}(x) = 1_{\{x>1-[2-2^{1-p}]\}}(x)$.

According to Proposition 1, $\rho_h[X] = VaR_{2-2^{1-p}}[X]$ is distortion risk measure corresponding to the given distortion function, i.e. known risk measure VaR with the confidence level changed in such a way. This risk measure grows fast with increasing confidence probability. For example, if the initial confidence level is $p = 0.95$, then $\rho_h[X] \approx VaR_{0.97}[X]$.

Example 3

We will look at sinusoidal distortion function $g(x) = \sin\frac{\pi}{2}x$, a concave distortion function, as well as at indicative concave distortion function $1_{\{x>1-p\}}$. Let's consider a distortion function built with this superposition: $1_{\{x>1-p\}}(g(x))$.

However, since $h(x) = 1_{\{x>1-p\}}(g(x)) = 1_{\{g(x)>1-p\}}(x)$

and inequality $\sin\frac{\pi}{2}x > 1 - p$ is equivalent to inequality $x > \frac{2}{\pi}\arcsin(1 - p)$, then

$h(x) = 1_{\{x>1-p\}}(g(x)) = 1_{\{x>\frac{2}{\pi}\arcsin(1-p)\}}(x) = 1_{\{x>1-[1-\frac{2}{\pi}\arcsin(1-p)]\}}(x)$.

According to Proposition 1, $\rho_h[X] = VaR_{1-\frac{2}{\pi}\arcsin(1-p)}[X]$ is distortion risk measure corresponding to the given distortion function, i.e. known risk measure VaR with the confidence level changed in such a way. This risk measure grows fast with increasing confidence probability. For example, if the initial confidence level is $p = 0.95$, then $\rho_h[X] \approx VaR_{0.9682}[X]$.

Example 4

We will consider power distortion function $g(x) = x^\alpha$, which is a concave distortion function at $0 < \alpha < 1$ and a convex distortion function at $\alpha > 1$, as well as indicator concave distortion function $1_{\{x>1-p\}}$.

Let's consider a distortion function built with this superposition $1_{\{x>1-p\}}(g(x))$.

However, since $h(x) = 1_{\{x>1-p\}}(g(x)) = 1_{\{g(x)>1-p\}}(x)$

and inequality $x^\alpha > 1 - p$ is equivalent to inequality $x > (1 - p)^{\frac{1}{\alpha}}$, then

$$h(x) = 1_{\{x>1-p\}}(g(x)) = 1_{\{x>(1-p)^{\frac{1}{\alpha}}\}}(x) = 1_{\{x>1-(1-(1-p)^{\frac{1}{\alpha}})\}}(x).$$

According to Proposition 1, $\rho_h[X] = VaR_{1-(1-p)^{\frac{1}{\alpha}}}[X]$ is distortion risk measure corresponding to the given distortion function, i.e. known risk measure VaR with the confidence level changed in such a way. The growth of these risk measures with increasing confidence probability strongly depends on the choice of parameter α. For example, if the initial confidence level is $p = 0.95$, then at $\alpha = 2$, $\rho_h[X] \approx VaR_{0.025}[X]$ this risk measure grows very slowly with increasing confidence probability; at $\alpha = 1$, $\rho_h[X] \approx VaR_{0.95}[X]$ it is standard VaR measure; and at $\alpha = \frac{1}{2}$, $\rho_h[X] \approx VaR_{0.9975}[X]$ this risk measure grows rapidly with increasing confidence probability.

Example 5

Let's consider function $g(x) = xe^{1-x}$, a concave distortion function, as well as indicative concave distortion function $1_{\{x>1-p\}}\ \{1\}$.

Let's consider a distortion function built with this superposition: $1_{\{x>1-p\}}(g(x))$.

However, since

$h(x) = 1_{\{x>1-p\}}(g(x)) = 1_{\{g(x)>1-p\}}(x)$ and inequality $xe^{1-x} > 1-p$ is equivalent to inequality $-xe^{-x} < -\frac{1-p}{e}$, from which it follows that $x > -W(-\frac{1-p}{e})$, where $W(x)$ is the well-known Lambert W-function (Corless et al., 1996), therefore

$$h(x) = 1_{\{x>1-p\}}(g(x)) = 1_{\{x>-W(-\frac{1-p}{e})\}}(x) = 1_{\{x>1-[1+W(-\frac{1-p}{e})]\}}(x).$$

According to Proposition 1, $\rho_h[X] = VaR_{1+W(-\frac{1-p}{e})}[X]$ is distortion risk measure corresponding to the given distortion function, i.e. known risk measure VaR with the confidence level changed in such a way. This risk measure grows fast with increasing confidence probability. For example, if the initial confidence level is $p = 0.95$, then $-\frac{1-p}{e} \approx -0.0184$ and then, using the well-known expansion of the Lambert W-function in a power series converging at $|x| < \frac{1}{e}$:

$$W(x) = \sum_{n=1}^{\infty} \frac{(-n)^{n-1}}{n!} x^n = x - x^2 + \frac{3}{2}x^3 - \frac{8}{3}x^4 + \frac{125}{24}x^5 - \ldots$$

we get $W(-0.0184) \approx -0.0187$ and thus,

$\rho_h[X] \approx VaR_{0.9813}[X]\ 0.9813$.

Example 6

Let's consider function $g(x) = \min\{\frac{x}{1-p}, 1\}$, a concave distortion function, as well as indicative concave distortion function $1_{\{x>1-p\}}(x)$.

Let's consider a distortion function built with this superposition:$1_{\{x>1-p\}}(g(x))$.

However,

$$h(x) = 1_{\{x>1-p\}}(g(x)) = \begin{cases} 1, \; if \; x > (1-p)^2 \\ 0, \; if \; 0 \leq x \leq (1-p)^2 \end{cases} = 1_{\{x>(1-p)^2\}}(x)$$

If we introduce concave distortion function $g_2(x) = x^{\frac{1}{2}}$ that belongs to the family of distortion functions studied in Example 4, then

$$1_{\{x>1-p\}}(g_2(x)) = 1_{\{x>(1-p)^2\}}(x).$$

Thus, distortion function $h(x)$ can also be represented as the following superposition:

$$h(x) = 1_{\{x>1-p\}}(g_2(x)) = \begin{cases} 1, \; if \; x > (1-p)^2 \\ 0, \; if \; 0 \leq x \leq (1-p)^2 \end{cases}$$
$$= 1_{\{x>(1-p)^2\}}(x) = 1_{\{x>1-(1-(1-p)^2\}}(x)$$

According to Proposition 1,

$\rho_h[X] = VaR_{1-(1-p)^2}[X]$ is distortion risk measure corresponding to the given distortion function, i.e. known risk measure VaR with the confidence level changed in such a way.

This risk measure grows fast with increasing confidence probability.

However, if we recall formula (6.2) for VaR squared, we get:

$$\rho_h[X] = VaR_p^{(2)}[X]$$

Thus, we found out that new risk measure VaR squared also belongs to the class of distortion risk measures, and it corresponds to the distortion function obtained as a superposition of function $1_{\{x>1-p\}}(x)$ with any distortion function: $g(x) = \min\{\frac{x}{1-p}, 1\}$ or $g_2(x) = x^{\frac{1}{2}}$.

We can prove that the following, more general definition is true.

Proposition 3

Risk measure VaR to the power of n (for any natural n) belongs to the class of distortion risk measures and corresponds to the distortion function obtained in any superposition of a function $1_{\{x>1-p\}}(x)$ with any distortion function: $g(x) = \min\{\frac{x}{1-p}, 1\}$ or $g_n(x) = x^{\frac{1}{n}}$:

$$h(x) = 1_{\{x>1-p\}}(\underbrace{g(g(...(g(x))}_{n-1-\text{times}} = 1_{\{x>1-p\}}(g_n(x))$$

i.e.

$$VaR_p^{(n)}[X] = \rho_h[X].$$

Proof We will consider function $g(x) = \min\{\frac{x}{1-p}, 1\}$ concave distortion function. The following superposition $\underbrace{g(g(...(g(x))}_{n-1-\text{times}}$ also represents a concave distortion function as follows:

$$\underbrace{g(g(...(g}_{k-1-\text{times}}(g_\alpha(x))...) = \begin{cases} 1, & \text{if } x > (1-p)^{k-1}(1-\alpha p) \\ \frac{x}{(1-p)^{k-1}(1-\alpha p)}, & \text{if } 0 \le x \le (1-p)^{k-1}(1-\alpha p) \end{cases}$$

concave distortion function $h(x) = 1_{\{x>1-p\}}(\underbrace{g(g(...(g(x))}_{n-1-\text{times}}$ is as follows:

$$\begin{aligned} h(x) &= 1_{\{x>1-p\}}(g_{k-1}(g_\alpha(x))) = 1_{\{x>(1-p)^k(1-\alpha p)\}}(x) \\ &= 1_{\{x>1-(1-(1-p)^k(1-\alpha p))\}}(x) \end{aligned}$$

If we introduce concave distortion function $g_n(x) = x^{\frac{1}{n}}$ that belongs to the family of distortion functions studied in Example 4, then

$$1_{\{x>1-p\}}(g_n(x)) = 1_{\{x>(1-p)^n\}}(x) = h(x)$$

Thus, distortion function $h(x)$ can also be represented as the following superposition:

$$h(x) = 1_{\{x>1-p\}}(g_n(x)) = 1_{\{x>(1-p)^n\}}(x) = 1_{\{x>1-(1-(1-p)^n\}}(x)$$

According to Proposition 1, $\rho_h[X] = VaR_{1-(1-p)^n}[X]$ distortion risk measure corresponding to the given distortion function, i.e. known risk measure VaR with the confidence level changed in such a way. This risk measure grows fast with increasing confidence probability.

However, if we recall formula (4) for VaR to the power of n, we get.

$$\rho_h[X] = VaR_p^{(n)}[X]$$

The Proposition is proved.

The more general statement is also valid for VaR risk measures to any power of $t \geq 1$.

Proposition 4

(Minasyan, 2020b)

Risk measure VaR to the power of t, $\mathrm{VaR}_p^{(t)}[X]$ (at any actual $t \geq 1$), where t is as follows: $t = k + \alpha$, where k is a natural number, and α is a real number, moreover $0 \leq \alpha < 1$, it is a distorted risk measure and it is obtained as a risk measure corresponding to the distortion function, which can be represented as superposition of distortion functions $1_{\{x>1-p\}}(x)$,$g(x) = \min\{\frac{x}{1-p}, 1\}$, and $g_\alpha(x) = \min\{\frac{x}{1-\alpha p}, 1\}$, and $g_{k-1}(x) = x^{\frac{1}{k-1}}$ in the following two ways:

$$h(x) = 1_{\{x>1-p\}}(\underbrace{g(g(\ldots(g}_{k-1-times}(g_\alpha(x)\ldots) = 1_{\{x>1-p\}}(g_{k-1}(g_\alpha(x))),$$

i.e.

$$VaR_p^{(t)}[X] = \rho_h[X]$$

Proof Functions $g(x) = \min\{\frac{x}{1-p}, 1\}$ and $g_\alpha(x) = \min\{\frac{x}{1-\alpha p}, 1\}$ are concave distortion functions. Next superposition $\underbrace{\mathrm{g(g(\ldots(g}}_{k-1-\mathrm{times}}(g_\alpha(x))\ldots)$ also represents a concave distortion function as follows:

$$\underbrace{\mathrm{g(g(\ldots(g}}_{k-1-\mathrm{times}}(g_\alpha(x))\ldots) = \begin{cases} 1, \text{ if } \mathrm{x} > (1-\mathrm{p})^{\mathrm{k}-1}(1-\alpha p) \\ \dfrac{x}{(1-p)^{k-1}(1-\alpha p)}, \text{ if } 0 \leq \mathrm{x} \leq (1-\mathrm{p})^{\mathrm{k}-1}(1-\alpha p) \end{cases}$$

and concave distortion function $h(x) = 1_{\{x>1-p\}}(\underbrace{g(g(\ldots(g}_{k-1-\text{times}}(g_\alpha(x)\ldots)$ is as follows:

$$h(x) = \begin{cases} 1, \ if \ x > (1-p)^k(1-\alpha p) \\ 0, \ if \ 0 \le x \le (1-p)^k(1-\alpha p) \end{cases} = 1_{\{x>(1-p)^k(1-\alpha p)\}}(x)$$

With function $g_{k-1}(x) = x^{\frac{1}{k-1}}$, the distortion function $h(x)$ can also be represented as the following superposition:

$$h(x) = \underbrace{g(g(\ldots(g(x))}_{n-times} = \begin{cases} \frac{x}{(1-p)^n}, \ if \ 0 \le x \le (1-p)^n \\ 1, \ if \ (1-p)^n < x \le 1 \end{cases}$$

According to Proposition 1, $\rho_h[X] = VaR_{1-(1-p)^k(1-\alpha p)}[X]$ is distortion risk measure corresponding to the given distortion function, i.e. known risk measure VaR with the confidence level changed in such a way. However, if we recall formula (9) for VaR to the power of t, we get $\rho_h[X] = VaR_p^{(t)}[X]$.

The Proposition is proved.

In general, any concave distortion function g gives the distribution tail more weight than the identical function $g(x) = x$, while any convex distortion function g gives the tail less weight than the identical function $g(x) = x$(Yin & Zhu, 2018). Therefore, in particular, any concave distortion function g gives the distribution tail more weight than any convex distortion function.

It is good to know when building a risk measure with the required properties.

The question is if risk measure $ES_p^{(2)}[X]$ is a distorted risk measure.

Example 6

We will consider function $g(x) = \min\{\frac{x}{1-p}, 1\}$ a concave distortion function, as well as distortion function built with superposition:$g(g(x))$.

It is easy to check,

$$h(x) = g(g(x)) = \begin{cases} 1, \; if \; x > (1-p)^2 \\ \dfrac{x}{(1-p)^2}, \; if \; 0 \leq x \leq (1-p)^2 \end{cases}$$

and

$$h'(x) = \begin{cases} 0, \; if \; x > (1-p)^2 \\ \dfrac{1}{(1-p)^2}, \; if \; 0 \leq x \leq (1-p)^2 \end{cases}$$

According to Theorem 2, the distorted risk measure corresponding to a given distortion function turns out to be a measure that can be represented as follows:

$$\rho_h[X] = \int\limits_{[0,(1-p)^2]} VaR_{1-q}[X]\frac{1}{(1-p)^2}dq + \int\limits_{[(1-p)^2,1]} VaR_{1-q}[X] \times 0dq$$

$$= \frac{1}{(1-p)^2} \int\limits_{[0,(1-p)^2]} VaR_{1-q}[X]dq = \frac{1}{(1-p)^2} \int\limits_{[1-(1-p)^2,1]} VaR_q[X]dq$$

However, if we recall formula (6.10) for ES squared, we get $\rho_h[X] = ES_p^{(2)}[X]$.

We found out that new risk measure ES squared, introduced in this paper, also belongs to the class of distortion risk measures, and it corresponds to the described distortion function.

The question is if risk measure $ES_p^{(n)}[X]$ is a distorted risk measure.

Proposition 5

Risk measure ES to the power of n (for any natural n) belongs to the class of distortion risk measures, and it corresponds to the distortion function obtained as any superposition of functions $g(x) = \min\{\frac{x}{1-p}, 1\}$ as follows:

$$h(x) = \underbrace{g(g(...(g(x)...)}_{n-\text{times}},$$

i.e.

$$ES_p^{(n)}[X] = \rho_h[X].$$

Proof Function $g(x) = \min\{\frac{x}{1-p}, 1\}$ is a concave distortion function. Next superposition $\underbrace{g(g(...(g(x)...)}_{n-\text{times}}$ also represents a concave distortion function as follows:

$$h(x) = \underbrace{g(g(...(g(x))}_{n-times} = \begin{cases} \dfrac{x}{(1-p)^n}, & if\ 0 \le x \le (1-p)^n \\ 1, & if\ (1-p)^n < x \le 1 \end{cases},$$

and

$$h'(x) = \begin{cases} 0, & if \quad x > (1-p)^2 \\ \frac{1}{(1-p)^2}, & if\ 0 \le x \le (1-p)^2 \end{cases}.$$

According to Theorem 2, the distorted risk measure corresponding to a given distortion function $h(x)$ turns out to be a measure that can be represented as follows:

$$\rho_h[X] = \int\limits_{[0,(1-p)^n]} VaR_{1-q}[X]\frac{1}{(1-p)^n}dq + \int\limits_{[(1-p)^n,1]} VaR_{1-q}[X] \times 0dq$$

$$= \frac{1}{(1-p)^n} \int\limits_{[0,(1-p)^n]} VaR_{1-q}[X]dq = \frac{1}{(1-p)^n} \int\limits_{[1-(1-p)^n,1]} VaR_q[X]dq$$

.

However, if we recall formula (11) for ES to the power of n, we get $\rho_h[X] = ES_p^{(n)}[X]$.

We found out that new risk measure ES to the power of n also belongs to the class of distortion risk measures. It corresponds to the described distortion function and is presented as usual risk measure ES with the confidence probability changed in a certain way.

The Proposition is proved.

The question is if risk measure $ES_p^{(t)}[X]$ is a distorted risk measure.

Proposition 6

(Minasyan, 2020b)

Risk measure ES in power of t for any real $t \geq 1$, represented as $t = k + \alpha$, where k is a natural number and α is a real number, $0 \leq \alpha < 1$, belongs to the class of distortion risk measures and corresponds to the distortion function obtained as any superposition of functions $g(x) = \min\{\frac{x}{1-p}, 1\}$ and $g_\alpha(x) = \min\{\frac{x}{1-\alpha p}, 1\}$ as follows:

$h(x) = \underbrace{\mathrm{g}(\mathrm{g}(\ldots(\mathrm{g}(}_{k-\text{times}} g_\alpha(x))\ldots),$

i.e.

$\mathrm{ES}_p^{(\mathrm{t})}[X] = \rho_h[X].$

Proof Function $g(x) = \min\{\frac{x}{1-p}, 1\}$ is a concave distortion function. Superposition $\underbrace{g(g(\ldots(g(}_{k-} g_\alpha(x))\ldots)$ also represents a concave distortion function as follows:

$$h(x) = \underbrace{\mathrm{g}(\mathrm{g}(\ldots(\mathrm{g}(}_{k-\text{times}} g_\alpha(x))\ldots) = \begin{cases} \dfrac{x}{(1-p)^k(1-\alpha p)}, & \text{if } 0 \leq \mathrm{x} \leq (1-\mathrm{p})^{\mathrm{k}}(1-\alpha p) \\ 1, \text{ if } (1-\mathrm{p})^{\mathrm{k}}(1-\alpha p) < x \leq 1 \end{cases}$$

and

$$h'(x) = \begin{cases} 0, \ if \ x > (1-p)^k(1-\alpha p) \\ \dfrac{1}{(1-p)^k(1-\alpha p)}, \ if \ 0 \leq x \leq (1-p)^k(1-\alpha p) \end{cases}.$$

According to Theorem 2, the distorted risk measure corresponding to a given distortion function $h(x)$ turns out to be a measure that can be represented as follows:

$$\begin{aligned}\rho_h[X] &= \int_{[0,(1-p)^k(1-\alpha p)]} VaR_{1-q}[X]\frac{1}{(1-p)^k(1-\alpha p)}dq \\ &\quad + \int_{[(1-p)^n,1]} VaR_{1-q}[X] \times 0dq \\ &= \frac{1}{(1-p)^k(1-\alpha p)} \int_{[0,(1-p)^k(1-\alpha p)]} VaR_{1-q}[X]dq \\ &= \frac{1}{(1-p)^k(1-\alpha p)} \int_{[1-(1-p)^k(1-\alpha p,1]} VaR_q[X]dq\end{aligned}$$

.

If we recall formula (6.13) for ES to the power of t, we get:
$\rho_h[X] = ES_p^{(t)}[X]$.

We found out that new risk measure ES to the power of t also belongs to the class of distortion risk measures. It corresponds to the described distortion function and is presented as usual risk measure ES with the confidence probability changed in a certain way.

The Proposition is proved.

We will now consider Example 7 of two random variables X and Υ with different discrete distribution laws, whose risks do not distinguish between the known risk measures VaR and ES (Yin & Zhu, 2018). Generalizing risk measure ES with random values of losses that obey discrete distribution laws has its own specifics. In particular, if the random loss X obeys a discrete distribution, then $ES_p[X]$ is expressed through the values of VaR and the expected value of the excess losses over VaR (Yin & Zhu, 2018):

$$\begin{aligned}ES_p[X] &= VaR_p[X] \\ &\quad + \frac{1 - F_X(VaR_p[X])}{1-p}E[X - VaR_p[X]|X \quad VaR_p[X]]. \quad (6.15)\end{aligned}$$

This example by C. Yin and D. Zhu (Yin & Zhu, 2018) shows that risk measures $VaR_p[X]$ and $ES_p[X]$ may not distinguish between the risks created by X and Υ. At the same time, an example of a certain risk measure that distinguishes between their risks is given. This measure coincides with risk measure $ES_p^{(2)}[X]$ introduced in this paper.

Example 7

Let us consider two random variables X and Υ that simulate risks with distribution functions, respectively:

$$F_X(x) = \begin{cases} 0 \quad if \quad x < 0 \\ 0.6, \ if \ 0 \le x < 100 \\ 0.975, \ if \ 100 \le x < 500 \\ 1, \quad if \quad x \ge 500 \end{cases}$$

and

$$F_Y(x) = \begin{cases} 0, \ if \quad x < 0, \\ 0.6, \ if \ 0 \le x < 100 \\ 0.99, \ if \ 100 \le x < 1100 \\ 1, \ if \quad x \ge 1100 \end{cases}$$

It is easy to check that $E(X) = E(\Upsilon) = 50$,

$VaR_{0,95}[X] = VaR_{0.96}[X] = 100, VaR_{0,95}[Y] = VaR_{0.96}[Y] = 100,$

ES can be calculated by formula (15) and we get: $ES_{0,95}[X] = ES_{0.95}[Y] = 300, ES_{0,96}[X] = ES_{0.96}[Y] = 350$. When $p = 0.95$ and $p = 0.96$, then according to the risk measures VaR and ES, both X and Υ have the same risk! However, the maximum loss for Υ (1100) more than doubles the loss for X (500), and it is clear that risk Υ is greater than risk X.

We now consider distortion measure ρ_h with distortion function искажения $h(x) = g(g(x))$ and $g(x) = \begin{cases} \frac{x}{1-p}, if \ 0 \le x \le 1-p \\ 1, if \ 1-p < x \le 1, \end{cases}$.

According to Example 6,

$$\rho_h[X] = \frac{1}{(1-p)^2} \int\limits_{[1-(1-p)^2,1]} VaR_q[X]dq = ES_p^{(2)}[X].$$

And numerically for $p = 0.95$

$$\rho_h[X] = \frac{1}{(0.05)^2} \int\limits_{[1-0.05^2,1]} VaR_q[X]dq = ES^{(2)}_{0.95}[X],$$

i.e.

$$\rho_h[X] = \frac{1}{0.0025} \int\limits_{[0.9975,1]} VaR_q[X]dq = \frac{500}{0.0025}(1 - 0.9975) = 500$$

and

$$\rho_h[Y] = \frac{1}{0.0025} \int\limits_{[0.9975,1]} VaR_q[X]dq = \frac{1100}{0.0025}(1 - 0.9975) = 1100.$$

Then at $p = 0.95$, $\rho_h[X] = ES^{(2)}_{0.95}[X] = 500$ and $\rho_h[Y] = ES^{(2)}_{0.95}[Y] = 1100$.

In this case, risk measure $\rho_h = ES^{(2)}_p$, distinguishing between different risk levels for X and Υ, turned out to be more suitable for risk management than usual risk measures VaR and ES.

6.4 Conclusions

A vigorous theoretical study of a class of distortion risk measures took place in the last decades. They have recently become widespread in financial and insurance applications due to their attractive properties. In his earlier works, the author introduced and investigated risk measure "VaR to the power of t" that allows identifying various financial catastrophic risks. In this paper, the author described and developed a composite method for creating a new class of distortion functions and corresponding distortion risk measures. By this method, the author proves that risk measure "VaR to the power of t" belongs to the class of distortion risk measures, and describes the corresponding distortion functions. Also, the author introduces a new class of risk measure "ES to the power of t", proves that they also belong to the class of distortion risk measures, and describes the corresponding distortion functions. Various cases illustrate the relevant concepts and results that demonstrate the importance of "VaR to the power of t" and "ES to the power of t" risk measures as subsets of distortion risk measures identifying various financial catastrophic risks. Distortion risk measures are currently well studied and have many useful and convenient properties. Thus, all the properties possessed by the distortion risk measures (Artzner et al., 1999) are also possessed by the families of measures "VaR to the power of t" and "ES to the power of t".

Acknowledgements This article is based on the budgetary-supported research 4.10 "Researching Methods for Measuring Risks at the Corporate and Macrofinancial Levels" according to the state task carried out by the Higher School of Finance and Management, Russian Presidential Academy of National Economy and Public Administration, Moscow, Russia.

References

Artzner, P., Delbaen, F., Eber, J.-M., & Heath, D. (1999). Coherent measures of risk. *Mathematical Finance, 9*(3), 203–228. https://doi.org/10.1111/1467-9965.00068

Artzner, P., Delbaen, F., Eber, J.-M., Heath, D. Thinking coherently. *Risk*, 10(11): 68–71.

Belles-Sampera, J., Guillén, M., & Santolino, M. (2014). Beyond value-at-risk: GlueVaR distortion risk measures. *Risk Analysis, 34*(1), 121–134. https://doi.org/10.1111/risa.12080

Belles-Sampera, J., Guillé, M., & Santolino, M. (2014). GlueVaR risk measures in capital allocation applications. *Insurance: Mathematics and Economics*, 58: 132–137. https://doi.org/10.1016/j.insmatheco.2014.06.014

Cherubini, U., & Mulinacci, S. (2014). Contagion-based distortion risk measures. *Applied Mathematics Letters, 27*, 85–89. https://doi.org/10.1016/j.aml.2013.07.007

Corless, R. M., Gonnet, G. H., Hare, D. E. G., Jeffrey, D. J., & Knuth, D.E. (1996). On the Lambert W function. *Advanced Computational Mathematics*, 5(1): 329–359. https://doi.org/10.1007/BF02124750

Crouhy M., Galai D., & Mark R. The essentials of risk management. New York: McGraw-Hill Book Co.; 2006. p. 414. (Russ. ed.: Crouhy M., Galai D., Mark R. Osnovy risk-menedzhmenta. Moscow: Urait; 2006. 414 p.).

Denuit, M., Dhaene, J., Goovaerts, M., & Kaas, R. (2005). *Actuarial theory for dependent risks: Measures, orders and models* (p. 440). John Wiley & Sons Ltd. https://doi.org/10.1002/0470016450

Dhaene, J., Kukush, A., Linders, D., & Tang, Q. (2012). Remarks on quantiles and distortion risk measures. *European Actuarial Journal, 2*(2), 319–328. https://doi.org/10.1007/s13385-012-0058-021

Denneberg, D. (1994). *Non-additive measure and integral* (p. 178). Dordrecht: Kluwer Academic Publishers. (Theory and Decision Library B. Vol. 27). https://doi.org/10.1007/978-94-017-2434-0

Hull, J. C. (2007). *Risk management and financial institutions* (p. 576). Pearson Education International.

Jorion, P. (2007). *Value at risk: The new benchmark for managing financial risk* (p. 624). McGraw-Hill Education.

Minasyan, V. B. (2019a). A new risk measure VaR squared and its calculation. The case of uniform and triangular loss distributions. *Upravlenie finansovymi riskami = Financial Risk Management Journal*, (3): 200–208. (In Russ.).

Minasyan, V. B. (2019b). A new risk measure VaR squared and its calculation. The case of the general law of loss distribution, comparison with other risk measures. *Upravlenie finansovymi riskami = Financial Risk Management Journal*, (4): 298–320. (In Russ.).

Minasyan, V. B. (2020a). New ways to measure catastrophic financial risk: "VaR to the power of t" measures and how to calculate them. *Finansy: teoriya i praktika = Finance: Theory and Practice*, 24(3): 92–109. (In Russ.). https://doi.org/10.26794/2587-5671-2020-24-3-92-109

Minasyan, V. B. (2020b). New ways of measuring catastrophic risks: measures "VaR to power t" and "ES to power t" their relationship with measures of risk distortion of expectations. *Finansy: teoriya i praktika = Finance: Theory and Practice*, 24(6): 92–107. (In Russ.). https://doi.org/10.26794/2587-5671-2020-24-6-92-107

Szegö, G. ed. (2004). *Risk measures for the 21st century* (p. 491). Chichester: John Wiley & Sons Ltd.

Wang, S. S. (2000). A class of distortion operators for pricing financial and insurance risks. *The Journal of Risk and Insurance, 67*(1), 15–36. https://doi.org/10.2307/253675

Wang, S., & Dhaene, J. (1998). Comonotonicity, correlation order and premium principles. *Insurance: Mathematics and Economics*, 22(3): 235–242. https://doi.org/10.1016/S0167-6687(97)00040-1

Wang, S. S. (1996). Premium calculation by transforming the layer premium density. *ASTIN Bulletin: The Journal of the IAA*. 26(1): 71–92. https://doi.org/10.2143/AST.26.1.563234

Yang, F. (2015). First- and second-order asymptotics for the tail distortion risk measure of extreme risks. *Communications in Statistics — Theory and Methods*, 44(3): 520–532. https://doi.org/10.1080/03610926.2012.751116

Yin, C., & Zhu, D. (2018). New class of distortion risk measures and their tail asymptotics with emphasis on VaR. *Journal of Financial Risk Management, 7*(1), 12–38. https://doi.org/10.4236/jfrm.2018.71002

Zhu, L., & Li, H. (2012). Tail distortion risk and its asymptotic analysis. *Insurance: Mathematics and Economics*, 51(1): 115–121. https://doi.org/10.1016/j.insmatheco.2012.03.010

CHAPTER 7

Measuring Market Liquidity and Liquidity Mismatches Across Sectors

Artur Akhmetov, Anna Burova, Natalia Makhankova, and Alexey Ponomarenko

7.1 Introduction

The development of financial markets is a hot topic in transitional economies since the possibility of fundraising using a variety of financial instruments is viewed as an important factor in ensuring investment growth and the sustainability of economic development.[1]

[1] In Russia, when discussing this topic, access to 'long money' is often mentioned. In our opinion, this term does not fully reflect the essence of the problem as the characteristics of financial instruments that determine their liquidity and the level of debt burden they create are not limited to maturity.

The views expressed herein are solely those of the authors. The content and results of this research should not be considered or referred to in any publications as the Bank of Russia's official position, official policy, or decisions. Any errors in this document are the responsibility of the authors.

A. Akhmetov · A. Burova · N. Makhankova · A. Ponomarenko (✉)
Research and Forecasting Department, Bank of Russia, Moscow, Russia
e-mail: ponomarenkoaa@cbr.ru

A. Karminsky and M. Stolbov (eds.), *Systemic Financial Risk*,
https://doi.org/10.1007/978-3-031-54809-3_7

Our work is aimed at systematising liquidity measurement concepts and the structure of financial markets, which allows to assess the development level of market segments. The main contribution of this work is the creation of tools that can be used to monitor and analyse liquidity and the structure of financial markets, which makes it possible to expand the discussion on promoting the accessibility of financing in Russia.

Liquidity is determined by a large number of factors, so it is difficult, albeit always appropriate to give a uniform definition. We consider the concept of liquidity from different perspectives and offer a toolkit for measuring it. On the basis of a cross-country comparison, we analyse the degree of liquidity of the stock and government bond markets.

Higher liquidity of financial markets is associated with a higher development level of these markets; however, this is fraught with liquidity risks when assets and liabilities may not correspond in terms of liquidity, which may lead to financial losses. In our work, we calculate liquidity indices (indicators of liquidity mismatch) that result from the operation of financial markets and assess the extent of risk taking by economic sectors. We also perform a cross-country comparison of liquidity indices based on data from financial accounts in the system of national accounts.

This work is structured as follows. In the literature review, we first show that when household savings are not automatically transformed into investments, it is important to create demand for long-term and risky financial instruments. This leads us to a discussion of the differences between bank-based and market-based financing. We also introduce the concept of market liquidity and the concept of a liquidity mismatch. Next, we move on to the empirical part where we first present the data used in our work. Then, we conduct an empirical analysis that allows to demonstrate the concept of market liquidity and the concept of liquidity mismatch and to interpret the values of liquidity indices in conjunction with the structure of the financial system. At the end, we draw up conclusions based on the results of our analysis.

7.2 Literature Review

In this section, we first show that economic development requires the development of various segments of the financial markets. We determine what type of financial system may be preferable for this. This will allow us to move on to the concept of liquidity as an indicator of financial instruments and financial markets development. Finally, we go on to focus on the liquidity mismatch concept as an indicator of liquidity risk taking by economic agents.

The Demand for Risky Financial Assets Is a Source of Investment Financing, While Savings Alone Are Not

A high level of household savings does not guarantee a high level of investments in the economy. Borio and Disyatat (2015) note that the systems of national saving accounts are, by definition, simply unused income, which is not the same as investment financing.[2] Jakab and Kumhof (2015) question the intermediary function of banks, that is, the function of banks to transform savings of some customers into borrowing for other economic agents. According to the authors, banks create money themselves by financing customers who are both borrowers and depositors. When issuing a loan to a customer, the bank recognises it on its balance sheet as an asset, simultaneously creating a new liability as the borrowed funds go to the customer's current or settlement account with the same bank (whereby they become deposit holders).[3] The authors argue that to issue loans, the bank does not need household savings, it is enough for it to have current and settlement accounts of customers, i.e., on-demand deposits, and liabilities created after the issuance of loans. Thus, savings in the form of deposits are a consequence of bank financing rather than the cause.

Speaking at the conferences on savings in 2016, Governor of the Bank of France Villeroy de Galhau noted that there was a high level of savings in France; however, most of those funds were placed in bank deposits at low interest rates. In such conditions, there is underinvestment in the innovation sector of the economy requiring long-term and riskier investments, which undermines the potential for economic growth (Villeroy de Galhau, 2016a). For the growth in investment, it is necessary to create demand for long-term financial instruments by offering savings products beneficial to households (Villeroy de Galhau, 2016b). The demand

[2] For the authors, this difference becomes fundamental when analysing the current transactions of the balance of payments. In particular, the authors assert that the current account tells us not about the real need for funding or the real willingness to finance the rest of the world but about how many resources are released by the economy to finance the rest of the world or held back to get credit from the rest of the world.

[3] Where a client takes a loan to purchase new goods or services, these funds become assets of other clients, who also keep their funds on current and settlement accounts with the bank—that is, the funds initially issued by the bank remain on the liability side in the form of deposits (if not of the same bank, then of the banking system as a whole).

for instruments riskier than bank deposits arises when the stock markets function well.

The Dominance of Market-Based Financing May Provide More Benefits than Bank-Based Financing

The structure of the financial system can be of two types, conditional on the ratio between bank-based and market-based financing. In a bank-based[4] financial system, financial intermediaries raise savings, issue loans and manage risks. In a market-based financial system, the stock and bond markets are the main source of funding. In this case, we are talking about the financing of the private non-financial sector.

Al Mamun et al. (2018) found that the stock market (as compared to the credit market) plays a more significant and positive role in expanding production in industries that require long-term investments with long payback periods, for example, to expand the production of clean energy. Fink et al. (2006) also assumed that raising large amounts of financing for long periods would more likely involve using stocks and bonds than bank loans.

There has been extensive debate in the academic community about which type of financial system is preferable for the economy. Demirgüç-Kunt and Levine (2001) and Levine (2002) showed that the structure of the financial system itself does not affect economic growth; the development of the financial system as a whole is much more important. Although this point of view has been criticised by (Luintel et al., 2008, 2016), the subsequent papers addressed narrower issues concerning the influence of the structure of the financial system on economic performance. In particular, it was shown that in bank-based economies the financial crisis had a greater adverse impact on the economy. Thus, Gambacorta et al. (2014) revealed that the impact of the financial crisis of 2008–2009 on the GDP of the countries with prevailing bank-based financing was three times more serious than in the countries primarily reliant on market-based financing. Langfield and Pagano (2016) found that during the real estate crisis the European bank-based financial system faced higher increases in systemic risks and lower economic growth than other countries.

[4] The terms 'bank-based' or 'market-based' are used as in Demirgüç-Kunt and Levine (2001), Bats and Houben (2017), Gambacorta et al. (2014).

Moreover, Bats and Houben (2017) showed that the predominance of bank-based financing contributes to the build-up of systemic risks. Highly leveraged banks may face difficulties in complying with regulatory requirements at a time of severe impairment of financial assets. Given that banks are interconnected through interbank transactions, risks of instability accumulate in the banking system. In market-based financing, risks are shared across multiple investors rather than within the banking system.

Non-bank financial institutions play an important role in the provision of financing. On the one hand, such organisations ensure the functioning of the stock and bond market, simultaneously acting as their participants. On the other hand, they issue loans to the private non-financial sector and securitise bank loans. Non-bank financial institutions that issue loans but are not subject to banking regulations form the shadow banking system. Unger (2016) described several forms of interaction in terms of creating a loan between banks and institutions related to the shadow banking system. First, a non-bank institution may use funds raised from the issuance of securities to redeem a mortgage from a bank and thereby receive a loan from this bank as an asset (for example, this is how government-sponsored enterprises operate in the USA). Second, a non-bank institution may for a start open a credit line with a bank to redeem the bank's credit asset and then issue securities backed by that asset. Third, a non-bank institution may raise financing by issuing securities and may issue loans on its own. In this case, the bank does not participate in issuing a loan but only allows the customer to keep free funds on its accounts. Moreover, Unger (2016) comes to the conclusion that the functioning of the shadow banking system in the USA in the 2000s, despite increasing the risks to financial stability due to the lack of banking regulation, was not a sufficient condition for a credit boom. Abramova and Mamuta (2014) noted that the spread of the shadow banking sector in Russia may pose risks to financial stability due to the emergence of unethical (predatory) consumer lending and the use of money laundering technologies by non-bank financial institutions.

Rojas-Suarez (BIS, 2014b) pointed to the complementarity of the capital and credit markets associated with the interaction of banks and non-bank financial institutions. Non-bank financial institutions may fund their inventories (in the form of securities) with bank credit lines. As a result, financial shocks affecting the banking system will have an effect on the non-bank financial sector. On the other hand, in emerging economies, the credit history of companies may reduce the informational asymmetry for investors planning to purchase securities of a given company.

It is worth noting an alternative view of the relationship between the financial system structure and economic growth. Unger (2018) showed that if in the economic growth regressions, financing distribution by economy sectors is controlled for, the importance of financial structure substantially weakens. Unger (2018) attributed the negative relationship between the share of bank financing and economic growth to the fact that a part of loans is issued to households, exhibiting an inverted U-shaped relationship between financing and economic growth. According to Unger (2016), as regards the influence of finance on economic growth, the distribution of such finance between non-financial corporations and households is much more important than the exact ways the financing is provided.

Let us also mention the articles by Kurronen (2015) and Allen et al. (2018) arguing that the structure of the real sector predetermines the structure of the financial sector. Allen et al. (2018) attributed this to the fact that capital-intensive companies tend to use bank lending (the risks of these companies are easier to assess, and it is possible to issue loans secured by tangible assets), while high-tech companies and companies with a high proportion of intangible assets tend to resort to the stock and bond markets. Kurronen (2015) notes that in the countries dependent on the export of resources large resource companies prevail, for which, on the one hand, it is easier to raise funds from the capital market as investors have larger access to information about the financial condition of the companies or their credit history than to information about small companies. On the other hand, it may be more difficult for large companies to obtain financing from one bank as the company's need may exceed the capabilities of a single bank, which, in addition, seeks to diversify its loan portfolio. It turns out that the financial sector meets the real sector's demand for financing; therefore, its structure adjusts to the real sector's requirements.

Thus, the comparison of financial systems based on different types of financing does not allow us to determine precisely which system is better. It should be noted that the transition to a market-based financing system may be preferable if there is a tangible demand for long-term financial instruments, on the one hand, and, on the other hand, it can prevent the accumulation of systemic risks through the use of stocks and bonds along with loans.

Speaking about the availability of various kinds of financing for borrowers and taking into account possible maturity and debt burden, it is important to identify market development indicators for certain financial instruments. One of the important market development indicators and instruments is their liquidity. On the one hand, liquid financial instruments facilitate transactions for the holders of these financial instruments; on the other hand, in developed financial markets, less liquid liabilities of companies are transformed into liquid financial instruments traded on the market. Therefore, measuring the liquidity of financial instruments of both issuers and holders makes it possible to judge about the development of financial markets. In the next section, we will look in more detail at the concept of liquidity.

Multidimensionality of the Concept of Liquidity in the Context of the Development of Financial Markets

The concept of liquidity is multifaceted; therefore, the same financial instrument may be viewed as both liquid and illiquid, conditional on whether a particular economic agent wants to buy/sell or issue this instrument. There are many approaches to determining liquidity focusing on various aspects of this phenomenon. We systematise the approaches that will be useful for us in comparing the development of financial markets in various countries.

First, it should be noted that the views on liquidity differ across regulators and investors. The first group of users includes international organisations that set the standards of financial regulation. Within the scope of ensuring financial stability, regulators identify the main criteria for liquidity as a capability to receive the maximum amount of monetary funds from assets at a given time and the current need to pay the maximum amount of monetary funds on its liabilities (Krishnamurthy et al., 2016). A group of practitioners represented by investors are interested in the liquidity of financial instruments they want to make profit from. Profit may be obtained both in the form of dividends or coupon payments for bonds (if any) and in the form of a change in the price of a financial instrument. The liquidity of an instrument is important if there is a need to buy or sell an instrument at a specific time to benefit from a price change. The possibility or impossibility of the quick sale of a financial instrument may affect its pricing due to the establishment of a liquidity premium.

Sarr and Lybek (2002) note that the concept of liquidity may differ depending on the object: an asset, the market for an asset, the financial market for an asset or the financial institutions in this market (in the latter case, we are talking about institutional liquidity). Below we will briefly explain the differences between these concepts of liquidity for each object.

As for the *liquidity of an asset*, one of the first definitions was by Fisher (1959). It says that liquidity is the ability of an asset to trade quickly and without loss in its value. Biais et al. (1997) argued that an asset is liquid if it can be sold quickly with low transaction costs and at a reasonable price. Sarr and Lybek (2002) summarised the existing definitions as follows: an asset is liquid if it can be easily converted into a legal tender.

Asset market liquidity is a broader concept, capturing the ease with which a large amount of assets can be placed in the market over a short period of time without changing the asset prices (IMF, 2018). Demsetz (1968) wrote that liquidity is determined by the price concession that a market participant agrees to in order to complete a transaction. Fleming (2003) defined a liquid market as a market in which a transaction can be completed with minimal transaction costs. In their fundamental research papers, Demsetz and Fleming point out only one aspect of market liquidity, i.e., the presence/absence of transaction costs. However, there are many more aspects of market liquidity, which will be discussed in more detail below.

Financial market liquidity, according to Sarr and Lybek (2002), depends on how interchangeable financial instruments are for investors. For example, differences in credit risk may impede the interchangeability of instruments and lead to market segmentation. Even if instruments are issued by the same issuer, they may still have different characteristics (for example, special rights on preferred shares), which makes it difficult to assess financial market liquidity.

Institutional liquidity reflects how easily financial institutions can conduct financial transactions to close the liquidity gap between assets and liabilities (Sarr & Lybek, 2002).

Of the liquidity objects mentioned above, financial market liquidity is the focus of the highest attention among researchers. In the research literature (Diaz & Escribano, 2020; Sarr & Lybek, 2002), there are five characteristics of a liquid financial market:

- Tightness is related to the volume of transaction costs. In tighter markets, transaction costs are lower, which is reflected in a smaller difference between the minimum selling price and the maximum purchase price. Tighter markets are more liquid.[5]
- Immediacy shows how quickly a financial instrument may be sold or bought, and how quickly a new financial instrument may be placed. Accordingly, the faster a transaction can be made, the higher the market liquidity is. Immediacy is an important aspect of liquidity for monetary authorities regulating banking. Banks' financial assets include not only stocks and bonds, with which market liquidity is associated, but also loans and deposits. To determine the liquidity of bank assets and liabilities, it is crucial to know how quickly a financial asset can be cashed out, or, conversely, how long it is possible to postpone repaying liabilities. However, not only the speed is important, but also the price of the transaction, which is more related to such aspects as the market breadth and resilience discussed below.
- Depth is defined through the number of buy and sell orders for an asset—that is, it is proposed to estimate how many orders exist at different prices (including at prices lower/higher than the one at which the instrument is actually traded). It is assumed that the financial market in which there is a wide range of prices at a given point of time is deeper (Sarr & Lybek, 2002). Market depth is associated with the risks of changes in inventories and demand pressure. The risks of changes in inventories are associated with an unexpected need to buy or sell a large amount of financial assets; if inventories are replenished or reduced easily, the market is deeper. Under the influence of regulatory measures for banking, after the crisis of 2008–2009, the inventories of banks' financial assets started to decline, which had an effect on the decrease in market depth (IMF, 2015).

[5] However, there is no consensus that a tight market is a more liquid market (as stated in Kyle [1985], Sarr and Lybek [2002], some authors use inverse interpretation: a tight market is a less liquid market [Diaz and Escribano, 2020; Dick-Nielsen et al., 2012]). It may stem from the fact that the authors more often use terms transaction costs and spread than tightness.

- Breadth indicates that, being large in volume and quantity, new orders have a minimal impact on the current price when they are sold, that is, new orders can be satisfied without significant price changes.
- Resilience indicates the market's ability to recover from unexpected events; in other words, resilience indicates how new orders can correct the imbalance of supply and demand without letting the price deviate from a fundamentally reasonable level. An imbalance may be associated with a shock caused by both a major market transaction and new information (for example, about the issuer of a financial asset or about the overall economic situation). This aspect also turns out to be key for monetary authorities as if bank liquidity evaporates in the event of any economic shock, this undermines the financial stability of the entire economy. Therefore, it is crucial to include the resilience aspect in the understanding of liquidity.

Bervas (2006), Hibbert et al. (2009), Diaz and Escribano (2020) presented a graphical visualisation of liquidity aspects. Let us look at Fig. 7.1 from Diaz and Escribano (2020), which is largely consistent with the description of the characteristics above. Q_A and Q_B are the number of seller orders at the asking price and the number of buyer orders at the bid price. As mentioned above, the number of orders reflects the market depth. The difference between the prices of the nearest orders reflects the tightness of the market: as the difference decreases, the prices of buyers and sellers approach the dotted line, which characterises the absolute liquidity of the asset. The volumes of assets that can be sold/bought at set prices without change determine the market breadth. The market ability to recover from unexpected shocks shows the market resilience. The time marks t_1 and t_2 indicate the time of the placement and execution of the order. Accordingly, the immediacy with which the order can be fulfilled will be equal to the differential $t_2 - t_1$.

To measure the characteristics of liquidity, 4 groups of indicators are distinguished: transaction cost indicators, volume-based indicators, price-based indicators and market-impact indicators. General information about these indicators is provided in Appendix 1. Below we consider in more detail four indicators that together cover the above-mentioned aspects of liquidity and allow further empirical analysis: bid-ask spread, turnover rate, Hui-Heubel Liquidity Ratio and Market Efficiency Coefficient.

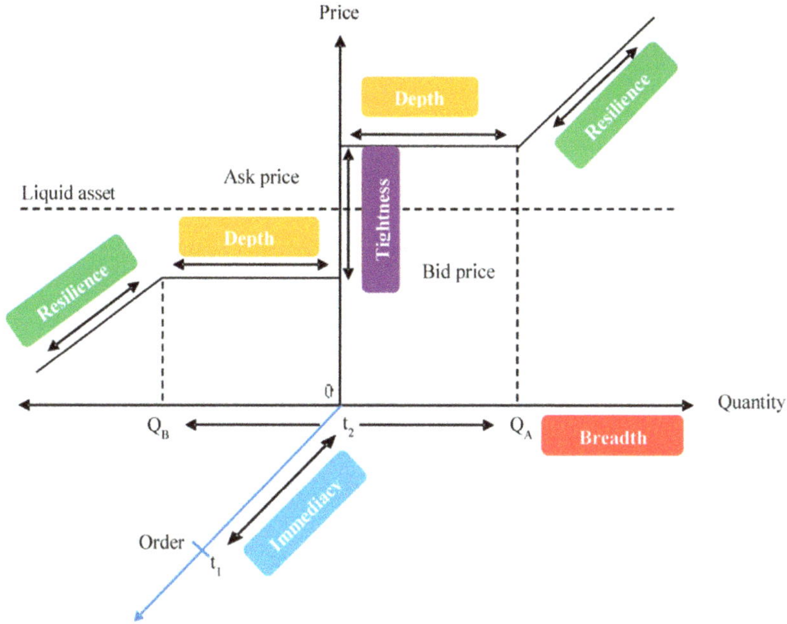

Fig. 7.1 Liquidity aspects (*Source* Diaz and Escribano [2020])

The market tightness indicator is the ***bid-ask spread***:

$$Bid - ask\,spread = \frac{P_A - P_B}{(P_A + P_B)/2}, \quad (7.1)$$

where P_A is the minimum selling price for the period (ask price), P_B is the maximum purchase price for the period (bid price).

In the absence of high-frequency data, closing ask and bid prices are used (Chung & Zhang, 2014). The bid-ask spread refers to the indicators that measure transaction costs. Accordingly, the lower the spread value is, the higher the market liquidity is.

The market depth indicator is the ***turnover rate*** (Gravelle, 1999):

$$Tn = \frac{V}{S * P} = \frac{\sum P_i * Q_i}{S * P} \quad (7.2)$$

where Tn is the turnover rate, V is the volume traded, P_i and Q_i are prices and quantities of the i trade during a specifies period, S is the outstanding stock of the asset, P is the average price of i trades.

The higher the turnover is, the more liquid the asset market is in terms of market depth.

The market breadth indicator is the ***Hui-Heubel Liquidity Ratio*** (Hui & Heubel, 1984), which is the inverse indicator of the asset turnover adjusted for the deviation of the maximum price from the minimum price:

$$L_{hh} = [(P_{max} - P_{min})/P_{min}]/\left[V/(S * \overline{P})\right], \tag{7.3}$$

where P_{max} is the maximum daily price for the last 5 days,

P_{min} is the lowest daily price for the last 5 days,
V is the traded volume of the asset for the last 5 days,
S is the outstanding stock of the asset,
$\overline{P}$ is the average closing price over the last 5 days.

The lower the value of the indicator is, the more liquid the asset is. It should be noted that in the literature Hui-Heubel LR refers not only to the market breadth indicators but also to the market depth and resilience.

The resilience indicator is the ***Market Efficiency Coefficient*** (MEC):

$$MEC = Var(R_t)/(T * Var(r_t)), \tag{7.4}$$

where $Var(R_t)$ is the variance of the long-term return logarithm,

$Var(r_t)$ is the variance of the short-term return logarithm,
T is the number of short-term periods in one long-term period.

In more resilient markets, MEC must be slightly less than 1, which means that prices are able to quickly approach the equilibrium level.

Research papers show an average decrease in transaction costs for the period from 1996 through 2014 on major world exchanges (NASDAQ, Bombay, Sao Paolo, Tokyo in paper [Fong et al., 2017]) despite the strong jump in transaction costs in 2008–2009 (Schestag et al., 2016). It is noted that after the crisis of 2008–2009 the resilience of the US government bond market was not fully restored, and there were episodes of collapses of the liquidity[6] of this market (Broto & Lamas, 2020). In recent years, there has been little research on measuring market liquidity, most of them focusing on the market of a single country (Będowska-Sójka & Echaust, 2020; Brandao-Marques & Danninger, 2016; Naik et al., 2020). We attempt to overcome this omission and in the empirical part of our work construct market liquidity indicators for ten countries during the period 2012–2020.

Trends in the Formation of Market Liquidity

The IMF Global financial stability report (IMF, 2015) identifies several trends determining the level of market liquidity after the 2008–2009 crisis.

First, there is the introduction of various regulatory requirements for banks' capital buffers and requirements for traded securities. As a result, banks began reducing their stocks of financial assets, including those acquired to operate as market makers, which made it possible to increase the resilience of systemically important banks. On the other hand, for banks, this led to an increase in the cost of services in the capital market, due to which market maker banks began to focus on a smaller number of customers, which affected the decrease in market liquidity.

Second, the introduction of algorithmic trading (including high-frequency trading) affects the liquidity of financial markets. Algorithmic trading allows computer programs to fulfil large orders by dividing them into several small ones with set price and volume characteristics. This leads to a decrease in the cost of order fulfilment and a reduction in the influence of a large order volume on the asset price (i.e., it contributes to an increase in the breadth of the market). However, during high-frequency trading, a large number of orders of the same type can be generated on various trading platforms (duplicate orders), some orders will be executed, and the other part (duplicates) will be closed after a short period of time. In this respect, ghost liquidity is discussed as in conditions of instant cancellation of orders created by the algorithm liquidity evaporates (Degryse et al., 2018). Massive cancellations of orders may also be triggered by an unexpected market shock. This makes the level of market liquidity unpredictable. Another consequence of high-frequency trading

[6] For example, the 'Flash Crash' in October 2014.

can be a decrease in market depth when the order volume is distributed across several venues, and the ability of individual venues to absorb a large counter order decreases.

Third, market liquidity is affected by unconventional monetary policy (purchase of financial assets). On the one hand, the buyout of financial assets by central banks leads to an increase in liquidity since the central bank is perceived as a large buyer capable of supporting demand in the market. On the other hand, the reduction in the supply of highly liquid and low-risk securities purchased by the central bank is pushing investors to buy less liquid financial assets, which affects the decrease in market liquidity.

Also, the IMF financial stability report reveals an increase in the number of institutions representing the buy-side in the capital market, in particular, an increase in the number of investment funds; moreover, mutual funds began to play an increasing role in financial intermediation.[7] These two facts lead to an increase in market liquidity.

Overall, market liquidity is shaped under the influence of multi-directional trends.

The Liquidity Mismatch Concept as an Indicator of Liquidity Risk Taking

It is important to assess the liquidity not only of stock market instruments but also of other instruments disclosed on the balance sheets of economic agents. Amidst financial crises, this seemed especially relevant for credit institutions. Inadequate and ineffective liquidity risk management is one of the reasons why financial stability may be undermined. Several approaches were proposed to monitor the level of banks' liquidity. Approaches were proposed both by regulators, in particular, the liquidity coverage ratio and the net stable funding ratio (BIS, 2014a, b), and by the academic community, such as the liquidity creation measures (Berger & Bouwman, 2009) and the liquidity mismatch index (Brunnermeier et al., 2013; Krishnamurthy et al., 2016).

In our work, we propose to compare the liquidity of assets and liabilities for different economic sectors. To that end, we provide a summary of the experience in measuring liquidity with respect to credit institutions.

[7] In Russia, mutual funds include exchange-traded mutual funds and open-ended mutual funds.

Berger and Bouwman (2009) proposed to divide all financial instruments into three groups: liquid, semi-liquid and illiquid. Loans were classified taking into account their maturity and their borrowers.[8] For deposits, how quickly money can be withdrawn from accounts is taken into consideration. Equity is recognised as completely illiquid. Also, recommendations are given on other asset and liability items. Based on the liquidity creation theory, each financial instrument receives one of three weights (–½, 0 or ½). It is said that the creation of liquidity in the economy occurs when a bank holds illiquid assets and provides liquid liabilities to the economy. Therefore, a positive weight is assigned to illiquid assets and liquid liabilities, and a negative weight is assigned to liquid assets and illiquid liabilities. Liquidity creation measures are a weighted sum of assets and liabilities. For example, when one conventional unit of an illiquid asset turns into one conventional unit of a liquid liability, one conventional unit of liquidity is created ($1*0.5 + 1*0.5 = 1$).

Krishnamurthy et al. (2016) criticised the approach of Berger and Bouwman (2009) for keeping the weights constant over time as the authors believed that during a crisis the liquidity of a given instrument changes. Based on the approach of Berger and Bouwman (2009), a liquidity mismatch index was proposed (Brunnermeier et al., 2013; Krishnamurthy et al., 2016). Like liquidity creation measures, the liquidity gap index shows the difference between liquidity-weighted assets and liquidity-weighted liabilities. The difference between the index and the liquidity creation measure is that the weights change over time due to the dependence of the weight of a financial instrument on the current market liquidity of this instrument. In particular, the authors use REPO haircuts as a proxy indicator of the asset liquidity. At the same time, the asset-side liquidity, according to the authors, reflects how easily a bank can get money for a financial asset. The liability-side liquidity is determined by how much counterparties may demand in the short-term in accordance with contract terms. The liability-side weights depend on the

[8] For example, consumer loans were recognised as semi-liquid, and corporate loans were illiquid since the former can easily be securitised, while the latter cannot.

liability maturity and on the spread between the overnight indexed swap and treasury bill.[9]

The Basel Committee proposed two indicators to measure liquidity: liquidity coverage ratio and the net stable funding ratio. The liquidity coverage ratio represents the ratio of the bank's high-quality liquid assets to the amount required to cover the increased outflow of funds from the bank within 30 days (BCBS, 2013).

The Net Stable Funding Ratio (NSFR) makes it possible to determine the relative amount of stable funding during the bank's continuous operation for the year under a specific stress scenario, where the bank is experiencing difficulties[10] that may become known to its customers and investors (BIS, 2009, 2014a, b). This ratio is the ratio of the share of available stable funding to required stable funding. Available stable funding is determined on the basis of the bank's resource base structure depending on its type and maturity and using the available stable funding factors (analogues of liquidity weights). The required stable funding is determined based on the structure of the bank's assets and off-balance sheet liabilities using the required stable funding factors. Thus, the amount of available and required stable funding depends on the maturity (long-term financial instruments are considered more stable than short-term ones) and the type of counterparty (for example, deposits provided by individuals and small- and medium-sized businesses are more stable than wholesale funding).

7.3 Data

Our empirical research applies the considered concepts of financial market liquidity and the liquidity mismatch to building liquidity indices for economic sectors based on country data.

To study various aspects of market liquidity, we analyse the stock and government bond markets. To that end, we use data from the Bloomberg

[9] The dependence of the liability-side liquidity on the OIS–Treasury Bill spread is associated with the assumption that at each point of time the bank solves an optimisation problem of maximising carry-trade profit, changing its level of liabilities, taking into account the likelihood of a period of low market liquidity.

[10] Namely, a significant drop in profitability or solvency as a result of an increased credit, market, operational risk and/or other risks; a possible downgrade of a debt, credit or deposit rating by an officially recognised rating agency; a serious event that questions the bank's reputation or creditworthiness (BIS, 2009).

system for 2012–2020. For financial instruments, we used the following indicators: closing price, bid price, ask price, daily trading volume, market capitalisation (for stocks), duration (for bonds) (for more details, see Table 7.4, Appendix 2). Since the number of listed shares is large, we work with the shares of companies included in the largest country indices at the end of 2020 (Table 7.5, Appendix 2). 10 countries are included in the sample: Bulgaria, Hungary, Germany, Denmark, Ireland, Russia, Slovakia, the USA, Finland and Sweden.

To study the liquidity mismatch, we build liquidity indices for economic sectors using the balances of financial assets and liabilities[11] of the system of national accounts (SNA 2008). We make calculations for various economic sectors of a particular country for 2019.[12] As financial instruments, we consider:

F1. Monetary gold and special drawing rights (SDR)
F2. Currency and deposits
F3. Debt securities classified into
F31. Short-term debt securities
F32. Long-term debt securities
F4. Loans classified into
F41. Short-term loans
F42. Long-term loans
F5. Equity and investment fund shares, including
F511. Listed shares[13]
F6. Insurance, pension and standardised guarantee schemes
F7. Financial derivatives and employee stock options
F8. Other accounts receivable and accounts payable.

At this stage, it is important to emphasise the specifics of the terminology used in the SNA 2008. In accordance with Clause 11.83 of the

[11] For methodology on compiling the balance sheets of financial assets and liabilities refer to (Bank of Russia, 2019; IMF et al., 2009).

[12] The most relevant and complete data at the time of the research.

[13] According to the SNA 2008 and the Russian methodology (Bank of Russia, 2019; IMF et al., 2009), listed shares are valued at market value. In addition, it was verified that, for example, in Russia, the volume of listed shares of non-financial corporations (according to the balance of financial assets and liabilities) is comparable to the value of the market capitalisation of non-financial companies traded on the Moscow Exchange.

SNA 2008 (IMF, 2009), 'equity is treated as a liability of the issuing institutional unit'—that is, we do not assume the division of liabilities into equity and liabilities, as is the case, for example, in corporate finance. Therefore, when we mention liabilities, we also include equity capital.

Due to the fact that we look at the values of liquidity indices that arise during the operation of the financial markets, we will be interested in instruments F1–F7, and we will not take into account other receivables and payables[14] (F8).

As economic sectors, we take:

S11—Non-financial corporations
S121 + S122—Monetary financial institutions[15] (Central Bank and deposit-taking corporations)
S124 + S125—Other financial institutions[16];
S128 + S129—Insurance corporations and pension funds (NCPF)
S13—Government
S14 + S15—Households and non-profit institutions serving households (NPISHs)
S2—Rest of the world.

It should be noted that the banking system, other financial institutions, insurance companies and pension funds form a single sector, S12—Financial corporations.

Balances of financial assets and liabilities allow the identification of counterparties, i.e., issuers of financial assets and holders of liabilities. This, in turn, allows to separate financial instruments traded between sectors from those traded within a sector, thereby performing a consolidation. We exclude instruments traded within a sector as they are not the result of the operation of the financial market.

[14] Accounts receivable/payable include debt related to the purchase and sale of securities, payment of dividends, rent, salary, taxes and utility bills as well as other debt. *Source* https://www.cbr.ru/statistics/macro_itm/households/metod/1.

[15] Hereinafter, for brevity and clarity, 'banking system'.

[16] Other financial institutions include investment funds, brokers, dealers, depositories and other professional securities market participants, microfinance organisations, pawnshops, consumer credit cooperatives, leasing companies, etc. (Bank of Russia, 2019).

The sources of information are the database 'QSA—ESA2010 quarterly financial and non-financial sector accounts'[17] for 26 European countries and statistical sections of the websites of the US Fed and the Bank of Russia.[18] The sample of countries includes Austria, Belgium, Bulgaria, Cyprus, the Czech Republic, Germany, Denmark, Estonia, Spain, Finland, France, Greece, Hungary, Ireland, Italy, Lithuania, Latvia, Malta, the Netherlands, Norway, Poland, Portugal, Romania, Sweden, Slovenia, Slovakia, the USA and Russia.

Let us note the limitations of our statistics. We faced certain difficulties in consolidating US and Russian data for the following sectors and financial instruments:

- Non-financial corporations: debt securities, loans, equity and investment fund shares (including listed shares)—for Russia and the USA.
- Banking system: debt securities, loans, equity and investment fund shares (including listed shares)—for Russia and the USA.
- Other financial institutions: debt securities, loans, equity and investment fund shares (including listed shares)—for Russia and the USA.
- Government: debt securities, loans—for Russia.

As a result, not all the lines of the USA and Russia are cleared of financial assets and liabilities traded within the sector.

Another limitation of our analysis is the difficulty for Russia to divide debt securities and loans into short-term and long-term and to separate Instrument F511—listed shares from Instrument F5—equity and investment fund shares. We did the following:

- For debt securities on the side of liabilities. From the Russian statistics, it is possible to obtain the volumes of debt securities issued *at par value* with a breakdown by sector and maturity. We assume that

[17] QSA—ESA2010 quarterly financial and non-financial sector accounts: https://sdw.ecb.europa.eu/browseExplanation.do?node=9689710.

[18] In particular, for Russia, the SNA balance sheets of financial assets and liabilities, the 'From-whom-to-whom' table and the Banking System Survey were used.

the ratio of short-to-long-term securities at par value is the same as their market value.

- In other cases, we assume that in Russia the shares of short- and long-term debt securities (loans) or listed shares in the total amount of debt securities (loans) or equity, respectively, coincide with the median shares in the sample of foreign countries.

We do not exploit absolute values of financial assets and liabilities; the information will be presented either as a share of GDP or as a share of the total value of sector assets. The line for GDP at current prices is obtained from the OECD database (OECD.Stat).[19]

7.4 Empirical Analysis of the Liquidity of Financial Assets and Liabilities for Various Structures of the Financial System

In this section, we illustrate the concepts presented in the literature review.

- First, we consider the structure of liabilities of non-financial corporations, which allows to assess which type of financial system different countries have.
- Second, we introduce the concept of market liquidity, taking into account its various aspects, by the example of the stock and government bond markets. We demonstrate that the market for a given instrument in one country may differ from a similar market in another country.
- Third, we show the application of the liquidity mismatch. In particular, we compare the values of the liquidity indices of economic sectors across countries with financial systems of different structures. We justify the selection of liquidity weights for calculating the liquidity index and consider how liquidity accounting may affect the liabilities of non-financial corporations. This allows to move on to analysing the values of the liquidity indices of economic sectors. We consistently analyse the values of liquidity indices for non-financial

[19] OECD.Stat: https://stats.oecd.org/.

and financial corporations, households and NPISHs, the government and the rest of the world.

Structure of Liabilities of Non-financial Corporations

Figure 7.2 shows the structure of liabilities of non-financial corporations (% of GDP) for 28 countries. On average, in the Eastern and Southern European countries, the liabilities of non-financial corporations account for a smaller share of GDP than in Western and Northern Europe. In Russia, the liabilities of non-financial corporations account for 185% of GDP, making Russia the median country in the sample.

Generally, liabilities are divided into loans (F4) and equity (F5). Loans account for 14% to 42% of all liabilities of non-financial corporations. Cyprus, Greece and Malta have the highest shares of loans in liabilities

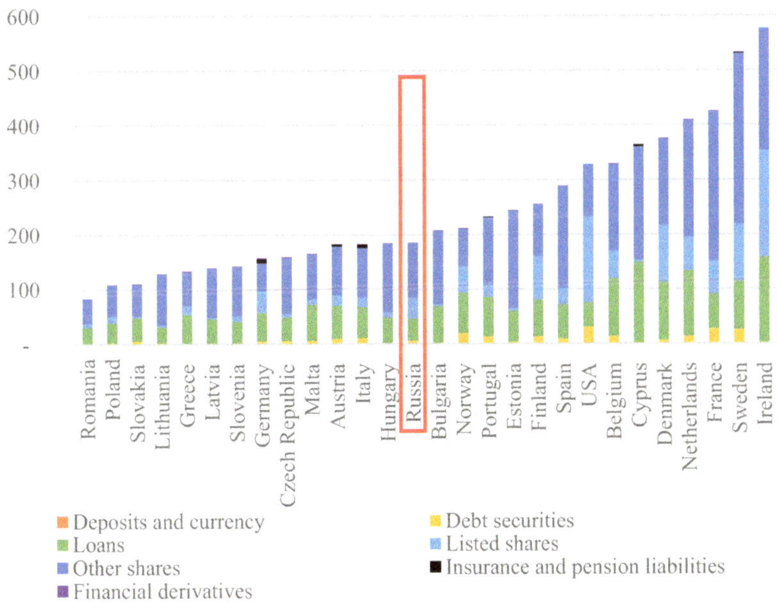

Fig. 7.2 Liabilities of non-financial corporations, 2019 (% of GDP) (*Source* compiled by the authors based on financial accounts)

(40–41%). The smallest share is observed in the USA (14%), where most of the liabilities are listed shares.

In Figs. 7.2 and 7.3, we see that the variation in the component of listed shares is higher than the variation in the component of debt instruments; it is this that leads to higher indicators of the balance sheet size of non-financial corporations. This may serve as an illustration of the point of view that if a corporation needs to expand its funding above a certain level, it is more likely to turn to the stock market. However, we cannot assert the existence of a causal relationship and will leave this issue outside the scope of our research.

Equity (F5) accounts for 55 to 77% of liabilities of non-financial corporations. At the same time, shares traded on the stock exchange (F511) make up 1 to 48% of liabilities (Table 7.1). The minimum percentage of listed shares in liabilities are observed in Bulgaria, Latvia, Cyprus (1% each), Slovakia and Estonia (2% each). The USA has the maximum percentage of listed shares in liabilities (48%) followed by Ireland (34%) and Finland (31%).

The percentage of listed shares in the company's liabilities allows to draw conclusions about the structure of the financial system of each country.[20] According to this indicator, the USA belongs to countries

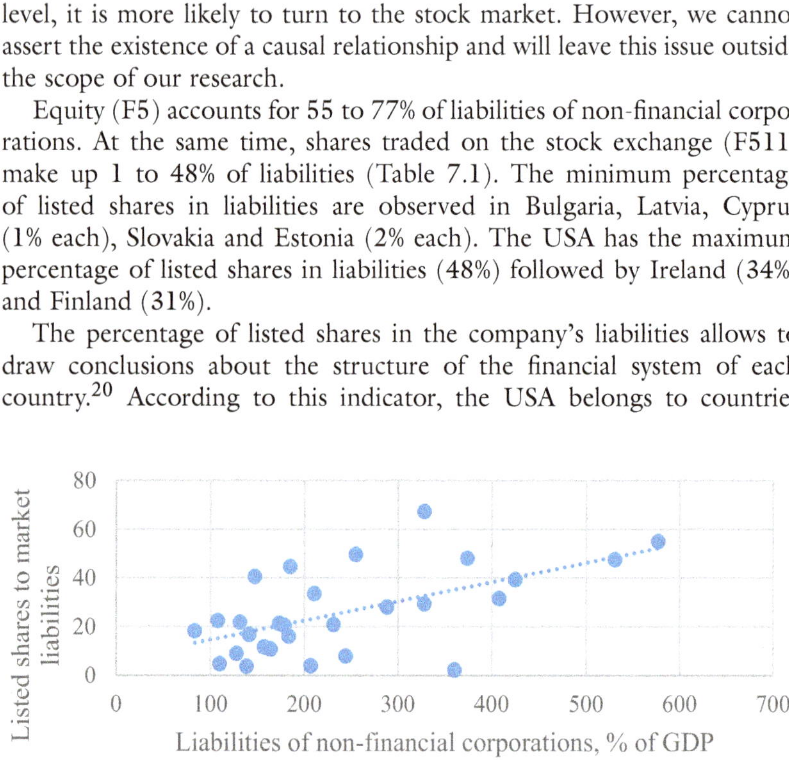

Fig. 7.3 Percentage of listed shares and liabilities of non-financial corporations, 2019 (% of GDP) (*Source* compiled by the authors. *Note* The percentage of listed shares is considered to be the ratio of the volume of listed shares to the sum of the volumes of listed shares, debt securities and loans)

[20] In the literature, the ratio of the market capitalisation of companies to GDP (Bats and Houben, 2017) or the ratio of market capitalisation to the volume of bank loans is

Table 7.1 Percentage of listed shares in the liabilities of non-financial corporations (%) (*Source* compiled by the authors)

Country	%	Part of Europe		Country	%	Part of Europe
USA	48			Spain	10	Southern
Ireland	34	Northern		Portugal	10	Southern
Finland	31	Northern		Italy	10	Southern
Denmark	28	Northern		Romania	8	Eastern
Germany	25	Western		Slovenia	6	Southern
Norway	22	Northern		Malta	5	Southern
Russia	20			Hungary	5	Eastern
Sweden	20	Northern		Czech Republic	4	Eastern
Belgium	15	Western		Lithuania	3	Eastern
Netherlands	15	Western		Slovakia	2	Eastern
France	14	Western		Estonia	2	Eastern
Greece	11	Southern		Bulgaria	1	Eastern
Poland	11	Eastern		Latvia	1	Eastern
Austria	10	Western		Cyprus	1	Southern

with market-based financing, while among other European countries bank-based financing is more common.

At the same time, Ireland, Finland, Denmark, Germany,[21] Norway, Sweden, Belgium, the Netherlands and France, despite the fact that they are countries in which bank-based financing prevails, have a relatively high percentage of listed shares in the liabilities of non-financial corporations (from 14 to 34% of liabilities). Moreover, these countries belong to Northern and Western Europe (according to the classification of the UN Statistics Division[22]). Other countries from our sample have a percentage of listed shares in liabilities ranging from 1 to 11%, i.e., these are countries with the least market-based financing. These include the Southern and Eastern European countries, with the exception of Austria, which belongs to Western Europe, and Lithuania, Latvia and Estonia, which may refer to both Eastern and Northern Europe.[23,24]

Next, we consider the weighing of liquidity liabilities. However, we understand that the markets for the same financial instrument may differ across countries. Therefore, before determining the weights, it was decided to analyse the market liquidity of financial instruments in different countries.

used as an indicator of the financial system's structure (Allen et al., 2018; Levine, 2002). Unger (2018) uses the ratio of market capitalisation of non-financial corporations to GDP, thereby excluding financial sector indicators. We go further and suggest looking at the ratio of market capitalisation to the liabilities of non-financial corporations to exclude the influence of the size of the non-financial corporate sector on the financial structure indicator.

[21] Unger (2018) also noted that although the German financial system is usually perceived as a classical example of a bank-based system other financing sources account for a large share in the liabilities of non-financial corporations.

[22] Standard country or area codes for statistical use (M49), Geographic Regions: https://unstats.un.org/unsd/methodology/m49/.

[23] The UN Statistics Division classifies these countries as Northern Europe, and the CIA's World Factbook classifies them as Eastern Europe (for details, see https://www.cia.gov/the-world-factbook/).

[24] As we can see, sorting countries by share of listed shares and sorting by geography have some similarities, so in the future, we will appeal to geography features to shortly describe a set of countries with similar financial system characteristics.

Market Liquidity of Financial Instruments in Different Countries

In this section, we examine the liquidity of stocks and government bonds to determine the maturity of these markets in different countries. The choice of financial instruments depends on the availability of data. Ten countries were selected for the analysis with different structures of the financial system. These are the USA as a country with market-based financing, Germany, Ireland, Finland, Denmark and Sweden as countries in which bank-based financing prevails, though capital market is developed fairly well. Finally, the sample covers Bulgaria, Slovakia and Hungary as credit-based countries with the least developed capital market. Russia is also included in the sample. For stocks, 4 indicators were calculated, namely: the bid-ask spread, the turnover rate, Hui-Heubel Liquidity Ratio (LR) and market-efficiency coefficient (MEC). For government bonds, the bid-ask spread and MEC were calculated.

Stock Markets

Appendix 3 provides the indicators of stock market liquidity for all the ten countries. The liquidity indicator for a specific year for a certain country is the average daily value of the indicator for the shares of companies included in the country stock exchange index (for example, for Russia, for companies included in the Moscow Exchange index, as of the end of 2020). Colour scales make it possible to visually correlate numerical values with each other, and one scale is created for each individual indicator and is common for all countries.

The Russian data show that the *bid-ask spread* has been declining since 2015, although in 2020 it turns out to be slightly higher than in 2019. A decrease in the spread indicates an increase in the liquidity of Russian stocks. At the same time, the spread values turn out to be higher than in the USA, Germany and Sweden, but lower than in other countries covered (Bulgaria, Hungary, Denmark, Ireland, Slovakia and Finland).

Turnover rate for Russia hovered around 0.0014 in 2016–2019 and increased to 0.0032 in 2020. An increase in the turnover means that ever-higher volumes are traded over a longer period of time. Asset turnover in Russia is lower than in the USA, Germany, Denmark and Sweden (countries with deeper markets) but higher than in Ireland, Finland, Bulgaria and Slovakia.

The *Hui-Heubel LR* in Russia indicates that in the period from 2015 through 2019 the market liquidity (its breadth) was growing (i.e., the influence of trading in large volumes on asset prices decreases). In terms of Hui-Heubel LR, the markets of the USA, Germany, Denmark and Sweden are more liquid than the Russian market.

The Russian *MEC* (resilience indicator) ranged from 70 to 74% in 2012–2018 and reached 76% and 78% in 2019 and 2020, respectively. This suggests that despite a slight increase in transaction costs in 2020 versus 2019 the market is becoming more resilient—that is, the variance of short-term fluctuations is close to the variance of long-term fluctuations. In terms of resilience, our indicators are close to those of the USA, Denmark, Sweden and Germany.

Thus, the Russian stock market turns out to be less liquid than those of the countries of North-Western Europe and the USA but more liquid and resilient than those of the countries of Eastern Europe. For all Russian liquidity indicators during the period from 2012 to 2020, there is an increase in liquidity. However, in the recent years, it is largely due to the massive influx of retail investors (Fig. 7.4).

The comparison of the USA and Germany shows that the lowest transaction costs are observed in the USA (in terms of the bid-ask spread). However, in terms of market breadth and depth (turnover rate and Hui-Heubel LR), the German market turns out to be more liquid than the US

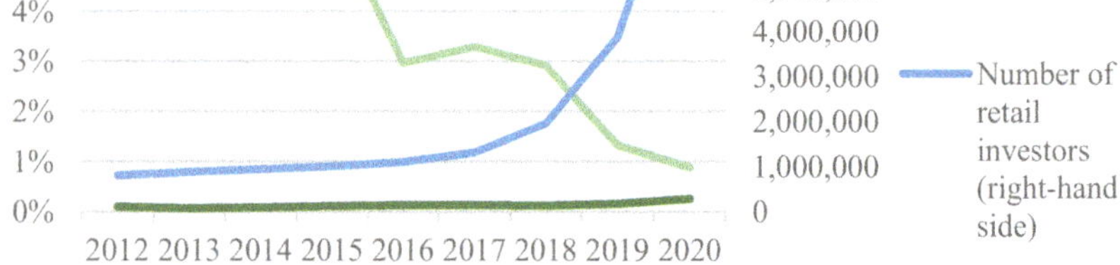

Fig. 7.4 Russian stock market liquidity and the number of retail investors (*Sources* Moscow Stock Exchange, author calculations)

market.[25] The resilience of the two markets is at a high level (on average 72% for the USA and 75% for Germany).

The analysis of other countries reveals that Slovakia, as the country with the least market financing, has the least liquid stock market, on the one hand, but, on the other hand, the liquidity indicators are the most volatile.

Government Bond Market

Appendix 4 presents liquidity indicators for government bonds of different countries. They are also daily average values of the indicators. For Russia, in addition to the bid-ask spread and MEC indicators, the turnover rate and Hui-Heubel LR indicators are computed.

Government bonds constitute a large part of government liabilities: in Russia and Hungary, the share of bonds in government liabilities reaches 87% and 89%, respectively, and for the ten countries, the number amounts on average to 75%, while the minimum level is observed in Sweden (48%) (Fig. 7.5).

Countries also differ by the ratio of the size of government bonds to the total financial assets of the government. This ratio makes it possible to assess how large the liabilities are (in the form of government bonds) compared to assets. The lowest indicators are achieved for Sweden (31%), Finland and Russia (37% each); the largest shares of bonds in assets are observed in the USA (438%), Hungary (281%) and Ireland (244%).

The *bid-ask spread* data for Russia are presented graphically in Fig. 7.6. The lowest values of transaction costs (in terms of the bid-ask spread) were observed in 2013 when access to the Russian government bonds (OFZ) was liberalised for non-residents (due to the opening of nominee accounts (with the central depository) for foreign clearance and settlement) (Mau et al., 2018). The highest values of the bid-ask spread were observed in 2014, which was the result of increased volatility in the domestic financial market and the introduction of international sanctions. In 2015, the government securities market became more liquid despite the expected downgrade of the Russian sovereign rating aided by a new

[25] When analysing the liquidity indicators, it should be borne in mind that in 2020 the German stock index included 30 companies, and the American S&P500 index comprised 505 companies. Therefore, the conclusions drawn for the companies included in the country stock exchange index must be interpreted with caution regarding the country as a whole.

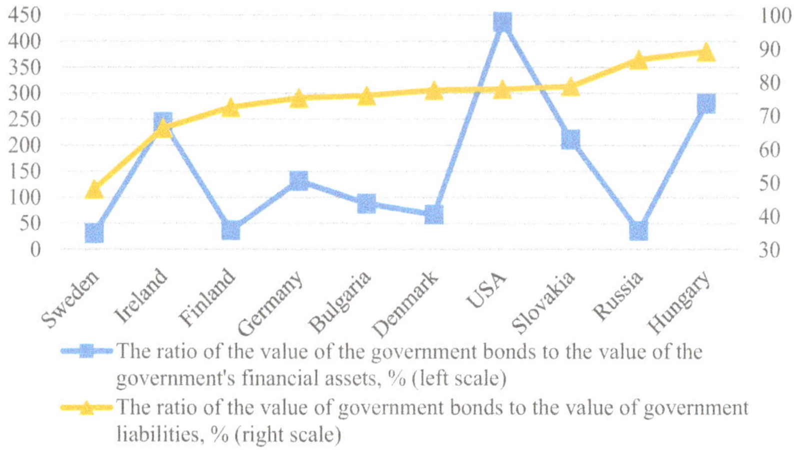

Fig. 7.5 Ratio of government bonds to assets and liabilities, 2019 (*Source* compiled by the authors based on the financial accounts from the government)

type of OFZ issue (inflation-indexed OFZ-IN and OFZ-PK (linked to the RUONIA)). There were local highs in the bid-ask spreads in 2018, which might be due to fears among non-residents about new sanctions, which didn't materialise (Mau et al., 2018). In 2020, despite the fears of non-resident withdrawal from OFZ and capital outflows from emerging markets due to the COVID-19 pandemic, liquidity performance across the curve remained better than in 2012–2018. We also see a natural increase in transaction costs with increasing duration, i.e., a decrease in liquidity for the 'longer-term' securities.

The bid-ask spread in the other countries under consideration (Appendix 4) is on average lower than in Russia. Bulgaria appears the only country having this indicator closest to that of Russia. The lowest bid-ask spreads are in Germany and in the USA, indicating that these countries' government bonds have the greatest liquidity. For Russia, we were also able to calculate the turnover rate and Hui-Heubel LR. The turnover rate of government bonds does not change much over time and averages 0.01 with the turnover rate expected to decrease with increasing duration. The highest turnover rate was in 2014 and 2020 for bonds with a duration of up to 3 months (0.07 and 0.05, respectively). In terms of Hui-Heubel LR, Russian government bonds were the least liquid in 2014 (value of

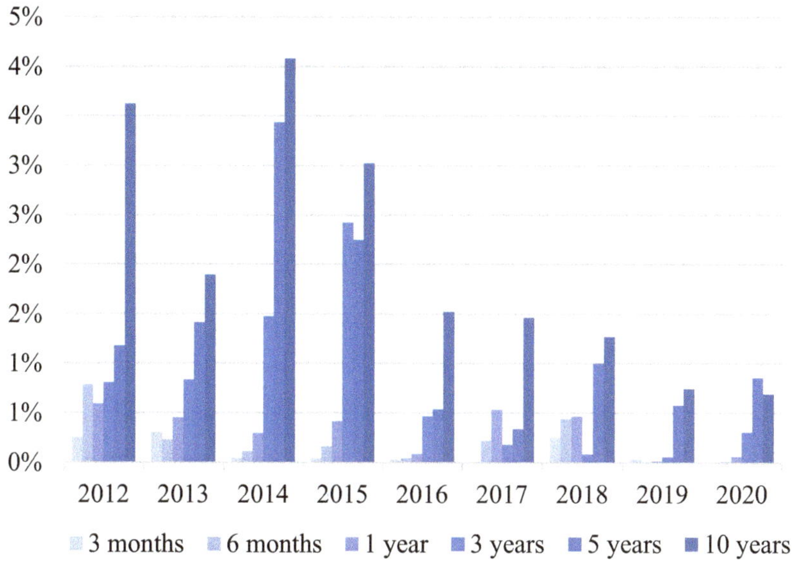

Fig. 7.6 Russia: bid-ask spread on government bonds (*Source* authors' calculations based on Moscow Exchange data)

1,794) and the most liquid in 2017 and 2019 (134 and 57, respectively). As duration increases, there is an increase in the Hui-Heubel LR indicator value.

The Russian market-efficiency coefficient averages 59% for Russian government securities, while the average yearly MEC was 48% in 2012 and 66% in 2020. On average, Russia has one of the lowest MEC values over the period of 2012–2020 (only Bulgaria and Slovakia are lower with 51%). In other countries, it ranges from 66% in Germany and in the USA to 88% in Hungary. As duration increases, the MEC rises, indicating a greater integrity of long-term government bonds. Thus, Russian government bonds prove to be the least liquid among European countries and the USA in various respects. Yet, the Russian securities have seen an increase in liquidity over the last eight years.

A study of stock and government bond market liquidity has assessed how markets for the same financial instrument differ across countries. The next section of the chapter focuses on the elaboration of liquidity indices.

Principles of the Liquidity Index Creation

We propose to estimate the amounts of financial assets and liabilities taking into account the liquidity of the financial instruments. The concept of the liquidity mismatch is useful for this purpose. As mentioned above, Berger and Bouwman (2009), Brunnermeier et al. (2013), Krishnamurthy et al. (2016) and BIS (2014) assert that rather than considering the simple sum of financial assets and liabilities, their weighted sum should be considered, where the degree of liquidity of the financial instrument is used as the weight:

$$Liquidityindex = \sum \alpha * financialasset_i - \sum \beta * libility_j$$

where $\alpha, \beta > 0$ are the liquidity weights for financial assets and liabilities, respectively.

In this section, we discuss the selection of the weights for calculating the weighted indicators. This discussion is based on the NSFR methodology for calculating net stable funding ratio (BIS, 2014a, b), the liquidity mismatch index (Brunnermeier et al., 2013; Krishnamurthy et al., 2016) and the concept of market liquidity. Note the specific feature of our terminology: we can consider both the liquidity of a financial instrument and its stability referring to the NSFR approach. Stability in line with the NSFR is interpreted as the least liquidity and instability—as perfect or complete liquidity. The net stable funding ratio varies from 0 to 100, where 0 corresponds to the least stable instrument (i.e., the most liquid one) and 100, to the most stable instrument (the least liquid one).

We have created a liquidity scale from 0 to 1, where 0 corresponds to a completely non-liquid instrument and 1 to a fully liquid instrument (in particular, cash). Tables 7.2 and 7.3 show the selection of weights for each financial instrument.[26] The economic interpretation of this weight selection is described below.

Monetary gold (F11) is an asset for the Central Bank only. According to the NSFR (BIS, 2014a, b), monetary gold is regarded as one of the

[26] Our empirical research is conducted for 2019, so we select static liquidity weights of financial instruments. Generally speaking, the liquidity of the instrument can change over time, so, at the peak of the crisis of 2007-2008, some instruments lost their liquidity (in particular, subprime mortgages). The change in the liquidity weight over time is implemented in the work (Krishnamurthy et al., 2016).

Table 7.2 Weights for calculating the liquidity index: assets (*Source* compiled by the authors)

Instrument		*Counterparty (issuer)*	*Weight: 0—non-liquid, 1—liquid*
F1	F11. Monetary gold		0.3
	F12. SDR		1
F2	F21. Currency		1
	F22–29. Deposits		0.9
F3	F31. Short-term debt securities	Government	0.9
		Other debt securities	0.7
	F32. Long-term debt securities	Government	0.9
		Other debt securities	0.7
F4	F41. Short-term loans		0.5
	F42. Long-term loans	Financial corporations	0.2
		Other	0.4
F5	F511. Listed shares		0.6
	Other		0
F6. Insurance, pension and standardised guarantee schemes			0
F7. Derivatives			0

Table 7.3 Weights for calculating the liquidity index: liabilities (*Source* compiled by the authors)

Instrument		*Counterparty (holder)*	*Weight: 0—non-liquid, 1—liquid*
F1	F12. SDR		1
F2	F21. Currency		1
	F22–29. Deposits	Households	0.5
		Financial corporations	0.9
		Other	0.7
F3	F31. Short-term debt securities		0.5
	F32. Long-term debt securities		0.3
F4	F41. Short-term loans		0.7
	F42. Long-term loans		0.4
F5. Equity and investment fund shares			0
F6. Insurance, pension and standardised guarantee schemes			0
F7. Derivatives			1

most stable financial instruments, so we have assigned a liquidity weight of 0.3 to this instrument.

Special Drawing Rights (SDR, F12) are only used by the Central Bank, which is part of the banking system. SDRs were created as an additional international reserve asset and are intended to provide additional liquidity. SDRs represent a guaranteed and unconditional right of the holder to receive other reserve assets. We, therefore, consider the SDR to be a fully liquid financial instrument (weight 1).

Currency (F21) is recognised as the most liquid (weight 1). Note that cash acts as a liability only for the Central Bank.

Weights for the following financial instruments will be considered separately for assets and for liabilities. Let us consider financial instruments on the ***asset*** side, in other words, from the point of view of the financial instrument holders (***investors***).

Deposits (F22–29) are assigned the weight of 0.9. On the one hand, deposits can be withdrawn at any time (indicating a high level of liquidity). On the other hand, withdrawal may involve the risk of losing accumulated interest, and, in addition, in the event of bankruptcy of the bank, the holder may not receive the whole amount, but only the government-insured part of it. As a result, we cannot speak of the perfect liquidity of deposits.

Debt securities (F3) are to be categorised as government securities and other securities. We assume that *government debt securities* are more liquid due to their higher reliability and lower risk, so we assign them the same weight as deposits—that is, 0.9.[27] We assign a lower weight of 0.7 to *non-government debt securities* (other debt securities).[28]

Loans (F4) are to be split into short-term (F41) and long-term (F42), and loans to financial corporations are singled out separately as part of long-term credits. Following the NSFR methodology (BIS, 2014a, b), we assign a weight of 0.5 to all *short-term loans*. We assume that *long-term loans* are a less liquid asset than short-term loans as their repayment

[27] NSFR assigns stability weights of 5 and 15 out of 100 to debt securities according to the Basel II Standardised Approach for credit risk. We have calculated the arithmetic mean of these weights (10) and obtained the weight of interest for us ((100 – 10)/100 = 0.9).

[28] NSFR assigns debt securities a weight of 15 and 50 depending on their quality (rating). We have rounded the average of these weights to 30 and obtained the liquidity weight of 0.7 (= (100 – 30)/100).

schedules differ. So, we assign a lower weight of 0.4 to long-term loans. NSFR defines *loans to financial corporations* as the most stable (least liquid) compared to other loans, so loans to financial corporations receive a minimum weight of 0.2.

Equity and investment fund shares (F5) should be divided into listed shares (F511) and other shares. We assign the weight of 0.6 to *listed shares* as we assume that equities are more liquid than short-term loans because they can be sold on the stock market, but less liquid than debt securities as the average variation in bond price is lower than that of listed shares, i.e., we assume that a debt security is more likely to be sold at the expected price.

Unlisted shares are assigned 0 weight, which means that the asset is completely non-liquid. The issuer is not obliged to buy back its own shares, so the cash received from the issue of the share remains with the issuer forever, and the holder of the share is unable to convert it into cash promptly.

Insurance, pension and standardised guarantee schemes (F6) receive the weight of 0, as we assume that the conditions for receiving benefits are so specific that these assets are completely non-liquid.

When estimating weights for ***financial derivatives*** (F7), we refer to the NSFR methodology (BIS, 2014a, b). NSFR proposes to calculate (derivatives receivable)—(derivatives payable). If the amount is positive (receivable is greater than payable), NSFR assigns the weight of 100% (i.e., it is a stable asset [non-liquid]); if the amount is negative (receivable is less than payable), NSFR assigns the weight of 0% (i.e., it is an unstable liability [liquid]). For simplicity, we assign 0 weight to derivatives if they are registered as assets and the weight of 1 if they are registered as liabilities.

Let us consider financial instruments on the ***liability*** side, i.e., from the ***issuer*** point of view.

Deposits (F22-29) are liabilities only for the banking system and the government. We assume that deposits are fairly stable liabilities. Meanwhile, household deposits are the least liquid (weight of 0.5), deposits from non-financial companies, the government and the rest of the world have the same weight as short-term loans (0.7), and deposits of financial corporations are the most liquid (0.9).[29]

[29] The liquidity ratio of deposits was determined in accordance with the methodology for calculating the liquidity coverage ratio (BIS, 2009).

Debt securities (F3) are proposed to be divided into short-term (F31) and long-term (F32). Short-term securities receive a higher liquidity weight than long-term securities: 0.5 for *short-term* securities and 0.3 for *long-term* securities because the probability that the full value of a short-term security is paid in the short-term is higher than that for long-term securities.

Loans (F4) are also to be divided into short-term (F41) and long-term (F42). Let us assume that short-term loans have a higher weight than long-term loans: 0.7 for *short-term* loans and 0.4 for *long-term* loans. The specific weights were chosen on the basis of the following considerations. First, the average weighting should be higher for loans than for debt securities (0.7 > 0.5 and 0.4 > 0.3) because each period interest is paid on the loan, and the principal is repaid, while only coupons are paid for debt securities. All other things being equal, the debt service cost is higher for loans; therefore, a loan is more liquid than a debt security. Second, we assume that a long-term loan is less liquid than a short-term bond (0.4 < 0.5) because the short-term bond pays both coupons and the original cost of the bond, while the long-term loan only pays interest, i.e., the debt service cost for the loan is lower.

Equity and investment fund shares (F5) are assigned 0 weight as the shares issued do not impose an obligation on their issuers to repurchase their shares making them a completely non-liquid liability.

Insurance, pension and standardised guarantee schemes (F6) are represented by only one sector—insurance corporations and pension funds. This type of liability has sale limitations for its holders, so we assign zero weight to insurance and pension liabilities (as a completely non-liquid financial instrument).

It is important to note that when we consider assets, we assign weights regardless of who holds those assets. For example, we assume that government bonds are equally liquid for both non-financial institutions and banks. Similarly, when we look at liabilities, it does not matter who the issuer of these liabilities is. In a similar vein, the shares issued will be equally non-liquid for both non-financial institutions and banks.

Liquidity Index of Non-financial Corporations

Let us first consider Fig. 7.7, which shows the weighted liabilities of non-financial corporations. Liquid liabilities are those that can be at least partially claimed by creditors in the short-term and are mainly represented by loans.

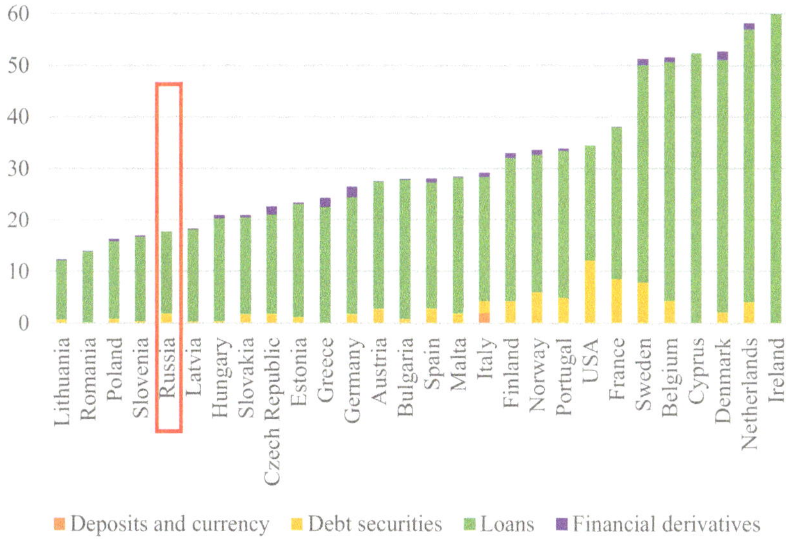

Fig. 7.7 Weighted liabilities of **non-financial corporations**, 2019, % of GDP (*Note* For Russia and the USA, the 'Debt Securities' and 'Loans' blocks are unconsolidated [include weighted liabilities where non-financial corporations are the issuer and holder]) *Source* compiled by the authors

Russia has relatively less liquid liabilities than other countries as it is the median country for the share of total liabilities in GDP. It is in the first quartile of the sample for the share of weighted liabilities in GDP.

Let us consider now not only the liabilities of non-financial corporations but also their assets. The analysis of weighted assets and liabilities will make it possible to compute ***the liquidity index***. The liquidity index is the difference between the weighted assets and the weighted liabilities. The liquidity index thus provides information on how much liquid financial assets exceed liquid liabilities. The lower the value of the liquidity index, the more risk this or that sector bears. By the risk, we mean the liquidity mismatch risk, i.e., the risk of losses caused by the mismatch between the maturity of assets and liabilities.

Figure 7.8 shows the weighted assets and liabilities of non-financial corporations. Assets are shown in the positive area, liabilities are shown in the negative area, and the liquidity index is shown on the chart as a black-dotted line.

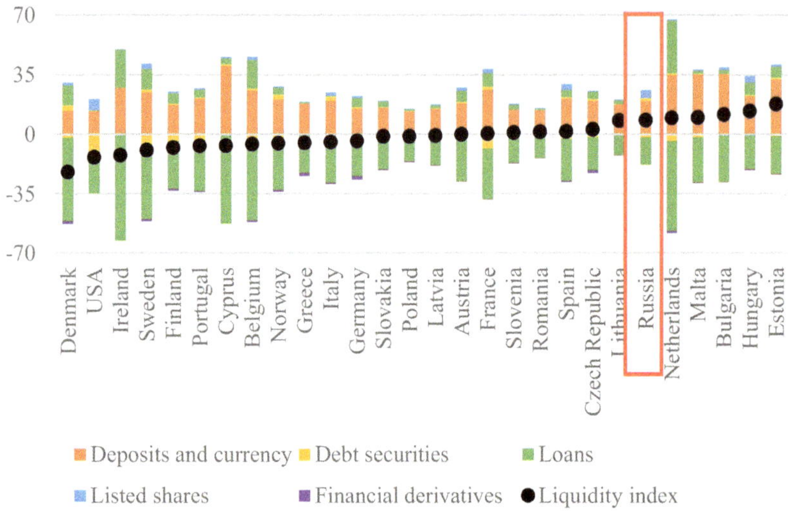

Fig. 7.8 Weighted financial assets (+) and liabilities (−) of **non-financial corporations**, 2019, % of GDP (*Source* compiled by the authors. *Note* For Russia and the USA, the 'Debt Securities' and 'Loans' blocks are unconsolidated [include weighted assets and liabilities where non-financial corporations are the issuer and holder])

Companies' weighted assets are mainly represented by deposits[30] and loans to other sectors of the economy (usually, loans to non-resident companies[31]). Liquidity index values range from −22% of GDP in Denmark to 18% of GDP in Estonia. In general, there is little variation in the liquidity index values. It is likely that regardless of their financial structure, companies seek to balance the liquidity of their assets and liabilities, thereby avoiding significant mismatches.

[30] For the sake of brevity, here and below, deposits will refer to deposits and currency, which corresponds to the orange column in the charts of weighted assets and liabilities of the sector.

[31] Loans from non-financial institutions to non-residents probably reflect loans to foreign companies included in the same group of companies. In this case, it would be logical to exclude them from the analysis, just as we do not include all intra-sectoral operations. When we do this, we get lower liquidity index values, although the overall conclusions for non-financial corporations do not change.

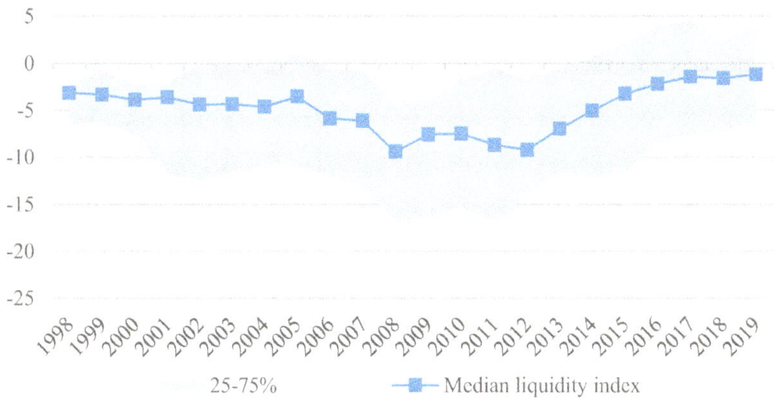

Fig. 7.9 Change in the liquidity index values of non-financial corporations, % of GDP (*Source* compiled by the authors)

Figure 7.9 shows the change in the liquidity index over time. Speaking of the level of the liquidity index value as the degree of the liquidity risk taking, the dynamics of the accumulation of financial imbalances can be traced. Before 2008, the liquidity index values were declining. During the financial crisis, they reached a minimum, and since the crisis the liquidity index values have risen to safer levels.

Liquidity Indices for Other Sectors of the Economy

We have considered the liquidity index values of non-financial corporations. Let us now look at the values of the liquidity indices for the other sectors of the economy. Figure 7.10 shows the box plot[32] for the liquidity indices for the main sectors of the economy.

[32] The upper and lower sides of the 'boxes' represent the upper and lower quartiles of the sample; the horizontal line inside the box represents the median; the crosses represent the sample mean; and the 'whiskers' represent the maximums and minimums (not including outliers).

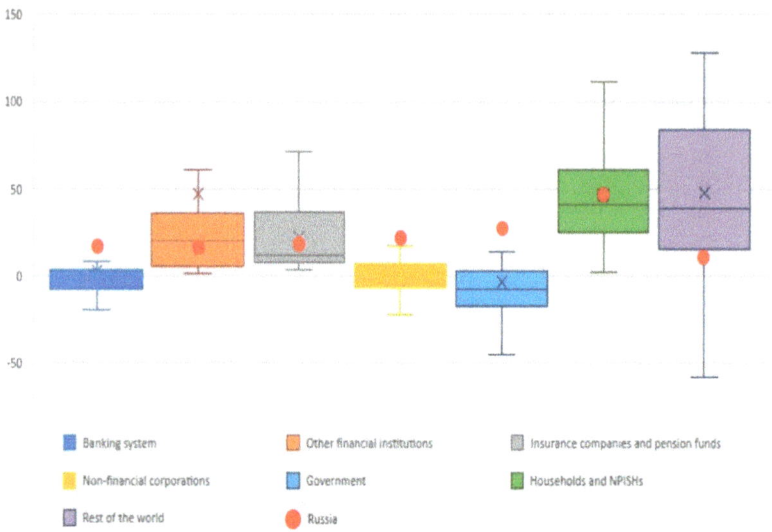

Fig. 7.10 Distribution of liquidity indices by sector, 2019, % of GDP (*Source* compiled by the authors)

Figure 7.10 shows[33] that the median value of the liquidity index of the banking system and non-financial corporations is around 0, and 'boxes' are skewed to the negative area. This suggests that the banking system and non-financial corporations are inclined to take on the liquidity mismatch risk. The government also most often takes on the liquidity mismatch risk, i.e., this sector's liabilities are more liquid than its assets (in Fig. 7.10, the 'box' is almost entirely in the negative area). A high liquidity index value is observed for insurance corporations and pension funds as well as other financial institutions indicating a relatively lower liquidity risk taking. The greatest values of the liquidity index are found for households and the rest of the world sector. However, the rest of the world's liquidity index

[33] It is important to note that in this case we observe some equilibrium values of liquidity indices. At the same time, we cannot judge about the nature of this equilibrium, that is, whether this equilibrium is a solution to the optimisation problem of the sector without restrictions (adoption by the sector of a certain business model) or a solution to the optimisation problem in terms of imperfect markets. We leave this question outside the scope of our study.

values vary more across countries than do the index values for any other sector of the economy.

Let us then look in more detail at each of the sectors: first, the financial corporations (banking system, other financial institutions, insurance companies and pension funds), then households and NPISHs, government and, finally, the rest of the world. Let us consider the weighted assets and liabilities as % of total financial assets of the sector. Changing the dimensions allows to capture the differences across countries on the graphs when the assets and liabilities as % of GDP of one country are several times higher than those of another country.[34]

The banking sector liquidity index (Fig. 7.11) rotates around zero in all countries, except Ireland. This is due to the fact that the banking sector is subject to strict regulatory liquidity requirements. Therefore, the extent to which the banking system takes liquidity risks does not depend on the financial system type in the country.

Ireland stands out in terms of its banking system liquidity index. On the one hand, foreign illiquid capital (equities) plays a significant role

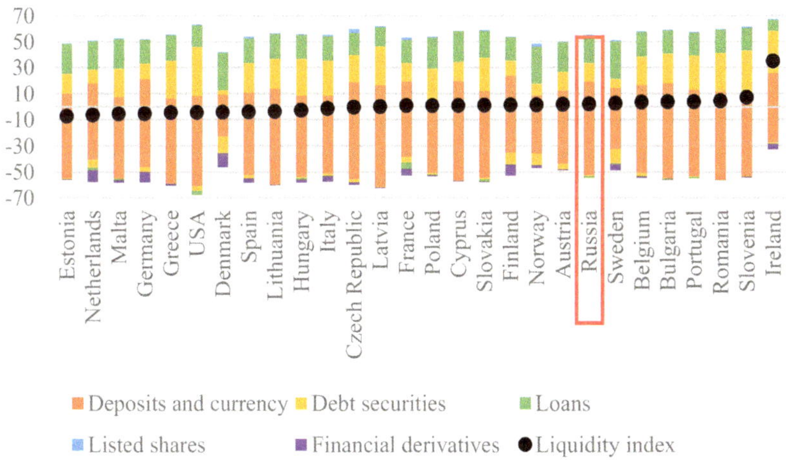

Fig. 7.11 Weighted financial assets (+) and liabilities (−) of the **banking system**, 2019, % of sector assets (*Source* compiled by the authors)

[34] We do not present a graph in % of the sector assets for non-financial corporations as the conclusions obtained are the same in different dimensions.

in the liabilities of Irish banks, whereas more liquid deposits dominate in other countries (see Fig. 7.18 in Appendix 5).[35] On the other hand, foreign deposits and debt securities account for a relatively large amount of assets. These two facts result in the high value of the liquidity index in Ireland.

In terms of the liquidity index structure, Denmark stands out with a small share of deposits in the bank's liabilities,[36] but given the small amount of bonds in the assets the liquidity index value is around zero. The low level of deposit investments in Denmark is due to the preference of households to invest in pension and insurance reserves.

Other financial institutions (excluding insurance companies and pension funds) have positive liquidity index values (Fig. 7.12). This is generally due to stable liabilities (in the form of equity and loans) and more liquid assets[37] (in the form of deposits, debt securities, listed shares) (Fig. 7.19 in Appendix 5). A positive liquidity index value indicates that other financial institutions do not take on liquidity risks. In contrast, sectors that make equity investments in other financial institutions, such as the household sector, take on liquidity risks. If we compare other financial institutions and the banking system, we can conclude that the former do not take the liquidity risks of the financial system.

Figure 7.12 also shows that the structure of weighted assets and liabilities varies greatly across countries. The differences in asset and liability structures are due to the fact that other financial institutions include a broad list of companies: professional securities market participants (brokers, dealers, depositories and other participants), stock exchanges, microfinance organisations, pawnshops, credit consumer cooperatives, leasing and factoring companies and public financial corporations.

The structure of financial instruments depends on which type of financial institution dominates the sector. It is beyond the scope of our study to assess the structure of the sector by country; however, at the end of 2020, liabilities of state financial corporations in Russia (VEB.RF, Deposit Insurance Agency, DOM.RF) totalled ₽7 trillion; investment

[35] Deposits account for 39% of the Irish banks' liabilities compared with the sample average of 74%.

[36] 30% of liabilities come from deposits, which is lower than in Ireland.

[37] Other financial institutions also have investments in illiquid equity in their assets, but the share of these investments in assets is much lower than the share of equity in the liabilities of other financial institutions.

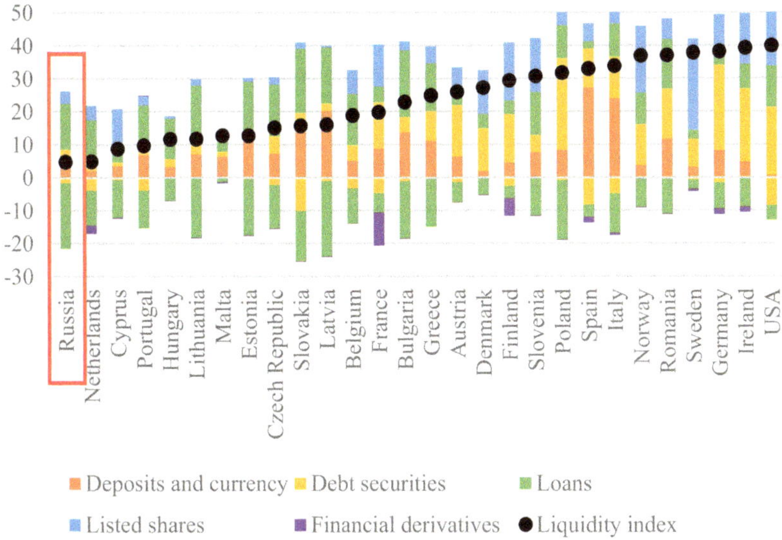

Fig. 7.12 Weighted financial assets (+) and liabilities (−) of **other financial institutions**, 2019, % of sector assets (*Source* compiled by the authors. *Note* For Russia and the USA, the 'Debt Securities' and 'Loans' blocks are unconsolidated [include weighted assets and liabilities where other financial institutions are the issuer and holder])

funds, ₽5.2 trillion; leasing companies, ₽5 trillion; stock exchanges, ₽4 trillion; professional securities market participants, ₽1.5 trillion; microfinance organisations, ₽0.25 trillion. The total liabilities of other financial institutions amounted to ₽54.4 trillion at the end of 2020. Russian financial institutions have the lowest liquidity index due to the high share of loans in both assets and liabilities.

Insurance corporations and pension funds (Fig. 7.13) have the highest liquidity index values as % of total sector assets. These companies have low-liquid liabilities and more liquid assets. That is why insurance corporations and pension funds have the potential to make long-term investments.

Most insurance corporations and pension funds invest in debt securities and, to a lesser extent, in deposits and equity. Cyprus, Ireland, the USA and Poland stand out in terms of the structure of the liquidity index. In Cyprus, insurance corporations and pension funds prefer to invest in

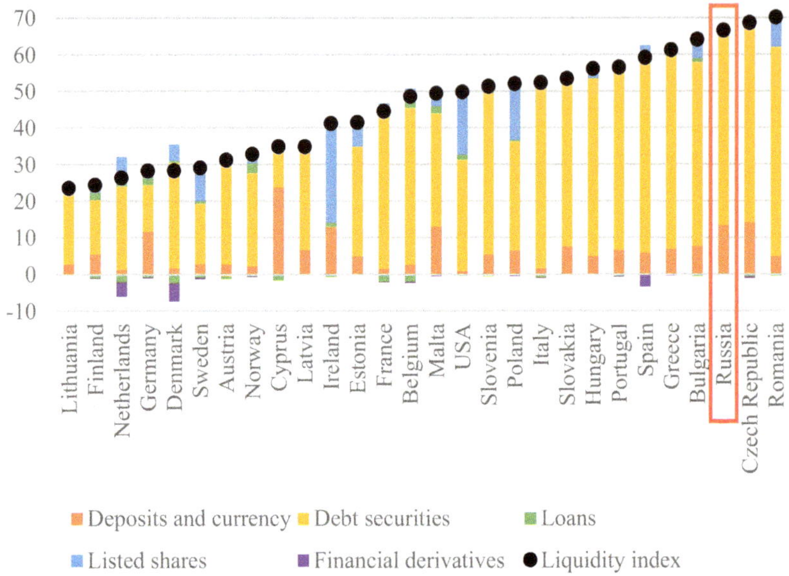

Fig. 7.13 Weighted financial assets (+) and liabilities (−) of **insurance corporations and pension funds**, 2019, % of sector assets (*Source* compiled by the authors)

deposits and less, in debt securities. There are virtually no investments in debt securities in Ireland, but there are investments in foreign deposits and equities. The USA and Poland are peculiar in terms of the share of investments in listed shares; their investment structure indicates that insurance and pension funds assume some of the liquidity risks of companies since firms have more opportunities to finance themselves with stocks rather than with less stable sources of funding, such as loans and debt securities.

Households and NPISHs (Fig. 7.14) have positive liquidity indices, which is explained by liquid deposits in assets on the one hand and less liquid loans in liabilities on the other. Russia has one of the highest liquidity indices, which can be explained by the low indebtedness of the population compared to other countries and the high level of investment in deposits.

The lowest liquidity index values are recorded in Norway, the Netherlands, Sweden and Denmark. This is due to the fact that people in these

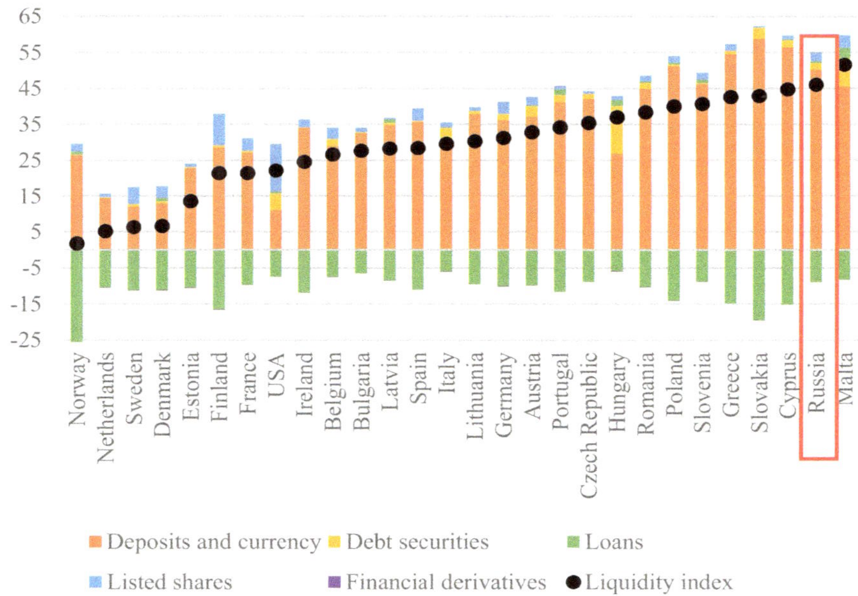

Fig. 7.14 Weighted financial assets (+) and liabilities (−) of **households and NPISHs**, 2019, % of sector assets (*Source* compiled by the authors)

countries prefer to invest in pension and insurance reserves, which are less liquid than deposits, debt securities and equities.

Speaking about different financial systems, we uncover a dilemma that the economy may face. On the one hand, the development of stock markets helps reduce liquidity risks for non-financial corporations as companies are able to finance themselves not only by using less stable funding sources such as loans, but also by using more stable sources, such as listed shares and bonds. Thus, the transition to a market-based financial system is favourable for non-financial corporations. On the other hand, this transition may be less favourable for households. It is worth keeping an eye on who is taking on liquidity risks as financial markets develop. Other financial institutions (including insurance companies and pension funds) are expected to cover the risks. However, the liabilities of other financial institutions, consisting mainly of equity, pension and insurance contributions, are sufficiently stable not to expose other financial institutions to the liquidity risk. Liquidity risks are therefore passed on to the owners of the liabilities of the financial institutions, i.e., households. Although the liquidity index of the households is always positive with a high proportion of investments in equity, pension and insurance reserves, the index value is lower than in other cases, i.e., liquidity risks begin to emerge.[38]

Let us illustrate the negative consequences of households' excessive taking of liquidity risks in Fig. 7.15. The figure shows the real growth index of the US household financial assets. For Russia, the series of real growth index in household deposits (given that deposits largely determine the dynamics of financial assets in case of households).

Figure 7.15 shows that the US household financial assets fell by 15% in real terms in the crisis year of 2008, while the real level of deposits remained unchanged in Russia. This illustrates the fact that as stock markets develop, the risks of liquidity mismatch for certain sectors of the economy, particularly households, increase. Monetary authorities should take this into account when promoting the development of stock markets.

[38] However, it should be understood that the greater risk of the instrument is reflected in its higher profitability. In this case, the development of the stock market allows market participants with long-term goals to invest in more highly profitable instruments, albeit taking on more liquidity risks. In this case, we are not trying to find out which financial structure is the best for the economy. For more information on the types of structure of the financial system and the role in the development of the economy, see the literature review (Sect. 2.2).

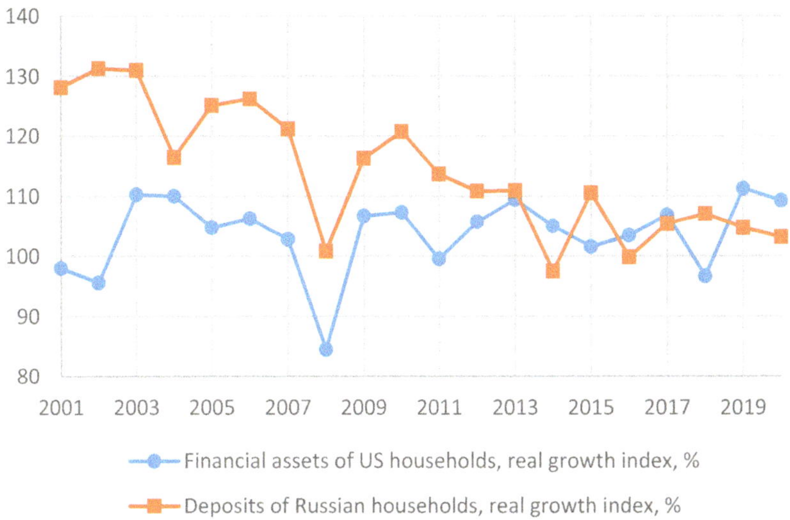

Fig. 7.15 Real growth index of financial assets of the US and Russian households (*Sources* US Financial Accounts [Fed], Banking sector survey [Bank of Russia])

The values for the ***government liquidity index*** are shown in Fig. 7.16. Most countries have a negative index value. On average, the government takes the risks of a liquidity mismatch between financial assets and liabilities. Such risk taking may have a negative impact on the integrity of public finances. In the context of high volatility in government revenue flows, a small negative value in the liquidity index could add more risks for the public sector and the economy as a whole.

Therefore, for countries whose public revenues depend on the exports of one or more important commodity, e.g., Russia and Norway, it is important to maintain a positive liquidity index.

The largest negative value in the liquidity index is that of Italy. This is due to a significant excess of liabilities over assets. Although the weighting of liabilities and assets has smoothed this excess, the absolute negative value of the index is still high compared to other countries.

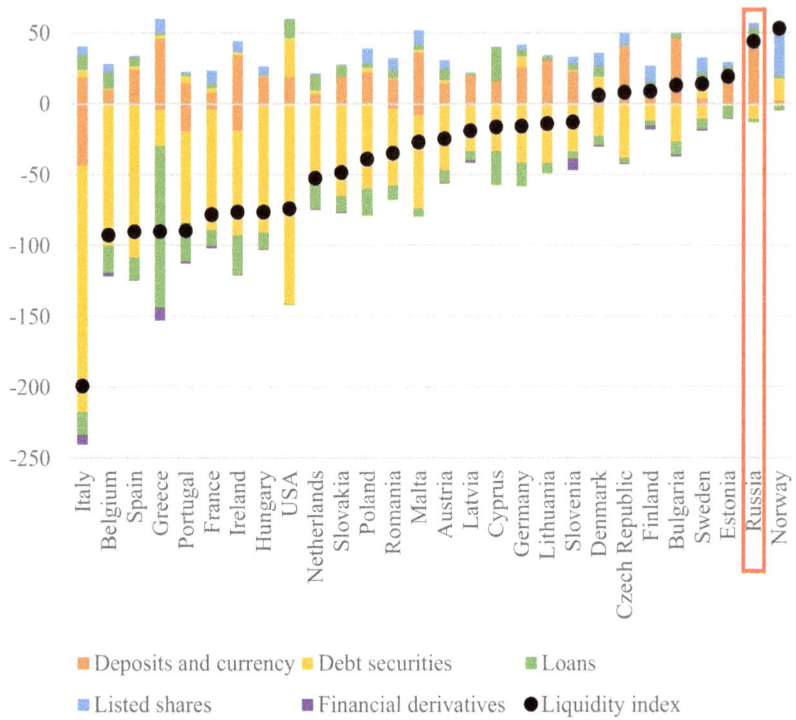

Fig. 7.16 Weighted financial assets (+) and liabilities (−) of the government, 2019, % of sector assets (*Source* compiled by the authors)

Figure 7.17 shows the liquidity-weighted assets and liabilities of the ***rest of the world***. For each individual country, the rest of the world represents a set of countries with which the selected country interacts. A positive value of the rest of the world's liquidity index can be interpreted as the presence of liquid external debt of a country that is not covered by the liquid external assets of that country. The liquidity index is positive in most countries. In Russia, the liquidity index is slightly negative. To a certain degree, this suggests that the rest of the world is taking over some of the liquidity mismatch risks. It should be taken into account, however, that when financial assets and liabilities are denominated in foreign currencies, transactions with the external sector involve not only the liquidity risk but also the exchange rate risk. In this context,

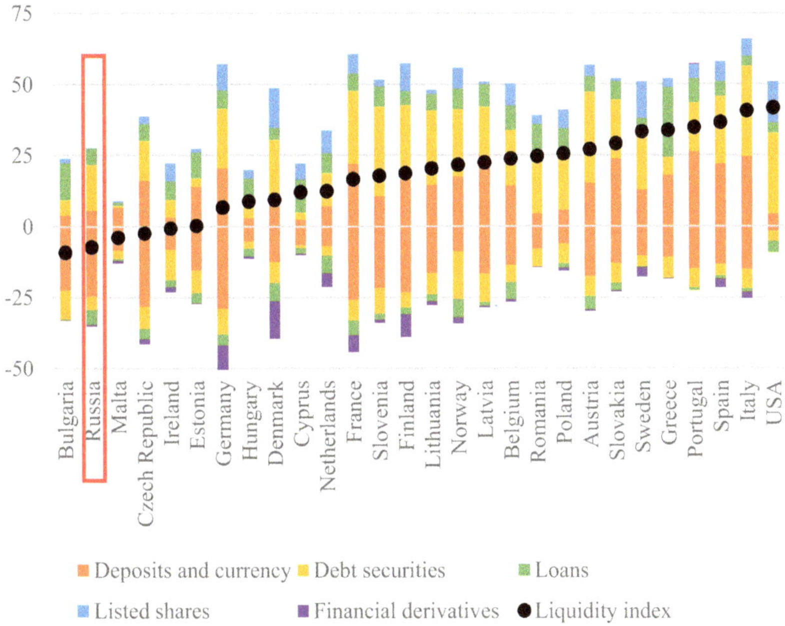

Fig. 7.17 Weighted financial assets (+) and liabilities (−) of the **rest of the world**, 2019, % of sector assets (*Source* compiled by the authors)

it may not be entirely correct to talk about the role of the external sector in the functioning of the domestic financial market on the basis of the liquidity index alone.

7.5 Conclusion

We have reviewed and made cross-country comparisons of financial market liquidity indicators and the structure of financial assets and the liabilities of economic sectors in terms of their liquidity.

The liquidity of financial markets is presented across five dimensions: tightness, immediacy, depth, breadth and resilience. There is a set of indicators to measure each of these aspects. Financial instruments vary in their liquidity across countries. In terms of tightness, depth and breadth, the Russian equity market proved more liquid than Eastern European equity markets but less liquid than Northern and Western European markets and that of the USA. Yet, the Russian market is comparable to the US and North-West European markets in terms of resilience. At the same time, the liquidity of Russian government bonds is low relative to most European and US securities.

The liquidity mismatch concept and the liquidity index values make it possible to assess how liquidity risk taking varies across economic sectors. A negative liquidity index value is a characteristic of the non-financial institutions sector and, to a lesser extent, of the banking system. However, in the countries where banks prevail in external financing provision, non-financial corporations nevertheless maintain the index at a high level by accumulating liquid assets.

The value of the liquidity index for the household sector varies considerably, depending on household participation in the stock market (including investments in pension funds and insurance corporations). If a country has a market-based financial system, the population of that country tends to take more liquidity risk. A strong decline in real financial assets in the USA in 2008 compared to the unchanged level of household deposits exemplifies that.

The transition to a market-based financial structure reduces the liquidity risks of non-financial corporations in terms of issuing liabilities, but it has implications for greater risk taking by other economic sectors, in particular, households.

Appendix 1: Market Liquidity Measurement

This section is an overview of market liquidity indicators. In practice, the choice of which indicator to measure depends on the availability of data of the required frequency. It is often said that liquidity indicators are used when using intraday data, and liquidity proxies are used when using less frequent data.

There are 4 groups of indicators to measure liquidity characteristics:

- ***Indicators that measure transaction costs*** make it possible to assess market tightness. These indicators include price spreads. The most common is the bid-ask spread, which is mentioned in the main body of the paper. Diaz and Escribano (2020) also mention such transaction cost indicators as the effective spread (Lee, 1993), the realised spread (Hong & Warga, 2000), the value of the deviation of the maximum price from the minimum price (Imputed Roundtrip Cost

(Dick-Nielsen et al., 2012)) and the Huang and Stoll (1996) ratio. In addition, a number of papers present proxies[39] for measuring transaction costs: the Roll indicator[40] in Roll (1984), the LOT, Zero, Zero2 indicators[41] in Lesmond et al. (1999), Holden and Effective tick in Goyenko et al. (2009), Gibbs, High-Low ratio, FHT in Schestag et al. (2016).

- ***Volume-based indicators*** measure the breadth and depth of the market. Sarr and Lybek (2002) examine the relation of the price growth rate (|%ΔP|) to the number of assets traded (N) or the volume of transactions (V), the turnover rate and the Hui-Heubel Liquidity Ratio.[42]

Volume-based indicators also embrace range measure (Downing et al., 2005), Martin index (Martin, 1975), Kyle's lambda (Kyle, 1985), traded volume of the asset (Kamara, 1994), market share of the asset (Diaz & Escribano, 2020), Amihud (Amihud, 2002) and Amivest (Cooper et al., 1985) indicators and other turnover indicators (Florackis et al., 2011).

- ***Price-based indicators*** make it possible to assess market resilience. These include the market-efficiency coefficient, which takes into account the ratio of the variance of long-term returns to the variance of short-term returns (Hasbrouck & Schwartz, 1988).

39 The abundance of different indicators is related to the specifics of the data we use, as noted above. The emergence of new indicators, especially proxy indicators, is accompanied by a correlation analysis, where the correlation of the indicator with a more fundamental indicator, for which data are not always available, is examined.

40 $Roll_i = 2\sqrt{-cov(\Delta p_t, \Delta p_{t-1})}$, where Δp_t is the price change in day t.

41 The idea behind the LOT, Zero, Zero2 indicators is that if transaction costs are high, investors will tend not to trade the asset, which increases the probability of zero return on the asset per day. So, the indicators take into account the number of days with zero return.

42 In particular, Sarr and Lybek (2002) analyse the price and volume performance of NASDAQ-listed stocks over the period 1996–2000. They note an increase in the absolute rate of price change (|%ΔP|) with a constant ratio of the growth rate to the number of shares traded (|%ΔP|/N) or the volume of transactions (|%ΔP|/V). The authors conclude that there is more market depth, i.e. more transactions can be made with minimal effect on average prices. At the same time, there is an increase in the ratio of the growth rate to turnover rate (|%ΔP|/(V/K)). In the context of rising turnover rate (V/K), this signals a shrinking market breadth.

Price-based indicators include the variance of returns (Houweling et al., 2005), price variance (Jankowitsch et al., 2011), inter-quartile price range indicator (Han & Zhou, 2008), Gamma indicator, which measures the covariance of price changes between transactions (Bao et al., 2011), Lambda[43] (Hasbrouck, 2009) and the following proxies: dispersion of quotes (Garbade & Silber, 1976), latent liquidity ratio (Mahanti et al., 2008), the indicators presented in Marsh and Rock (1986), Pastor and Stambaugh (2003), Abdi and Ranaldo (2017), Broto and Lamas (2020).

- Indicators that measure ***exposure to price changes*** related to changes in ***market liquidity***, excluding other effects (e.g., excluding information on the onset of a crisis that affects all assets at once). Sarr and Lybek (2002), for example, consider market-adjusted liquidity.[44]

Diaz and Escribano (2020) also distinguish a category of trade frequency indicators. These include the trading volume for a certain period, including per day (Fleming, 2003), the number of trades per day (Chordia et al., 2001), the proportion of days when the instrument was not traded (relevant, for example, for bonds) (Dick-Nielsen et al., 2012).

Appendix 2: Bloomberg Data

See Tables 7.4 and 7.5.

[43] The index is estimated by regressing the return on the asset by the square root of the volume of the asset taking into account the sign of the transaction: $r_t = \lambda * \sum_k sign(V_{t,k}) * \sqrt{V_{t,k}} + \varepsilon_t$, where $V_{t,k}$ is the volume of the transaction k in period t.

[44] To calculate this indicator, it is first necessary to estimate the CAPM model and then regress the squares of the CAPM model residuals on the change in traded asset volumes. The lower the coefficient of the volume change indicator, the lower the impact of trading volumes on price dispersion, and the higher the liquidity of the asset.

Table 7.4 Indicators for measuring the liquidity aspects of securities (*Source* Bloomberg)

Indicator	*Variable name in the Bloomberg system*
Closing price	PX_LAST
Bid price	PX_BID
Ask price	PX_ASK
Trading volume for the day	PX_VOLUME
Market capitalisation (for shares)	CUR_MKT_CAP
Duration (for bonds)	DUR_ADJ_OAS_BID

Table 7.5 Market indices (*Source* Bloomberg)

Country	*Market index*
Russia	MOEX Russia Index
USA	S&P 500 (SPX)
Germany	DAX
Finland	HEX
Ireland	ISEQ
Hungary	BUX
Slovakia	SKSM
Bulgaria	SOFIX
Denmark	KFX
Sweden	OMX

Appendix 3: Liquidity Aspects of the Stock Market

Year	Number of fin. instruments	Number of observations	Bid-Ask spread	Turnover rate	Hui-Heubel	MEC
Russia						
2012	29	7373	0.00185	0.00222	30.2	72%
2013	31	7480	0.00169	0.00172	22.0	72%
2014	31	7740	0.00180	0.00247	18.8	74%
2015	33	8063	0.00200	0.00182	34.9	73%
2016	34	8447	0.00158	0.00142	29.8	72%
2017	35	8792	0.00126	0.00130	17.1	72%
2018	35	8890	0.00103	0.00134	12.4	70%
2019	35	8820	0.00071	0.00141	7.5	76%
2020	35	8750	0.00084	0.00323	5.5	78%
Total		**74355**	**0.00139**	**0.00187**	**19.4**	**73%**
USA						
2012	505	114196	0.00043	0.00227	3.5	75%
2013	461	117006	0.00034	0.00196	3.7	72%
2014	469	119745	0.00030	0.00196	3.6	73%
2015	477	122341	0.00032	0.00215	3.8	71%
2016	481	123705	0.00031	0.00239	4.0	71%
2017	486	124129	0.00025	0.00213	2.9	71%
2018	492	125539	0.00023	0.00240	3.7	73%
2019	498	127978	0.00028	0.00225	3.5	73%
2020	503	129680	0.00046	0.00294	5.1	69%
Total		**1104319**	**0.00032**	**0.00228**	**3.8**	**72%**
Germany						
2012	25	6350	0.00069	0.00391	2.2	72%
2013	26	6445	0.00073	0.00330	2.7	70%
2014	26	6552	0.00075	0.00323	2.3	78%
2015	27	6638	0.00082	0.00366	2.6	72%
2016	27	6885	0.00075	0.00329	2.8	79%
2017	28	6931	0.00073	0.00288	2.5	76%
2018	29	7070	0.00063	0.00355	2.1	76%
2019	29	7279	0.00055	0.00322	2.2	78%
2020	30	7432	0.00074	0.00395	3.0	72%
Total		**61582**	**0.00071**	**0.00344**	**2.5**	**75%**
Ireland						
2012	33	5621	0.05315	0.00113	963.7	58%
2013	25	5778	0.05468	0.00117	580.5	61%
2014	27	6732	0.05900	0.00125	470.9	61%
2015	28	7055	0.06979	0.00147	581.4	61%
2016	29	7116	0.09050	0.00126	1986.9	67%
2017	31	7366	0.05756	0.00116	7116.2	62%
2018	33	8194	0.05282	0.00123	1004.3	60%
2019	34	8533	0.08219	0.00129	2799.2	66%
2020	34	8725	0.06723	0.00165	929.4	71%
Total		**65120**	**0.06591**	**0.00130**	**1890.0**	**63%**
Finland						
2012	138	26104	0.02102	0.00120	127.6	59%
2013	109	26769	0.01815	0.00110	76.1	63%
2014	113	28047	0.01720	0.00128	55.5	63%
2015	120	29287	0.01382	0.00144	59.3	66%
2016	123	30880	0.01220	0.00124	61.4	62%
2017	127	31187	0.00848	0.00134	44.2	65%
2018	133	32445	0.01142	0.00116	63.5	66%
2019	134	33266	0.01130	0.00113	65.4	68%
2020	135	33992	0.00806	0.00165	41.0	70%
Total		**271977**	**0.01315**	**0.00129**	**64.2**	**65%**

Year	Number of fin. instruments	Number of observations	Bid-Ask spread	Turnover rate	Hui-Heubel	MEC
Denmark						
2012	20	4569	0.00359	0.00264	5.6	69%
2013	18	4554	0.00267	0.00264	4.0	69%
2014	19	4758	0.00211	0.00284	3.7	78%
2015	19	4807	0.00185	0.00276	3.9	70%
2016	20	4935	0.00120	0.00231	4.3	78%
2017	20	5020	0.00106	0.00236	3.1	69%
2018	20	4960	0.00096	0.00269	3.4	75%
2019	20	4960	0.00088	0.00253	3.4	67%
2020	20	5000	0.00100	0.00303	4.1	71%
Total		**43563**	**0.00166**	**0.00264**	**3.9**	**72%**
Sweden						
2012	28	7112	0.00137	0.00295	3.4	70%
2013	28	7084	0.00108	0.00267	3.2	74%
2014	28	7084	0.00094	0.00272	3.4	75%
2015	29	7283	0.00112	0.00289	4.6	72%
2016	29	7337	0.00092	0.00268	4.5	71%
2017	30	7418	0.00086	0.00263	3.0	69%
2018	30	7500	0.00060	0.00290	3.6	75%
2019	30	7500	0.00069	0.00247	3.9	81%
2020	30	7560	0.00075	0.00299	4.5	71%
Total		**65878**	**0.00092**	**0.00277**	**3.8**	**73%**
Bulgaria						
2012	15	2474	0.03124	0.00030	447.9	51%
2013	11	2493	0.03349	0.00047	385.4	58%
2014	11	2728	0.02726	0.00039	224.9	59%
2015	12	2733	0.03014	0.00028	324.1	50%
2016	13	2974	0.03238	0.00028	265.9	54%
2017	13	3224	0.02161	0.00042	139.7	59%
2018	14	3298	0.02098	0.00024	244.6	44%
2019	14	3444	0.02246	0.00018	344.0	46%
2020	15	3601		0.00027	224.8	54%
Total		**26969**	**0.02735**	**0.00031**	**281.9**	**53%**
Slovakia						
2012	8	1972	0.09903	0.00009	515.2	81%
2013	8	1992	0.06556	0.00005	1459.0	8839%
2014	8	2061	0.34476	0.00002	1302.8	530%
2015	8	2045	0.20328	0.00001	1663.7	163605%
2016	8	2013	0.13771	0.00001	3302.8	115%
2017	8	1972	0.09616	0.00002	68679.0	72%
2018	8	2055	0.14048	0.00002	150003.8	109%
2019	8	2068	0.21858	0.00002	52672.7	72%
2020	8	1992	0.11705	0.00002	79039.9	311%
Total		**18170**	**0.17129**	**0.00003**	**36503.8**	**22237%**
Hungary						
2012	14	3130		0.00188	88.3	57%
2013	15	3571	0.03623	0.00174	129.9	59%
2014	15	3720	0.01565	0.00118	3395.1	62%
2015	15	3735	0.01702	0.00116	492.5	84%
2016	15	3780	0.01547	0.00097	91.3	72%
2017	16	3889	0.01454	0.00301	52.9	63%
2018	16	3904	0.00983	0.00247	28.2	61%
2019	16	3936	0.00726	0.00147	12.7	63%
2020	16	4032	0.00909	0.00141	17.3	68%
Total		**33697**	**0.01417**	**0.00170**	**450.9**	**66%**

Appendix 4: Liquidity Aspects of Government Bonds

See Tables 7.6, 7.7, 7.8, 7.9, 7.10 and 7.11.

Table 7.6 Government bonds: bid-ask spread (by year)

	Russia	USA	Germany	Bulgaria	Hungary	Denmark	Ireland	Slovakia	Finland	Sweden
Average annual number of issues traded	43	347	15	23	21	10	26	19	18	11
2012	0.0153	0.0002	0.0001	0.0096	0.0063	0.0034	0.0147	0.0098	0.0014	0.0028
2013	0.0132	0.0002	0.0001	0.0107	0.0055	0.0024	0.0050	0.0084	0.0007	0.0021
2014	0.0275	0.0002	0.0002	0.0115	0.0050	0.0014	0.0014	0.0074	0.0004	0.0015
2015	0.0229	0.0003	0.0002	0.0146	0.0060	0.0047	0.0028	0.0072	0.0005	0.0026
2016	0.0083	0.0003	0.0003	0.0110	0.0033	0.0035	0.0040	0.0067	0.0008	0.0024
2017	0.0074	0.0003	0.0005	0.0104	0.0026	0.0017	0.0043	0.0066	0.0014	0.0024
2018	0.0084	0.0004	0.0006	0.0102	0.0031	0.0013	0.0030	0.0067	0.0015	0.0023
2019	0.0049	0.0005	0.0003	0.0110	0.0036	0.0013	0.0015	0.0069	0.0015	0.0023
2020	0.0059	0.0011	0.0005	0.0081	0.0046	0.0032	0.0012	0.0087	0.0018	0.0053
Total	**0.0118**	**0.0004**	**0.0003**	**0.0110**	**0.0043**	**0.0025**	**0.0035**	**0.0076**	**0.0012**	**0.0026**

Table 7.7 Government bonds: bid-ask spread (by duration)

Duration	Russia	USA	Germany	Bulgaria	Hungary	Denmark	Ireland	Slovakia	Finland	Sweden
Up to 3 m.	0.0013	0.0003	0.0005	0.0007	0.0014	0.0002	0.0014	0.0037	0.0008	0.0001
3-6 m.	0.0030	0.0003	0.0004	0.0016	0.0017	0.0005	0.0017	0.0038	0.0008	0.0003
0.5-1 y.	0.0037	0.0003	0.0004	0.0029	0.0009	0.0010	0.0019	0.0048	0.0008	0.0004
1-3 y.	0.0074	0.0003	0.0002	0.0066	0.0020	0.0023	0.0023	0.0053	0.0008	0.0006
3-5 y.	0.0125	0.0003	0.0002	0.0120	0.0037	0.0045	0.0026	0.0070	0.0009	0.0011
Over 5 y.	0.0172	0.0006	0.0003	0.0188	0.0079	0.0086	0.0041	0.0085	0.0014	0.0039
Total	**0.0118**	**0.0004**	**0.0003**	**0.0110**	**0.0043**	**0.0043**	**0.0035**	**0.0076**	**0.0012**	**0.0026**

Table 7.8 Government bonds: market-efficiency coefficient (by year)

	Russia	USA	Germany	Bulgaria	Hungary	Denmark	Ireland	Slovakia	Finland	Sweden
Average annual number of issues traded	43	347	15	23	21	10	26	19	18	11
2012	48%	72%	66%	57%	74%	75%	88%	61%	75%	80%
2013	55%	67%	68%	52%	77%	70%	91%	65%	75%	79%
2014	47%	62%	46%	57%	75%	53%	89%	49%	54%	69%
2015	57%	60%	61%	56%	85%	67%	129%	64%	69%	83%
2016	62%	72%	69%	47%	100%	61%	75%	62%	68%	84%
2017	56%	62%	83%	49%	104%	70%	84%	116%	80%	87%
2018	64%	67%	70%	42%	92%	62%	81%	67%	65%	82%
2019	61%	73%	68%	41%	83%	68%	67%	68%	66%	89%
2020	66%	64%	72%	58%	93%	78%	75%	60%	70%	87%
Total	**59%**	**66%**	**66%**	**51%**	**88%**	**67%**	**85%**	**69%**	**69%**	**82%**

Table 7.9 Government bonds: market-efficiency coefficient (by duration)

Duration	Россия	США	Германия	Болгария	Венгрия	Дания	Ирландия	Словакия	Финляндия	Швеция
Up to 3 m.	46%	41%	42%	35%	80%	40%	29%	292%	30%	32%
3-6 m.	44%	59%	45%	44%	64%	52%	43%	38%	43%	44%
0.5-1 y.	49%	72%	60%	45%	65%	62%	54%	43%	51%	43%
1-3 y.	53%	66%	70%	46%	92%	82%	71%	45%	68%	80%
3-5 y.	60%	67%	70%	56%	92%	90%	113%	59%	69%	88%
Over 5 y.	66%	68%	75%	55%	92%	90%	84%	70%	73%	87%
Total	**59%**	**66%**	**66%**	**51%**	**88%**	**81%**	**85%**	**69%**	**69%**	**82%**

Table 7.10 Russian government bonds: liquidity aspects by year

Russia	Number of instruments	Number of observations	Bid-ask spread	Turnover rate	Hui-Heubel LR	MEC
2012	40	8 135	0.0153	0.0128	1	48%
2013	41	8 671	0.0132	0.0114	493	55%
2014	36	8 667	0.0275	0.0119	1794	47%
2015	40	9 428	0.0229	0.0089	1003	57%
2016	42	9 324	0.0083	0.0118	576	62%
2017	42	9 908	0.0074	0.0128	134	56%
2018	43	10 066	0.0084	0.0132	730	64%
2019	46	9 781	0.0049	0.0114	57	61%
2020	55	11 138	0.0059	0.0089	337	66%
Total			**0.0118**	**0.0114**	**571**	**59%**

Table 7.11 Russian government bonds: liquidity aspects by duration

Russia	Number of instruments	Number of observations	Bid-ask spread	Turnover rate	Hui-Heubel LR	MEC
3m	40	2 335	0.0013	0.0284	12	46%
6m	40	2 633	0.0030	0.0200	100	44%
1y	38	5 312	0.0037	0.0141	76	49%
3y	45	19 449	0.0074	0.0102	418	53%
5y	43	20 158	0.0125	0.0098	788	60%
10y	57	35 231	0.0172	0.0105	700	66%
Total			**0.0118**	**0.0114**	**571**	**59%**

Appendix 5: Financial Assets and Liabilities of Economic Sectors

See Figs. 7.18, 7.19, 7.20, 7.21, 7.22, 7.23 and 7.24.

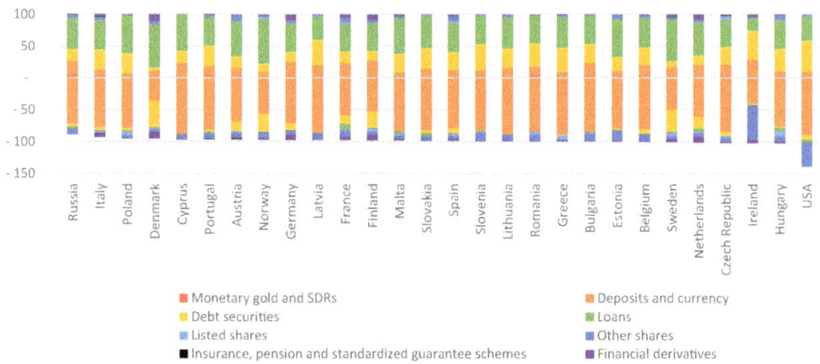

Fig. 7.18 Financial assets (+) and liabilities (−) of the banking system, % of sector assets

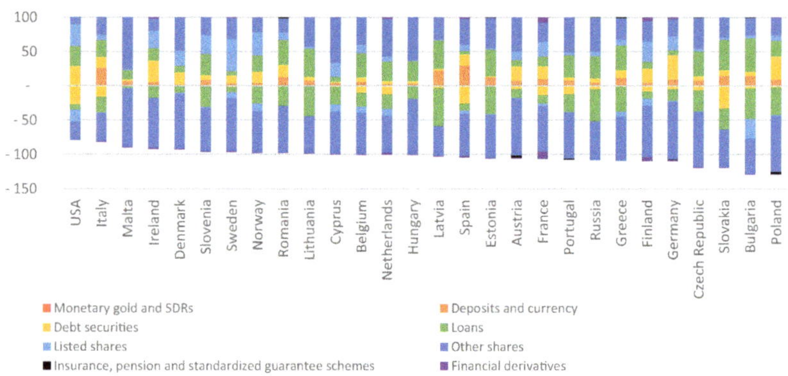

Fig. 7.19 Financial assets (+) and liabilities (−) of other financial institutions, % of sector assets

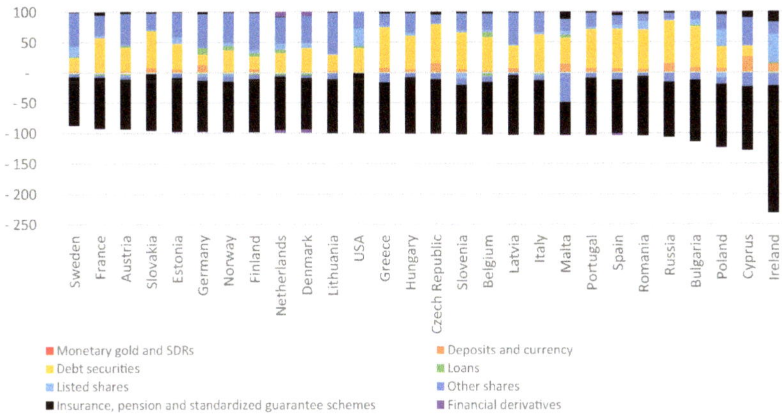

Fig. 7.20 Financial assets (+) and liabilities (−) of insurance corporations and pension funds, % of sector assets

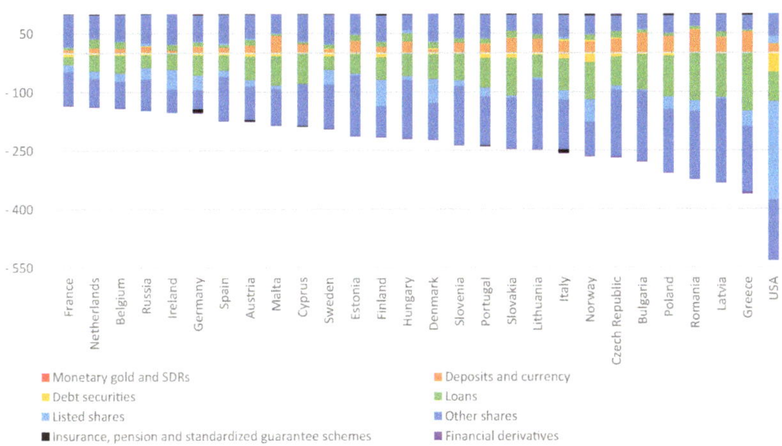

Fig. 7.21 Financial assets (+) and liabilities (−) of non-financial corporations, % of sector assets

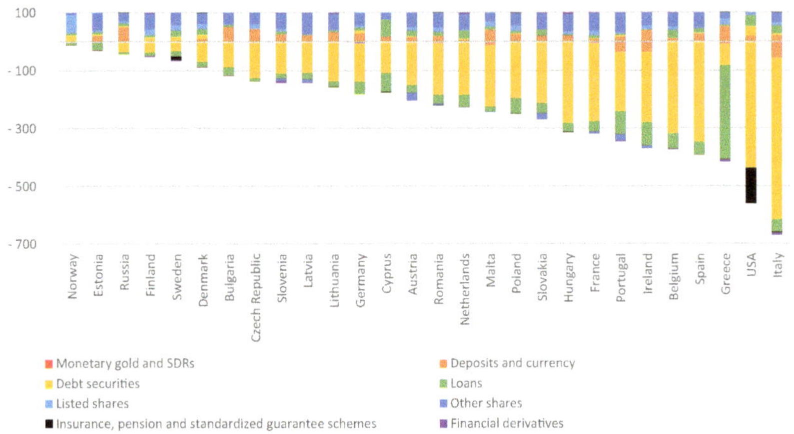

Fig. 7.22 Financial assets (+) and liabilities (−) of the government, % of sector assets

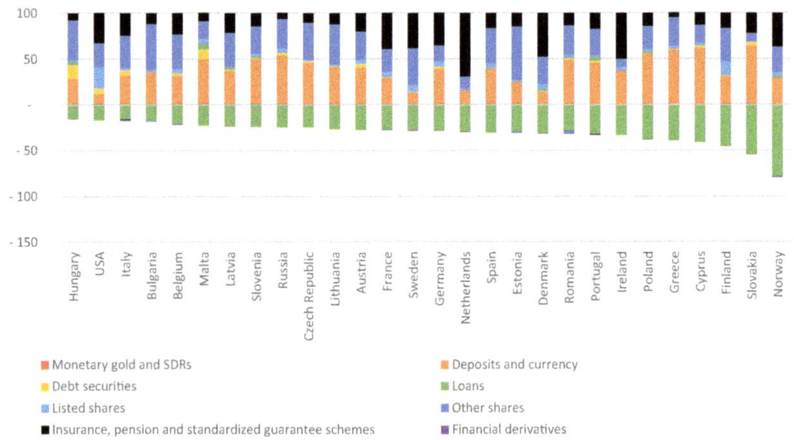

Fig. 7.23 Financial assets (+) and liabilities (−) of households and NPISHs, % of sector assets

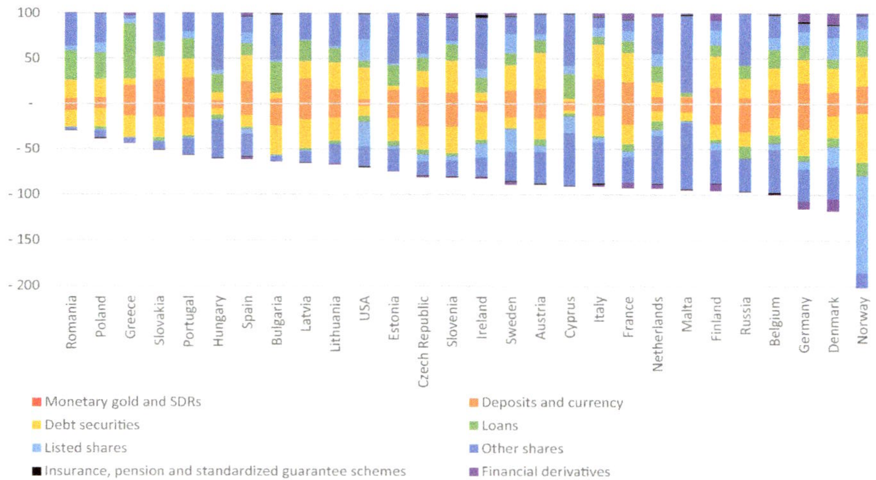

Fig. 7.24 Financial assets (+) and liabilities (−) of the rest of the world, % of sector assets

References

Abdi, F., & Ranaldo, A. (2017). A simple estimation of bid-ask spreads from daily close, high, and low prices. *The Review of Financial Studies, 12*, 4437–4480.

Abramova, M. & Mamuta, M. (2014). Shadow Banking in Russia: factors of propagation, possibilities of regulation. *Finance: Theory and Practice, 5*, 55–62.

Al Mamun, M., Sohag, K., Shahbaz, M., & Hammoudeh, S. (2018). Financial markets, innovations and cleaner energy production in OECD countries. *Energy Economics, 72*, 236–254.

Allen, F., Bartiloro, L., Gu, X., & Kowalewski, O. (2018). Does economic structure determine financial structure? *Journal of International Economics, 114*, 389–409.

Amihud, Y. (2002). Illiquidity and stock returns: Cross-section and time-series effects. *Journal of Financial Markets, 1*, 31–56.

Bank of Russia. (2019). Methodology of financial accounts and balances of financial assets and liabilities in the Russian system of national accounts.

Bao, J., Pan, J., & Wang, J. (2011). The illiquidity of corporate bonds. *The Journal of Finance, 3*, 911–946.

Bats, J., & Houben, A. (2017). *Bank-based versus market-based financing: implications for systemic risk* (De Nederlandsche Bank. Eurosystem. Working Paper, Vol. 577).

BCBS. (2013). *Basel III: The liquidity coverage ratio and liquidity risk monitoring tools*. s.l.: Basel Committee on Banking Supervision Policy Paper.

Będowska-Sójka, B., & Echaust, K. (2020). What is the best proxy for liquidity in the presence of extreme illiquidity?. *Emerging Markets Review,* (43), 100695.

Berger, A. N., & Bouwman, C. H. (2009). Bank liquidity creation. *The Review of Financial Studies, 22*(9), 3779–3837.

Bervas, A. (2006). Market liquidity and its incorporation into risk management. *Financial Stability Review*, May, pp. 63–79.

Biais, B., Foucault, T., & Hillion, P. (1997). *Microstructure des marchés financiers: Institutions, modèles et tests empiriques*. Presses universitaires de France.

BIS. (2009). International framework for liquidity risk measurement, standards and monitoring. [Online] Available at: https://www.bis.org/publ/bcbs165.pdf

BIS. (2014a). *Basel III: The net stable funding ratio*. s.l.:s.n.

BIS. (2014b). *Long term finance: can emerging capital markets help?*(BIS Papers, № 75).

Borio, C. E., & Disyatat, P. (2015). *Capital flows and the current account: Taking financing (more) seriously* (BIS Working Papers).

Brandao-Marques, M. L., & Danninger, S. (2016). *Stock market liquidity in Chile*. International Monetary Fund, Vol. 223.

Broto, C., & Lamas, M. (2020). Is market liquidity less resilient after the financial crisis? Evidence for US Treasuries. *Economic Modelling*, pp. 217–229.

Brunnermeier, M. K., Gorton, G., & Krishnamurthy, A. (2013). *Liquidity mismatch*. Risk Topography.

Chordia, T., Roll, R., & Subrahmanyam, A. (2001). Market liquidity and trading activity. *The Journal of Finance, 2*, 501–530.

Chung, K. H., & Zhang, H. (2014). A simple approximation of intraday spreads using daily data. *Journal of Financial Markets*, 94–120.

Cooper, S. K., Groth, J. C., & Avera, W. E. (1985). Liquidity, exchange listing, and common stock performance. *Journal of Economics and Business, 1*, 19–33.

Degryse, H., De Winne, R., Gresse, C., & Payne, R. (2018). *High frequency trading and ghost liquidity*. s.l.:s.n.

Demirgüç-Kunt, A., & Levine, R. (2001). *Financial structure and economic growth: A cross-country comparison of banks, markets, and development*. MIT press.

Demsetz, H. (1968). The cost of transacting. *The Quarterly Journal of Economics, 82*(1), 33–53.

Diaz, A., & Escribano, A. (2020). Measuring the multi-faceted dimension of liquidity in financial markets: A literature review. *Research in International Business and Finance, 51*(101079).

Dick-Nielsen, J., Feldhütter, P., & Lando, D. (2012). Corporate bond liquidity before and after the onset of the subprime crisis. *Journal of Financial Economics, 3*, 471–492.

Downing, C., Underwood, S., & Xing, Y. (2005). *Is Liquidity risk priced in the corporate bond market?* (Working Paper). Rice University.

Fink, G., Haiss, P. R., & Hristoforova, S. (2006). *Credit, bonds, stocks and growth in seven large economies* (EI Working Papers).

Fisher, L. (1959). Determinants of risk premiums on corporate bonds. *Journal of Political Economy, 67*(3), 217–237.

Fleming, M. J. (2003). Measuring treasury market liquidity. *Economic Policy Review*, pp. 83–108.

Florackis, C., Gregoriou, A., & Kostakis, A. (2011). Trading frequency and asset pricing on the London Stock Exchange: Evidence from a new price impact ratio. *Journal of Banking & Finance, 12*, 3335–3350.

Fong, K. Y., Holden, C. W., & Trzcinka, C. A. (2017). What are the best liquidity proxies for global research? *Review of Finance, 4*, 1355–1401.

Gambacorta, L., Yang, J., & Tsatsaronis, K. (2014). Financial structure and growth. *BIS Quarterly Review.*

Garbade, K. D., & Silber, W. L. (1976). Price dispersion in the government securities market. *Journal of Political Economy, 4*, Part 1, 721–740.

Goyenko, R., Holden, C., & Trzinka, C. (2009). Do liquidity measures measure liquidity? *Journal of Financial Economics*, 153–181.

Gravelle, T. (1999). *Liquidity of the government of Canada securities market: stylized facts and some market microstructure comparisons to the United States treasury market* (Working Paper). Bank of Canada.

Han, S., & Zhou, H. (2008O. *Effects of liquidity on the non-default component of corporate yield spreads: Evidence from intraday transactions data* (Working Paper).

Hasbrouck, J. (2009). Trading costs and returns for US equities: Estimating effective costs from daily data. *The Journal of Finance*, 1445–1477.

Hasbrouck, J., & Schwartz, R. A. (1988). Liquidity and execution costs in equity markets. *Journal of Portfolio Management, 3*, 10–16.

Hibbert, J., Kirchner, A., Kretzschmar, G., & Li, R. (2009). *Liquidity premium: Literature review of theoretical and empirical evidence* (Barrie & Hibbert research report).

Hong, G., & Warga, A. (2000). An empirical study of bond market transactions. *Financial Analysts Journal, 2*, 32–46.

Houweling, P., Mentink, A., & Vorst, T. (2005). Comparing possible proxies of corporate bond liquidity. *Journal of Banking & Finance*, 1331–1358.

Huang, R. D., & Stoll, H. R. (1996). Dealer versus auction markets: A paired comparison of execution costs on NASDAQ and the NYSE. *Journal of Financial Economics, 3*, 313–357.

Hui, B., & Heubel, B. (1984). Comparative liquidity advantages Among major US stock markets. *Financial Information Group Study Series.*

IMF. (2015). *Global financial stability report.* s.l.:s.n.

IMF. (2018). *Global financial stability report.*

IMF, et al. (2009). *System of national accounts 2008.* ISBN 978-92-1-161522-7 ed. New York: s.n.

Jakab, Z. & Kumhof, M. (2015). *Banks are not intermediaries of loanable funds–and why this matters* (Bank of England Working Paper Series).

Jankowitsch, R., Nashikkar, A., & Subrahmanyam, M. G. (2011). Price dispersion in OTC markets: A new measure of liquidity. *Journal of Banking & Finance, 2*, 343–357.

Kamara, A. (1994). Liquidity, taxes, and short-term treasury yields. *The Journal of Financial and Quantitative Analysis, 3*, 403–417.

Krishnamurthy, A., Bai, J., & Weymuller, C. H. (2016). Measuring liquidity mismatch in the banking sector. *National Bureau of Economic Research.*

Kurronen, S. (2015). Financial sector in resource-dependent economies. *Emerging Markets Review, 23*, 208–229.

Kyle, A. S. (1985). Continuous auctions and insider trading. *Econometrica: Journal of the Econometric Society*, 1315–1335.

Langfield, S., & Pagano, M. (2016). Bank bias in Europe: Effects on systemic risk and growth. *Economic Policy, 31*(85), 51–106.

Lee, C. M. C. (1993). Market integration and price execution for NYSE-listed securities. *The Journal of Finance*, 1009–1038.

Lesmond, D. A., Ogden, J. P., & Trzincka, C. A. (1999). A new estimate of transaction costs. *The Review of Financial Studies, 5*, 1113–1141.

Levine, R. (2002). Bank-based or market-based financial systems: Which is better? *Journal of Financial Intermediation, 11*(4), 398–428.

Luintel, K. B., Khan, M., Arestis, P., & Theodorid, K. (2008). Financial structure and economic growth. *Journal of Development Economics, 86*(1), 181–200.

Luintel, K. B., Khan, M., Leon-Gonzalez, R., & Li, G. (2016). (2016). Financial development, structure and growth: New data, method and results. *Journal of International Financial Markets, Institutions and Money, 43*, 95–112.

Mahanti, S. et al. (2008). Latent liquidity: A new measure of liquidity, with an application to corporate bonds. *Journal of Financial Economics*, 272–298.

Marsh, T. A., & Rock, K. (1986). Exchange listing and liquidity: A comparison of the american stock exchange with the NASDAQ national market system. *American Stock Exchange.*

Martin, P. (1975). *Analysis of the impact of competitive rates on the liquidity of NYSE stocks* (Economic Staff Paper, Vol. 3).

Mau, V., Sinelnikov-Murylev, S., & Radygin, A. (2018). *Russian economy in 2017. Trends and OUTLOOKS.* Gaidar Institute Publishers ed. Moscow: Gaidar Institute for Economic Policy.

Naik, P., Poornima, B. G., & Reddy, Y. V. (2020). Measuring liquidity in Indian stock market: A dimensional perspective. *PLoS ONE, 15*(9).

Pastor, L., & Stambaugh, R. (2003). Liquidity risk and expected stock returns. *Journal of Political Economy*, 642–685.

Roll, R. (1984). A simple implicit measure of the effective bid-ask spread in an efficient market. *The Journal of Finance, 4*, 1127–1139.

Sarr, A., & Lybek, T. (2002). *Measuring liquidity in financial markets* (IMF Working Papers, Issue 02/232).

Schestag, R., Schuster, P., & Uhrig-Homburg, M. (2016). Measuring liquidity in bond markets. *The Review of Financial Studies, 5*, 1170–1219.

Unger, R. (2016). *Traditional banks, shadow banks and the US credit boom: Credit origination versus financing* (Bundesbank Discussion Paper Series, Vol. 11).

Unger, R. (2018). *Revisiting the finance and growth nexus: A deeper look at sectors and instruments* (Bundesbank Discussion Paper Series, Vol. 55).

Villeroy de Galhau, F. (2016a). *Identifying various forms of savings in France. Speech at the 25th Parliamentary Conference on Savings, Paris.* [Online] Available at: https://www.bis.org/review/r160216e.htm [Accessed August 16, 2021].

Villeroy de Galhau, F. (2016b). *Savings glut, or investment deficit? Speech at "The future of savings" conference.* [Online] Available at: https://www.bis.org/review/r161109d.htm [Accessed August 20, 2021].

CHAPTER 8

The Impact of Macroeconomic Factors on Capital Adequacy of the Russian Banking Sector in the Context of Countercyclical Banking Regulation

Olga Miroshnichenko and *Maria Vyshkovskaia*

8.1 Introduction

The consequences of the global financial crisis of 2008–2009 were represented by the bankruptcy of many banks, including those of global importance, and in this regard, forced a significant revision of the regulatory and supervisory authorities' policy regarding the stability of the banking system. According to the Basel Committee on Banking Supervision (BCBS), the main reason for the banking sector crisis was the

O. Miroshnichenko (✉)
Tyumen State University, Tyumen, Russia
e-mail: o.s.miroshnichenko@utmn.ru

M. Vyshkovskaia
Citibank, Moscow, Russia

A. Karminsky and M. Stolbov (eds.), *Systemic Financial Risk*,
https://doi.org/10.1007/978-3-031-54809-3_8

aggressive policy of banks, taking excessive unsecured risks and, therefore, the rapid growth of subprime debt during the periods of economic expansion.

In order to mitigate the consequences of future crises, there is a need for countercyclical regulation of bank capital adequacy as one of the most important indicators of the banking system stability, which is affected by many factors formed in the financial and non-financial sectors of the economy. This study aims to assess the impact of macroeconomic factors on banking capital adequacy as an important indicator of the stability of the Russian banking sector, considering the cyclical nature of the economy.

8.2 Bank Capital Adequacy, State of Economy and Credit Cycles

Capital Adequacy in the Assessment of Banking Stability

Capital adequacy is a widely recognized indicator of a bank's financial soundness. The international unification of approaches to the use of the banking capital adequacy ratio enshrined in the Basel Capital Agreement of 1988 (Basel I) and the further transformation of the Basel Accords, due to understanding of the causes of the global financial crisis and the following Great Recession, confirm the expediency of using this indicator as a primary one in banking regulation. The need for a major reform of the Basel I was discussed at the highest level—at the summit of the world's leading states G-8 in 2009. The final set of reforms was introduced as the Basel III Accord.

This transformation of the Basel Accords was embedded in the introduction of the concepts of core and additional regulatory capital, besides the traditional total capital adequacy (the so-called Cook's ratio), and their inclusion in the list of mandatory indicators recommended for supervision, as well as the implementation of a countercyclical approach in regulation. In addition, other indicators are being introduced into the supervisory toolkit, including the indicator of financial leverage. At the macro level, capital adequacy of the banking sector acts as a macroprudential indicator used by the supervisory authority for making regulatory decisions (Financial Stability Indicators, IMF).

The theory and practice of banking regulation and supervision has not developed an alternative indicator or indicators that are fully capable of replacing regulatory capital and its adequacy. Despite all the criticism, they are still the pillars of financial regulation. The results of relevant research suggest that the higher levels of capital adequacy ratios during crises contribute to safeguarding banking stability by increasing the ability to counter increased risks (Krüger et al., 2018; Mishchenko et al., 2021). In turn, strengthening of the banks' capital base is enhanced by stability of the macroeconomic situation and economic growth (Miroshnichenko, Tarasova, 2018). Indicators of total and Tier 1 capital adequacy ratios make it possible to reliably assess the vulnerability of the financial sector (Lepers, Serrano, 2020). Moreover, a study based on the data from the banking sectors of European countries showed an increase in the exposure to systemic risk of the largest banks, which is associated with the utilization of internal models for determining credit and market risk, affecting capital adequacy ratios (Gehrig, Iannino, 2021).

Thus, the development of the economic capital concept and the expansion of its use in the banking risk management did not lead to a widespread rejection of the Basel Accords application. Bank capital and its adequacy assessment remain the main instruments of banking regulation. Recently, requirements for the formation of so-called capital buffers suggested by the Basel III framework have been introduced into the regulatory practice by the national supervisory authorities all over the world. This new set of regulatory instruments includes countercyclical capital buffer. Its size is determined by each national regulator independently based on the current phase of the credit cycle, taking into account a number of macroeconomic indicators. It is generally accepted that the search for predictors of crises in order to adequately respond to threats in terms of the formation or liquidation of capital buffers should be based on the aggregate changes in credit indicators and asset prices (see, for example, Misina et al., 2008; Slingenberg et al., 2011).

Therefore, this study complements the existing literature by providing the evidence on predicting ability of such macroeconomic indicators in the Russian economy.

Banking Crisis Predictors

In recent years, based on the evidence from different countries, the need to take into account macroeconomic factors and the impact of credit cycles when forecasting and managing risks in financial markets was recognized (Donetskova, 2021; Karminsky, Dyachkova, 2020; Rahman et al., 2022). Previous studies find the interdependence among the real economy, the household sector and the financial sector. Namely, it is shown that the economic situation in the real sector can determine the stability of the banking system. Therefore, there is a potential opportunity to predict changes in the level of banking stability based on macroeconomic data.

Critical reviews of the literature aiming to identify the causes of banking crises are provided by Frankel and Saravelos (2012), Kauko (2014), Truong et al. (2021). Researchers pay attention to such macroeconomic and socio-economic factors that affect the banking sector and can act as predictors of banking crises, such as lending indicators, arrears on total loans and by counterparties (firms and households), indicators of banking sector balance sheet structure, exchange rate, stock market, unemployment, inflation, interest rates, monetary aggregates, GDP dynamics, sovereign debt indicators, Gini coefficient, real estate prices and others. At the same time, there is no consensus in the literature about the predictive ability of the factors mentioned above. Modern research tends to confirm the absence of common factors that can be universally used as indicators of future crises. Moreover, it is argued that the factors of different crises may vary, and it is very likely that other causes not studied in the existing literature will be relevant for future crises (Alessi, Detken, 2018; Vasicek et al., 2017). In this regard, the search for financial and macroeconomic variables that could be used to assess the stability of the banking sector, predict the crisis, identify phases of the credit cycle and implement countercyclical regulation continues. Finally, when examining the macroeconomic factors affecting the banking sector, one should not ignore the national characteristics determined by the structure of the economy (Allen Franklin et al., 2018; Gryzunova et al., 2019), in particular, the recognized impact of oil prices on financial sector indicators (Alsamara et al., 2019; Flori et al., 2021; Nazlioglu & Soytas, 2015). Thus, related studies develop approaches for the identification of indicators that are able to determine the stages of the credit cycle, assess the stability of the banking sector and predict, if not the crises themselves, then the buildup of imbalances and risks.

Indicators of Cyclicality in the Economy and the Financial Sector Affecting Banking Stability

In accordance with the studies emphasizing the importance of identifying the stages of credit cycles for financial stability (Arnold et al., 2012; Drehmann et al., 2011) and after the introduction of the countercyclical capital buffer, national regulators calculate and publish the indicators of credit cycle, in particular, credit gap indicators recommended by the BCBS. The countercyclical regulation introduced into the supervisory practice is at the stage of approbation. At this stage, there is no unified empirically confirmed approach to determining the stage of the credit cycle and the corresponding capital buffer size. To determine the stages of the credit cycle, such indicators as the growth rate of the ratio of loans to households and non-financial organizations adjusted for inflation and GDP, growth rates of housing loans to GDP, public debt-to-GDP ratio, real estate price-to-income ratio, real estate price gap, money supply gap, debt service ratio, annual growth rates of credit and real estate prices are used (see e.g. Alessi L., Detken C., 2018; Borio et al., 2020; Galati et al., 2016). It is recognized that indicators that are significant for predicting the state of the banking system vary due to country specific characteristics (Dawood et al., 2017; Vasicek et al., 2017). In this regard, there is a need to study the issue individually in each country or, at least, in groups of countries sharing similar economic and financial characteristics.

The credit-to-GDP gap indicator proposed by the Basel Committee has been criticized in the literature (Alessi & Detken, 2018; Repullo & Saurina, 2011). In response to the criticism, Drehmann and Tsatsaronis (2014) emphasize the informational nature of the indicator, which should not be used as a guide to action, but should help make right decisions, taking into account other factors recognized as important by regulator at a particular point of time. Based on this logic, the impact of various macroeconomic, financial and socio-economic indicators, including the indicators of the credit cycle, on the capital adequacy of the Russian banking sector is further examined.

Credit Cycle Indicators of the Bank of Russia

The composition of the national macroprudential indicators of the credit cycleby the Central Bank of the Russian Federation includes indicators of the banking sector, credit conditions and credit gap indicators.

The banking sector performance indicators include indicators of capital adequacy (total, as well as Common Equity Tier 1 and Additional Tier 1), and the ratio of loans to GDP. The composition of indicators, determining the conditions of lending, includes growth rate of loans to non-financial organizations and individuals, share of loans to non-financial organizations in foreign currency, share of overdue debt and non-performing loans to non-financial organizations and individuals. Credit gap indicators include "Credit gap (broad definition of a credit supply)", "Credit gap (narrow definition of a credit supply)", "Credit gap (narrow definition of a credit supply to non-financial organizations)", "Credit gap (loans provided to individuals)".

Obviously, the indicators themselves tend to correlate with each other. The relationship between overdue debt indicators and capital adequacy indicators is generally recognized, since overdue debt reflects the result of the realization of risks, primarily credit risks, leading to capital losses. It is of interest to identify the relationship between the credit gap and capital adequacy indicators. The credit gap as an indicator of the credit cycle should indicate the stages of growth, in which the banking sector accumulates imbalances and risks, and the stages of decline, when the accumulated imbalances and risks are materialized. The realized risks are reflected in the banking capital and its adequacy. To overcome the shortcomings of credit gap indicators identified by other authors, this paper also examines the feasibility of using other gap and general macroeconomic indicators that allow to assess the impact of macroeconomic factors on the capital adequacy of the Russian banking sector in the context of countercyclical banking regulation.

8.3 Data and Methodology

Data Description

The study adopts quarterly time series data of the Tier 1 capital adequacy ratio (N1.2) and the total bank's own funds (N1.0) indicators, as well as macroeconomic and socio-economic indicators that are considered potential regressors in the model. The time span for the study is from 2008 to 2019.

The period is determined by the availability of comparable data, primarily data on the credit gap indicators from the Bank of Russia, which have been published since April 2008.

The study does not include the data after the year 2020, since the period of the COVID-19 pandemic is characterized by an unprecedented situation for the global economy, the widespread introduction of lockdowns, breaking and rebuilding established economic and financial ties, and therefore requires a separate study. However, the results obtained in this study can serve as a basis for the further research. Since the statistical significance of nominal variables was established in the previous literature on banking sector studies (Gambera, 2000; Hanschel, Monnin, 2005), nominal variables are also used in this paper. The data sources used in the study are the official websites of the Federal State Statistics Service and the Central Bank of the Russian Federation.

Dependent Variables

Dependent variables are Tier 1 capital adequacy ratio (N1.2) and total capital adequacy ratio (N1.0). These capital adequacy ratios having a standardized calculation method and allowing to assess the aggregate level of capital adequacy of all credit institutions in the sector were found the most consistent with the purpose of the study. In addition, comparing the impact of macroeconomic indicators on different levels of capital helps develop a deeper understanding of the investigated research question.

Descriptive statistics of the dependent variables are presented in Appendix 1, the dynamics of actual annual averages is illustrated in Fig. 8.1.

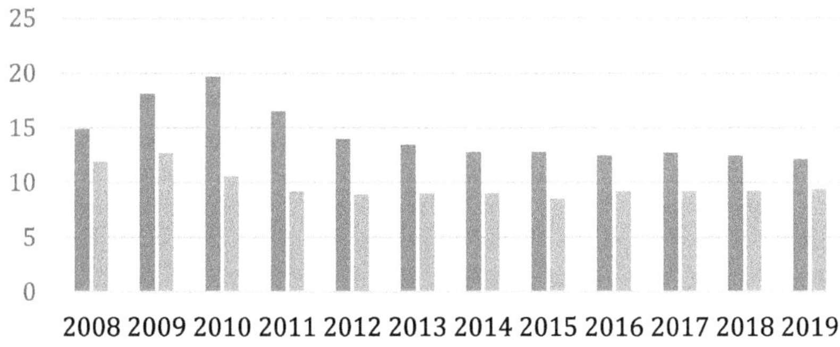

Fig. 8.1 Capital adequacy ratios dynamics, %

Based on Fig. 8.1, we can conclude that the capital adequacy ratios of the Russian banking sector are quite stable. At the same time, the total capital adequacy ratio is relatively more volatile than the Tier 1 capital adequacy ratio, which became especially evident during the global economic crisis that occurred in the Russian economy in 2008–2009.

Explanatory Variables
The database of macroeconomic variables potentially capable of explaining the dynamics of capital adequacy ratios relies on the existing studies, taking into account the availability of statistical data.

These variables include credit gap indicators published by the Bank of Russia and proposed by the BCBS as the main indicators to determine the size of the countercyclical capital premium. Furthermore, data on the indicators of household income, unemployment, oil prices and the stock market index proposed in a number of studies as alternative indicators of the credit cycle have been collected. The indicators determining the interaction between the real and financial sectors are represented by the volume of loans and deposits as well as by the ability of non-financial organizations and households to fulfill their debt obligations.

The study calculates the gap indicators for several macroeconomic ratios, such as the gap for the ratio of household debt-to-income, and others. The calculated gap indicators are determined as the difference between the current value of the indicator and its long-term trend. In order to extract the long-term trend from the time series, the one-sided Hodrick-Prescott filter with the parameter $\lambda = 400{,}000$ is used.

The other gap indicators for macroeconomic ratios (gap for the ratio of household debt-to-income and gap for the ratio of household income-to-housing price) have been computed by the authors. The calculated gap indicators are determined as the difference between the current value of the indicator and its long-term trend. In order to isolate the long-term trend from the time series, the one-sided Hodrick-Prescott filter with the parameter $\lambda = 400{,}000$ is used. It is recommended by the Basel Committee to extract the credit cycle and is utilized by the Bank of Russia (Basel Committee, 2010; Bank of Russia, 2019). Finally, as a control indicator determining the state of the financial sector, the volume of interbank lending is used.

Methodology

The research methodology involves estimating regression models based on time series data that explain the relationship between capital adequacy ratios and macroeconomic indicators of the non-financial sector.

The selection of explanatory variables for the final models is arranged in two stages. First, the presence of significant relationships between the explanatory variables is tested in order to mitigate the problem of multicollinearity. This effect can affect the reliability of the obtained coefficients and the quality of the models. Thus, if several correlated explanatory variables are identified, only one of them should be introduced into the model. During testing, a number of significant relationships between explanatory variables were found. In this regard, indicators with a correlation of more than 90% were combined into separate groups. The grouping of explanatory variables is presented in Appendix 2.

The first group is represented by the indicators of household income, the volume of household loans and deposits as well as housing prices. All of them are significantly correlated with each other. This suggests that the indicators of the banking services demand volume also indirectly gauge the size of the household income. It can also be concluded that demand and, accordingly, the price of housing are related to the household income. Despite the proximity of the increase in household loans per capita to the first group, it has a weaker correlation with other indicators of banking services demand and, for this reason, enters a separate group.

Furthermore, despite the conceptual connection between unemployment and household income, the correlation between these indicators appears rather weak and, when used together in the model, they can improve its explanatory power. Therefore, the unemployment rate indicator constitutes its own group.

As expected, there is a significant relationship between the grouped indicators of arrears. The importance of the oil price dynamics for economic growth in Russia (Ono, 2017) entails the inclusion of this indicator in the set of the explanatory variables. In addition to oil price, the fifth group also includes the stock market index dynamics. Credit gap indicators in broad and narrow definitions form the seventh group. The remaining indicators follow rather distinctive patterns. Thus, each of them can be included in the final model if there is a statistically significant relationship with the dependent variable.

At the next stage of regression models estimation, an indicator that has the highest correlation with the dependent variable is selected from each group. Thus, by identifying the strongest relationships between explanatory variables and capital adequacy ratios, we come up with two models.

The first model, in which the total capital adequacy ratio of banks acts as a dependent variable, includes six regressors:

$$\begin{aligned} N1.1_t &= \alpha + \beta_1 Household\,income_{t-1} \\ &+ \beta_2 NPL\,ratio_{t-1} + \beta_3 Unemployment\,rate_{t-1} \\ &+ \beta_4 Interbank\,loans\,ratio_{t-1} + \beta_6 Oil\ price_{t-1} \\ &+ \beta_7 Increase\,in\,loans\,to\,households\ per\ capita_{t-1} + \varepsilon_t \end{aligned} \quad (8.1)$$

where:

t - time period.

l - lag number of the variable.

The second model explaining the changes in the Tier 1 capital adequacy ratio is as follows:

$$\begin{aligned} N1.1_t &= \alpha + \beta_1 Household\,income_{t-1} + \beta_2 NPL\,ratio_{t-1} \\ &+ \beta_3 Unemployment\,rate_{t-1} + \beta_4 Interbank\,loans\,ratio_{t-1} \\ &+ \beta_5 Household\,income\,to\,hou\sin g\ price\,ratio\,gap_{t-1} \\ &+ \beta_6 Oil\ price_{t-1} \\ &+ \beta_7 Increase\,in\,loans\,to\,households\ per\ capita_{t-1} + \varepsilon_t \end{aligned} \quad (8.2)$$

where:

t - time period.

l - lag number of the variable.

The interbank loans indicator is calculated as the share of loans issued to other banks in total liabilities. We also use logarithms and apply lags to the explanatory variables, which allows us to test the predictive power of the model. The model uses robust standard errors to eliminate heteroscedasticity.

8.4 Empirical Results

This section presents the results of our empirical analysis. Table 8.1 presents the results for the first model, in which the dependent variable is the total capital adequacy ratio (N1.0). The table indicates that the basic conditions for the model quality are met. Four coefficients have a significance level of 1%. The coefficients of corporate and household NPL ratio and oil price are significant at the 5% level. The R-squared is 0.96. The reliability of the coefficients of the model is also verified by the absence of multicollinearity, as confirmed by the test results.

Lags of explanatory variables range from two quarters for the household income per capita to six quarters for the interbank lending indicator. The model shows that there is a statistically significant negative effect of household income and the growth rate of household loans per capita on the total capital adequacy ratio. The results also suggest that an increase

Table 8.1 Macroeconomic factors and total capital adequacy ratio model

Model 1	***N1.0***
Log household income per capita (−3)	−2.562***
	(0.592)
Unemployment rate (−2)	1.039***
	(0.176)
Corporate and household NPL rate	0.197**
	(0.091)
Interbank loans (−6)	0.484***
	(0.080)
Oil price	0.014**
	(0.006)
Loans to households per capita (growth rate)	−10.006***
	(2.385)
Constant	26.472***
	(5.839)
Observations	46
R-squared	0.958

Notes The table shows a regression model based on time series of quarterly data for the period 2008–2019. The dependent variable is represented by the total capital adequacy ratio. Three independent variables have lags (in brackets after the variable). For the variable Log household income per capita, the lag is 3 quarters. The Unemployment rate and Interbank loans variables have lags of 2 and 6 quarters, respectively. Interbank loans are calculated as the share of loans issued to other banks in total labilities. Robust standard errors of the variables are given in brackets. *, ** and *** denote the significance level of 10%, 5% and 1%, respectively in unemployment rate, non-performing loans, interbank lending and oil prices leads to a higher level of capital adequacy ratio. The explanation for the revealed relationships could be found in the following. The growth in household income is accompanied by an increase in lending and the subsequent buildup of imbalances and risks taken into account in the formula for calculating the total capital adequacy ratio, which determines the decrease in the value of the indicator. Unemployment as well as the increased arrears are the natural indicators for the banking sector that reflect the presence of difficulties in the economy.

The classical response of banks in such a situation is to reduce risks, which leads to a reduction in the denominator of the total capital adequacy ratio and an increase in the value of the indicator itself. In an effort to keep working assets on the balance sheet, banks are moving into a sector of less risky interbank lending that simultaneously generates income and does not pose a threat to liquidity.

The model presented in Table 8.2 determines the relationship between macroeconomic variables and Tier 1 capital adequacy ratio. In this model, six variables have a significance level of 1%, while the variable for growth in household loans per capita is significant at the 10% level.

As in the previous model, the variables of the household income per capita and the volume of interbank lending have lags. However, in this case, the lag of variables is one quarter, which indicates that the Tier 1 capital adequacy ratio reacts to the changes in these indicators faster than the similar indicator for total capital. In this model, non-performing loans ratio to households and enterprises has the largest lag which is 5 quarters.

The signs of the coefficients, and hence the direction of the relationship between the explanatory variables and capital adequacy ratios of different levels, also differ. Thus, unlike the first model, the volume of non-performing loans and the oil price negatively affect the Tier 1 capital adequacy ratio, while the increase in per capita household loans has a positive coefficient.

Thus, out of all the tested macroeconomic indicators, only the variable of household income per capita has lags in the two obtained models, which indicates a high predictive potential of this indicator. Traditional approaches to the banking sector studies suggest a direct relationship between the dynamics of household income and the financial well-being of the economy as a whole and the financial sector in particular, which, to a large extent, is expressed in increasing the level of capital adequacy. However, as a result of the recent global financial crisis (GFC), a revision

Table 8.2 Macroeconomic factors and Tier 1 capital adequacy ratio model

Model 2	*N1.2*
Log household income per capita (−1)	−2.691***
	(0.906)
Unemployment rate	0.616***
	(0.211)
Corporate and household NPL rate (−5)	−0.221***
	(0.042)
Interbank loans (−1)	0.314***
	(0.064)
Household income-to-housing price ratio gap	12.798***
	(3.494)
Oil price	−0.014***
	(0.005)
Loans to households per capita (growth rate)	6.829*
	(3.609)
Constant	26.642***
	(7.778)
Observations	47
R-squared	0.890

Note The table shows a regression model based on time series of quarterly data for the period 2008–2019. The dependent variable is represented by the Tier 1 capital adequacy ratio. Three independent variables have lags (in brackets after the variable). For the variable Log household income per capita, the lag is 1 quarter. The variables Corporate and household NPL rate and Interbank loans have lags of 5 and 1 quarter, respectively. Interbank loans are calculated as the share of loans issued to other banks in total labilities. Robust standard errors of the variables are given in brackets. *, ** and *** denote the significance level of 10%, 5% and 1%, respectively

of the traditional approach is required. In case of the GFC, there was no decrease in income, but at the same time, the risks of lending to individuals increased sharply, which was due to an ease in the requirements for the solvency of mortgage borrowers. Thus, the inverse relationship between the expansion of lending volumes and the level of capital adequacy is explained by the cyclicality of lending (Borio, Lowe, 2002; Demirgüç-Kunt et al., 2006). The expansion of lending contributes to the accumulation of imbalances and the realization of risks associated with an increase in the volume of non-performing loans and credit losses, leading to a decrease in the level of bank capital.

At the same time, there is evidence of cyclicality being inherent not only in the dynamics of the lending volume, but also in the household income (Büyükkarabacak, Valev, 2010). It has been found that favorable economic conditions have a positive effect on household demand for banking services (Allen, Wood, 2006), which is reflected through banks' balance sheets. In this regard, it can be assumed that the indicator of household income is also a potential predictor of the level of capital adequacy in the banking sector. Based on the assumption that there is a time lag for households to build confidence in their financial position in the face of positive income dynamics and materialize this confidence in expanding interaction with credit institutions, it is reasonable to consider household income indicators as having predictive power for capital adequacy in addition to credit cycle indicators.

The results of the obtained model confirm the above assumptions. The household income variable has a negative coefficient. The lag for this variable is three quarters in the first model and one quarter in the second model. This suggests that a commensurate decline in the level of capital adequacy occurs soon after the increase in the household income per capita.

Another macroeconomic indicator that has shown its predictive ability in the models is unemployment rate. Unlike the household income per capita, the unemployment rate has a lag only in the model in which the dependent variable is the total capital adequacy ratio (Model 1). The positive coefficient of the variable of this indicator also supports the hypothesis that economic growth, accompanied by a decrease in unemployment, is a precursor of a credit boom and subsequent recession, which in turn implies a decrease in capital adequacy in the banking sector.

The bigger lag of the household income per capita compared to the unemployment rate indicates its ability to provide an earlier warning. At the same time, comparing the two models, we can also see that the Tier 1 capital adequacy ratio responds to the changes in the mentioned macroeconomic indicators faster than the total capital adequacy ratio. Changes in household income anticipate commensurate changes in Tier 1 capital adequacy by only one quarter, while the unemployment rate completely loses its predictive ability. This may be explained by the fact that it is easier for banks to maintain the level of total capital by increasing its lower quality sources, such as subordinate loans. Tier 1 capital, containing higher quality sources, including a significant fraction of bank profits, however, is more sensitive to macroeconomic changes. It is notable that there is a significant difference in the predictive ability of the share of non-performing loans variable for capital adequacy ratios of different levels. However, in the case of the total capital adequacy ratio, the coefficient of the variable has a positive sign, which contradicts the economic sense. Based on this, it can be assumed that the mentioned problem of the presence of lower quality sources in total capital distorts the impact of the share of non-performing loans on the total capital adequacy ratio of banks and does not allow for its reliable assessment. At the same time, the negative coefficient and the lag of 5 quarters indicate a high predictive ability of the share of non-performing loans variable in relation to the Tier 1 capital adequacy ratio. Finally, it is worth noting the ability of the interbank lending volume indicator to predict changes in the level of capital adequacy. As expected, the positive dynamics in the interbank lending market anticipates a favorable financial situation in the banking sector, which is proxied by the growth of first the Tier 1 capital, and then that of the total capital. However, this indicator is the most sensitive to the endogeneity problem, since it is itself an indicator of the financial sector. It is possible that it is the increase in the level of capital adequacy that causes the expansion of interbank lending.

It should be stated that the final model has limitations. First, the explanatory variables included in the model largely, but not fully, explain the dynamics of the capital adequacy levels in the banking sector. They are not the only factors underlying the banking sector. Other factors can also affect the change in the capital adequacy ratios, but they are not included in the model.

8.5 Conclusions

The study revealed significant relationships between explanatory variables—macroeconomic indicators, and the indicators of the capital adequacy of Russian banks, as well as determined the ability of these indicators to predict changes in the level of capital adequacy in the Russian banking sector.

The results of the empirical analysis carried out with the aid of regression models suggest that there is a negative relationship between household income per capita and the level of capital adequacy of banks, which confirms the hypothesis of cyclical lending.

The models also confirm the predictive ability of household income per capita, unemployment rate, non-performing loans ratio and interbank lending volume indicators. At the same time, the indicator of household income per capita appears more universal for predicting the capital adequacy of banks, since it predicts changes in the different levels of capital, while unemployment rate and the share of non-performing loans could be used to predict only the total capital adequacy level. Although the indicator of interbank lending reveals a good predictive ability in relation to both indicators of capital adequacy, we suggest using it with caution, as it may be subject to the endogeneity problem due to the fact that it reflects the behavior of the banks themselves. In conclusion, the analysis showed that it is more difficult to predict changes in Tier 1 capital adequacy than the dynamics of total capital adequacy. The N1.2 coefficient reacts to the changes in macroeconomic indicators faster by two quarters in the case of household income and unemployment rate and by 5 quarters in the case of interbank loans than the N1.0. Thus, the targeted level of bank capital is of great importance in forecasting its adequacy. Apparently, banks use different strategies when targeting the internal amount of capital of different levels, based on the current economic situation. Namely, it is easier for banks to maintain capital adequacy by attracting lower quality sources in a stagnant economy. This demonstrates the importance of timely accumulation of capital buffers, consisting of the highest quality sources, in favorable economic conditions and confirms the need for countercyclical regulation of bank capital.

Thus, the results of the study are relevant for timely identification of instability in the national banking sector and limiting banks' exposure to increased risks by adjusting the requirements for their capital adequacy, which not only allows the banking sector to accumulate a capital cushion, but also mitigates the adverse effects of financial instability.

Appendix 1: Summary Statistics

Variables	*Mean*	*Median*	*Standard deviation*	*Minimum*	*Maximum*
N1.0	14.311	13.300	2.534	11.733	20.900
N1.2	9.695	9.233	1.315	8.133	13.300
Household income (per capita)	19,041.280	18,619.700	10,668.080	3062.000	41,111.200

(continued)

(continued)

Variables	*Mean*	*Median*	*Standard deviation*	*Minimum*	*Maximum*
Loans to households (per capita)	1257.735	918.034	1089.500	9.211	3727.734
Household deposits (per capita)	1874.663	1456.091	1528.309	77.900	4937.302
Housing	42,347.710	52,961.620	18,414.770	7300.880	59,997.540
Loans to households per capita (growth rate)	0.087	0.062	0.093	−0.061	0.349
Corporate and household NPL rate	6.056	6.285	3.936	1.293	13.112
Household NPL rate	7.036	6.518	5.156	1.118	17.523
Corporate NPL rate	4.747	5.411	2.873	0.976	9.212
Interbank loans	9.846	9.629	1.982	6.428	14.973
Oil price	65.322	62.773	29.844	19.803	126.323
RTSI	1127.830	1142.798	518.177	169.250	2295.240
Unemployment rate	6.696	6.200	1.576	4.400	10.600
Credit gap (broad definition)	−3.336	−4.045	5.559	−11.306	9.467
Credit gap (narrow definition)	−2.545	−2.627	2.746	−6.433	3.362
Household debt-to-income ratio gap	0.000	0.000	0.003	−0.007	0.010
Household income-to-housing price ratio gap	0.000	0.012	0.073	−0.155	0.131

Appendix 2: Explanatory Variable Groups

Group 1
Household income (per capita)
Loans to households (per capita)

(continued)

(continued)

Household deposits (per capita)
Housing price
Group 2
Loans to households per capita (growth rate)
Group 3
Corporate and household NPL rate
Household NPL rate
Corporate NPL rate
Group 4
Interbank loans
Group 5
Oil price
RTSI
Group 6
Unemployment rate
Group 7
Credit gap (broad definition)
Credit gap (narrow definition)
Group 8
Household debt-to-income ratio gap
Group 9
Household income-to-housing price ratio gap

References

Alessi L., & Detken C. (2018). Identifying excessive credit growth and leverage. *Journal of Financial Stability* (36): 39–52. https://doi.org/10.1016/j.jfs.2017.06.005

Allen Franklin, Laura Bartiloro, Xian Gu. (2018). Oskar Kowalewski Does economic structure determine financial structure? *Journal of International Economics*, 114: 389–409. https://doi.org/10.1016/j.jinteco.2018.08.004

Allen, W. A., & Wood, G. (2006). Defining and achieving financial stability. *Journal of Financial Stability, 2*(2), 152–172. https://doi.org/10.1016/j.jfs.2005.10.001

Alsamara, M., Mrabet, Z., Jarallah, S., & Barkat, K. (2019, August). The switching impact of financial stability and economic growth in Qatar: Evidence from an oil-rich country. *The Quarterly Review of Economics and Finance, 73*, 205–216. https://doi.org/10.1016/j.qref.2018.05.008

Arnold, B. R., Borio, C., Ellis, L., & Moshirian, F. (2012). Systemic risk, Basel III, global financial stability and regulation. *Journal of Banking & Finance, 36*(12), 3123–3124. https://doi.org/10.1016/j.jbankfin.2012.07.025

Borio, C., Drehmann, M., & Xia, F. D. (2020, December). Forecasting recessions: The importance of the financial cycle. *Journal of Macroeconomics, 66*, 103258.

Borio C., & Lowe P. (2002). Asset prices, financial and monetary stability: exploring the nexus. *BIS Working Papers*. No 114. Bank for International Settlements.

Büyükkarabacak, B., & Valev, N. T. (2010). The role of household and business credit in banking crises. *Journal of Banking & Finance*, 34 (6): 1247–1256. https://doi.org/10.1016/j.jbankfin.2009.11.022

Dawood, M., Horsewood, N., & Strobel, F. (2017). Predicting sovereign debt crises: An Early Warning System approach. *Journal of Financial Stability*, (28): 16–28.

Demirgüç-Kunt, A., Detragiache, E., & Tressel, T. (2006). Banking on the principles: Compliance with basel core principles and bank soundness. *Journal of Financial Intermediation*, 17 (4): 511–542.

Donetskova, O.Yu. (2021). Interbank competition in the Russian banking market. *Finance: Theory and Practice*, 25 (1): 143–156. https://doi.org/10.26794/2587-5671-2021-25-1-143-156

Drehmann, M., Claudio, Borio., & Kostas, Tsatsaronis. (2011, December). Anchoring countercyclical capital buffers: The role of credit aggregates. *International Journal of Central Banking*. https://www.ijcb.org/journal/ijcb11q4a8.pdf

Drehmann, M., & Tsatsaronis, K. (2014). The credit-to-GDP gap and countercyclical capital buffers: questions and answers. *BIS Quarterly Review*. https://www.bis.org/publ/qtrpdf/r_qt1403g.pdf

Financial Soundness Indicators (FSIs): IMF. https://data.imf.org/?sk=51B096FA-2CD2-40C2-8D09-0699CC1764DA

Flori, A., Pammolli, F., & Spelta, A. (2021, June). Commodity prices co-movements and financial stability: A multidimensional visibility nexus with climate conditions. *Journal of Financial Stability, 54*, 100876.

Frankel, J., & Saravelos, G. (2012, July). Can leading indicators assess country vulnerability? Evidence from the 2008–09 global financial crisis. *Journal of International Economics*, 87 (2): 216–231 https://doi.org/10.1016/j.jinteco.2011.12.009

Galati, G. (2016, August). Irma Hindrayanto, Siem Jan Koopman, Marente Vlekke Measuring financial cycles in a model-based analysis: Empirical evidence for the United States and the euro area. *Economics Letters, 145*, 83–87. https://doi.org/10.1016/j.econlet.2016.05.034

Gambera, M. (2000, April). Simple forecasts of bank loan quality in the business cycle. *Emerging Issues Series*. Supervision and Regulation Department. Federal Reserve Bank of Chicago.

Gehrig, T., & Iannino, M. C. (2021, August). Did the basel process of capital regulation enhance the resiliency of European banks? *Journal of Financial Stability*, 55: 100904. https://doi.org/10.1016/j.jfs.2021.100904

Gryzunova, N. V., Pyatanova, V. I., Manuylenko, V. V., & Ordov, K. V. (2019). Models of credit limit-setting for companies as means of encouraging competitiveness. *Entrepreneurship and Sustainability Issues, 7*(1), 615–625. https://doi.org/10.9770/jesi.2019.7.1(43)

Guidance for national authorities operating the countercyclical capital buffer. (2010). Basel Committee—Basel, Switzerland. https://www.bis.org/publ/bcbs187.htm

Hanschel, E., & Monnin, P. (2005). Measuring and forecasting stress in the banking sector: evidence from Switzerland. *BIS Working Papers*. No 22., pp. 431–449. Bank for International Settlements.

Karminsky, A. M., & Dyachkova, N. F. (2020). Empirical study of the relationship between credit cycles and changes in credit ratings. *Journal of the New Economic Association*, 4 (48).

Kauko, K. (2014). How to foresee banking crises? *A Survey of the Empirical Literature Economic Systems, 38*(3), 289–308. https://doi.org/10.1016/j.ecosys.2014.01.001

Krüger, S., Rösch, D., & Scheule, H. (2018). The impact of loan loss provisioning on bank capital requirements. *Journal of Financial Stability, 36*, 114–129. https://doi.org/10.1016/j.jfs.2018.02.009

Lepers, E., & Serrano, A. S. (2000, January). Decomposing financial (in)stability in emerging economies. *Research in International Business and Finance*, 51: 101068 https://doi.org/10.1016/j.ribaf.2019.101068

Miroshnichenko, O. S., & Tarasova, A. N. (2018). Sources of regional banks capitalization. *Ekonomika Regiona [economy of Region], 14*(1), 303–314. (in Russ.).

Svitlana, M., Naumenkova, S., Mishchenko, V., & Dorofeiev, D. (2021). Innovation risk management in financial institutions. *Investment Management and Financial Innovations, 18*(1), 190–202. https://doi.org/10.21511/imfi.18(1).2021.16

Misina, M., Pierre, St-Amant, & Greg, Tkacz. (2008, December). Credit, asset prices, and financial stress in Canada Reports Bank of Canada. *Financial System Review*. https://www.bankofcanada.ca/wp-content/uploads/2012/01/fsr-1208-misina.pdf

Nazlioglu, S., Soytas, U., & Gupta, R. (2015). Oil prices and financial stress: A volatility spillover analysis. *Energy Policy, 82*, 278–288.

Ono, S. (2017). Financial development and economic growth Nexus in Russia. *Russian Journal of Economics, 3*(3), 321–332. https://doi.org/10.1016/j.ruje.2017.09.006

Rahman, Md. L. (2022, January). Victor Troster, Gazi Salah Uddin, Muhammad Yahya Systemic risk contribution of banks and non-bank financial institutions across frequencies: The Australian experience. *International Review of Financial Analysis, 79*, 101992. https://doi.org/10.1016/j.irfa.2021.101992

Repullo, Rafael and Saurina Salas, Jesus, The Countercyclical Capital Buffer of Basel III: A Critical Assessment (2011, March). Available at SSRN: https://ssrn.com/abstract=1794894

Slingenberg, Jan, Willem., & de Haan, Jakob and de Haan, Jakob, Forecasting Financial Stress (2011, April 1). De Nederlandsche Bank Working Paper No. 292, Available at SSRN: https://ssrn.com/abstract=1951800 or https://doi.org/10.2139/ssrn.1951800

Truong C., Sheen, J., Trück, S., & Villafuerte, J. (2021, May 19). Early warning systems using dynamic factor models: An application to Asian economies. *Journal of Financial Stability, 58*, 100885. https://doi.org/10.1016/j.jfs.2021.100885

Vašíček, B., Žigraiová, D., Hoeberichts, M., Vermeulen, R., Šmídková, K., & Haan, J. (2017). Leading indicators of financial stress: New evidence. *Journal of Financial Stability*, (28): 240–257. https://doi.org/10.1016/j.jfs.2016.05.005

Determining the credit cycle phase and establishing a national countercyclical capital buffer. Consultation paper. Bank of Russia. 2019 (in Russ.) http://www.cbr.ru/content/document/file/72455/consultation_paper_190617.pdf.

CHAPTER 9

Assessing the Probability of Default During the COVID-19 Pandemic: The Case of Airlines

Elizaveta Markovskaya and Elena Smolina

9.1 Introduction

As defined by Kaufman (1995), systemic risk is the likelihood of an event that triggers a chain of counterparty defaults (domino effect). The idea of our research is related to the fact that for systemically important banks actively involved in financing large infrastructure projects with state participation, it makes sense to add a focus related to a more detailed analysis of the likelihood of insolvency and bankruptcy of large borrowers, taking into account their industry specifics, in order to timely prevent credit risks and thereby prevent a chain of defaults. Systemically important banks are the most important financial institutions on which the stability of the entire banking system depends. Since their bankruptcy can have serious consequences both for the banking system and for the economy

E. Markovskaya (✉) · E. Smolina
Department of Finance, National Research University
Higher School of Economics, Saint Petersburg, Russia
e-mail: emarkovskaya@hse.ru

A. Karminsky and M. Stolbov (eds.), *Systemic Financial Risk*,
https://doi.org/10.1007/978-3-031-54809-3_9

as a whole, their activities must comply with strict criteria determined by states and international financial organizations.

There are 13 systemically important banks in Russia. Systemically important credit institutions are required to comply with additional capital adequacy requirements in accordance with Basel III. Thus, the Bank of Russia established a capital adequacy premium for systemic importance from January 1, 2016 at 0.15% of risk-weighted assets, with an annual increase to reach 1% (from January 1, 2020). For example, now the minimum size of the capital adequacy ratio (N1.0) of the bank is 8%. Taking into account the minimum requirements for the capital adequacy premium (2.5%) and the minimum systemic importance (1%), the N1.0 ratio for systemically important credit institutions should be at least 11.5%.

In our opinion, focusing on large borrowers and modeling the likelihood of insolvency and bankruptcy as a part of the system for monitoring and controlling systemic risks are very important for Russian banks, which, as a rule, assess the creditworthiness of potential borrowers and monitor the financial conditions of current borrowers from the point of view of general standards and criteria. This is also becoming especially important because on January 1, 2022, systemically important banks will have to switch to a new standard for assessing the risk of large clients designed to prevent situations when the default of a large counterparty of the bank may lead to the insolvency of other clients. Market participants, in particular, will need to monitor related borrowers and assume that the risk of one such client is equal to the risk of the entire group. Russian banks are already obliged to calculate the borrower concentration ratio (N6). The new N30 standard will take into account the universe of credit requirements without weighing them up by risk level. It will be calculated as the ratio of all credit requirements to a client or a group of related clients to the amount of the bank's main capital, not the total capital. N30 will not be able to exceed 25% of equity. Banks will have to calculate the concentration ratio for all counterparties.

In this case, it is advisable to take into account the following:

1. that the well-known models for assessing the likelihood of insolvency and bankruptcy may not take into account the industry specifics and therefore may not "work" for companies in some industries.

2. New factors appear that are to be included in the model. For example, the pandemic opens up space for new research in the field of modeling and assessing the likelihood of bankruptcy.

We developed the research algorithm that can be used by banks to model the likelihood of bankruptcy for groups of major companies from certain industries.

The algorithm is as follows:

1. The existing basic models that assess the likelihood of bankruptcy in the analyzed industry have been determined.
2. Indicators have been identified that are significant for companies from these industries, which should be included in the model.
3. Model verification.
4. Determination of standard values (optimal and critical) indicators included in the model.
5. Integration of the model into the organizational and economic mechanism for assessing the creditworthiness of the bank.

Our research is based on a sample of European airline carriers in order to build a model to assess the likelihood of bankruptcy.

The pandemic caused serious problems for the most of businesses and the worst one is their bankruptcy. Speaking more precisely, world airline industry lost $328 billion (40% of the previous year's level) of revenues in the year 2021. Shares of airline companies dropped dramatically, and it is unknown when their quotes will return to the pre-crisis level. The most serious factor of the pandemic crisis is the uncertainty.

A lot of airlines all over the world faced the financial problems connected with the cancellation of flights and closure of borders and were forced to consider going bankrupt. Thus, in the current situation, one of the most important problems is the need of support from governments to maintain the solvency of the airlines. That is why, bankruptcy prediction is a very important issue not only for consumers, investors and governments but also for creditors and management of companies.

Against this backdrop, the goal of the current research is to develop the approaches and in particular, the model of the bankruptcy prediction for airline companies. The sample consists of the major players of European countries. The following are the main hypotheses of the current research.

H0: The existing global model of bankruptcy prediction of the European companies is inaccurate in the prediction of the European airlines' defaults.

H1: The existing model of bankruptcy prediction of the European airlines developed in 2012 retains its relevance.

H2: An increased probability of bankruptcy of the European airlines is directly connected with the decrease in the sales to total assets ratio.

Thus, to achieve the goal of this study, several stages of research will be performed:

1. To study the main approaches of bankruptcy prediction,
2. To select companies for the analysis,
3. To collect data for the analysis,
4. To calculate necessary financial indicators,
5. To build regression models of bankruptcy prediction,
6. To choose the model with the best predictive power,
7. To apply the new model to the data sample and to compare the results to the real position of the companies,
8. To define the normative values for all significant variables for this industry on the basis of the analysis conducted in the current research,
9. To develop the approach of bankruptcy prediction for the European airlines.

Thus, the object of this research is the European airlines, the subject—the approach to assessing the probability of bankruptcy.

During the current investigation, several methods of analysis were applied. First, we review several relevant research papers on the topic. Second, the necessary information was collected on the selected airlines. Third, the financial indicators for each company were calculated. Fourth, regression analysis was carried out using the Stata package. Fifth, a mathematical model for assessing the financial position was elaborated on the basis of selected significant indicators. Based on the model, normative values (thresholds) for airlines were calculated. Finally, the computed thresholds were compared to normative values established in the international practice. As a result, based on the findings, the most effective algorithm for assessing the probability of European airlines' bankruptcy was developed.

9.2 Literature Review of Existing Models of Bankruptcy Prediction

The Concept of Bankruptcy and Global Bankruptcy Prediction Models

Bankruptcy risk is one of the types of financial risks as well as market, exchange rate, credit, liquidity risk and others. Bankruptcy means the situation of insolvency when the company cannot pay its debts and thus cannot survive among its competitors in the market. This inability can be reflected, for example, in the dismissal of its employees, low productivity and asset destruction (Aleksanyan & Huiban, 2016). In the global financial environment, the bankruptcy risk of the companies is measured by applying different models to assess the probability of the companies' bankruptcy in the nearest future. It is necessary to get this assessment timely both to investors to make right decisions and to managers to propose an appropriate anti-crisis policy. In addition, banks and rating agencies are interested in it (Ouenniche & Tone, 2017).

In the international practice, a lot of methods of bankruptcy prediction have been developed. Most of them are similar to Altman's Z-score or Ohlson's default model. But, all of them have their own disadvantages and limitations, which is the reason for the attempts to identify which method is the most effective and, speaking about financial institutions, which method can provide the most accurate assessment of the borrower's creditworthiness to minimize their possible risks and losses.

The first generation of bankruptcy prediction models includes those by Beaver (1966), Altman (1968) and Ohlson (1980), which represent 3 types of the most cited methods. The Beaver's model implies simple calculations and the comparison of companies' individual financial indicators during several periods of time to analyze their dynamics. Altman's and Ohlson's models are linear, and they allow to make a conclusion about the firm (healthy or bankrupt) on the basis of financial ratios. Altman's model is known as Z-score, which is based on the multiple discriminant analysis. Initially, Altman used 22 ratios in the model, from which 5 most significant indicators were chosen. Each coefficient has its own weight according to its impact on the probability of default and non-repayment of debtor's obligations. The main indicator is the coefficient of the default probability (Z), which can be calculated as:

$$\text{Z-score} = 0,012\,X1 + 0,014\,X2 + 0,033\,X3 + 0,006\,X4 + 0,999\,X5 \quad (9.1)$$

where:

X1 = Working capital/Total assets,
X2 = Retained Earnings/Total assets,
X3 = Earnings before interest and tax/Total assets,
X4 = Market value equity/Book value of total debt,
X5 = Sales/Total assets.

This model has the predictive power of 95% for 1-year period and 82% for 2-year period.

Altman's model was improved repeatedly and in 1993, it was optimized by change of the weights and the use of the book value instead the market one in X4:

$$\text{Z2-score} = 0,717\,X1 + 0,847\,X2 + 3,107\,X3 - 0,420\,X4 + 0,998\,X5 \quad (9.2)$$

The meaning of Z2 > 2,9 means the Safe zone for the company, 1.23 < Z2 < 2,9 Grey zone and Z2 < 1,23 the high probability of bankruptcy (Distress zone). In 2006, Aziz and Dar conducted a study, in which they tried to define which model was the most popular in 89 papers in 10 countries from 1968 to 2003 and it was precisely Altman's Z-score.

Ohlson's model is one of the most famous representatives of the logistic regression (LR) approach and it can be provided as a sigmoid function: $f(x) = 1/(1+e^{-x})$ with the binary output which can provide a conclusion if the company is close to bankruptcy or not. This model has the predictive power around 94%.

Nowadays, there is an abundance of different models and there are disputes in the scientific literature about their relevance, efficiency and the scope of application. Thus, for example, Ashraf et al. (2019) consider that Altman's model is very useful in predicting the bankruptcy in emerging markets. Elviani et al. (2020) conclude that the models created by Altman, Ohlson, Zmijevski and Springate are accurate in the prediction of the financial distress of the Indonesian trade companies. Salehi and Pour (2016) consider that traditional prediction models can be applied only to several industries. Shonfeld et al. (2018) and Slefendorfas (2016) argue that these models cannot be used to provide the accurate prediction of possible distress of modern companies because of the independence of businesses and changing economic environment. The defined advantages and limitations of the several existing models are shown in Table 9.1.

Thus, all models have their own advantages and limitations. On the one hand, all traditional models are based on the simple calculations of several linear indicators which capture a company's financial results. Alaka et al. (2018) state that even though MDA are less accurate than neural network models, due to more simple calculations, they are more efficient than alternative models. From the point of view of Ul Hassan et al. (2017), MDA studies only the dependence of linear indicators and probability of bankruptcy, but changes in the economic environment are much more complicated. Also, in the scientific literature, there are a lot of discussions about the number of indicators which can be used in bankruptcy models to provide the most accurate prediction. One of the most famous investigations was made by Tomczak and Radosinski (2017). They conclude that the optimal number of financial indicators in bankruptcy models is from 3 to 5 indicators, while adding more of them decreases the accuracy of models. The conclusion by Fedorova et al. (2016) states that the most efficient models are those that can be applied to the specific industry and they can be different according to the country and the economic sector. Glezakos et al. (2010) consider that logistic regression models are the most efficient as they can be adapted to the economic environment. The opinions about neural networks models are rather distinctive.

Some economists, e.g. Belas et al. (2017), argue that these models can provide more useful information than traditional models. In contrast, others like Bredart (2014) conclude that using such models per se decreases the accuracy of the prediction and, as a disadvantage, he points out that these models are very data- and time-intensive.

Although there are many different models of bankruptcy prediction, they all tend to have quite similar explanatory variables. Du Jardin (2009) points out that there are 3 types of variables usually used in bankruptcy models which characterize:

Table 9.1 Advantages and limitations of models of bankruptcy prediction

Bankruptcy prediction models		*Advantages*	*Limitations*
Traditional	MDA (Models of discriminant analysis) (Altman, 1968; Edmister, 1972; Fulmer et al., 1984; Springate, 1978)	+High accuracy +Simple calculations +Long-lasting usage in practice	– Dependence of only linear indicators is analyzed – Macroeconomic changes, company's financial position, trends of development are not considered – The most accurate assessment can be achieved only for short period (mostly, 1 year) – Models are usually unrelated to the company's sector and its features
	Logistic regression models (Chesser, 1974; Ohlson, 1980; Zavgren, 1985)	+Considering the economic environment	– Similar to MDA – Accuracy of these models for the period more than 1 year is lower than MDA
Alternative	Neural networks models (Iturriaga & Sanz, 2015)	+High accuracy +considering company's specific features +Possibility of usage of complex non-linear functions and broad sets of composite data	– Less studied and reliable than traditional models – Special computer software is needed, which increases the company's costs – Difficulties in defining the most accurate neural network

Source Authors' elaboration

1. Firm's financial position through the calculation of different indicators and variables which reflect firm's structure, strategy, management, etc.
2. Company's economic environment through the indicators related to it in general (like interest rate) or to the whole industry.
3. Information from financial markets to evaluate bankruptcy risk.

Du Jardin (2009) thoroughly surveyed 190 studies on bankruptcy prediction models and identified the most widespread variables, which are shown in the Table 9.2.

The most used variable in the sample of models analyzed by Du Jardin (2009) is financial ratios: 93% of studies include financial indicators, nearly 53% of them are based only on this type of variable and 78% include this one along with other types of variables. But, there is an opinion that it is important to evaluate the size of the company to analyze its ratios and compare them to other firms' indicators. Thus, for example, Gupta (1969) points out that the bigger the company is, the higher are the profitability and the liquidity ratios and the lower the leverage and turnover ratios. Some economists, like Horrigan (1983), assert that the size of the company is a very important financial characteristic, and it should be considered in the bankruptcy prediction model.

Other 5 types of variables are rarely used in models in comparison to financial ratios. The second type on the list is a statistical variable. This type presents the mathematical or statistical functions of financial variables like logarithm, mean, variance, etc. to standardize data. The calculation of logarithm of total assets is widely adopted in bankruptcy prediction. Then come variation variables which allow to analyze the position of the firm in dynamics. The next are non-financial variables which present quantitative and qualitative indicators that can broaden the field of bankruptcy prediction by assessing the quality of firm management, position in the market,

Table 9.2 The most common variables of the existing bankruptcy models

The most used variables in bankruptcy prediction models	
Variables	*Frequency of use (%)*
Financial indicator (ratio)	93
Statistical variable (variance, mean, logarithm, standard deviation, etc.) calculated with financial ratios	28
Variation variable (changes of financial ratios over different time periods)	14
Non-financial variable (company's: long-term strategy, market share, size, etc. or its environment's features: interest rate, sector profitability, availability of loans, etc.)	13
Market variable (ratio related to stock price or return)	6
Financial variable (data from financial reports)	5

Source Du Jardin (2009)

size, availability of funds, the current situation of the sector, etc. The so-called market variables are used in 6% of models and they are based on the stock prices or returns. Finally, standard accounting items are used in 5% of models, containing information from financial statements and reports like the size of total assets, inventories, debt, etc. They can be used alone or to calculate financial ratios.

The most common indicators in bankruptcy models, namely financial ratios, are used not because of their predictive power, but because of their economic nature. Also, this information is easy to get in comparison to market information which is available only for publicly traded firms. A lot of studies have been done to compare models to different types of used variables. Keasey and Watson (1987) conclude that the models with both financial and non-financial indicators are more accurate than the models which use only one of these types of variables. Besides, models with ratios outperform those with only non-financial indicators. Lussier (1995) concludes that models with only qualitative variables lag behind in prediction because they identified healthy companies with the probability of only 73% and distressed firms with 65%. Atiya (2001) pointed out that models with financial ratios gave more accurate results than models with market variables. Pérez (2002) and Pompe and Bilderbeek (2005) concluded that absolute values had the more predictive power than their variations over time.

Review of the Approaches to Predicting Bankruptcy in the European Countries

In this part of the study, the approaches to assessing the probability of bankruptcy are reviewed. The first approach was proposed by Alaminos et al. (2016) who studied 440 companies (bankrupt and solvent) of different industries in Europe, Asia and America and found that the consideration of the regional factor increased the accuracy of bankruptcy prediction. That is, they provided models for each region and a unified global model for all of them and concluded that the factors which influenced the probability of distress were not the same in the different regions and that the global model could assess it less accurately than the models which were specified for a specific region.

For instance, the model based on the sample of European companies, according to their research, is as follows:

$$P = -1,465 + 1,852 * X1 + 2,166 * X2 - 16,299 * X3 + 0,803 * X4 + 3,468 * X5 \quad (9.3)$$

where

P—the probability of bankruptcy (binary variable, 1-bankrupt, 0-solvent),
X1—Working Capital/Total assets,
X2—Retained earnings/Total assets,
X3—EBIT/Total assets,
X4—Sales/Total assets,
X5—Total debt/Total assets.

This result means that higher the indicators X1, X2, X4, X5 are, the higher the probability of distress is. The connection between X3 and P is negative. Also, Current assets/Current liabilities and Current assets/Total assets ratios were calculated, but they were defined as insignificant concerning the European companies.

The second approach was proposed by Lee and Hooy (2012) who studied airline companies in Europe, Asia and Northern America from 1990 to 2010. They used 5-factor asset pricing model in their analysis, which implied the calculation of these indicators:

X1—the size of total assets,
X2—quick liquidity ratio,
X3—return on assets,
X4—total debt to total assets,
X5—operational leverage (change of EBIT divided by change of Sales),
X6—the change of EBIT (%),
X7—operating lease costs.

Lee and Hooy (2012) concluded that risk of bankruptcy of the European airlines had a positive relationship with the operational leverage, but a negative one with the EBIT growth. It is important to notice that only one indicator (Total debt/Total assets) is the same in the global approach and in the methodology aimed at airlines' bankruptcy prediction. This result proves that bankruptcy prediction is a very complicated task which depends not only on the region, but also on the industry of the companies.

9.3 Materials and Method: Development of the Approaches of Bankruptcy Prediction of the European Airlines in a Pandemic

Data and Methodology

In the current research, 8 European airline companies (6 of them still operating and 2 bankrupt) are analyzed. The list of the companies is provided below in Table 9.3. The major players of the European airline industry were selected since their bankruptcy could produce the strongest adverse effect on the economy of the European region and their respective country. Also, the motivation behind the companies' selection was the availability of all necessary data. The data were borrowed from the «Thomson Reuters Eikon» for a 5-year period, from 2016 to 2020 (for bankrupt companies—till the year when they filed for bankruptcy).

The dependent variable of our model is binary and denotes the probability of bankruptcy (P). For already bankrupt companies, it is equal 0, for still operating, 1. The model will represent the mathematical expression of several financial indicators (independent variables) with their own weights. If the result exceeds 1, it means that the probability of the firm's bankruptcy is low, or otherwise, the company's position is sustainable. If

Table 9.3 List of the companies

	Company		
Region	*Not bankrupt*	*Bankrupt*	*Year of bankruptcy*
Europe	Deutch Lufthansa	Air Berlin	2017
	Aegean Airlines	Monarch Airlines	2017
	Air France-KLM		
	Finnair		
	Ryanair		
	Norwegian air		

Source Made by the authors

the result is less than 1, it means that the company is not stable, and it has a high probability of distress.

The independent variables used in the research are divided into 3 groups. First, there is a group of indicators from the existing global model of bankruptcy prediction of the European countries, proposed by Alaminos in 2016. Thus, these indicators will be used to test if the global model is significant for the specific industry, in our case, airline companies, or it is more suitable to assess every industry separately to create a model with higher predictive power which accounts for the features of the specific industry. As independent variables, we adopt all the ratios calculated by Alaminos, including:

X1—Current assets/Current liabilities,
X2—Working Capital/Total assets,
X3—EBIT/Total assets,
X4—Sales/Total assets,
X5—Total debt/Total assets,
X6—Current assets/Total assets,
X7—Retained earnings/Total assets.

The second group of indicators, or Z-group, is borrowed from Lee's model specified for airline companies. It encompasses the following ratios:

Z1—the size of total assets,
Z2—quick liquidity ratio,
Z3—return on assets,
Z4—operational leverage,
Z5—the change of EBIT.

Finally, the third group integrates the indicators which can lead to the instability of the airlines but do not enter the previous groups. Namely, both models considered do not take into account turnover ratios, mainly accounts receivable and accounts payable turnover ratios (in days). These indicators can influence the probability of distress because their high levels or the increases of the deferral of repayments mean that customers are not able to pay for the company's services in time or the company cannot pay to its creditors, which means that the company certainly faces financial problems. Besides, total equity/total assets ratio can show how well the company is equipped with its own funds. Finally, return on assets ratio can be useful in bankruptcy prediction as the indicator indicates how efficiently the company utilizes its assets. Overall, the proposed ratios can constitute the Y-group:

Y1—Accounts receivable turnover,
Y2—Accounts payable turnover,
Y3—Total equity/Total assets,
Y4—Return on assets (ROA).

Descriptive Statistics

For all the selected airlines and the 17 indicators from groups X, Y, Z, the descriptives are calculated for the 5-year period from 2016 to 2020.

They are presented on Fig. 9.1. It can be noted that the greatest standard deviations and spreads between maximum and minimum values are observed in variables Y1, Y2, Z1, Z3, Z4 and Z5. Probably, some of these differences can be explained by the financial position of the companies (bankrupt or not), the difference in the size of the companies (for Z1) or settlement terms (for Y1, Y2), etc.

To define more precisely, if the standard deviation can be explained by the financial position, separate tables of descriptive statistics for both bankrupt and solvent companies have been built.

Descriptive statistics of operating companies are presented on Fig. 9.2 It can be established that, in general, the standard deviations do not vary significantly, except for the small decrease of Y1 and Y2, which means that the great spreads between minimum and maximum values of the indicators are unlikely to arise because of bankruptcy.

Concerning already bankrupt companies (Fig. 9.3), the greatest standard deviations are shown in Y1, Y2, Z3 and Z4. Thus, one can conclude that the descriptive statistics are not sufficiently informative and do not allow to make any clear-cut conclusions or predictions in case of the present study.

Variable	Obs	Mean	Std. Dev.	Min	Max
X1	32	.9049609	.4501604	.1746032	1.858934
X2	32	-.0795802	.2545807	-1.124153	.1676867
X3	32	-.0135852	.2174273	-.9173292	.1556255
X4	32	.8274943	.5682608	.0695652	2.865937
X5	32	.3769945	.1926466	.0313253	1.008892
X6	32	.3441918	.18434	.0316885	.6988984
X7	32	-.0112883	.4357729	-1.826949	.3299213
Y1	32	21.55732	20.45882	1.129681	111.84
Y2	32	28.68447	22.53969	3.195374	87.69
Y3	32	.1239859	.3320133	-1.062927	.4080908
Y4	32	-.0242864	.2008767	-.82	.2177686
Z1	32	17.87149	15.92057	.4416742	48.56
Z2	32	.5031625	.3592472	.0692063	1.734587
Z3	32	-1.523661	5.780311	-16.50764	7.037769
Z4	32	.2511753	3.01469	-9.413631	8.383187
Z5	32	.4890025	4.182496	-9.67509	5.401515

Fig. 9.1 Descriptive statistics of bankrupt and not bankrupt airlines (*Source* Obtained by the authors)

9.4 Results and Discussion

Model Development

The first step is to check if the existing global model for bankruptcy prediction of the European countries (Alaminos et al., 2016) can apply to the airline companies of the same region and, if so, what predictive power it has.

Let us check the dependence between the probabilities of bankruptcy from the whole X-group of indicators, which were theoretically proposed by Alaminos et al. (2016).

Let us re-estimate the model using only significant variables. Thus, the model based only on X2, X3, X4, X5 and X7 is built. The results on Fig. 9.4 indicate that X2 does not become significant, and the predictive

Variable	Obs	Mean	Std. Dev.	Min	Max
X1	32	.9049609	.4501604	.1746032	1.858934
X2	32	-.0795802	.2545807	-1.124153	.1676867
X3	32	-.0135852	.2174273	-.9173292	.1556255
X4	32	.8274943	.5682608	.0695652	2.865937
X5	32	.3769945	.1926466	.0313253	1.008892
X6	32	.3441918	.18434	.0316885	.6988984
X7	32	-.0112883	.4357729	-1.826949	.3299213
Y1	32	21.55732	20.45882	1.129681	111.84
Y2	32	28.68447	22.53969	3.195374	87.69
Y3	32	.1239859	.3320133	-1.062927	.4080908
Y4	32	-.0242864	.2008767	-.82	.2177686
Z1	32	17.87149	15.92057	.4416742	48.56
Z2	32	.5031625	.3592472	.0692063	1.734587
Z3	32	-1.523661	5.780311	-16.50764	7.037769
Z4	32	.2511753	3.01469	-9.413631	8.383187
Z5	32	.4890025	4.182496	-9.67509	5.401515

Fig. 9.2 Descriptive statistics of not bankrupt airlines (*Source* Obtained by the authors)

power of the model practically does not change. This model cannot be accepted because the indicator X2 has no influence on bankruptcy in this model (Fig. 9.5).

The second step is to test the indicators of Z-group, which concern the existing approach of bankruptcy prediction of the European countries (Lee et al., 2012). The model incorporating these variables has a very low predictive power—25,14%. The results on Fig. 9.6 show us that only Z3 and Z5 are significant in this model as their p-value < 0,05. It can indicate that the period from 2016 to 2020 differs substantially from the events which influenced the airlines before 2012. Therefore, this model cannot be accepted either. Thus, H1 is rejected.

In the third step, only the ratios of Y-group are tested. The model with only these indicators has better predictive power than Z-based model

Variable	Obs	Mean	Std. Dev.	Min	Max
X1	12	1.253273	.7140003	.53	2.34
X2	12	-.0126707	.3548512	-.61	.41
X3	12	-.2107956	.3468431	-.9173292	.3068531
X4	12	2.172925	.4547924	1.524658	2.920696
X5	12	.5944237	.1518782	.4381982	1.008892
X6	12	.5962406	.1403366	.3650563	.804494
X7	12	-.5502793	.6083282	-1.826949	.1013119
Y1	12	62.2825	37.02386	20.45	111.84
Y2	12	49.96417	29.74757	11.61	87.69
Y3	12	-.2761964	.4078923	-1.062927	.1517782
Y4	12	-.2381576	.2865315	-.82	.008
Z1	12	1.398615	.9882085	.4416742	2.925
Z2	12	1.230833	.7322252	.53	2.34
Z3	12	-3.019298	11.44964	-36.63273	7.037769
Z4	12	-2.874704	11.94747	-38.70929	8.383187
Z5	12	10.44352	43.9666	-15.84346	148.372

Fig. 9.3 Descriptive statistics of bankrupt airlines (*Source* Obtained by the authors)

but less than X-based one. This model, in general, can explain 82% of bankruptcies, but it cannot be accepted due to the insignificance of Y1 and Y2 (Fig. 9.7).

It can be concluded that all the models are not a good fit to assess the probability of possible distress of the European airlines from 2016 to 2020. Also, all the models considered above face the problems of multicollinearity and heteroxedactness. Thus, a newly proposed model should rule out these problems. We begin by presenting a correlation matrix between Bankruptcy (P) and all independent variables of X, Z, Y groups. From Fig. 9.8, it is shown that P has the strongest correlation with X3, Y3, Y4, X7 and weak negative correlation with Z2. Besides this, the absolute values of correlation between several variables exceed 0,7, which means that there is multicollinearity. After that, it is necessary to examine all the indicators for normality by plotting the distribution and visually comparing it to the normal one, as well as conducting the

Source	SS	df	MS			
				Number of obs	=	32
				F(7, 24)	=	67.37
Model	1.78419634	7	.254885191	Prob > F	=	0.0000
Residual	.090803661	24	.003783486	R-squared	=	0.9516
				Adj R-squared	=	0.9374
Total	1.875	31	.060483871	Root MSE	=	.06151

Bankruptcy	Coef.	Std. Err.	t	P>|t|	[95% Conf.	Interval]
X1	.1126652	.0678187	1.66	0.110	-.0273056	.252636
X2	-.1771328	.1060126	-1.67	0.108	-.395932	.0416665
X3	.9252264	.1575752	5.87	0.000	.6000072	1.250446
X4	-.3037398	.0644656	-4.71	0.000	-.4367903	-.1706893
X5	-.5320963	.1452987	-3.66	0.001	-.8319782	-.2322145
X6	.0090386	.1856077	0.05	0.962	-.3740369	.392114
X7	-.2672189	.1270473	-2.10	0.046	-.5294317	-.0050061
_cons	1.279828	.0793339	16.13	0.000	1.116091	1.443565

Fig. 9.4 Model 1 on the base of X-group indicators

Source	SS	df	MS			
				Number of obs	=	32
				F(5, 26)	=	74.55
Model	1.75274786	5	.350549572	Prob > F	=	0.0000
Residual	.122252142	26	.004702005	R-squared	=	0.9348
				Adj R-squared	=	0.9223
Total	1.875	31	.060483871	Root MSE	=	.06857

Bankruptcy	Coef.	Std. Err.	t	P>|t|	[95% Conf.	Interval]
X2	-.0036139	.0606274	-0.06	0.953	-.1282353	.1210076
X3	.6930412	.148191	4.68	0.000	.3884303	.997652
X4	-.2451504	.0495262	-4.95	0.000	-.3469531	-.1433478
X5	-.3789808	.1391656	-2.72	0.011	-.6650397	-.0929219
X7	-.0959836	.1250719	-0.77	0.450	-.3530726	.1611054
_cons	1.291278	.0879648	14.68	0.000	1.110464	1.472092

Fig. 9.5 Model 2 on the base of X-group indicators

Source	SS	df	MS			
				Number of obs	=	32
				F(5, 26)	=	1.75
Model	.471459891	5	.094291978	Prob > F	=	0.1593
Residual	1.40354011	26	.053982312	R-squared	=	0.2514
				Adj R-squared	=	0.1075
Total	1.875	31	.060483871	Root MSE	=	.23234

Bankruptcy	Coef.	Std. Err.	t	P>|t|	[95% Conf.	Interval]
Z1	.0027357	.0027504	0.99	0.329	-.0029179	.0083894
Z2	-.0740099	.1363365	-0.54	0.592	-.3542537	.2062338
Z3	-.0521124	.0258013	-2.02	0.054	-.1051477	.000923
Z4	.0724131	.0388238	1.87	0.073	-.0073903	.1522165
Z5	.0418871	.0173878	2.41	0.023	.0061459	.0776283
_cons	.8077744	.0986614	8.19	0.000	.6049729	1.010576

Fig. 9.6 Model 3 on the base of Z-group indicators

Source	SS	df	MS			
				Number of obs	=	32
				F(4, 27)	=	31.03
Model	1.53998039	4	.384995098	Prob > F	=	0.0000
Residual	.335019606	27	.012408134	R-squared	=	0.8213
				Adj R-squared	=	0.7949
Total	1.875	31	.060483871	Root MSE	=	.11139

Bankruptcy	Coef.	Std. Err.	t	P>|t|	[95% Conf.	Interval]
Y1	.0004876	.0015174	0.32	0.750	-.0026258	.003601
Y2	-.000405	.0015234	-0.27	0.792	-.0035308	.0027207
Y3	.3040107	.1331465	2.28	0.031	.0308167	.5772047
Y4	.6501702	.1972988	3.30	0.003	.2453465	1.054994
_cons	.9167042	.0553485	16.56	0.000	.8031385	1.03027

Fig. 9.7 Model 3 on the base of Y-group indicators

Shapiro-France test. Thus, all indicators except X1, X5, Y2, Y1, Z2 have normal distribution. For variables X1, X5, Y2, Y1, Z2, the logarithm of their values will be used to build models.

Dozens of models were tried and three with the best predictive performance were chosen. The first model (Model A) includes three regressors. They are operational leverage (Z3), sales to total assets ratio (X4), total

	Bankru~y	X1	X3	X4	X5	X6	Y1	Y2	Y3	Y4	X7	Z1	Z2
Bankruptcy	1.0000												
X1	0.1945	1.0000											
X3	0.8593	0.1792	1.0000										
X4	-0.6879	0.0236	-0.3566	1.0000									
X5	-0.5982	-0.1954	-0.6567	0.0340	1.0000								
X6	-0.4735	0.4421	-0.3243	0.7578	-0.0970	1.0000							
Y1	-0.6102	-0.0783	-0.6941	0.4267	0.1309	0.4694	1.0000						
Y2	-0.6653	-0.2583	-0.6607	0.5756	0.3404	0.4245	0.7235	1.0000					
Y3	0.8644	0.1558	0.8412	-0.5775	-0.6303	-0.4169	-0.6653	-0.7550	1.0000				
Y4	0.8786	0.0776	0.9417	-0.4106	-0.6856	-0.3824	-0.6607	-0.6547	0.8530	1.0000			
X7	0.9246	0.2168	0.8715	-0.6282	-0.6961	-0.3986	-0.6026	-0.7763	0.9450	0.8760	1.0000		
Z1	0.2682	-0.2750	0.1441	-0.2666	-0.2336	-0.4650	-0.0067	0.1836	0.0908	0.2560	0.1460	1.0000	
Z2	-0.1036	0.6699	-0.1655	0.2620	0.0117	0.4589	0.1305	0.1629	-0.0777	-0.2384	-0.1516	-0.1861	1.0000
Z3	0.0468	-0.1759	0.5007	0.4099	-0.2181	0.0627	-0.2830	-0.0637	0.1382	0.4031	0.1256	-0.0687	-0.3312
Z4	0.0667	-0.0469	0.4941	0.3607	-0.0319	0.0054	-0.5001	-0.1144	0.1219	0.3883	0.0656	-0.0818	-0.1190
Z5	0.2679	-0.1450	0.4942	-0.0281	-0.3522	-0.2389	-0.0901	-0.2297	0.3219	0.4253	0.3593	0.0833	-0.3685

	Z3	Z4	Z5
Z3	1.0000		
Z4	0.8740	1.0000	
Z5	0.6629	0.3525	1.0000

Fig. 9.8 Correlation matrix

debt to total assets (logX5). These indicators were chosen because they show the position of the company from different aspects, namely its debt burden, the ability to generate revenue with high gross margin and low operational costs and the ability of using the profit (revenue) in the correct way. Our survey shows us that all the variables are significant at the 5% significance level. *P*-value for *F*-statistic equals 0, which means that the model is significant in general. *R*-squared is also quite high (88,35%).

Although the Model A is significant, it is necessary to check this model for the correctness of specification, which, in turn, will ensure that there is no heteroxedactness and biased estimates. To do this, the Ramsey test is conducted, which implies constructing an auxiliary regression of the dependent variable on itself, its square, cube, and fourth power, which should be insignificant, in other words, the coefficients for the regressors should be zero. From Fig. 9.9, we can see that *p*-value for *F*-statistics is less than 0,05, thus, the H0 about the right model specification is rejected (Fig. 9.10).

Next, it is necessary to check this model for heteroxedactness, in other words, heterogeneity of observations with a predominance of variance and error, which leads to bias and inconsistency of the covariance matrix estimation and inefficiency of the estimation results. For greater accuracy, we will perform 3 tests for heteroxedactness. The first of the heteroxedactness tests is the Breusch–Pagan test, which is used to construct the

Source	SS	df	MS			
Model	1.65663183	3	.552210609	Number of obs	=	32
Residual	.218368173	28	.007798863	F(3, 28)	=	70.81
				Prob > F	=	0.0000
Total	1.875	31	.060483871	R-squared	=	0.8835
				Adj R-squared	=	0.8711
				Root MSE	=	.08831

Bankruptcy	Coef.	Std. Err.	t	P>|t|	[95% Conf.	Interval]
logX5	-.1897955	.0231158	-8.21	0.000	-.2371462	-.1424449
X4	-.4284931	.0314801	-13.61	0.000	-.4929772	-.3640091
Z3	.0135222	.0030349	4.46	0.000	.0073056	.0197389
_cons	1.092875	.0381219	28.67	0.000	1.014786	1.170965

Fig. 9.9 Model A

```
Ramsey RESET test using powers of the fitted values of Bankruptcy
       Ho:  model has no omitted variables
                  F(3, 25) =  17530.93
                  Prob > F =      0.0000
```

Fig. 9.10 Ramsey test for Model A

dependence of the square of the residuals on the predicted values of the dependent variable (Fig. 9.11).

This test shows us that *p*-value is less than 0,05, which means that the Ho about the homoskedacticity is rejected and the problem of heteroxedactness is presented in the Model A.

```
Breusch-Pagan / Cook-Weisberg test for heteroskedasticity
         Ho: Constant variance
         Variables: fitted values of Bankruptcy

         chi2(1)      =    11.02
         Prob > chi2  =   0.0009
```

Fig. 9.11 Breusch–Pagan test for Model A

```
Breusch-Pagan / Cook-Weisberg test for heteroskedasticity
         Ho: Constant variance
         Variables: logX5 X4 Z3

         chi2(3)      =    14.09
         Prob > chi2  =   0.0028
```

Fig. 9.12 Breusch–Pagan test 2 for Model A

The second test is the Breusch–Pagan test 2 (hettest, rhs), which involves constructing a regression of the squares of residuals on explanatory variables (Fig. 9.12). The null hypothesis is similar to the previous test. The result of the second test is the same as in the first one and points on the problem of the heteroskedasticity.

The White test allows to detect the presence of heteroscedasticity of any form by constructing the error squared on the explanatory variables, their squares, as well as all or some of their pairwise products (Fig. 9.13). The null hypothesis is the same as the one of the previous tests. This test also confirms the presence of heteroskedasticity.

The next step is to check the model for multicollinearity, which characterizes the presence of a linear relationship between the variables (Fig. 9.14). To do this, we perform the VIF test. To detect the presence of multicollinearity, it is necessary to compare the *R*-squared = 0.8835 of the model to the value 1–1/VIFmax = 1 − 0,89 = 0,11. Thus, *R*-squared > 1–1/VIFmax, which means that there is no multicollinearity.

Let us now build the second model (Model B), which includes the set of the independent variables of model A plus working capital/total assets (X2). Model B presented on the Fig. 9.15 has all indicators significant

Cameron & Trivedi's decomposition of IM-test

Source	chi2	df	p
Heteroskedasticity	29.31	9	0.0006
Skewness	18.80	3	0.0003
Kurtosis	0.51	1	0.4747
Total	48.63	13	0.0000

Fig. 9.13 White test 2 for Model A

Fig. 9.14 Multicollinearity test for Model A

Variable	VIF	1/VIF
X4	1.27	0.786144
Z3	1.22	0.817498
logX5	1.12	0.890383
Mean VIF	1.21	

at the 5% level and is significant in general (*p*-value of *F*-statistics equals 0). The variables of this model explain the probability of bankruptcy a bit better than Model A, its predictive power is rather high and equals to 89,49%.

The three tests for heteroskedasticity are represented on Fig. 9.16. All of them detect heteroskedasticity because *p*-value is less than the critical value. The test for multicollinearity shows that the value 1–1/VIFmax = 1–0,205 = 0,154 is less than *R*-squared of Model B = 0,8949, which points to the absence of the multicollinearity in this model (Fig. 9.17).

However, the Ramsey test shows that there can be errors in the model specification (Fig. 9.18).

The third model (Model C) includes accounts payable turnover (logY2), change of EBIT in % (Z4), sales to total assets ratio (X4) and total debt to total assets (log X5).

This model can be a better fit than the others because it additionally takes into consideration the indicators of profitability and changes in

Source	SS	df	MS		
				Number of obs	= 32
				F(4, 27)	= 57.47
Model	1.67792782	4	.419481954	Prob > F	= 0.0000
Residual	.197072182	27	.00729897	R-squared	= 0.8949
				Adj R-squared	= 0.8793
Total	1.875	31	.060483871	Root MSE	= .08543

Bankruptcy	Coef.	Std. Err.	t	P>|t|	[95% Conf.	Interval]
logX5	-.1700841	.0251647	-6.76	0.000	-.2217177	-.1184504
X2	.1186888	.0694851	1.71	0.099	-.0238828	.2612604
X4	-.4136891	.0316637	-13.07	0.000	-.4786576	-.3487206
Z3	.0126794	.0029772	4.26	0.000	.0065708	.0187881
_cons	1.111614	.038477	28.89	0.000	1.032666	1.190562

Fig. 9.15 Model B

```
. hettest

Breusch-Pagan / Cook-Weisberg test for heteroskedasticity
         Ho: Constant variance
         Variables: fitted values of Bankruptcy

         chi2(1)      =     8.87
         Prob > chi2  =   0.0029

. hettest,rhs

Breusch-Pagan / Cook-Weisberg test for heteroskedasticity
         Ho: Constant variance
         Variables: logX5 X2 X4 Z3

         chi2(4)      =    14.48
         Prob > chi2  =   0.0059

. imtest

Cameron & Trivedi's decomposition of IM-test
```

Source	chi2	df	p
Heteroskedasticity	29.72	14	0.0083
Skewness	19.44	4	0.0006
Kurtosis	0.20	1	0.6557
Total	49.36	19	0.0002

Fig. 9.16 Heteroskedasticity tests for Model B

Variable	VIF	1/VIF
logX5	1.42	0.703144
X4	1.38	0.727246
X2	1.33	0.752429
Z3	1.26	0.795044
Mean VIF	1.35	

Fig. 9.17 Multicollinearity test for Model B

```
Ramsey RESET test using powers of the fitted values of Bankruptcy
       Ho:  model has no omitted variables
                 F(3, 24) =  47503.90
                 Prob > F =      0.0000
```

Fig. 9.18 Ramsey test for Model B

EBIT compared to the previous period as well as the debt burden. The results are shown on Fig. 9.19.

Regressors of Model C have the greatest predictive power among all the three models, and they explain 92,67% of the dependent variable variance. All the regressors are significant at the 5% level. The model is significant in general as the *p*-value of *F*-statics equals to 0.

Let us provide 3 tests of heteroskedasticity (Fig. 9.20). In all of them, *p*-value exceeds the critical *p*-value, which means that Ho is accepted and there is homoskedasticity in Model C. Test for multicollinearity defines that 1–1/VIFmax = 1 − 0,2197 = 0,7803 is less than R-squared of the model = 0,9267, which means that there is no multicollinearity in Model (Fig. 9.21).

Source	SS	df	MS		
				Number of obs =	32
				F(4, 27) =	85.28
Model	1.73747675	4	.434369187	Prob > F =	0.0000
Residual	.137523254	27	.005093454	R-squared =	0.9267
				Adj R-squared =	0.9158
Total	1.875	31	.060483871	Root MSE =	.07137

Bankruptcy	Coef.	Std. Err.	t	P>|t|	[95% Conf.	Interval]
logY2	.0437732	.0170725	2.56	0.016	.0087433	.0788031
logX5	-.2102407	.0188294	-11.17	0.000	-.2488754	-.1716061
Z4	.0330897	.0048666	6.80	0.000	.0231042	.0430753
X4	-.4778683	.0309869	-15.42	0.000	-.5414482	-.4142883
_cons	.9497639	.0494168	19.22	0.000	.848369	1.051159

Fig. 9.19 Model C

```
. hettest

Breusch-Pagan / Cook-Weisberg test for heteroskedasticity
         Ho: Constant variance
         Variables: fitted values of Bankruptcy

         chi2(1)      =     0.62
         Prob > chi2  =   0.4323

. hettest,rhs

Breusch-Pagan / Cook-Weisberg test for heteroskedasticity
         Ho: Constant variance
         Variables: logY2 logX5 Z4 X4

         chi2(4)      =     0.64
         Prob > chi2  =   0.9582

. imtest

Cameron & Trivedi's decomposition of IM-test
```

Source	chi2	df	p
Heteroskedasticity	18.49	14	0.1852
Skewness	5.74	4	0.2197
Kurtosis	2.04	1	0.1537
Total	26.27	19	0.1230

Fig. 9.20 Heteroskedasticity tests for Model C

However, according to the Ramsey test, there are errors in the model specification because *p*-value equals to 0 (Fig. 9.22).

Thus, let us summarize the results of the three models in Table 9.4 by coding with «1» if the model has the best predictive power, no heteroskedasticity, multicollinearity and specification errors, otherwise the value is set to «0».

Variable	VIF	1/VIF
X4	1.89	0.529905
logY2	1.53	0.653729
Z4	1.31	0.763318
logX5	1.14	0.876407
Mean VIF	1.47	

Fig. 9.21 Multicollinearity test for Model C

```
Ramsey RESET test using powers of the fitted values of Bankruptcy
      Ho:  model has no omitted variables
                 F(3, 24) =  16790.40
                 Prob > F =      0.0000
```

Fig. 9.22 Ramsey test for Model C

Table 9.4 Comparison of 3 models

Criteria	*Model A*	*Model B*	*Model C*
Heteroskedasticity	0	0	1
Multicollinearity	0	0	1
Specification	0	0	0
Adj R-squared	0	0	1

As Model C has a higher predictive power, no heteroskedasticity and multicollinearity, it is chosen as the best one.

Thus, the scoring model for bankruptcy prediction for the European countries looks as follows:

$$P = 0,949 + 0,044\ \log X1 - 0,21\log X2 + 0,033X3 - 0,478X4 \quad (9.4)$$

where

X1—accounts payable turnover,
X2—total debt/total assets,
X3—change in EBIT in %,
X4—sales/total assets.
If P>=1—healthy company,

if $P<1$—company has financial problems and the increasing possibility of bankruptcy.

The signs before the variables are easy to interpret. Firstly, a positive sign before X1 means that the increase of accounts payable turnover does not imply the deterioration of the financial position of airlines companies. A negative sign before debt to total assets ratio (X2) shows that a high debt burden can be a signal of future bankruptcy. The increase of EBIT for airline companies means that company consolidates its sustainability. For airlines, it is better when sales to total assets ratio (X4) is smaller because airlines tend to have a large asset basis which are financed by revenues. Thus, H2 is rejected.

It is reasonable to try applying this model to the data of the current research. It points that several companies have the sharp decline of P in 2020 and it becomes less than 1, which is the sign of instability. The information that these companies really have serious problems is widely known.

The first company with P = 1,53 in 2019 and 0,31 in 2020 is Lufthansa. At the end of 2020, there were rumors about the bankruptcy of the company instead of the public support provision. Nowadays, there is no new information about the company's intentions.

Secondly, Finnair's P in 2019 equals 1,36 and in 2020 it is 0,11. The information about its possible bankruptcy has not been commented by the official representatives to the mass media, but it is obvious that such great decline can be a negative sign for the company.

Thirdly, P of Norwegian Air in 2019 equals to 1,36 and 0,11 in 2020. In 2020, Norwegian airlines claimed about its possible bankruptcy because the COVID-19 caused the crisis in the company due to huge amounts of debt and the termination of transatlantic transportation. But in May 2021, the company officially declared that it managed to prevent a default and began to work as a regional carrier. The company reduced its fleet threefold and its debt from the pre-pandemic 156 billion Norwegian crowns to 18 billion crowns.

Air France KLM has the worst situation, which was also announced in the media and known all over the world because of the huge loss in 2020 equal to 7 billion euros. It is the only company in the sample which P was very close to zero in 2020. Nowadays, the French government tries to help the company to maintain solvency. Last year, it allocated 7 billion euros to Air France to cover its losses of the year 2020.

For all the four companies, the serious decline in P from 2019 to 2020 is explained mostly by the decrease of sales/total assets and negative change in EBIT.

Aegean airlines' position was not so crucial in 2020 and P equaled to 0,9. Only Ryanair has P more than 1 and, moreover, its EBIT remained positive in 2020.

Development of the Economic Approach to Assessing the Probability of Bankruptcy

The proposed regression model takes into consideration a number of factors, but it omits two groups of indicators which should be considered in the assessment of financial position of the company and its dynamics. First, it is important to consider the indicator of current liquidity since it is a key factor in assessing the short-term financial stability of airlines. With its help, it is possible to assess not only its ability to repay short-term obligations at the expense of funds in various accounts, but also its ability to mobilize available resources for the repayment of the most urgent obligations. Thus, the calculation of the current liquidity ratio allows to assess the ability of the company to immediately repay the obligations at the expense of various available funds.

Secondly, the debt to EBITDA ratio can provide the effective assessment of the period for which the cash flows cover the existing debt. Moreover, it is one of the most important indicators used by commercial banks in their assessment of borrowers' creditworthiness.

Additionally, it is necessary not only to assess how fast the company repays its creditors but also if its customers pay on time, that is why it is advised to consider accounts receivable turnover.

Thus, in the overall model of bankruptcy prediction for European airline companies, seven financial indicators are to be considered. Now, we set the standard values for the selected indicators. To do this, the data of the companies is divided into 2 groups. The first group is made up of the years when companies had financial problems or bankruptcy according to the constructed model, while the second group embraces the periods when their financial position was assessed as stable. The normative values are set in such a way that the values of the indicators of the first group will act as the optimal values for the industry, and the average values of the corresponding indicators in the second group as critical. However, the average of all indicators should not be extracted from the second group, but only those that are worse than the average values of the first group. Thus, the average value in the second group should consist of those indicators that are less than the average of the first group, except for the turnover of accounts payable and receivables, sales to total assets (according to the industry), debt to EBITDA. For the mentioned indicators, the higher their value is, the worse is the financial position.

Thus, based on the calculations performed, the following critical and optimal values of financial indicators are obtained (Table 9.5) along with the standard values of these indicators according to the global international practice.

From Table 9.5, it can be established that, in general, the optimal and critical values for airline companies are within the internationally established bounds. But also airlines have their own peculiarities. First, the average optimal liquidity ratio is less than the established normative ratio and is equal to 0,93. Second, the normative value for sales to total assets is not defined in the global practice because it depends on the industry. In the sample of the airlines, it is found that companies facing financial problems have a higher level of this ratio than healthy firms. It can be concluded that airlines tend to have the great amounts of total assets which mostly consist of the non-current assets, mainly fixed assets (PP&E), which proves the assumption about the smaller liquidity ratio in comparison to the one established in the international practice. Third,

Table 9.5 Normative values of financial indicators according to the developed model for bankruptcy prediction

Ratio	*Optimal value*	*Critical value*	*International practice (max value)*
Current liquidity ratio	0,93	0,59	1
Sales to total assets ratio	0,82	2,3	Depends on industry
Total debt to total assets	0,31	0,6	0,4
Accounts receivable turnover (days)	18	43	30
Accounts payable turnover (days)	25	61	30
EBIT change	14%	<0	
Debt to EBITDA	2,6	<0	5

accounts receivable and payable turnovers are within the bounds of the established normative values, but it is important to notice that it is necessary to analyze the terms of contracts with customers and creditors to make a right conclusion about timely fulfillment of obligations. The indicator of change in EBIT has not been defined in world practice, but the sample shows that healthy companies have the growth of EBIT from year to year, while the companies which have problems witness the decrease of their EBIT or mostly negative values of EBIT and EBITDA. Concerning the debt to EBITDA ratio, the value depends on the industry, but it is often in the range between 4 and 5. According to the model, the optimal value for the European countries is equal to 2,6. Thus, it is reasonable to establish the normative upper bound of this indicator at 5.

Summing up, we can conclude that the assessment of bankruptcy of the European airlines has its own specific features, such as accounting for current liquidity ratio and total sales to total assets ratio. Thus, it is advisable to divide the assessment of the possible bankruptcy of the European airlines into several stages.

At the first stage, it is necessary to define if the company is stable and does not have serious problems ($P>=1$) or not ($P<1$) using the formula

$$P = 0,949 + 0,044\log X1 - 0,21\log X2 + 0,033X3 - 0,478X4 \quad (9.5)$$

At the second stage, 7 financial indicators of the company are compared to the normative values.

The greatest emphasis is placed on the method of the bankruptcy prediction. If the values of the calculated financial ratios fully correspond to the optimal values established in the industry, the company is recognized healthy. If the values of the indicators coincide with the critical values, it can be a sign of financial problems. If the values do not completely match, the priority of the analysis should be given to the four regression model indicators. For the airline to be recognized healthy, it is necessary that the values of these 4 indicators are in the optimal range. Thus, based on two existing models of bankruptcy prediction as well as regression analysis, the coefficient methodology has been improved and the approach for bankruptcy prediction of the European airlines has been developed, taking into account their industry characteristics.

9.5 Conclusion

Bankruptcy prediction is one of the most important issues for a wide number of stakeholders: company's management, investors, creditors, banks and government, especially in terms of economic crises, including the pandemic COVID-19. Airline industry was strongly affected all over the world during the pandemic period. Our research was devoted to the development of such model based on the data from 2016 to 2020 and accounted for the regional factor. This model can be useful for all interested entities to carry out a timely assessment of the financial problems and to make right decisions about the need for public financial support and the future of the company in general. Thus, in this study, the industry-specific features of the European airlines were identified and analyzed. This was achieved by conducting a multi-step analysis. First, 11 financial indicators, used in the existing models and 5 additional ratios which can trigger filing for bankruptcy according to the authors' assumption, were calculated for 7 biggest European airlines. Then, several regression models were constructed, among which the best one was determined, containing the most significant indicators for the industry:

$$\mathrm{P} = 0,949 + 0,044\,\mathrm{log X1} - 0,21\,\mathrm{log X2} + 0,033\mathrm{X3} - 0,478\mathrm{X4}$$

where

X1—accounts payable turnover,
X2—total debt/total assets,
X3—change in EBIT in %,
X4—sales/total assets.
If P>=1—healthy company,
if P<1—company has financial problems and the increasing possibility of bankruptcy.

Further, three more indicators were added to the analysis from the point of view of economic feasibility. After that, based on all 7 coefficients, their optimal and critical values for the industry were calculated. Then, they were compared to the standards established in the international practice, based on which the thresholds for the indicators of current liquidity and sales to total assets were identified.

Next, the approaches for assessing the possibility of bankruptcy of the European airlines were developed. So first, the mathematical scoring model should be applied, $P = 0,949 + 0,044\,\log X1 - 0,21\,\log X2 + 0,033X3 - 0,478X4$, to determine if the company is stable in the current year (P>1) or not (P<1).

Then it was found that it is appropriate to recognize the company as healthy in two cases:

1. If the values of the calculated financial indicators fully correspond to the established optimal ones for the industry.
2. If the values of 4 regressors used in the regression model fully correspond to the optimal ones.

Otherwise, the risk of the deterioration of the company's financial position or even future bankruptcy emerges.

The three hypotheses stated in the Introduction have different results. H0 is accepted as the global existing model of the bankruptcy prediction of the European companies is inaccurate in the prediction of the European airlines since several indicators are found insignificant. H1 is rejected as the existing model of bankruptcy prediction of the European airlines developed in 2012 lost its significance for the observation period in question. H2 is rejected as low sales to total assets ratio is the feature of the airlines because they tend to have large amounts of PP&E.

Summing up the results of this study, the goal has been achieved, since the approaches of bankruptcy prediction for the European airlines have been developed, allowing to determine the financial position of the companies in this industry more accurately, which, in turn, will help reduce credit risk.

References

Alaka, H. A., Oyedele, L. O., Owolabi, H. A., Kumar, V., Ajayi, S. O., Akinade, O. O., & Bilal, M. (2018). Systematic review of bankruptcy prediction models: Towards a framework for tool selection. *Expert Systems with Applications, 94*, 164–184.

Alaminos, D., Del Castillo, A., & Fernandez, M. A. (2016). A global model for bankruptcy prediction. *PLoS One, 11*, 1–18.

Aleksanyan, L., & Huiban, J.-P. (2016). Economic and financial determinants of firm bankruptcy: Evidence from the French food industry. *Review of Agricultural, Food and Environmental Studies, 97*, 89–108.

Altman, E. I. (1968). Financial ratios, discriminant analysis and the prediction of corporate bankruptcy. *The Journal of Finance, XXIII*, 589–609.

Ashraf, S., Félix, E. G. S., & Serrasqueiro, Z. (2019). Do traditional financial distress prediction models predict the early warning signs of financial distress? *Journal of Risk and Financial Management, 12*, 55.

Atiya, A. F. (2001). Bankruptcy prediction for credit risk using neural networks: A survey and new results. *IEEE Transactions on Neural Networks, 12*(4), 929–935.

Aziz, M. A., & Dar, H. A. (2006). Predicting corporate bankruptcy: Where we stand? *Corporate Governance, 6*, 18–33.

Beaver, W. H. (1966). Financial ratios as predictors of failure. *Journal of Accounting Research, 4*, 71–111.

Belas, J., Misankova, M., Schonfeld, J., & Gavurova, B. (2017). Credit risk management: Financial safety and sustainability aspects. *Journal of Security and Sustainability Issues, 7*, 79–93.

Bredart, X. (2014). Bankruptcy prediction model using neural networks. *Accounting and Finance Research, 3*, 124–128.

Chesser, D. L. (1974). Predicting loan noncompliance. *The Journal of Commercial Bank Lending, 56*, 28–38.

Du Jardin, P. (2009, January–February). Bankruptcy prediction models: How to choose the most relevant variables? *Bankers, Markets & Investors, 98*, 39–46.

Edmister, R. O. (1972). An empirical test of financial ratio analysis for small business failure prediction. *Journal of Financial and Quantitative Analysis, 7*, 1477–1493.

Elviani, S., Simbolon, R., Riana, Z., Khairani, F., Puspa Dewi, S., & Fauzi, F. (2020). The accuracy of the Altman, Ohlson, Springate and Zmejewski models in bankruptcy predicting trade sector companies in Indonesia. *Budapest International Research and Critics Institute (BIRCI-Journal), 3*, 334–347.

Fedorova, E. A., Dovzhenko, S. E., & Fedorov, F. Y. (2016). Bankruptcy-prediction models for Russian enterprises: Specific sector-related characteristics. *Studies on Russian Economic Development, 27*, 254–261.

Fulmer, J. G., Moon, J. E., Gavin, T. A., & Erwin, M. (1984). A bankruptcy classification model for small firms. *Journal of Commercial Bank Lending, 66*, 25–37.

Glezakos, M., Mylonakis, J., & Oikonomou, K. (2010). An empirical research on early bankruptcy forecasting models: Does logit analysis enhance business failure predictability? *European Journal of Finance & Banking Research, 3*, 1–15.

Gupta, M. C. (1969). The effect of size, growth, and industry on the financial structure of manufacturing companies. *Journal of Finance, 24*(3), 517–529.

Horrigan, J. O. (1983). Methodological implications of non-normally distributed financial ratios factors associated with insolvency amongst small firms. *Journal of Business Finance and Accounting, 10*(4), 683–689.

Iturriaga, F. J. L., & Sanz, I. P. (2015). Bankruptcy visualization and prediction using neural networks: A study of US commercial banks. *Expert Systems with Applications, 42*, 2857–2869.

Kaufman, G. G. (1995). Comment on systemic risk. *Research in financial services: Banking, financial markets, and systemic risk* (Vol. 7, pp.47–52).

Keasey, K., & Watson, R. (1987). Non-financial symptoms and the prediction of small company failure: A test of Argenti's hypothesis. *Journal of Business Finance and Accounting, 14*(3), 335–354.

Lee, C.-H., Hooy, C.-W. (2012). Determinants of systematic financial risk exposures of airlines in North America, Europe and Asia. *Journal of Air Transport Management, 24*, 31–35.

Lussier, R. N. (1995). A nonfinancial business success versus failure prediction model for young firms. *Journal of Small Business Management, 33*(1), 8–20.

Ohlson, J. A. (1980). Financial ratios and the probabilistic prediction of bankruptcy. *Journal of Accounting Research, 18*, 109–131.

Ouenniche, J., & Tone, K. (2017). An out-of-sample evaluation framework for DEA with application in bankruptcy prediction. *Annals of Operations Research, 254*, 235–250.

Pérez, M. (2002). De l'analyse de la performance à la prévision de défaillance: les apports de la classification neuronale, Thèse de doctorat, Université Jean-Moulin, Lyon III.

Pompe, P. P. M., & Bilderbeek, J. (2005). The prediction of bankruptcy of small- and medium-sized industrial firms. *Journal of Business Venturing, 20*(6), 847–868.

Thomson Reuters Eikon. https://eikon.thomsonreuters.com/index.html. Assessed at 10 April 2021.

Salehi, M., & Davoudi Pour, M. (2016). Bankruptcy prediction of listed companies on the Tehran Stock exchange. *International Journal of Law and Management, 58*, 545–561.

Schonfeld, J., Kudej, M., & Smrcka, L. (2018). Financial health of enterprises introducing safeguard procedure based on bankruptcy models. *Journal of Business Economics and Management, 19*, 692–705.

Slefendorfas, G. (2016). Bankruptcy prediction model for private limited companies of Lithuania. *Ekonomika, 95*, 134–152.

Springate, G. (1978). *Predicting the possibility of failure in a Canadian firm.* Master's Thesis, Simon Fraser University, Burnaby, BC, Canada.

Tomczak, S. K., & Radosinski, E. (2017). The effectiveness of discriminant models based on the example of the manufacturing sector. *Operations Research and Decisions, 27*, 81–97.

Ul Hassan, E., Zainuddin, Z., & Nordin, S. (2017). A review of financial distress prediction models: Logistic regression and multivariate discriminant analysis. *Indian-Pacific Journal of Accounting and Finance, 3*: 13–23

Zavgren, C. V. (1985). Assessing the vulnerability to failure of American industrial firms: A logistic analysis. *Journal of Business Finance & Accounting, 12*, 19–45.

PART III

New Challenges in Systemic Risk Assessment and Regulation

CHAPTER 10

Macroprudential Policy: Tools and Evaluation of the Effectiveness of Measures for Systemic Risks Management

Ekaterina Seryakova

Indicators of systemic banking risks, when reaching certain values, act as triggers for macroprudential policy measures. The Bank for International Settlements defines systemic risk as the possibility of a disruption in the functioning of the financial sector, which leads to the deterioration of the entire banking sector and entails negative consequences for the real economy. Systemic risk in a broad sense is understood as a simultaneous deterioration in main performance indicators of banking institutions, which also negatively affects the dynamics of the real sector markets.[1] In the foreign literature, systemic risk is more often characterized as a risk that originates in the banking sector (due to insolvency or a lack of liquidity of systemically important banks), which creates a dysfunction

[1] Ayvazyan, S., Andrievskaya, I., Connolly, R., & Penikas, G. (2011). Identification of systemically important financial institutions: a review of methodologies. *Money and credit*.

E. Seryakova (✉)
Sberbank, Moscow, Russia
e-mail: ekaterinaseryakova@yandex.ru

A. Karminsky and M. Stolbov (eds.), *Systemic Financial Risk*,
https://doi.org/10.1007/978-3-031-54809-3_10

(imbalances) of the entire banking sector and has negative consequences for the real sector of the economy. Systemic risk is also often understood as the probability of losses of the entire banking system.[2] Systemic banking risk can also be understood as the loss of financial stability by the banking sector, the main sources of which are systemically important banks.

The stages of distribution of systemic banking risks include: (1) The occurrence of the initial shock; (2) Spread of the shock across the banking sector; (3) Violation of the functioning of the banking sector.

The main channels for the spread of systemic banking risks within the national banking sector and its transmission to other national banking sectors are:

- interbank channel due to the presence of mutual requirements and obligations of banks;
- price channel of assets;
- channel of infection due to the presence of a common creditor.

Table 10.1 shows the classification of quantitative indicators for assessing systemic banking risk into four groups.

Let us consider in more detail the first two groups of indicators from Table 10.1, which are most often encountered in practice.

1. *Indices of financial (in)stability.* Despite the wide experience of using indicators of financial instability in the G20 countries (CISS, FSCI), there is still no recognized single indicator of financial instability. The following examples can be singled out as Russian and foreign experience in developing such indices: an indicator of financial instability based on high-frequency data[3]; an indicator of systemic risks of the Russian financial market, proposed by the DFS of the Bank of Russia in 2017; early warning indicators of financial instability[4]; financial stress index proposed by the Analytical Credit Rating Agency (ACRA) in 2017; Financial Stress Index

[2] Hurd TR Contagion! The spread of systemic risk in financial networks, March, 2015.

[3] Pestova A. A., Pankova, V. A., Akhmetov, R. R., & I. O. Goloshchapova. (2017). Development of a system of indicators of financial instability based on high-frequency data. *Money and credit,* (6). - 49–58ss.

[4] Solntsev, O. G., Pestova, A. A., Mamonov, M. E. & Magomedova, Z. (2011). Experience in developing an early warning system for financial crises and forecasting

Table 10.1 General classification of systemic risk indicators

Indicator group	*Indicators*
Indicators of the "contribution" of each participant to the systemic risk	• CoVaR • MES (Marginal Expected Shortfall) • CES (Conditional Expected Shortfall) • DIP (Distress Insurance Premium) • SRISK (Systemic Risk) • Distress Spillovers(DS) • Systemic Liquidity Risk Indicator(SLRI) • Index of the contribution of systemically important banks to the systemic liquidity risk of the Russian banking sector
Index indicators	• Indicator of systemic risks of the Russian financial market, proposed by the Department of Financial Stability (DFS -further) of the Bank of Russia in 2017 • Financial instability indicator based on high-frequency data • Financial stress indices: proposed by the Analytical Credit Rating Agency (ACRA) in 2017 CISS (Composite Indicator of Systemic Stress) St. Lois Fed FSI (Financial Stress Index) Kansas City Fed FSI CLIFS • Leading indicators of financial instability; • Financial condition indicators: OECD FCI (Financial Conditions Index) Goldman Sachs FCI Bloomberg FCI Chicago Fed FCI • Mahalanobis distance index
Indicators stress—risk testing	• StressVaR, dNIIstress (percentage risk) • PDstress, EDF (credit risk) • Capital adequacy ratios • Liquidity Buffer
network models	• Variation decomposition indicators (volatility spillovers) (Diebold-Yilmaz (DY))

Source compiled by the author

(FSI); Composite Indicator of Systemic Stress (CISS); Financial instability index based on the Mahalanobis distance.

2. *Parametric metrics (VaR - metrics)*.The indicators of this group are designed to assess the share of each participant's contribution to the spread of systemic banking risks. The CoVaR metric was proposed in 2008 by American scientists T. Adrian and M. Brunnermeier. This indicator is calculated for each financial institution and determines the losses of the banking sector, subject to the deterioration of the financial stability of a particular bank. Also, after that, the indicator ΔCoVaR is calculated, which shows the bank's marginal contribution to the systemic banking risk, which is the difference between CoVaR under conditions of financial instability and and CoVaR under normal operating conditions of the same bank. Within the group of parametric metrics, there are four indicators derived from the ES (Expected shortfall) metric: MES, CES, SES, LRMES. In modern risk-management practice, the ES indicator is understood as the average expected loss in α-% worst cases. In other words, ES shows the average losses exceeding VaR (Value-at-Risk)—the maximum possible losses on the confidence (1-α)% interval during the selected period. The ES metric is calculated by the largest banks and is more informative than the VaR (Value-at-Risk) metric. MES shows the level of losses in the capital of the bank in the event of a shock in the financial (stock) market over a certain period of time.[5] LRMES (long-run MES) represents the average of a bank's MES for various crisis scenarios, taking into account the weight of each scenario:

$$LRMES = 1,69 * MES. \tag{10.1}$$

The SRISK indicator, unlike MES, means the required amount of capital that a bank may need in the event of a systemic crisis in the banking sector and is an absolute value:

$$SRISK_{it} = \max(0; k * D_{it} - (1 - k) * W_{it} * (1 - LRMES_{it}), \tag{10.2}$$

where k is the ratio of assets to capital (bank multiplier);

the development of the Russian banking sector for 2012. *Journal of the New Economic Association*, (12), 41–76.

[5] http://vlab.stern.nyu.edu/(website of the Volatility Institute (V-LAB)).

Dit is the indicator of liabilities of bank i in period t;

Wit is an indicator of the net assets of bank i in period t.

Thus, in a normal situation, SRISK should be 0 for a bank, and that should be the prudential requirement for its value. Let us further consider how systemic banking risks and the realization of financial instability are connected. *Firstly*, due to the interconnectedness of the banking sector participants at the national and cross-border levels, exposure to common risk factors and the procyclicity of their activities, the threat of a systemic banking crisis is increasing. To prevent the beginning of systemic crises in advance, it is important to assess the level of systemic banking risks. Secondly, it is important to understand what the sources and channels for the spread of systemic risk in the banking sector are and its impact on the real sector of the economy. The realized systemic risks affect the financial stability of the banking sector, leading to a decrease in lending, a shortage of liquidity and, as a result, to a slowdown in economic growth. *Third*, there are methodological prerequisites for further development of the concept of systemic banking risk. In this regard, it is still relevant to develop proposals for quantitative assessments of systemic banking risk, upon reaching certain values, it is possible to identify the financial instability of the banking sector.

The issue of assessing the effectiveness of the applied macroprudential policy measures to minimize systemic banking risks is also becoming important. The relevance of assessing the effectiveness of measures to regulate the credit market is associated with the need to ensure the countercyclical nature of macroprudential policy, the timely recalibration of its tools and the determination of side effects from its implementation. At present, the world practice mainly evaluates the effectiveness of the use of instruments that affect banking assets, and the study of the effectiveness of the use of instruments that affect the capital and liquidity of banks is limited to a small number of studies. There is no unequivocal answer to which instruments are more effective for regulating the growth rates of loans and real estate prices: for example, whether to apply differentiated risk weights or the maximum limit on the ratio of the volume of loans to the value of collateral (LTV).

Having considered the main definitions of systemic banking risk—the object of macroprudential policy—we can proceed to the analysis of tools and measures of macroprudential policy, which can be defined as a policy aimed at preventing financial instability, in other words, minimizing systemic banking crises. According to experts of the Bank for International Settlements, macroprudential policy is aimed at limiting systemic risks, and should also be of a countercyclical nature, i.e., to counteract the trend of underestimation of risks by the participants of the banking sector during the period of economic expansion and, accordingly, their overestimation during periods of recession and economic downturn. **The main objectives of macroprudential policy** in relation to the banking sector are:

1. mitigating the procyclicity of the banking sector and the impact of procyclicity on financial and business cycles (the time aspect of systemic banking risks);
2. strengthening the financial stability of participants in the banking sector, increasing the ability of the banking sector to quickly cope with financial and economic shocks without creating imbalances in the banking sector (structural aspect of systemic risk).

At the same time, one of the tasks of a macroprudential policy should be a system of control over government spending to restore the financial stability of individual banks after the realization of the crisis. Macroprudential policy should be carried out primarily in relation to systemically important banks, which are considered by banking regulators around the world as the main sources of systemic banking risks. Having defined the concept and main goals of macroprudential policy, it is important to consider deeply **the tools of macroprudential policy**. They can be divided into two categories: those aimed at curbing the manifestation of the dynamic (temporary) aspect of systemic banking risks and the structural (cyclical) aspect of systemic banking risks. The first category includes instruments regulating credit expansion (restrictions on the growth rate of loans, LTV, DTI, reserve requirements) and measures aimed at regulating capital (countercyclical capital buffer, dynamic provisioning, restrictions on profit distribution, capital conservation buffer). The second group includes concentration limits by borrowers/industries, limits on the duration of assets and liabilities, restrictions on lending in foreign currency.

Table 10.2 provides a classification of macroprudential policy instruments used in international banking practice.

Table 10.2 Macroprudential policy instruments used in international and Russian practice and the purposes of their application

Tool group	*Tool*
Instruments affecting capital	Capital buffers Sectoral capital requirements Base Capital Supplement for Systemically Important Banks
Tools, affecting liquidity	Limits on maturity gaps between assets and liabilities Market premiums for securities collateral for repo transactions Loan to Deposit Ratio (LDR) Limits LCL-indicator of short-term liquidity PPSF is an indicator of net stable funding
Instruments affecting assets	LTV (loan-to-value)/LTI (loan-to-income) Foreign currency lending restrictions Required reservations

Source compiled by the author

Macroprudential policy instruments can also be classified in more detail: by types of systemic banking risks, by objects of influence (bank assets, banks' capital, bank liquidity) and by macroprudential policy objectives. This classification is shown in Table 10.3.

It is also important to look into **foreign experience in the use of macroprudential policy instruments and the application of appropriate measures in relation to them**. In foreign practice, the vast majority of studies are related to the assessment of the influence of instruments based on the impact on assets: on the growth rate of lending, mortgage lending and real estate prices.[6] Using the statistics of loan applications from 2000 to 2012 some experts in macro prudential regulation conclude that dynamic provisioning as a countercyclical macro-prudential policy tool applied to Spanish banks is effective in smoothing the credit cycle. Dynamic provisioning involves banks building up reserves during periods of increased profits, which creates an additional buffer for use in times of crises. However, this measure works only during periods of

[6] Jimenez, G., Ongena, S., Peydro, J. L., & Saurina, J. (2013). *Macroprudential policy, countercyclical bank capital buffers and credit supply: Evidence from the Spanish dynamic provisioning experiments* (European Banking Center Discussion Paper, No. 2012-011)

Table 10.3 Macroprudential policy instruments in international and Russian practice and the purposes of their application

Tool group	*Tools*	*Objectives of macroprudential policy Risk targeted by the instrument*
Instruments affecting capital		
Capital buffers	Countercyclical capital buffer Conservation capital buffer Buffer for a bank's systemic importance	Easing the bank's pro-cyclical activity in the short term Credit risk: reducing the growth of the loan portfolio through more expensive funding (domestic)
Sector capital requirements	Indicators of volumes and prices of credits by instruments; Limits of industry concentration of borrowers; Position limits in securities	
CET 1 surcharge for systemically important banks	CET 1 surcharge for systemically important banks (O-SII)	Increasing the ability of the capital of systemically important banks to cover unexpected losses Significant risks for SIBs
Instruments affecting liquidity		
Countercyclical liquidity requirements	LCR (short-term liquidity indicator); NSFR (Net Stable Funding Index); Maximum Limit on Loan to Deposit Ratio (LTD) Limits on the duration of assets and liabilities	Regulation: current liquidity; Long term liquidity; Shares of unstable funding; balance sheet liquidity risk;
Currency balance	Limits on an open currency position	Currency risk
Market premiums and discounts	Discounts for collateral for loans; Liquidity premium; Financial Market Depth Indicators	Market liquidity risk

(continued)

Table 10.3 (continued)

Tool group	*Tools*	*Objectives of macroprudential policy Risk targeted by the instrument*
Instruments affecting assets		
LTV (loan-to-value)/LTI (loan-to-value); Restrictions on lending in foreign currency; Required reservations	Loan to collateral ratio; The ratio of the loan to the income of the borrower	Decrease in LGD of banks Decreased borrower PD and corporate portfolio credit risk

Source compiled by the author

recession to contain a further downturn, while in preventing the buildup of systemic credit risk and containing a credit boom this measure is ineffective. Kim (2013)[7] studied the impact of LTV and DTI restrictions on mortgage lending volumes and residential real estate prices in Korea during the period 2003–2012 and came to the conclusion that these measures are countercyclical in nature and successfully regulate the credit cycle, as well as curb the growth of real estate prices. Restrictions on the level of leverage, in his opinion, lead to the reduction in short-term borrowing by banks. At the same time, he notes that a little-studied area is the interaction of monetary and macroprudential policies.

The study, taking into account specific country characteristics, was presented by S. Claessens, S. Ghosh and R. Mikhet.[8] The authors shown that the intensity of application of macroprudential policy instruments by developing countries is higher due to exposure to higher systemic banking risks, which is associated with larger accumulated domestic imbalances, more frequent external shocks, foreign exchange risks and liquidity shortages. Such problems explain the choice of developing countries in favor of instruments aimed at regulating liquidity (restrictions on external borrowing, restrictions on open foreign exchange positions,

[7] Kim Ch. *Macroprudential policies: Korea's experiences. Rethinking macro policy II: First steps and early lessons*. Conference hosted by the IMF. Washington, DC, April 16–17, 2013.

[8] Claessens, S., Ghosh, S. R., & Mihet, R. (2014). Macro-prudential policies to mitigate financial system vulnerabilities (IMF Working paper No. 155), Access mode: http://www.imf.org/external/pubs/ft/wp/2014/wp14155.pdf

mandatory reserve requirements). Developed countries mainly use tools aimed at restraining the procyclicity of banks' behavior (restrictions on loan portfolio growth rates, LTV, DTI).

In their study, L. Zhang and E. Zoli[9] show the need for macroprudential policy in Asian countries in addition to monetary policy due to different cycles of inflation and asset price cycles, as well as the high cost of monetary policy to regulate a particular sector/industry (for example, only mortgage lending) and the problem of high volatility of capital inflows observed after the global financial and banking crisis.

Next, consider the macroprudential policy tools used in various countries—developed, dynamically developing, developing, since 2000 by impact groups[10]:

1. *Instruments affecting banking assets.* This group will consider two instruments of influencing borrowers (LTV and DTI) (see Table 10.4) and five instruments of influencing assets (concentration limits on assets, limits on interbank loans, limits on the growth of the loan portfolio, limits on the growth of the foreign currency loan portfolio, required mandatory reserve ratios) (see Table 10.5).

2. *Instruments affecting capital.* This group will consider four tools for affecting bank capital (see Table 10.6): countercyclical capital buffer, dynamic provisioning for possible losses, minimum limit on financial leverage, additional capital requirements for systemically important banks.

The practical analysis of measures (tightening/easing) in relation to the instruments of countercyclical and conservation capital buffers based on ESRB data also seem interesting.[11] An overview of these measures will be presented in Tables 10.7 and 10.8.

[9] Zhang, L. & Zoli, E. (2014).*Leaning against the wind: macroprudential policy in Asia* (IMF Working Papers No. 22).

[10] Countries not included in the tables for each instrument did not take action on that instrument.

[11] Kochanska, U. (2018). *ESRB Macroprudential Measures Database (MPMDB) and indicators of the usage of macroprudential instruments*. ESRB, IFC Workshop.

Table 10.4 Use of instruments affecting borrowers, by country, periods of activation (tightening)

Tool	*Country*[12]	*Activation (tightening) period, years*
DTI	Chile (Develop.); Colombia (Develop.); Bahrain (Develop.); Tunisia (Develop.); Hong Kong (EMEs)	2000–2017
	Lebanon (Develop.)	2001–2017
	Ecuador (Develop.)	2002–2017
	–	2003–2017
	Bahamas (Develop.); Kuwait (Develop.); China (EMEs); Serbia (CEE); Romania (CEE)	2004–2017 2004–2017 2004–2017 2004–2012 2004–2017
	South Korea (Develop.); Pakistan (Develop.); Greece(SE)	2005–2017
	Saudi Arabia (Develop.);	2006–2017
	Turkey (Develop.); Kenya (Develop.);	2007–2017
	Canada (Adv.); Algeria (Develop.)	2008–2017
	–	2009–2017
	Norway (WNE); Poland (CEE); Hungary (CEE); Kyrgyzstan (Develop.); Bolivia (Develop.); Qatar (Develop.)	2010–2017
	UAE (Develop.); Lithuania (CEE)	2011–2017
	Brunei (Develop.); Oman (Develop.)	2012–2017
	Netherlands (WNE); Israel (Develop.); Singapore (EMEs); Azerbaijan (CIS); Mongolia (Develop.)	2013–2017
	Bhutan (Develop.); Mauritius (Develop.); Kazakhstan (CIS)	2014–2017
	Estonia (WNE); Kosovo (CEE); Tanzania (Develop.); Curacao (Develop.)	2015–2017
	Slovenia (CEE); Costa Rica (Develop.); Cyprus (SE); Egypt (Develop.); Tuvalu (Develop.)	2016–2017
	Slovakia (CEE);	2017–present
LTV Cap	Austria (WNE); Spain (SE); Chile (Develop.); Colombia (Develop.); Bahamas (Develop.); Curacao (Develop.); Hong Kong (EMEs); Malaysia (Develop.); Pakistan (Develop.); Singapore (EMEs);	2000–2017
	–	2001–2017
	South Korea (Develop.)	2002–2017
	Cyprus (SE); Denmark (WNE); Thailand (Develop.)	2003–2017
	Bangladesh (Develop.); China (EMES); Romania (CEE)	2004–2017
	Costa Rica (Develop.)	2005–2017
	–	2006–2017

(continued)

[12] Each country will be assigned to a group of countries: developed (Adv.), including CEE countries (CEE), countries of Northern and Western Europe (WNE), for the USA, Australia and Canada (Adv.); dynamically developing (EMEs); developing (Develop.); CIS countries (CIS).

Table 10.4 (continued)

Tool	*Country*	*Activation (tightening) period, years*
	Algiers (Develop.); Latvia (WNE)	2007–2017
	Canada (Adv.); Lebanon (Develop.); Oman (Develop.)	2008–2017
	Nepal (Develop.)	2009–2017
	Norway (WNE); Sweden (WNE); Hungary (CEE)	2010–2017
	Turkey (Develop.); India (EMES); Serbia (WNE); Lithuania (WNE); Qatar (Develop.)	2011–2017
	Israel (Develop.); Brunei (Develop.); Indonesia (Develop.)	2012–2017
	Netherlands (WNE); New Zealand (WNE); Brazil (EMES); Kuwait (Develop.); Mongolia (Develop.); Guatemala (Develop.); UAE (EMEs); Saudi Arabia (EMEs)	2013–2017
	Italy (SE); Butane (Develop.); Mauritius (Develop.); Czech Republic (CEE); Slovakia (CEE); Poland (CEE)	2014–2017
	Ireland (WNE); Estonia (WNE); Kosovo (CEE); Sri Lanka (Develop.); Tanzania (Develop.)	2015–2017
	Finland (WNE); Tunisia (Develop.); Slovenia (CEE); Iran (Develop.)	2016–2017
LTV Cap	Iceland (Develop.); Namibia (Develop.)	2017–present

Source compiled by the author

Let us also consider the most relevant measures currently in place regarding the use of the capital buffer for systemic importance (see Table 10.9).

The use of tools to influence liquidity is covered in the analytical materials of the Bank for International Settlements.[13] The intensity of use of this group of instruments is considered in relation to eight instruments: (1) limits on gaps between assets and liabilities in different currencies; (2) restrictions on asset and liability maturity gaps by currency; (3) minimum discount requirements for collateral; (4) short-term liquidity ratio (LCR); (5) Net Stable Funding Ratio (NSFR); (6) short-term foreign exchange liquidity ratio (FECR); (7) currency net stable funding ratio (FFAR); and (8) minimum loan-to-deposit ratio (LDR) requirement. It is interesting to note that all instruments are aimed at

[13] BIS Papers Macroprudential frameworks, December 2017.

Table 10.5 Use of instruments affecting banking assets by countries, periods of activation (tightening)

Tool	*Country*[14]	*Activation (tightening) period, years*
Limits on the growth rate of lending in the national currency	Argentina (Develop.); Ecuador (Develop.); Paraguay (Develop.); Kuwait (Develop.); Lesotho (EMEs)	2000–2017
	Mozambique (Develop.)	2001–2017
	–	2002–2017
	–	2003–2017
	Bangladesh (Develop.); Kyrgyzstan (CIS)	2004–2017
	South Korea (Develop.); Pakistan (Develop.); Greece (SE)	2005–2017
	–	2006–2017
	–	2007–2017
	Pakistan (Develop.); Philippines (Develop.); Moldova (CIS)	2008–2017
	Solomon Islands	2009–2017
	–	2010–2017
	–	2011–2017
	Vietnam (Develop.)	2012–2017
	Oman (Develop.)	2013–2017
	Australia (Adv.)	2014–2017
	China (EMES)	2015–2017
	Nepal (Develop.)	2016–2017
	Ethiopia (Develop.); Iraq (Develop.);	2017–present
Concentration limits for certain asset classes (financial instruments; loans)		2000–2017
	USA (Adv.); Ecuador (Develop.)	2001–2017

(continued)

[14] Each country will be assigned to a group of countries: developed (Adv.), including CEE countries (CEE), countries of Northern and Western Europe (WNE), countries of Southern Europe (SE), for the USA, Canada and Australia (Adv.); dynamically developing (EMEs); developing (Develop.); CIS countries (CIS).

Table 10.5 (continued)

Tool	*Country*	*Activation (tightening) period, years*
	Dominican Republic (Develop.); Singapore (EMES)	2002–2017
	Serbia (WNE); Finland (WNE); Romania (CEE); Australia (Adv.); DRC (Develop.); Georgia (CIS); Namibia (Develop.)	2003–2017
	Sudan (Develop.); Afghanistan (Develop.); Nigeria (Develop.); Iraq (Develop.);	2004–2017
	Honduras (Develop.); Brunei (Develop.); Indonesia (Develop.); Uganda (Develop.); Bahms (Develop.); Saint Kitts and Nevis (Develop.)	2005–2017
	Malta (SE); Slovenia (CEE); Albania (CEE); Malawi (Develop.)	2006–2017
	Switzerland (WNE); Luxembourg (WNE); Angola (Develop.);	2007–2017
	Thailand (Develop.); Montenegro (CEE); Trinidad and Tobago (Develop.); Rwanda (Develop.); South Africa (EMEs);	2008–2017
	Denmark (WNE); Solomon Islands (Develop.); Maldives (Develop.)	2009–2017
	San Marino (WNE); Croatia (CEE)	2010–2017
	Liberia (Develop.)	2011–2017
	Ethiopia (Develop.); Sierra Leone (Develop.); Kosovo (CEE); Papua New Guinea (Develop.)	2012–2017
	Ivory Coast (Develop.)	2013–2017

(continued)

Table 10.5 (continued)

Tool	*Country*	*Activation (tightening) period, years*
	United Kingdom (WNE); Austria (WNE); Germany (WNE); Netherlands (WNE); Ireland (WNE); Estonia (CEE); Latvia (CEE); Lithuania (CEE); Tanzania (Develop.)	2014–2017
	Saudi Arabia (Develop.);Iran (Develop.)	2015–2017
	Oman(Develop.); Qatar (Develop.); Djibouti (Develop.);Benin (Develop.);Myanmar (Develop.)	2016–2017
	Vietnam (Develop.); Tongo (Develop.); Guinea-Bissau (Develop.)	2017–present
Limits on growth rates of lending in foreign currency	Brazil (Develop.); Colombia (Develop.); Jordan (Develop.); Kuwait (Develop.); Pakistan (Develop.); Morocco (Develop.); Moldova (CIS); Tunisia (Develop.); Malawi (Develop..);	2000–2017
	Iceland (WNE); Haiti (Develop.)	2001–2017
	–	2002–2017
	Argentina (Develop.);	2003–2017
	Dominican Republic (Develop.); Ukraine (CIS);	2004–2017
	Fiji (Develop.); Romania (CEE)	2005–2017
	–	2006–2017
	South Korea (Develop.);	2007–2017
	Albania (CEE)	2008–2017
	Turkey (Develop.);	2009–2017
	Austria (WNE); Uganda (Develop.)	2010–2017
	Liberia (Develop.); Hungary (CEE); Serbia (CEE); Belarus (CIS)	2011–2017
	–	2012–2017
	Malta (SE); China (EMEs)	2013–2017

(continued)

Table 10.5 (continued)

Tool	*Country*	*Activation (tightening) period, years*
	Gambia (Develop.); Tanzania (Develop.); Nigeria (Develop.); Oman (Develop.)	2014–2017
	Bosnia and Herzegovina (CEE); Vietnam (Develop.);Papua and New Guinea (Develop.)	2015–2017
	Chile (Develop.); Rwanda (Develop.); Samui (Develop.);Kyrgyzstan (CIS);	2016–2017
	Bangladesh (Develop.); Iran (Develop.); Namibia (Develop.); Poland (CEE)	2017–present
Minimum limits on reserve requirements	Brazil (Develop.); Peru (Develop.); Lebanon (Develop.); Cambodia (Develop.); Pakistan (Develop.); Burundi (Develop.); Mozambique (Develop.); Sudan (Develop.); Mongolia (Develop.); Vietnam (Develop.); Uruguay (Develop.); Libya (Develop.); Solomon Islands (Develop.); Fiji (Develop.); Macedonia (CEE); Armenia (CIS); Belarus (CIS); Georgia (CIS); Kazakhstan (CIS);Ukraine (CIS);	2000–2017
	Argentina (Develop.)	2001–2017
	–	2002–2017
	–	2003–2017
	–	2004–2017
	Bulgaria (CEE);	2005–2007
	Romania (CEE);	2005–2017
	Serbia (CEE)	2005–2017
	–	2006–2017
	–	2007–2017
	Haiti (Develop.)	2008–2017
	–	2009–2017
	Turkey (Develop.)	2010–2017
	Liberia (Develop.); Hungary (CEE); Serbia (CEE);Belarus (CIS)	2011–2017
	Tajikistan (CIS)	2012–2017

(continued)

Table 10.5 (continued)

Tool	*Country*	*Activation (tightening) period, years*
	Malta (SE);China (EMES)	2013–2017
	Indonesia (Develop.);	2014–2017
	China (EMEs); Kyrgyzstan (CIS)	2015–2017
	Russia (EMES);	2016–2017

Source compiled by the author

restraining the structural systemic liquidity risk caused by internal imbalances in banks. Tables 10.10 and 10.11 show the countries that use the liquidity impact toolkit.

From Table 10.11, we can conclude that LCR is the most popular instrument from the liquidity impact group. There are some features of tightening the requirements for LCR: in Sweden, for example, the minimum requirements for LCR (100%) are set by currency (dollars, euros, all currencies). Also in Norway there is a gradual increase in the minimum LCR (from 70% from 01/01/2016 to 100% from 01/01/2018), in Russia—the same, but with a fixed annual step of 10% (70% from 01/01/2016 to 100% from 01/01/2019).

Analysis of practical data allows us to draw conclusions by the following groups of countries—BRICS, countries of the "Big 7" (G7) and EU countries (developed countries)—as well as highlight the following features:

1. **BRICS Countries** (Brazil, Russia, India, China, South Africa):

- equally use the tools, having impact on banking assets and on capital. From the second group of instruments, all five countries have now introduced additional capital requirements for systemically important banks: the first country was China (since 2013), Russia—since 2016. It is worth noting that none of the BRICS countries uses a countercyclical capital buffer, and the use of two other instruments of the group is also weakly expressed: dynamic provisioning has been used

Table 10.6 Use of instruments affecting bank capital

Tool	*Country*[15]	*Activation (tightening) period, years*
Countercyclical capital buffer (CCyB)	Pakistan (Develop.); Serbia (CEE)	2008–2017
	–	2009–2017
	–	2010–2017
	Peru (Develop.)	2011–2017
	–	2012–2017
	Norway (WNE)	2013–2017
	Sweden (WNE)	2014–2017
	–	2015–2017
	Hong Kong (EMEs); Qatar (Develop.); Iceland (WNE)	2016–2017
	Czech Republic (CEE); Slovakia (CEE)	2017–present
Dynamic provisioning for possible loan losses	Spain (WNE); Brazil (EMEs); Nepal (Develop.); Burundi (Develop.)	2000–2017
	–	2001–2017
	–	2002–2017
	China (EMES);	2003–2017
	Kyrgyzstan (CIS); Croatia (CEE)	2004–2017
	Bulgaria (Develop.);	2005–2017
	Turkey (Develop.)	2006–2017
	Australia (Adv.); Columbia (Develop.); Kuwait (Develop.)	2007–2017
	Peru (Develop.);	2008–2017
	Dominican Republic (Develop.); Maldives (Develop.)	2009–2017
	Chile (Develop.)	2010–2017
	Thailand (Develop.); Bolivia (Develop.);	2011–2017
	Ecuador (Develop.); Qatar (Develop.)	2012–2017
	Mexico (Develop.);	2013–2017
	Vietnam (Develop.);	2013–2017
	Kazakhstan (CIS)	2013–2016
	Bhutan (Develop.); Panama (Develop.); Uruguay (Develop.); Tanzania (Develop.)	2014–2017
	Costa Rica (Develop.)	2015–2017

(continued)

[15] Each country will be assigned to a group of countries: developed (Adv.), including CEE countries (CEE), countries of Northern and Western Europe (WNE), for the USA, Canada, Australia and Japan (Adv.); dynamically developing (EMEs); developing (Develop.); CIS countries (CIS).

Table 10.6 (continued)

Tool	*Country*	*Activation (tightening) period, years*
	–	2016–2017
	–	2017–present
Minimum requirements for financial leverage	USA (Adv.); Canada (Adv); Chile (Develop.); Paraguay (Develop.); Saint Kitts and Nevis (Develop.); Bahrain (Develop.); Saudi Arabia (Develop.); Zambia (Develop.);	2000–2017
	Ecuador (Develop.)	2001–2017
	–	2002–2017
	Jordan (Develop.); Papua New Guinea (Develop.)	2003–2017
	Jamaica (Develop.); Kyrgyzstan (CIS);	2004–2017
	–	2005–2017
	–	2006–2017
	–	2007–2017
	Switzerland (WNE); Gambia (Develop.); Trinidad and Tobago (Develop.);	2008–2013 2008–2017 2008–2017
	Maldives (Develop.); Namibia (Develop.)	2009–2017
	Azerbaijan (CIS)	2010–2017
	–	2011–2017
	China (EMEs); Kosovo (Develop.); Uruguay (Develop.);	2012–2017
	South Africa (EMES); Uganda (Develop.); Libya (Develop.);	2013–2017
	Singapore (EMES)	only in 2013
	Turkey (Develop.);Qatar (Develop.);Kuwait (Develop.);Bhutan (Develop.)	2014–2017
	Bangladesh (Develop.);	2015–2017
	United Kingdom (WNE); Belarus (CIS); Nicaragua (Develop.); Panama (Develop.);	2016–2017

(continued)

Table 10.6 (continued)

Tool	*Country*	*Activation (tightening) period, years*
	Norway (WNE); Serbia (CEE); Honduras (Develop.); Bahamas (Develop.); Rwanda (Develop.)	2017–present
Additional capital requirements for systemically important banks	Peru (Develop.); Mongolia (Develop.); Uruguay (Develop.)	2012–2017
	Switzerland (WNE); Singapore (EMEs) China (EMEs)	2013–2017
	Czech Republic (WNE); Kuwait (Develop.); Bangladesh (Develop.);	2014–2017
	Norway (WNE); Canada (Adv.); Mexico (Develop.); India (Develop.); Philippines (Develop.);Latvia (CIS); Lithuania (CIS); Denmark (WNE); Nigeria (Develop.)	2015–2017
	Albania (CEE)	Only in 2016

(continued)

Table 10.6 (continued)

Tool	*Country*	*Activation (tightening) period, years*
	US (Adv.); UK (WNE); Austria (WNE); Belgium (WNE); France (WNE); Germany (WNE); Italy (WNE); Netherlands (WNE); Sweden (WNE); Finland (WNE); Iceland (WNE); Malta (SE); Spain (SE); Turkey (Develop.); Japan (Adv.); Australia (Adv.); South Africa (Develop.); Paraguay (Develop.); Saudi Arabia Hong Kong (EMEs); Indonesia (Develop.); South Korea (Develop.); Malawi (Develop.); Mauritius (Develop.); Uganda (Develop.); Russia (EMEs); Slovakia (CEE); Estonia (CEE); Croatia (CEE); Slovenia (CEE); Romania (CEE); Luxembourg (WNE); Qatar (Develop.);	2016–2017
	Brazil (EMEs); Israel (Develop.); Jordan (Develop.); Sri Lanka (Develop.); Kazakhstan (CIS); Bulgaria (CEE); Serbia (CEE); Hungary (CEE); Macedonia (CEE); Poland (CEE); Oman (Develop.)	2017–present

Source compiled by the author

in Brazil since 2000 and in China since 2003; minimum requirements for financial leverage—China (since 2012) and South Africa (since 2013)

- instruments of the group of influence on borrowers are used more seldom than instruments of influence on banking assets. Thus, the reduction of the maximum limit on LTV occurred only in China (since 2004), in India (since 2011) and Brazil (since 2013), on DTI—only in China in 2004. Describing the use of strict measures by the BRICS countries in relation to instruments of influence on banking assets, it can be noted that China is the only country that

Table 10.7 Use of the Countercyclical capital buffer (CCyB) by EU countries

Tool	*Countries*	*Meaning (as of 2019)*	*Validity*	*Changing the actual value*
Countercyclical capital buffer (CCyB)	Austria	0%	01/01/2016–present	
	Belgium		01/01/2016–present	
	Bulgaria		01/01/2016–10/01/2019	0.5%: from 10/01/2019
	Croatia		01/01/2016–present	
	Ireland		01/01/2016–05/07/2019	1%: from 07/05/2019
	Cyprus		01/01/2016–present	
	Estonia		01/01/2016–present	
	Finland		03/16/2015–present	
	France		12/30/2015–07/01/2019	0.25%: from 07/01/2019
	Germany		01/01/2016–present	
	Greece		01/01/2016–present	
	Hungary		01/01/2016–present	
	Latvia		02/01/2016–present	
	Luxembourg		01/01/2016–01/01/2020	0.25%: 01/01/2020
	Malta		01/01/2016–present	
	Netherlands		01/01/2016–present	
	Poland		01/01/2016–present	
	Portugal		01/01/2016–present	

(continued)

Table 10.7 (continued)

Tool	*Countries*	*Meaning (as of 2019)*	*Validity*	*Changing the actual value*
	Romania		01/01/2016–present	
	Spain		01/01/2016–present	
	Slovenia		01/01/2016–present	
	Italy		01/01/2016–present	
	Lithuania	0.5%	12/31/2018–06/30/2019	1%: from 06/30/2019
	Denmark		03/31/2019–09/30/2019	1%: from 09/30/2019
	Great Britain	1%	–	–
	Slovakia	1.25%	01/01/2018–01/01/2019	
	Czech Republic		01/01/2019–07/01/2019	1.5%:07/01/2019–01/01/2020 1.75%: from 01.01.2010
	Sweden	2%	03/19/2017–03/19/2019	2.5%: from 03/19/2019
	Norway		12/31/2017–12/31/2019	2.5%: from 12/31/2019

applies all instruments at the same time (from 2015 to the present). Brazil, China and Russia simultaneously used restrictive measures both in relation to instruments regulating the structural component of systemic risk (concentration limits) and temporary (requirements for reserves for possible losses on loans and limits on lending rates). In this group, concentration limits have been used in all BRICS countries since 2000, except for South Africa (South Africa—since 2008); limits on interbank lending positions—in India (since 2007), in China (since 2014), in Russia (since 2017). On the whole, it

Table 10.8 Use of Conservation Capital Buffer (CCoB) by EU countries

Tool	*Countries*	*Meaning (as of 2019) %*	*Validity*	*Changing the actual value*
Conservation capital buffer (CCoB)	Austria	2.5	From 01/01/2015–0%; From 01/01/2016–0.625%; From 01/01/2017–1.25%; From 01/01/2018–1.875%; From 01/01/2019–2.5%;	
	Belgium	2.5	From 01/01/2015–0%; From 01/01/2016–0.625%; From 01.01.2017–1.25%; From 01/01/2018–1.875%; From 01/01/2019–2.5%;	
	Bulgaria	2.5	Since November 2014	
	Croatia	2.5	Since July 2014	
	Ireland	2.5	From 01/01/2015–0%; From 01/01/2016–0.625%; From 01/01/2017–1.25%; From 01/01/2018–1.875%; From 01/01/2019–2.5%;	
	Cyprus	2.5	Since January 2013	
	Iceland	2.5	From June 2016	
	Estonia	2.5	From May 2014	
	Finland	2.5	Since January 2014	

(continued)

Table 10.8 (continued)

Tool	*Countries*	*Meaning (as of 2019) %*	*Validity*	*Changing the actual value*
	France	2.5	From 01/01/2015–0%; From 01/01/2016–0.625%; From 01/01/2017–1.25%; From 01/01/2018–1.875%; From 01/01/2019–2.5%;	
	Germany	2.5	From 01/01/2015–0%; From 01/01/2016–0.625%; From 01/01/2017–1.25%; From 01/01/2018–1.875%; From 01/01/2019–2.5%;	
	Greece	2.5	From 01/01/2015–0%; From 01/01/2016–0.625%; From 01/01/2017–1.25%; From 01/01/2018–1.875%; From 01/01/2019–2.5%;	
	Hungary	2.5	From 01/01/2015–0%; From 01/01/2016–0.625%; From 01/01/2017–1.25%; From 01/01/2018–1.875%; From 01/01/2019–2.5%;	
	Latvia	2.5	From June 2015	
	Luxembourg	2.5	Since January 2014	

(continued)

Table 10.8 (continued)

Tool	*Countries*	*Meaning (as of 2019) %*	*Validity*	*Changing the actual value*
	Liechtenstein	no information	From March 2015	
	Malta	2.5	From 01/01/2015–0%; From 01/01/2016–0.625%; From 01/01/2017–1.25%; From 01/01/2018–1.875%; From 01/01/2019–2.5%;	
	Netherlands	2.5	From 01/01/2015–0%; From 01/01/2016–0.625%; From 01/01/2017–1.25%; From 01/01/2018–1.875%; From 01/01/2019–2.5%;	
	Portugal	2.5	Since September 2015	
	Romania	2.5	From 01/01/2015–0%; From 01/01/2016–0.625%; From 01/01/2017–1.25%; From 01/01/2018–1.875%; From 01/01/2019–2.5%;	

(continued)

Table 10.8 (continued)

Tool	*Countries*	*Meaning (as of 2019) %*	*Validity*	*Changing the actual value*
	Spain	2.5	From 01/01/2015–0%; From 01/01/2016–0.625%; From 01/01/2017–1.25%; From 01/01/2018–1.875%; From 01/01/2019–2.5%;	
	Slovenia	2.5	From 01/01/2015–0%; From 01/01/2016–0.625%; From 01/01/2017–1.25%; From 01/01/2018–1.875%; From 01/01/2019–2.5%;	
	Italy	2.5	From May 2015	
	Lithuania	2.5	From April 2015	
	Denmark	2.5	From 01/01/2015–0%; From 01/01/2016–0.625%; From 01/01/2017–1.25%; From 01/01/2018–1.875%; From 01/01/2019–2.5%;	
	Great Britain	2.5	From 01/01/2015–0%; From 01/01/2016–0.625%; From 01/01/2017–1.25%; From 01/01/2018–1.875%; From 01/01/2019–2.5%;	

(continued)

Table 10.8 (continued)

Tool	*Countries*	*Meaning (as of 2019) %*	*Validity*	*Changing the actual value*
	Slovakia	No information	Since November 2014	
	Czech Republic	2.5	Since July 2014	
	Sweden	2.5	Since November 2014	
	Norway	2.5	From July 2013	

Source compiled by the author

can be concluded that the BRICS countries applied more intensively measures in relation to instruments of influence on assets that restrain the spread of systemic concentration risk, which depends on intra-bank relations and is transmitted through the price channel and the channel of the interbank lending market. Russia is one of the BRICS countries that began tightening measures on two macro-prudential regulation instruments—limits on interbank loans and minimum reserve requirements—quite late, since 2016. South Africa is the country with the least developed practice of applying macro-prudential policy instruments compared to all BRICS countries: in this country, restrictive measures have been observed only in relation to the concentration limits since 2008. Administrative instruments (taxes on net income) were not applied in these countries.

2. **EU Countries, incl. G7 Countries (Developed):**

- there are no measures related to the instruments of influence on assets that restrain the spread of systemic risk over time. At the same time, in all G7 countries, tightening measures are applied in relation

Table 10.9 Use of instruments by EU countries that affect bank capital

Country	*SRB value as of 2019, % of RWA*	*Measure activation date*	*Systemically important banks in each country*
Austria	Max 2% for 13 banks	From 01/01/2019	
Bulgaria	1.5% for all national banks	From 10/31/2017	
Croatia	3% and 3% depending on the market share in terms of assets: less than 5% and more than 5% respectively	From 19/05/2014	
Czech Republic	In the range from 1 to 3% for 5 banks	From 01/01/2019	
Denmark	In the range from 0.5% to 3% for 7 banks depending on their systemic importance	From 01/01/2019	
Estonia	1% for all banks	From 04/17/2018	
Iceland	3% for 8 banks	From 04/01/2016	
Liechtenstein	2.5% for 3 banks	From 01/01/2019	
Netherlands	3% for 3 banks	From 11/01/2018	
Norway	2% for banks recognized by O-SIIs; 3% for all other banks	From 07/01/2016	
Poland	3% for all banks	From 01/01/2018	
Romania	From 0 to 2% of NPLs for the period June 2017-June 2018 for all banks	From 01/01/2019	

(continued)

Table 10.9 (continued)

Country	*SRB value as of 2019, % of RWA*	*Measure activation date*	*Systemically important banks in each country*
Slovakia	1.5% or 2% dd for O-SIIs	From 01/01/2018	
Sweden	3% for 4 banks	From 01/01/2015	

Source compiled by the author

Table 10.10 Countries using instruments to influence liquidity

Country	*Restrictions on gaps between assets and liabilities in different currencies*	*Restrictions on maturity gaps of assets and liabilities by currency*	*Minimum discount requirements for collateral*
Argentina	■		

Source compiled by the author

Table 10.11 Countries using instruments to influence liquidity (continued)

Country	*LCR*	*NSFR*	*FECR*	*FFAR*	*LDR*
Hungary			■	■	
Saudi Arabia	■	■			■
Bulgaria	■				
Norway	■				
Poland	■	■			
Slovenia					■
Sweden	■				

Source compiled by the author

to limits on interbank loans and concentration limits, which characterizes the high connectedness of banks through interbank channels and the exposure of banks in the G7 countries to the same risk factors.

- the use of tools to influence the borrower has been observed only in Canada since 2008, in Italy—only a reduction in the upper limit (tightening) on LTV since 2014.
- among the EU countries, the tightening of measures on instruments impacting banking assets is represented more intensively in Eastern Europe countries than in Western Europe and Southern Europe.
- the least popular instrument from the capital impact group is the countercyclical capital buffer; the activation of measures in relation to this instrument began only during the beginning of the global financial crisis (since 2008).
- there has been a sharp increase in the intensity of using additional capital requirements for systemically important banks since 2015, mainly in the EU and dynamically developing countries.
- only three of the G7 countries apply capital requirements for systemic importance (Canada since 2015; others since 2016).
- slightly more than a third of the EU countries have applied restrictive measures since 01/01/2016 in relation to the countercyclical capital buffer.[16]
- conservation capital buffer in half of the EU countries was applied with a gradual tightening ("time-varying"), in others—using a fixed value ("fixed").
- Also, from the analysis carried out, it is possible to identify the features of the application of macroprudential policy instruments in developed, dynamically developing and developing countries (in accordance with the UN classification):
- the minimum leverage requirement is used primarily in developing countries
- macroprudential policy instruments applied to the borrower (including industry-specific restrictions, for example, on the loan-to-value ratio (LTV) or risk weight depending on the asset class, are most widely used in developed countries, while application of instruments impacting banking assets are on average higher in all group of countries compared with instruments impacting liquidity and capital;
- the minimum leverage requirement is used primarily in developing countries;

[16] Information on CCyB is available on the ESRB website. Access mode: https://www.esrb.europa.eu/national_policy/ccb/html/index.en.html.

- there has been a sharp increase in the use of additional capital requirements for systemically important banks since 2015, mainly in the EU and dynamically developing countries;
- in the BRICS countries, the instruments of the group of influence on borrowers are used to a much lesser extent than the instruments of influence on bank assets;
- LCR is the most commonly used instrument for influencing liquidity, regardless of whether a country belongs to the group of developed or developing countries.

Before proceeding to the evaluation of the effectiveness of measures of a number of macroprudential policy instruments on the loan portfolio of the Russian banking sector, we will present the measures of the macroprudential policy of the Bank of Russia, starting in 2013 (Table 10.12).

The most important element of macroprudential policy is **assessment of the effectiveness of measures in relation to macroprudential policy instruments.** The criteria for evaluating the effectiveness of macroprudential policy measures can be systematized as follows:

- preventing the accumulation of systemic banking risks in the banking sector
- the ratio of benefits and costs after the implementation of measures in relation to macroprudential policy instruments
- timely application of measures by the banking regulator
- the degree of impact on the expectations of financial market participants after the introduction of instruments
- changing approaches to building a risk-management system in banks
- assessment of leaks from the application of macroprudential policy measures (banks leaving for the shadow banking sector).[17]

The choice of instruments of macroprudential policy is currently quite difficult due to a number of reasons. First, there is no universal basis

[17] Systemic risk of the financial sector: assessment and regulation: monograph / Karminsky A.M., Stolbov M.I., Shchepeleva M.A. ed. A.M. Karminsky.M.: Scientific Library, 2017-284 p.

Table 10.12 Measures of the Bank of Russia's macroprudential policy

Period of macroprudential actions	*Measures concerning macroprusential instruments taken by Central Bank of Russia*
4–1 Q 2012/2013	The need to stimulate lending in conditions of low interest rates in the markets of developing countries by increasing the maximum levels of LTV and DTI indicators.
2–3 Q 2013	The Bank of Russia increased the coefficients for calculating RWA
4–1 Q 2013/2014	Possible introduction of a countercyclical capital buffer after the credit gap has grown to 2%
2–3 Q 2014	Differentiation of risk weights for mortgage loans depending on LTV: the higher the LTV, the higher the risk, and the higher the coefficient for calculating RWA is introduced)
2–3 Q 2015	Reduction of risk coefficients in the calculation for loans to small and medium-sized businesses
2–3 Q 2016	Increase of risk coefficients on foreign currency loans Raising the standards of mandatory reserves for banks' liabilities in foreign currency
4–1 Q 2016/2017	Introduction of a new scale of risk weights for calculating RWA for consumer loans
4–1 Q 2017/2018	Reduction of loans with an initial high contribution requires a decrease in the upper limit on LTV Possible increase in requirements for the share of high-liquid assets in the total assets of the bank From 01.08.2018, the Bank of Russia increases the mandatory reserve ratio by 1 p.p. for obligations in foreign currency (up to 7% for obligations of retail clients and up to 8% on other obligations)
2–3 Q 2018 г	Since 01.01.2018, the risk coefficients for calculating RWA for loans with LTV < 80% have been increased From 01.10.2019, it is planned to introduce a mandatory debt burden indicator (PD) in banks Since 01.05.2018, the risk coefficients for consumer loans with the full loan cost from 15–25% have been increased, from 01.09.2018 further increases are planned Gradual refusal from credit lines from Bank of Russia by all banks by 01.01.2021

(continued)

Table 10.12 (continued)

Period of macroprudential actions	*Measures concerning macroprusential instruments taken by Central Bank of Russia*
4–1 Q 2018/2019	Since 01.04.2019 the surcharges to the risk coefficients on consumer loans with full clean cost from 10 to 30% have been increased In the fourth quarter of 2018, the allowances to the risk coefficients for mortgage loans granted after 01.01.2019 with an initial payment of 10% to 20% were increased Raising the mandatory reservation for obligations to individuals in foreign currency is considered
2–3 Q 2019	In June 2019, surcharges were established to the risk coefficients for consumer loans, depending on the full loan cost and the borrower's PD, which apply to loans issued from 01.10.2019
2–3 Q 2020	Allowances for new unsecured consumer loans were reduced in order to supportretail lending In accordance with the countercyclical approach of the macroprudential policy, allowances to risk coefficients for unsecured consumer loans in rubles issued before 31.08.2019 were canceled The decision not to consider the reduction of the actual value of the standard N26 (N27) of the SIBs as a result of the lack of highly liquid assets and other alternative instruments due to the limited possibility of prolongation or raising funds for a period of more than 30 calendar days was canceled due to the improvement of the liquidity situation in the banking sector
2–3 Q 2021	Since 01.10.2021I, allowances to risk coefficients for unsecured consumer loans in rubles have been increased Surcharges to risk coefficients for loans with a high value of the total cost of the loan and loans provided to borrowers with a high debt burden have been increased
2–3 Q 2022	Macroprudential limits were set for loans granted to borrowers with full debt burden of more than 80%, including loans with a credit limit, at the level of 25% Macroprudential limits for loans issued for a period of more than 5 years were set at the level of 10%

for choosing specific macroprudential policy measures in different situations. Secondly, macroprudential policy as a scientific concept is quite young and sufficient experience in using the tools has not yet been formed. Thirdly, it is difficult to conduct a quantitative analysis of the effectiveness of macroprudential policy measures due to an insufficient statistical base. Fourth, there are questions about the interchangeability and complementarity of the application of monetary policy instruments and macroprudential policy, as well as the consistency in the consequences for the regulation of the credit market of the simultaneous application of several macroprudential policy instruments by regulators.

Due to little experience in quantifying the effectiveness of measures of the macroprudential policy in the Russian banking sector, **this article proposes a model for evaluating the effectiveness of macroprudential policy measures to regulate lending growth in order to minimize systemic credit risk**. The model evaluates the impact of macro indicators, indicators of market risk factors, as well as a number of balance sheet indicators and the constructed index of macroprudential policy on: the real growth rate of loans in the Russian economy (Real credit growtht) and the volume of banking loans (Δln(Loansbanks,t). The macroprudential policy index is constructed on measures for two instruments: **currency-differentiated minimum reserve requirements and increased risk weights for calculating risk-weighted loans.**

The following autoregressive model specifications have been proposed to assess the impact of the above described factors on the dependant variables and evaluate the effectiveness of measures relating these two instruments of the macroprudential policy.

Model №1 specification:

$$\begin{aligned} \text{Re}al\,credit\,growth\; &= £ * \text{Re}al\,credit\,growth - 1 \\ &+ \sum \rho * MPPIndex * GDP\,growth \\ &+ \sum \gamma * GDPgrowth + \sum \beta * Interestratet \\ &+ VIXIt + dVIXt + C + \varepsilon_t \end{aligned}$$

Model №2 specification is as follows:

$$\begin{aligned} Loansbanks, t &= £ * Loansbanks, t - 1 + \sum \beta * Interestratet - 1 \\ &+ \Sigma\gamma * GDPgrowthk, t - 2 \end{aligned}$$

Table 10.13 Variables of the model for evaluating the effectiveness of macroprudential policy measures of the Bank of Russia

Variable	*Description*
Real credit growth	Lending growth rate at time t (total loan portfolio of the Russian banking sector by legal entities, individuals and banks)
MPP Index	Variable reflecting the adoption of measures in relation to the two macroprudential policy instruments considered in the model
*MPP Index*GDP growth*	Variable reflecting the adoption of the two macroprudential policies considered in the model, adjusted for quarterly GDP growth rates
GDP_growtht	Quarterly growth rates of Russia's real GDP at time *t*
interest rate	The value of the market interest rate at time t (the model used Mosprime 3M)
Loansbankst	Issued by all banks Russian banking sector loans at time *t*
Equity/ Assetsbanks, t-1	Ratio of capital to assets banking sector Russia at time *t*-1
Deposits/ Creditsbanks, t-1	The ratio of customer deposits to the total loan portfolio banking sector Russia at time *t*-1

Source compiled by the author

$$
\begin{aligned}
&+ \Sigma\rho * MPPIndexk, t-3 \\
&+ \Sigma\Omega * Equity/Assetsbanks, t-1 \\
&+ \Sigma\delta * Deposits/Loansbanks, t-1 + C + \varepsilon_t
\end{aligned}
$$

Table 10.13 presents the description of the variables of the presented model specifications.

Table 10.14 shows the values of the studied macroprudential policy measures from 07/01/2007 to 02/01/17.

The cumulative index of macroprudential policy, shown in Fig. 10.1, is calculated for each month as the sum of the values of measures in respect of these two instruments accumulated to that month.

The main conclusions obtained as a result of calculations for autoregressive models in specification №1 are the following:

1. The adopted macroprudential policy measures, adjusted for quarterly GDP growth rates, are not statistically significant in explaining the growth rate of loans: thus, it is likely that the impact of macroprudential policy measures should be considered without reference to GDP growth rates, as presented in Specification №2.

Table 10.14 Values of studied macroprudential policy measures from 01.07.2007 until 01.02.17

Month and year of the action *1: restrictive measure;* *−1: mitigating measure;* *0: no action taken*	*Differentiated reserve requirements*	*Risk weights to calculate RWA*
July 2007	1	0
October 2007	−1	0
January 2008	1	0
March 2008	1	0
July 2008	1	0
09/01/2008–09/17/2008	1	0
09/18/2008–09/30/2008	−1	0
October 2008	−1	0
May 2009	0	−1
February 2011	1	0
March 2011	1	0
April 2011	1	0
October 2011	0	1
March 2013	−1	0
July 2013	0	1
January 2014	0	1
May 2014	0	−1
December 2014	0	−1
January 2015	0	−1
February 2015	0	−1
April 2015	0	1
August 2015	0	1
January 2016	0	−1
April 2016	1	0
May 2016	0	1
July 2016	1	0
August 2016	1	0
January 2017	−1	0
December 2017	0	1
January 2018	1	0

2. The VIX indicator, which is used as an alternative to the global financial instability index, has a significant impact on the real growth rates of loans in the 99% confidence interval, which indicates a high degree of reaction of the national banking sector to the volatility of

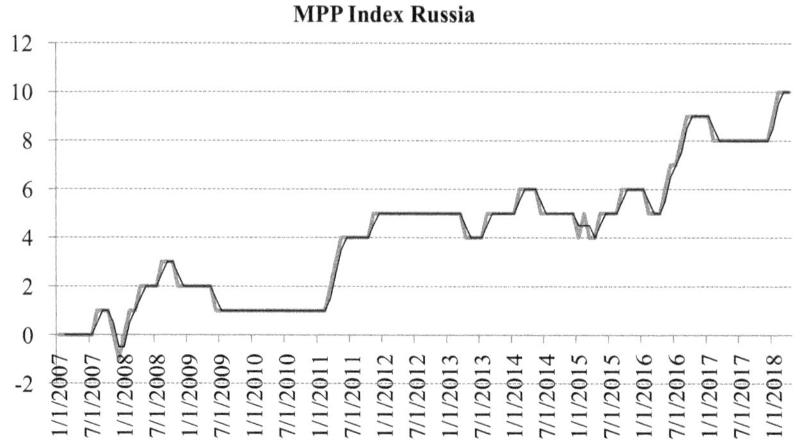

Fig. 10.1 Cumulative index of macroprudential policy built on two instruments of macroprudential policy aimed at regulating the pace of the volume of loans and the absolute volume of the loan portfolio (*Source* compiled by the author)

Table 10.15 Significance of explanatory variables of Specification #1

	Regression coefficients	*Standard error of the t-statistic*
Constant (trendline)	−0.017	0.08
First Difference VIX	0.42***	0.13
Second difference Mosprime 3 M	0.701***	0.19
Index of macroprudential policy at time t, adjusted for quarterly GDP growth rates at time t	−0.012	0.06
GDP growth rate at time t	0.035	0.06
The total volume of banking sector loans at time t-1	0.554***	0.08

Source compiled by the author

the global financial market. We present the obtained coefficients for explanatory variables for the first specification in Table 10.15.

The conclusions obtained for specification №2 of the AR-model are the following:

3. The added variables with a time lag for the 3-month Mosprime rate become less statistically significant for the total loan portfolio, which is logical for short-term money market interest rates.
4. The impact of introducing a macroprudential policy index appropriate for regulating the total volume of loans has a significant statistically significant negative impact with a single lag at a confidence level of 95%. As the lags increase, the statistical significance weakens due to the fast response of the dependant variable to the measures taken by the regulator.
5. Single lags of balance sheet variables (Capital/Assetsbanks, *t*-1, Deposits/Creditsbanks, *t*-1) which characterize the financial condition of the entire banking sector in the model turn out to be statistically significant at a 90%-confidence interval.
6. GDP growth rates do not have a significant impact on the total volume of loans regardless of the lag.

Thus, from both specifications of the model, it can be concluded that the application of reserve requirements and risk weights for calculating risk-weighted assets to regulate the credit market in the Russian banking sector significantly affects the total volume of loans on the confidence horizon of 90% with a lag of one quarter. At the same time, as the lags increase, the statistical significance of the macroprudential policy index weakens which indicates a high degree of reaction of the credit market to the application of currency-differentiated requirements for mandatory reserves and increased risk weights for calculating risk-weighted assets. Also in both specifications, short-term money market rates at time t turn out to be statistically significant on the confidence horizon $\gamma = 99\%$ and the dependence is positive ($k = 0.06$). At the same time, for money market rates with a lag of one quarter, the coefficient for the factor variable "3-month Mosprime" is negative ($k = -0.03$): this can be explained by the fact that with an increase in the cost of short-term funding in

Table 10.16 Significance of explanatory variables of Specification #2

	Regression coefficients	*Standard error of the t-statistic*
Constant	0.023***	0.01
The ratio of capital to assets at time *t*-1	0.02*	0.01
The ratio of deposits to loans at time *t*-1	0.02*	0.01
Mosprime 3 M at time *t*	0.06***	0.01
Mosprime 3 M at time *t*-1	−0.03**	0.01
Macroprudential policy index at time *t*-1	−0.06**	0.03
Macroprudential policy index at time *t*-2	0.058*	0.03

Source compiled by the author

the previous quarter, interest rates on loans by the time t will already be increased, which will lead to a reduction in the demand for loans. With an increase in rates at time t, lending rates will remain at the same level at time t which will stimulate credit demand at time t in anticipation of their subsequent increase. We present all significant explanatory variables for the total volume of loans from the second specification of the model in Table 10.16.[18]

Conclusion

The contributions of the study are as follows:

- The chapter presents the author's classification of indicators for assessing systemic banking risks used by national and foreign regulators of the banking sector;
- defines the concept, goals of macroprudential policy and its instruments classifications;
- researches the practical aspects of the application of macroprudential policy instruments in the EU, BRICS and developing countries since 2000;
- presents the model of the effectiveness of measures in relation to two instruments of macroprudential policy and of a number of balance

18 *** - significance level $\alpha=1\%$; **-significance level $\alpha=5\%$; *-significance level $\alpha=10\%$.

sheet and macro-indicators for regulating the Russian credit market in order to prevent the buildup of systemic credit risk in the banking sector.

References

Cerutti, E., Correa, R., Fiorentino, E., & Segalla, E. (2017). Changes in prudential policy instruments: A new cross-country database. *International Journal of Central Banking, 13*(1), 477–503.

Claessens, S., Ghosh, S. R., & Mihet, R. (2014). *Macro-prudential policies to mitigate financial system vulnerabilities* (IMF Working paper No. 155).

ESRB. (2014). The ESRB handbook on operationalising macro-prudential policy in the banking sector.

Hurd, T. R. (2015). *Contagion! The spread of systemic risk in financial networks.*

Key aspects of Macroprudential Policy. IMF Policy Paper, 2013.

Kim, C. (2013, April). Macroprudential policies: Korea's experiences. *Rethinking macro policy II: First steps and early lessons conference hosted by the IMF*, pp. 16–17.

Laeven, L., & Levine, R. (2009). Bank governance, regulation and risk taking. *Journal of Financial Economics, 93*(2), 259–275.

Leonard T. Stern. (2015). *How to measure and regulate systemic risk.*

Mishkin, F. (2000). *Financial stability and the Macroeconomy.* (Working Paper No. 09). Central Bank of Iceland, Department of Economics.

CHAPTER 11

Financial Resolution of Banks in Distress: International Evidence

Nataliya Kovaleva and Oksana Petrova

11.1 Introductory Notes

The banking sector was heavily influenced by the financial crisis in 2008. During this crisis, several years which followed banks were subject to a strong financial pressure and stricter regulation. According to Baudino et al. (2019), between 2008 and 2013, nearly 500 American banks went bankrupt which resulted in the outlays from the Deposit Insurance Fund equal to about US$73 billion. In the Eurozone, during 2008–2014, governments spent 8% of GDP to support the financial sector (Baudino et al., 2018).

This made both banks and regulators revise the ways they treat the institutions in trouble to improve the systemic consequences management and maintain confidence in the banking sector.

N. Kovaleva (✉) · O. Petrova
Moscow, Russia
e-mail: NKovaleva@fa.ru

O. Petrova
e-mail: ONPetrova@fa.ru

A. Karminsky and M. Stolbov (eds.), *Systemic Financial Risk*,
https://doi.org/10.1007/978-3-031-54809-3_11

The objective of banking supervision and regulation is to ensure the safe and sound functioning of banks but the methods applied are not of preventive nature. If a bank is no longer sound, the national regulator faces a trade-off between launching the procedure of insolvency (bankruptcy and liquidation) and the process of solving its problems to re-launch this bank's activities (financial recovery).

In the latter case, the legislation in many countries stipulates certain measures and instruments to support troubled banks. It is worth noting that some instruments are used by credit institutions themselves, their shareholders and depositors without involving regulators or governments. Other measures are the oversight bodies' responsibility, and sometimes governments take charge to help credit institutions. Let us consider the international practices and tools to support banks at different levels of responsibility.

According to the study conducted by the Financial Stability Institute among national banking authorities, as summarized by Baudino et al. (2018), the main drivers of bank insolvency are the loss of both short-term and long-term liquidity, lack of balance sheet liquidity, violation of performance standards and insufficient capitalization.

Depending on the systemic importance of a failing or failed bank and on how critical its functions are, the authorities may take a decision to either resolve or liquidate it. The main goal of such decision is to minimize the impact of the bank's insolvency on the financial system and the economy as a whole. If resolved, the bank will keep its functions. If the bank is of no systemic significance, it is liquidated. Even if the decision is made to support the bank, for example, because a part of the business can be sold in liquidation, the main goal of such a sale is to maximize the value for the lender or to minimize costs for the deposit insurer. International authorities prioritize risks and challenges in international bank failures.

11.2 Measures of Financial Recovery Applied by Banking Institutions

A liquidation of a bank directly affects depositors and borrowers, resulting in irreversible consequences for both banking and financial sectors. That is why it is necessary to provide a timely financial support to insufficiently sound banks or the banks with the first signs of financial insolvency.

The analysis of documents published by international supervisors, in particular the study of the International Monetary Fund "Euro area policies..." (IMF, 2018), the Directive on the Restoration and Resolution of Banks in the European Union (hereafter referred to as BRRD) (see Official Journal of the European Union, 2014) has made it possible to single out the following measures in modern banking practices which banks apply independently when facing difficulties.

Preparing a Bank's Recovery Plan

Within the bank resolution framework, the BRRD included, special attention is paid to the development of a financial recovery plan being an important measure in the recovery of credit institutions. The Financial Stability Board has even issued a special instruction: FSB SIFI Recommendations—Recovery and Resolution Planning for Systematically Important Financial Institutions (FSB, 2013). The Basel Committee on Banking Supervision conducted a survey among national regulators about the existence of legal national framework of designing financial recovery and resolution plans) (BCBS, 2011). National legal frameworks related to recovery plans differ across the countries. Most of the surveyed regulators assert they already have the requirements to the contingency plans in order to maintain the stability of business and continue critically important operations in crisis times. Several respondents including those from the United States have official regimes of working out financial recovery and resolution plans requiring that banks should prepare the plans of quick and streamlined recovery in case there is a major financial crisis or bankruptcy. A number of respondents, for instance from South Africa, Switzerland and the United Kingdom, are engaged in elaborating legal provisions for making financial recovery and resolution plans, whereas some others participate in the work of crisis management groups which develop financial recovery and resolution plans for large international banks. It is worth noting that the development of the recovery plan is an interactive and recurring process involving constant cooperation and information exchange between regulators and banks. The primary objective of this plan is to stabilize the troubled bank and to develop recovery scenarios. A financial recovery plan should combine measures tailored for a particular bank and make it possible to shape a structured approach to collecting and analyzing the information about the bank, as well as to identify the gaps for a wide range of indicators compared to their target values. According to Financial Services Authority (FSA) of Great Britain, the financial recovery plan should include scenarios to manage both bank-specific and market stress along with instruments and measures targeted at replenishing the lack of capital and liquidity in order to recover the bank (FSA, 2011). Thus, international banking regulators believe that banks and national regulators should necessarily have pre-prepared templates of financial recovery plans which could be quickly adapted and applied, should banks demonstrate signs of instability and insolvency.

Bail-in Mechanism

Large-scale reforms in regulation which follow the global financial crisis (GFC) have improved the concept of sharing the costs related to bank recovery between its creditors and governments. In this regard, the most preferable is the bail-in mechanism. The bail-in mechanism is a scheme to rescue a failing bank by attracting funds from large creditors—depositors and other account holders. They are invited to convert their accounts into bank shares or a subordinated loan to replenish bank's capital. Investors and depositors undoubtedly would prefer to keep the solvency of the institution rather than face a trade-off losing the complete value of their investments or deposits in crisis times. This tool can be used as a part of measures undertaken for recovery, and independently by banks without the involvement of the banking supervisor. The most impressive example of the independent use of bail-in in the Russian practice is the case of "Trust" bank, which converted large deposit accounts into subordinated loans between 2011 and 2014.

The adoption of the BRRD in 2014 made a significant contribution to the development and strengthening of national legislation regarding the bail-in mechanism. According to Restoy (2018), at least 8% of the bank's liabilities must be restructured via the application of a bail-in mechanism. The German authorities were among the first to begin strengthening the legal frameworks of the bail-in regime under the BRRD and, in particular, they adopted legislative subordination of creditors' claims based on a multi-level approach. Similar legislative initiatives were undertaken in France, Italy, Belgium and Spain.

A bail-in mechanism is duly practiced in developing countries as well. Researches refer to the successful experience in using this mechanism to rescue troubled banks in African countries (Havemann, 2019).

The use of the bail-in mechanism has also been announced in Russia: the Deposit Insurance Agency proposes to use bail-in as a tool in the resolution of weak banks (Kornilova, 2017).

However, this mechanism has both advantages and disadvantages. Its great advantage is that it provides the opportunity for a bank to avoid license revocation and bankruptcy. It also allows to save public funds. As a result, this mechanism makes it possible not only to improve the position of creditors, but also to reduce the government's costs on the resolution of a failing bank when it is recapitalized.

The advantage of bail-in becomes evident when compared with an alternative mechanism of quick disposal of assets given the strategy of the troubled bank activity is adjusted. In this case, the bail-in mechanism is more attractive because the alternative mechanism of disposing assets is only applicable when there are no restrictions in antitrust legislation but there is a competitive market of corporate control.

The disadvantage of the bail-in mechanism is that its application may be interpreted as a signal that the bank is facing significant problems. The market perceives this fact negatively, and the application of the mechanism acts as an impetus for the outflow of depositors. Thus, the use of the bail-in mechanism by the bank leads to an increase in strategic risk.

Restructuring Plans of Bad Assets and Liabilities

The mechanism of nonperforming loans securitization (hereafter referred to as NPL-securitization) is now widely used along with other standard measures of restructuring bad assets and liabilities. This is another instrument designed to share the burden of assistance to a stressed bank between itself and public authorities. The state and responsible supervisory bodies provide the governmental guarantee on restructured financial instruments. The scheme involves combining bad loans subject to securitization and transferring them to a SPV (Special Purpose Vehicle) for further issuing debt instruments in several tranches.

The government underwrites the senior tranche as a CDS (Credit Default Swap) between the state and a SPV. The schemes backed by the state usually ensure more beneficial prices than market deals and hence minimize potential losses for initiating banks. The securitization of bad loans is not a new instrument in the banks' toolkit to cope with nonperforming loans. In North America and in many European countries securitization legislation dates back to the previous century. According to

Deloitte research «NPL securitizations and related governmental guarantee schemes in Europe» between 2003 and 2007, there was a series of large deals on securitization of nonperforming loans in Italy, Belgium, Portugal and Germany amounting to 19.9 mln euros (Delloitte, 2020).

Earlier, a similar mechanism was used in the United States during the Savings and Loan Crisis in the 1980s and the Asian crisis in 1990s. Nowadays, NPL-securitization is most widely used in Italy and Greece, which is explained by the considerable support the governments provide to these schemes such as Italian Garanzia Cartolarizzazione Sofferenze (GACS) and Greek scheme of assets protection (HAPS). Between 2016 and 2020, such transactions in Europe totaled 88.8bln. euros in GBV (gross balance value) and 28.2 bln. euros in face value. Italy's share is 75% followed by Greece (13%), Ireland (10%), Portugal and Spain—1% each. More than 70% of deals involve the governmental guarantee while the rest are backed by non-government organizations. The most striking recent example is the case of Banca Monte dei Paschi di Siena S.p.A (hereafter referred to as MPS). MPS is one of the five largest banks in Italy and has a long history of taking resolution actions against failing—precautionary recapitalization, government bailouts and using other resolution tools.

The results of stress testing in 2016 showed that MPS had a large amount of nonperforming NPL loans on its balance sheet. After that MPS sold a bad loan portfolio for about 26 billion euros through a securitization scheme (IMF, 2018). The main advantages of NPL-securitization for banks are as follows: reducing NPL portfolio, decreasing costs of financial recovery, creating liquidity and reducing the burden on capital. The recent deals have given an impetus to the development of regulatory control over NPL-securitization in the European Union and other countries.

Revision and Adjustment Strategy of the Bank's Activities

A revision and adjustment strategy of the bank's activities and allocation of assets are made to identify unprofitable and loss-making business lines and dispose of these business lines. The sale of bank assets and even business lines is aimed at preserving their value and recovery of the bank's activity. The procedure is carried out in the way that will most likely maximize the value for creditors. This instrument is included in the mandatory list for unstable banks. The practice of selling assets by large banks is quite interesting. The large banks which are recognized "too big to fail" have to set up a separate holding company to manage assets and certain liabilities. This company is a temporary entity (Kornilova, 2017) and will operate until a right buyer comes along. When the buyer is found, the proceeds from the sale of assets and business lines are spent on repaying the debts to creditors or replenishing the capital.

Attracting a New Investor

This measure is widely used for bank recovery in many countries. For example, such Italian banks as Veneto Banca and Banca Popolare di Vicenza had a history of poor profitability, high level of nonperforming loans and capital shortfalls. In 2016, the private fund "Atlante" acquired almost a 100% stake in the bank (IMF, 2018). One may find many similar examples in other countries, as well as in Russia (Andryushin & Kuznetsova, 2017).

11.3 Financial Recovery Measures Applied by the Supervisory Authorities

Banks are complicated entities regulated in a specific way. That is why oversight authorities can take timely intervention measures to minimize the impact of a bank's failure on the financial system. In case of a stressed bank, it is extremely important to make a decision quickly to prevent a bank run and avoid panics among depositors so that the bank may continue its economic activity (Svoronos, 2018). Today supervisory authorities tend to play a proactive role in the resolution of banking institutions' insolvency.

In the international practice, the Deposit Insurance Schemes (hereafter referred to as DIS) are used not only to pay out the insured deposits of failed banks, but also to support member banks financially (hereafter referred to as "alternative measures"). In 2019, the Financial Stability Institute conducted a survey, received responses from 53 countries and prepared a review about using DIS resources to finance alternative measures (Baudino et al., 2019). About 60% of respondents confirmed that it is possible to use the Deposit Insurance Fund to finance alternative measures. Alternative measures include the following types of financial assistance:

Capital Support

DIS may provide capital support to member banks either to prevent insolvency, or to address insolvency resolution, or in both cases. The DIS of Brazil, Italy and Spain can provide capital support to the banks on the brink of insolvency. The DIS of Colombia, Indonesia, Mexico and Turkey may provide capital support to scheme members in resolution. The legal frameworks of Deposit Insurance Funds in such countries as Germany, Canada, Norway, Korea and Morocco allow the provision of capital support to DIS member banks both to avert bankruptcy and in the process of insolvency resolution.

Liquidity Support and Liquidity Assistance

In practice, several sources may be combined when the measures to support the liquidity of financial stressed banks are implemented. In many countries, DIS can provide the liquidity assistance to member banks before bankruptcy and to those that are in the process of resolution, for example, in Canada, Germany, Korea and Nigeria.

Some countries, such as Brazil, provide liquidity support from the Deposit Insurance Fund as a preventive measure to banks before their insolvency occurs on condition they preserve the capacity to pay. Sometimes the provision of liquidity is carried out in cooperation with the mechanisms of the central banks (Mexico, Jamaica, Turkey and Indonesia).

Funding for Purchase and Assumption Transactions (P&A)

This mechanism involves a full or partial transfer of deposits and other liabilities from a stressed bank to a solvent bank. The transferred liabilities are backed with the assets of the failing bank. If there is a shortfall of assets, funding from DIS resources is provided as financial assistance to the acquiring bank. There are several forms of funding P&A transactions using DIS resources: cash, asset purchase, loss-sharing agreements, provision guarantees and loans against securities. DIS in different countries provides financial support for certain types of P&A transactions: when transferring insured deposits, when transferring uninsured deposits, and when transferring liabilities. In Canada, Italy, Mexico and in four other countries DIS resources can be used to finance the transfer of all deposits and liabilities of a failed bank.

In other countries, only certain types of P&A transactions are supported. In international practice, there is a wide range of forms to provide financial assistance: providing cash to the acquiring bank (Serbia, Indonesia), buying assets from an insolvent bank (Japan, Korea), loss-sharing agreements (Canada, United States, Mexico and Singapore), providing secured loans (Jamaica, Sri Lanka). The experience of the United States is the most developed. In recent years, the United States has used P&A transactions as the main tool in bank resolution. P&A transactions in the United States fall into four categories: Basic P&A, Whole-bank P&A, Loss-share P&A, P&A with loan pools, see FDIC (2017). The first type under consideration is called the main one. It involves the transfer of deposits (all or only insured ones) and highly liquid assets (cash, securities) to the acquiring bank. The second type is known as a general banking one.

All deposits and liabilities are transferred to the acquiring bank, and it buys all the assets on a discounted basis. The third type is loss sharing. This type of transaction is similar to the previous one, an additional condition being an agreement with the Federal Deposit Insurance Corporation[1] (hereafter referred to as FDIC) on loss sharing.

The fourth type is transactions with a credit pool. The acquiring bank takes on deposits and purchases assets—cash, cash equivalents, securities and pools of loans (other assets). Applications are submitted and evaluated separately for each credit pool. This arrangement allows the FDIC to pool assets and deposits from several stressed banks. The disadvantage of this scheme is the operational complexity and associated risks. In Russia P&A transactions are also practiced (Andryushin & Kuznetsova, 2017).

Financing a Bridge Bank (BB) Transaction

A bridge bank is a bank temporarily created where assets and liabilities of a failed bank are transferred. In specific cases, when a P&A transaction is impossible, the deposits and selected liabilities backed by the assets of a failed bank are transferred to a bridge bank. The bridge bank manages the transferred assets and liabilities until a suitable buyer is found. Thus, this

[1] Deposit Insurance Fund in the United States.

mechanism is a sort of reorganization or a partial resolution: the national supervisor revokes the license of the insolvent bank, it is liquidated, and a new bank, i.e., a bridge bank, is founded. The main purpose of the new bank is the accumulation of the working assets of the insolvent bank and its selected liabilities for resale to the third party. The gap between assets and liabilities to be transferred from the failed bank is funded using DIS resources. Typically, the transfer process is managed by the Deposit Insurance Agency, which determines which assets and liabilities should be transferred to the bridge bank. Alternatively, the financial stressed bank is bought by a solvent bank. The provision of DIS resources to a bridge bank can take different forms: monetary grants, asset purchases and capital injections. The banking authorities of twenty-one countries provide various schemes for reorganization of insolvent banks by means of a bridge bank transaction. The schemes with the greatest coverage, involving the transfer of deposits, assets and liabilities, operate in the United States, Mexico, Italy, Nigeria, Jamaica, Germany, Canada and Colombia. This mechanism was also used in Russia, bank "Trust" being an example of such a bridge bank.

Thus, we have considered some alternative measures to support banks with DIS being a funding source. In international practice, there are other sources of funding. According to the Financial Stability Institute' review (Baudino et al., 2019), in more than 40% of the fifty-three countries surveyed, bank resolution funds[2] distinctive from the DIS have been established in addition to the DIS. The objective of a bank resolution fund's activity is to resolve bank failures, i.e., their financial recovery. In this case, resources for financial assistance are provided by a bank resolution fund. Such bank resolution funds have been established in Australia, Norway, Poland, Finland, Germany and in some other countries. A similar practice has been in operation in the Russian Federation since 2017, when the Fund of Banking Sector Consolidation was established.

[2] Fund of Banking Sector Consolidation in Russia.

11.4 Financial Recovery Measures Applied by Governments and International Banking Authorities

If a very large bank fails, the DIS resources may turn out insufficient and that calls for the use of backup funding. In the international practice, backup funding arrangements involve public and private sources. In the former case, sources include government financial assistance, i.e., government loans, central bank loans and an access to private markets, for example, through issuing bonds. Let us consider government funding in more detail. Baudino et al. (2019) refer to these measures as "emergency funding» which is sourced from government loans or funding from the governments. In some cases, the failed bank may be temporarily brought into the state ownership. A significant number of countries mentioned in this review, both developed and developing, have access to the above-described mechanism of using public sources. Among them are such countries as Australia, the United States, the UK, Norway, Turkey, Poland, Uruguay, Colombia, Moldova, Indonesia, Mexico and Russia.

In the period of the post-crisis recovery, regionalization of financial regulation aimed at providing a response to the unresolved problem of safeguarding national financial systems against financial risks is taking shape. The Eurozone countries demonstrated a highly illustrative experience having launched in November 2014, the unified supervisory mechanism based on the system of bank regulation and recovery institutions. In the European Union, there are special arrangements to help financially stressed banks. Some arrangements are described in the BRRD mentioned above. Baudino et al. (2018) argue that resolution tools in the BRRD are applied to systematically significant institutions, and less significant institutions recover by themselves. They use resolution tools available to their management within the framework of the national insolvency treatment or are liquidated after corresponding bankruptcy procedures.

The European Union now operates the European Stability Mechanism (hereafter referred to as ESM). This is a financial stabilization fund for the Eurozone countries. It was established in 2012 as a result of reforming the European Financial Stability Facility and the European Financial Stability Facility (ESFS). The ESM has a landing cap of 500 billion EUR credit limit, in paid-in shares EUR 80 billion worth and EUR 620 billion worth of callable shares. It can finance itself from the market and from member states (IMF, 2018).

Thus, 41 billion euros was allocated to the Spanish banking sector. In January and April 2017, 10 billion euros were provided to support liquidity to the Italian banks Veneto Banca and Banca Popolare di Vicenza, since the measures of recapitalization and the participation of a new investor had been unsuccessful (IMF, 2018). Member States are required to contribute to the ESM. The decision to allocate assistance under the ESM is based on a special evaluation procedure and stress tests. It is mandatory to draw up a bank recovery plan for the use of ESM funds and establish post-resolution monitoring.

Such a system which includes the bank recovery mechanisms may also be applicable in the Eurasian Economic Union (EAEU) (Shayakhmetova et al., 2021; Zvonar, 2017). Although currently Eurasian integration mainly has a nonfinancial sector involved, there is no doubt that the financial sphere along with banking regulation mechanisms, prudential oversight and financial recovery should also be integrated. There are already certain integration moves in this direction. By 2025, a supranational financial regulator is to be created using the experience of the European Banking Union. Nevertheless, though the institutional structure of banking supervision in Eurasian countries is mostly identical being the competence of the Central banks, there are considerable differences in economic aspects which may slow down the process of delegating authority to the supranational level and delay the creation of the unified Eurasian regulator of the financial market. The unification of financial recovery and rehabilitation procedures for banking institutions will be a must. The recent events proved that this process should be based on the unified principles of anti-crisis, stabilization model of regulation and methodological agreed-upon fundamentals. It will contribute to the enhancement of systemic stability in the EAEU financial sphere, to the formation of the banking union of the EAEU and the system of supranational banking regulation.

The setting up of the complex effective system of banking regulation in the EAEU is aimed at enhancing stress resistance and financial stability of national banking organizations within the EAEU, the earlier identification of systemic risks in the region, harmonization of competitive environment and improvement of cooperation between banks and national banking regulators.

11.5 Recovery Mechanism

In modern international practice, when making a decision about administrative bank resolution, special attention is paid to the fact of systemic importance, social and economic significance of a credit institution. In this case, critical functions of the bank are preserved, i.e., they do not disappear because of the intervention of a competent authority. The main goal of such a decision is to minimize the impact of the bank's insolvency on the financial system and the economy as a whole. In the case of less significant institution, the bank is closed, is put into liquidation, and does not preserve critical functions in the society, as noted by Baudino et al. (2018).

As mentioned earlier, in response to the global financial crisis, in 2014, the European Union adopted the BRRD Directive. The BRRD established a pan-European procedure about bank resolution, tools and powers and "normal" insolvency. It explains the notion of resolution and defines the conditions for its initiation. A resolution is a combination of special measures that should be used by the authorities for resolution of an insolvent bank in case of its significant importance, meaning that its financial problems can damage the stability of the banking sector.

In legal frameworks, significant financial institutions are called "systemically important credit institutions." Accordingly, an immediate decision is made on whether the bank will be subject to resolution or whether the national insolvency regime will be applied, i.e., liquidation. Normal insolvency regime remains within the competence of the national authorities. The resolution uses the tools and measures previously described. The choice of instruments depends on the degree of bank insolvency.

11.6 Conclusion

The analysis of international practices of recovering financially troubled banks reveals that nowadays, the tools used for this purpose are quite distinctive. The banks able to resume their activities without regulators' intervention may use the following instruments: bail-in, restructuring of assets and liabilities, adjusting their strategy and separating assets, along with attracting new investors. The instruments chosen for the recovery of a particular bank are included in the plan of its financial recovery. Recently in the European Union, the bail-in mechanism has been developed. This mechanism also widely applies in the resolution procedure. Systemically, socially and economically important banks can rely on the support by the banking supervisor, and in certain cases, by the government. Supervisory authorities may make use of the following instruments: capital support, liquidity assistance, funding P&A transactions and financing a bridge bank transaction. To provide financial assistance through these instruments, the banking regulator resorts to various sources. In most countries, the main source is the Deposit Insurance Fund. In some countries, a bank resolution fund has been established for this purpose. In exceptional cases, backup funding from the central bank and/or the government is provided. In the European Banking Union, there exists the interesting experience of combining national and supranational mechanisms of banking supervision and bank assistance to financially stressed banks. The similar mechanisms of financial recovery are now being created in the EAEU.

References

Andryushin, S. A., & Kuznetsova, V. V. (2017). *Banks' rehabilitation: International experience and the Russian practice*. Economic strategies (Vol. 7). http://www.inesnet.ru/article/sanaciya-bankov-mezhdunarodnyj-opyt-i-rossijskaya-praktika/

Basel Committee on Banking Supervision. (2011). *Resolution policies and frameworks—Progress so far*. https://www.bis.org/publ/bcbs200.pdf

Baudino, P., Defina, R., Fernández Real, J. M., Hajra, K., & Walters, R. (2019). *Bank failure management—The role of deposit insurance*. Bank for International Settlements. Financial Stability Institute. FSI Insights, No17. www.bis.org/fsi/publ/insights17.pdf

Baudino, P., Gagliano, A., Rulli, E., & Walters, R. (2018). *How to manage failures of non-systemic banks? A review of country practices*. Bank for International Settlements. Financial Stability Institute. FSI Insights, No10. www.bis.org/fsi/publ/insights10.pdf

Delloitte. (2020). *NPL securitisations and related governmental guarantee schemes in Europe*. https://www2.deloitte.com/content/dam/Deloitte/uk/Documents/corporate-finance/deloitte-uk-npl-securitisation-report.pdf

Federal Deposit Insurance Corporation. (2017, November). *Crisis and response. An FDIC history, 2008–2013*. www.fdic.gov/bank/historical/crisis/crisis-complete.pdf

Financial Services Authority. (2011). *Recovery and resolution plans* (Consultation Paper 11/16). https://www.fca.org.uk/publication/consultation/cp11_16.pdf

Financial Stability Board. (2013). *Recovery and resolution planning for systematically important financial institutions: Guidance on identification of critical function and critical shared services.* https://www.fsb.org/wp-content/uploads/r_130716a.pdf

Havemann, R. (2019). Can creditor bail-in trigger contagion? The experience of an emerging market. *Review of Finance*, 1155–1180. https://doi.org/10.1093/rof/rfy023. https://watermark.silverchair.com/

International Monetary Fund. (2018). *Euro area policies: Financial sector assessment program. Technical note-bank resolution and crisis management.* https://www.imf.org/en/Publications/CR/Issues/2018/07/19/Euro-Area-Policies-Financial-Sector-Assessment-Program-Technical-Note-Bank-Resolution-and-46106

Kornilova, E. V. (2017). The bail-in tool and prospects for its application in Russia. *Finance and Credits, 23*(5). http://213.226.126.9/fc/2017/fc05/fc0517-259.pdf

Official Journal of the European Union. (2014, May). *Directive 2014/59/EU establishing a framework for the recovery and resolution of credit institutions and investment firms (BRRD).* europa.eu

Restoy, F. (2018, March 23). *Bail-in in the new bank resolution framework: Is there an issue with the middle class?* Bank for International Settlements. IADI-ERC International Conference: "Resolution and deposit guarantee schemes in Europe: Incomplete processes and uncertain outcomes", Naples, Italy. https://www.bis.org/speeches/sp180323.pdf

Shayakhmetova, K. O., Usipbekov, A. A., Sarygulova, R. K., & Shynybaev, A. A. (2021). *The possibilities of integrating the banking sector into EAEU*. Bulletin of the Kirgiz National University named after Zhusup Balagazin. No 4(108). https://www.elibrary.ru/item.asp?id=48066572

Svoronos, J.-P. (2018). *Early intervention regimes for weak banks.* Bank for International Settlements. Financial Stability Institute. FSI Insights, No 6. www.bis.org/fsi/publ/insights6.pdf

Zvonar, V. K. (2017). Establishment of a signal regulator for the purpose of regulation of banking activities in the Eurasian Economic Union. *Economics: Yesterday, Today, Tomorrow, 7*(7A). https://www.elibrary.ru/item.asp?id=32337583

CHAPTER 12

Digital Systemic Financial Risks in the Russian Banking Sector

Sergey Dubinin

12.1 Introduction

Both banks and non-bank financial institutions aim to secure sustainability of their activities in serving retail and corporate clients. Commercial banks are targeting to change their business models to meet the challenges. The major Russian banks have implemented a customer-oriented business model. In 2022, the special military operation in Ukraine created a new hard situation for the Russian economy as a whole and for the financial sector in particular. The pressure arisen from the economic sanctions is significantly concentrated on the banking sector and IT sector. Thus, the financial sanctions are playing an important role among the measures designed to undermine the Russian economy. "The leading sanctions are financial. On the top of the list are the effective freezing of assets held abroad by the Bank of Russia and selected Russian commercial banks, and the expulsion of key Russian financial intermediaries from the SWIFT

S. Dubinin (✉)
Head of Finance and Credit Department, Faculty of Economics, Lomonosov Moscow State University, Moscow, Russia
e-mail: fincred@econ.msu.ru

A. Karminsky and M. Stolbov (eds.), *Systemic Financial Risk*,
https://doi.org/10.1007/978-3-031-54809-3_12

messaging system" (Berner et al., 2022). The strategic scope of the financial sanctions aims at provoking systemic risks and eventually a full-fledged crisis on all financial markets.

In view of the geopolitical tension, the vague macroeconomic prospects and the economic climate deteriorations have become the main challenge. Uncertainty and a lack of mutual trust among market participants appeared as a strong disruptive factor for economic growth. The volume of direct investment dropped following the shrinkage in demand. The threat of corporate sector insolvency, as a result of supply chain fractures and the ban on international money payments, created credit and market risks for banking business in the medium-term perspective. The systemic financial risks are transforming into a significant danger.

> Systemic risk refers to the risk or probability or breakdowns in an entire system, as opposed to breakdowns in individual parts or components, and is evidence by co-movements (correlation) among most or all the parts. Thus, systemic risk in banking is evidenced by high correlation and clustering of bank failures in a single country, in a number of countries, or throughout the world. Systemic risk also may occur in other parts of the financial sector…Systemic risk may be domestic or transnational. (Kaufman & Scott, 2003)

12.2 Financial Sector Digital Transformation

In accordance with the current financial market development, risk function is challenged by various factors (Boehm et al., 2021):

- Ever-changing monetary policies: countries often adjust their monetary policies, and the banking risk function should adapt to these policy changes.
- Volatility in regulatory demands: the laws that govern the operations of banks are changing very rapidly.
- Retreating from globalization: countries are now scaling back from globalization to major recessions that have hit the world economy. The volatile stock market adds to the uncertainty of the global economy. Maintaining a static risk function in this highly volatile environment is a great challenge.

- Introduction of fintechs: fintech companies combine finance and technology to cater to changing customer needs. The introduction of technology into finance has introduced a new set of challenges for banks: an increase in transaction volume, third-party APIs, and cyberattacks.

Financial market institutions stand behind a large fraction of demand for information services in today's economy. Those also provide financial services to the widest range of customers, which by their form and technological nature, are information services. In this specialized sector, telecommunications powered by information technologies (IT) characterized by continuous modification have led to the development of numerous financial and non-financial risks lying at the crossroads between financial institutions, including banks, and their customers.

The modern global financial and monetary system, including banking and non-bank institutions in both developed and emerging markets, has acquired new quality and structure resulting from two innovative trends.

On the one hand, financial information technology (Fintech) has created a network for transmitting data on financial transactions. These information flows have scaled up unprecedentedly. The general evolution trend of modern Fintech is the transition from payment and settlement relations to digital lending with the application of customer data processing methods and further to customer-oriented business models in the field of digital finance. On the other hand, the offer of new financial instruments has become a response to the customers' growing demand for the services of relevant institutions and markets. One type of innovation—the technological one, stemming from the technological revolution—is to lose its economic significance without the other one, i.e., financial innovation.

The IMF experts stated: "*As digital transformation is a business decision, the goal is to boost an individual bank's competitiveness, strength, and ultimately its long-term profitability. The size of the bank, its profit margins, capital positions and business models could all influence the success and long-term benefits of digital transformation. For example, the nature of new technologies and the necessary large initial investment tend to favor large banks with stronger balance sheets rather than smaller banks with weaker balance sheets. In addition, although a bank's profitability could also be an important consideration in its decision on digital transformation, the impact could be uncertain. That is, a highly profitable bank could be in a better position in financing investment in digital technology, but it also may feel less pressure to digitalize as a means to boost its future profitability*" (IMF Working Paper, 2021).

One can discern the following stages of digitalization in the international monetary and financial system:

- 1980–1990. Creation of business Internet. Electronic communication and international transactions system (Society of World-wide Interbank Financial Telecommunications—SWIFT). The first Fintech—financial technologies.
- 1991–2000. "The Big Bang": reorganization of the London Stock Exchange; the market transition to remote access. Telebanking: conclusion of remote financial transactions.
- 2001–2006. Development of the derivative market. Shadow banking in the world financial markets based on Telebanking: conclusion of remote financial transactions.
- 2007–2009. Financial crisis and the Great Recession.
- 2010–2021. Market competition of financial conglomerates. Banking groups and bank holdings. Fintech based on processing Big data. Entry of e-commerce and information technology companies (Big Tech and eCommerce companies) into the financial sector.
- From 2020 to date. Accelerated customization of financial services—customer-oriented service. Transition to marketplaces powered by information platforms. Creation of Ecosystems as a financial business model.

The banking business model is currently using Fintech to a greater extent. The main areas of Fintech today are quite diverse. They complement each other:

- Electronic communications and settlement systems (*interbank financial telecommunications*);
- Online investment advice (*online consulting*);
- Online issue of shares in investment funds, investment management (*passive and active investing*);
- Personal data processing, storage, and protection (*personal data storage and cyber security*);
- Big data systems and the use of information (*Big data operations*);

- Use of open banking and API (*open banking and Application Programming Interface—API*);
- Cloud-based information technology and banking (*iCloud technologies banking*);
- Processing data on customer lending to assess the customer creditworthiness (*customer credits scoring*);
- *Artificial intelligence and machine learning;*
- Robot trading in securities *(Robot-trading);*
- Comprehensive customer service. C*ustomer-oriented business-model;*
- IT ecosystems (*Cyber-ecosystems*).

The official report by the Bank of Russia provides the following data:

- In 2020, Russia ranked 8th in terms of the number of Internet users and 6th in terms of mobile devices penetration into the consumer's daily life. Thus, as of December 2020, 80.9% of Russian consumers have access to the Internet (64.7% worldwide), whereas the smartphone penetration level in Russia is 67.8% as of September 2020 (53.3% worldwide).
- In 2019, Russia ranked 3rd in terms of Fintech penetration; since 2017, this index has almost doubled to amount 82% (64% worldwide). At the same time, payments are the most widespread application for Fintech solutions. Russia ranks 1st in the world in terms of awareness of Fintech solutions in the field of payments.
- Russia is one of the most advanced markets worldwide in terms of providing digital services: thus, according to 2020 data, 87% of bank clients in Russia used digital channels; 30% of Russians planned to reduce the number of visits to bank offices or even refuse to visit them after the end of the COVID-19 pandemic (12% worldwide).
- In 2020, Russia ranked 4th in terms of transition to cashless payments during the pandemic.

According to the Bank of Russia report that presents the results of a survey among financial market stakeholders, the most promising technologies used in the course of service digitalization in 2021 were mobile technologies (73% of respondents), open API (64%), artificial intelligence and machine learning (64%), cloud computing (58%), and chatbots (54%) (Bank of Russia, 2021b).

The Russian banking sector has launched a variety of innovative financial instruments and information technologies (Fintech). The digital ecosystem formed the modern customer-oriented business model. The leading roles on this arena are played by 30 major banks, including 13 systemically important credit institutions. They control more than 80% of total assets in the banking system. These banks are forming their digital ecosystem, based on their own information platforms. Today, the banks act as the core of financial conglomerates. They coordinate the operations of investment and pension funds, consulting and insurance companies, which are included in the banking groups and holdings.

Similar observations are confirmed by other digital banking experts. Deloitte, a consulting and auditing company, has prepared the fourth edition of its international review of the commercial banks digitalization. According to the company's representatives and analysts, more than 180 consultants and analysts from Deloitte offices around the world acted as "mystery shoppers" to compare over 1,000 functional features and technical specifications of 318 banks in 39 countries (Russia is the world's top 10 in terms of digital banking. The banks' digital maturity level, 2020).

The main results and conclusions are stated as follows: "*After classifying banks in terms of their digitalization level, compliance with customer requests, and positive customer experience, Deloitte experts identified 4 groups of banks: Latecomers, Adopters, Smart Followers, and Champions. Circa 10% of banks fell into the 'Champions' category. First and utmost, these are high-tech banks offering their customers a wide range of services and a positive customer experience. These are some kind of industry's engines whose portfolio includes the best market practices and the best user solutions. Three Russian banks take their place among the world-level 'Champions.' Their key advantages (among many other service options) are the following features: opening a debit card online; tracking the percentage of completing the customer questionnaire and pop-up error messages that indicate problems with filling in an online form… Russia was put on the list of top ten leading countries in global digital banking, along with Japan, Singapore, Norway, Spain, Belgium, Turkey, Poland, Saudi Arabia, and Qatar.*"

«Classical» Banking Risks in the Digital Age

Under modern conditions, many authors consider cost management as a way to increase bank competitiveness. In turn, it serves to ensure both the financial stability of individual credit institutions (banking risk management) and the banking sector stability in general (systemic risk management) (Gospodarchuk & Amosova, 2020). From the macroprudential regulation point of view, digital risks should be compared with the traditional list of banking risks: liquidity risk; credit risk; interest rate risk; market risk; foreign exchange risk; operational risk. The last one includes the main part of digital risks. The operational risk has become the most catchall digital business model challenge. Before the beginning of digitalization process, the banking sector development tended to depend mainly on staff and customers behavior more than on IT or financial market innovations. However, the situation has changed dramatically.

> An increase in the number of operational risk sources is due to the use of new technologies, in particular artificial intelligence and machine learning, the distributed ledger technology, and a greater number and variety of services provided online. Ecosystems, including bank-based ones, can be a significant source of operational risk, due to the need for coordination between stakeholders, the lack of sufficient control with banks over the actions of their partners, and sophisticated architecture of information technology and business processes. (Bank of Russia, 2021b)

Digital security experts explain how operational risk at a banking institution can snowball from a single mistake by an individual employee into a severe systemic problem for the bank as a whole. American experts made a natural conclusion: "*...with every opportunity digital technology has provided to banks, customer and counterparties, it has also transformed existing risk and often introduced new risk*" (RSA Security). They listed the following features as the most common ones for digital risks in the banking business (RSA Security):

- Dynamically emerging digital risk as an unexpected outcome of innovation.
- Greater inherent risk impact: errors and fraud may extend to every transaction in the process.
- Increased velocity of risk: risk can emerge so quickly that risk control turns no longer effective.
- Broad, more complex sources of threat: primarily the threat of external cyberattack.

- Higher-impact business interruptions: the length and cost of the interruption are highly dependent upon how well the bank prepares for business interruption scenarios.
- Consumer privacy: banks bear the legal responsibility for clients' information security.
- Unknown, emerging, and transformed regulations: a bank which is the first to launch an innovation could face a strict regulation or an absence of any regulation, which represents a substantial business risk.
- Third-party risk: banks can enter into outsourcing arrangements, but cannot outsource their digital risk.

In accordance with Basel II&III agreements standards, the predominant potential losses, linked with the operational/ digital risks, are the result of internal factors—mainly staff behavior. But the external factors are important as well, e.g., a criminal fraud attack.

1. Criminal Cyberattack risks.
    - Personal data loss risk.
    - Business deals information abuse risk.
    - Money laundering risk.
    - Fake libelous news risk.
2. The business model choice and enforcement risk.
    - Information platform ecosystem low efficiency.
    - Banking groups business-lines lack of coordination.
    - Business-lines financial losses damage.
    - Low attractiveness for customers.
    - Big data false interpretation.
3. Hard and soft technological risks for business.
    - Low customer-orientation risk.
    - Unfriendly interface risk.
    - Retail customers coring misinterpretation risk.
    - Corporate customer scoring misinterpretation risk.
    - Big data false interpretation.
    - Artificial Intelligence on the base of Machine Learning wrong decision-making.

Many experts on digital risk management emphasize their connection, primarily, with technological innovations.

> There are several non-financial banking risks. Technology risk is one of them. It includes cybersecurity risks, the risk of non-compliance with data protection regulations, and the risk of legacy systems. While banks develop thorough plans for dealing with financial risks, they may not be aware of technological risks. (Boehm et al., 2021)

However, it is not only IT that is prone to this issue. "*Several banking risks may arise due to a lack of data governance (/reference-center/what-is-data-governance) plans. Financial organizations often have data in disconnected silos and teams making decisions based on partial data…The future risk functions should leverage advancements in technology like big data, …artificial intelligence, and improved analytics. These technologies allow risk functions to make better decisions. They also help create a data infrastructure that enables enterprises to spend more time analyzing their data rather than managing it*" (Boehm et al., 2021).

S. Partha is analyzing how Fintech has created new sources of risks (S. Partha):

1. Core data vs distributed data systems. New technological innovations have experimented with existing core banking solutions, which results in data being stored in external nodes exposed to exploitation.
2. Paper data vis-à-vis digital data. AI, machine learning compromise exposes digitally validated and stored data which can be interpreted by information system.
3. High fraud exposure. The digitization increases the risk of fraud and account takeovers leaving customer's helpless.
4. Paper data vis-à-vis digital data. AI, machine learning compromise exposes digitally validated and stored data which can be interpreted by information system.
5. Regulatory Sanctions. Fintech is very luring with the innovation. Regulators can apply sanctions or disallow the business case and end bypassing attempts.
6. Uncontrolled data sharing. Fintech is exposed to 3rd party applications and shared by banks with broken social and privacy data security.

7. Algo manipulation as a threat to insider fraud. Algo Trading is the buzzword for the last 4–5 years. How Fintech has created new sources of risks.
8. Biometric, retina, and fiscal scan expose new-age risk exposures. These bio-scan and bio-sensitive voice pattern validation and user verification may lead to account takeover risks.
9. Agile systems are not always secure (open applications). Banks are using data to analyze customers' behavior and offer them targeted suggestions, anticipating their needs. This exposes nodes to cyber threat.
10. High Speed of execution. "Fintech is all about speed."
11. Core data vs distributed data systems. New technological innovations have experimented with existing core banking solutions, which results in data being stored in external nodes exposed to exploitation.
12. Paper data vis-à-vis digital data. AI, machine learning compromise exposes digitally validated and stored data which can be interpreted by information system.
13. High fraud exposure. The digitization increases the risk of fraud and account takeovers leaving customers helpless.
14. Paper data vis-à-vis digital data. AI, machine learning compromise exposes digitally validated and stored data which can be interpreted by information system.
15. High fraud exposure. The digitization increases the risk of fraud and account takeovers leaving customers helpless.
16. Regulatory Sanctions. Fintech is very luring with the innovation. Regulators can apply sanctions or disallow the business case and end bypassing attempts.
17. Cyber threat. Fintech platform firms in partnership with banks are vulnerable for cyberattack.
18. Uncontrolled data sharing. Fintech is exposed to 3rd party applications and shared by banks with broken social and privacy data security.
19. Algo manipulation as a threat to insider fraud. Algo Trading is the buzzword for the last 4–5 years.

F.Z. Aguayo and B. Slusarczyk give the following description of systemic banking risk management:

Diversification of bank risks is one of the main methods for the sustainable development of banks in the global economy...

Electronic banking services include:

1. Account statements for a customer;
2. Information on banking products (deposits, loans, securities);
3. Applications for opening deposits and obtaining loans and bank cards;
4. Internal transfers to bank accounts;
5. Transfer to accounts in other banks;
6. Currency conversion...

The implementation of Basel II (that is, recommendations for managing operational risk) becomes a key factor that raises bank's reliability rating and arouses investor confidence and interest. Therefore, the study used optimized approach to measurement (AMA) under Basel II, which allowed the authors to simulate the operational risk of the study object (Santander Bank). The model includes indicators such as:

- Threat of defects and failures;
- Threat of loss of data integrity and unauthorized access to customer data;
- Threat of violation of technical system in an information space;
- Threat of cyberattacks;
- Level of annual defects;
- Current annual loss from defects;
- Current annual loss of data integrity and unauthorized access to customer data...

Operational risk management is based on identifying sources operational risk, identifying operational risks, assessing operational risks, monitoring operational risks, and controlling and minimizing operational risks. The research design and its procedures were built on these elements. (Aguayo & Slusarczyk, 2020)

12.3 Systemic Risk Control

The practice of the financial sanctions has brought about so-called Geo-Economic Fragmentation (GEF) in the international monetary system. The Russian cross-border banking model is reliant on short-term wholesale funding. Under the financial sanctions, this model faced the stalemate of market regionalization. "...Under GEF, crises may be more severe. Given lower international risk-sharing, higher financing costs, reduced scope for policy coordination across countries, and more fragmented global liquidity backstop …the severity crises may be greater unless regional or domestic risk mitigation policies play a larger role" (IMF, 2023).

The task to elaborate the anti-crisis financial policy has become pressing for the Russian financial authorities. The Bank of Russia's systemic risk control strategy is based on the following pillars:

1. The sustainable and unsustainable banks decoupling and banking sector "cleaning."
2. Stress-testing scenarios analysis. Top-down and bottom up stress-tests with crisis full down estimate for the banking sector.
3. The Basel I, II, III agreements principles enforcement. Risk and capital management. Corporate governance and compliance.

The financial regulation state authorities are gradually migrating to the use of information technology for prudential supervision and regulation of financial institutions' activities.

SupTech (Supervisory Technology) means technologies used by regulators to improve the efficiency of control and supervision over the activities of financial market stakeholders.

RegTech (Regulatory Technology) means technologies used by financial institutions to improve efficiency in complying with the regulator's requirements.

Professor Xavier Vives (IESE Business School) prepared an analytical review for the OECD on the impact of digitalization on increased competition in the financial markets for credit, securities, and cash transactions. In this report, he concludes that although the business partnership and interaction of traditional banks with BigTech firms and FinTech start-ups is a promising area for their strategic development, the new types of systemic risk in the financial sector are created by the impact of digital failures and disturbances.

> With regard to potential impacts on systemic risk, there are several sources of concern. First, there is the possibility of development of a parallel payment system not adequately monitored by central banks, which could take place if BigTech firms deposit customer funds directly with banks, as is the case in China. Second, a proportion of financial institutions may rely on a BigTech firm (or a few of them) that provides third-party services

(e.g. data storage, transmission, or analytics), some of them in the cloud. In this case, a cyberattack or operational failure may pose a systemic risk. Third, the very existence of large online money market funds, such as Yu'ebao in China, which are not in principle insured, leaves them vulnerable to runs (which are possible, as we learned in the United States during the 2007–2008 financial crisis). On the bright side, FinTech start-ups may manage to operate with less leverage than traditional banks... Fourth, if BigTech enters the core of banking, than systemic concerns will increase, since trouble in the nonbank business of the firm may contaminate the bank and would be very likely to be systemic. (OECD, 2020)

According to the Bank of Russia experts, the main risks inherent to the development of the platform economy should be categorized in the following way (Bank of Russia, 2021a):

- risks for individual ecosystem customers;
- risks for individual not being ecosystem customers;
- risks for providers being ecosystem participants producing services or goods;
- risks for services or goods providers not included into ecosystem;
- risks for economy as a whole;
- risks related to monopoly over technological decisions.

In the Annual Report by the Bank of Russia for 2020, it is stated that "*...In the context of ecosystem development, there is a risk of market monopolization as the growing popularity of individual participants may lead to an excessive strengthening of their competitive position even in new business areas...Taking into account the possible growth of risks, the Bank of Russia is working on ecosystem regulation to maintain a balance between the development of financial innovations, the development of domestic ecosystems in the context of global competition, and the limitation of risks for bank customers and financial system as a whole*" (Bank of Russia Annual Report for 2020).

In its report on the issues of digitalization, the Bank of Russia stated that "*For financial market stakeholders, the main challenge of digital transformation is associated with high time and financial costs that not all institutions can afford (71% of respondents), system integration issues (66%), and obsolete engineering infrastructure that needs to be updated (62%).*

...According to a Financial Stability Board survey of 41 regulators from 25 countries [conducted in 2020], 30 regulators already have an approved

SupTech strategy or are in the process of developing one. In addition, about a third of the surveyed regulators actively support the development of RegTech solutions to implement the use of digital technology by supervised institutions, primarily, in the field of compliance with the requirements on countermeasures to combat legalization (laundering) of illegally obtained proceeds and financing of terrorism and for regulatory reporting (Bank of Russia, 2021b).

According to KPMG and McKinsey experts' global banking fraud surveys, "*banks readily recognize the importance of digitizing risk… 69% of our survey respondents report that senior management has paid a moderate level of attention to risk digitization efforts, and 11% see it as a high priority. According to the analysis, 22% of banks around the world have invested more than 25% of their annual budget to digitize risk management 34% of respondents specify regulatory burdens as a key challenge. In combination, several of these challenges can defeat the main thrust of digital risk: the development and adoption of new technologies. Other functions can adopt cutting-edge technologies, develop beta versions of new offerings, or test and refine minimum viable products in production.* [These regulation methods taken in the aggregate can weather the digital risk storm—this is how the development and adaptation/mastering of the new technology occurs. For other functions, adoption of cutting-edge technology, emerging of beta versions of new offers, or testing and refining the existing economically viable products may be needed.] *But this might not be feasible for all risk activities, since one misstep could lead to potentially serious disruptions in core risk activities or even affect a bank's stability… 56% of respondents state that regulations are a main challenge when adopting new technologies*" (Institute of International Finance, 2017). The Future of Risk Management in KPMG Report (2020). The Bank of Russia report presents the results of a survey on the development of financial technologies, conducted in October–November 2020 among market stakeholders by the Fintech Association together with the Accenture consulting company. It consisted of a series of 30 interviews with financial sector experts and leaders, including CEOs of major market players, industry associations, and development institutions. At the same time, they conducted an open survey among representatives of the Fintech market in the format of an online questionnaire involving 79 institutions from different market segments. The survey identified 12 priority areas for the development of financial technologies in Russia (Bank of Russia, 2021b):

1. Safe financial market: creating and developing effective mechanisms and tools to counter cyber threats and fraud in the financial market; the development of quantum cryptography technologies;
2. Development of data access mechanisms: developing common data access mechanisms; creating new opportunities to use data to maintain competition in the market and to promote the emergence of new business models;
3. Financial literacy in the digital world: developing joint programs and common mechanisms to enhance digital, financial literacy, and confidence in the financial market;
4. End-to-end digitalization of the financial market: providing a full range of financial services and operations in digital form;
5. Payment environment development: developing convenient, transparent, fast, and secure digital payment services based on an efficient and reliable payment infrastructure;
6. Environment for developing Fintech innovations: creating conditions to support the innovation development by new and current stakeholders from idea to piloting, effective interaction between market players, and development of talents and competencies;
7. Freedom of choice for consumers: creating opportunities and mechanisms for the free choice of financial products or services by consumers and easy switching between financial service providers;
8. Invisible finance: easy and seamless integration of financial products and services into non-financial services (the "financial services as a service" model);
9. Cloud services: the use of high-tech commercial B2B solutions and services by financial players, including secure public cloud services for financial institutions;
10. Development of blockchain technologies: creating shared infrastructure for distributed ledger technologies as a tool for developing new industry solutions for the financial and non-financial markets;
11. Competition development and regulation of ecosystems: introducing cross-industry regulation, standards, and norms with due consideration of the development of digital platforms and the evolution of closed ecosystems;
12. New generation financial services based on new technologies: creating conditions and incentives for the application of new technologies (including artificial intelligence and machine learning, Internet of Things, etc.) to digitalize interaction with the client, to

develop new high-tech services, algorithmic smart products, and ethical tools for financial management.

12.4 Conclusion

Transformation of the banking business model affected both financial services for corporate and retail clients. Fintech (financial technologies) has become a general term to describe such innovative solutions. The development of information financial technologies (Fintech) has expanded swiftly. Fintech has opened a door to a dramatic expansion of the customers' choice, both in passive and active operations.

In terms of macroeconomic parameters, digitalization has a significant effect on systemic risks in the banking sector as a whole. Based on assessing the possibility of credit market contagion, the increased likelihood of a rapid spread of financial distress can be noted.

From the economic point of view, there appeared new thrusts of the digital systemic financial risks:

1. Oligopolistic structure of the IT sector. Banking platforms business commissions and tariffs agreements.
2. Big Tech approach to use the personal client information databases for rent-oriented business profitability on marketplaces and platforms.
3. The threat of technological standards divergence. Political and economic rivalry between the United States and China.
4. "Cyberwars" and mutual sanctions in the US-China rivalry.
5. De-globalization and protectionism in the international financial markets. National government regulation pressure on digitalization process.
6. Social and national inequality worldwide.
7. Inadequacy of international agreements for financial payments and regulation of business deals.

The Fintech approach essentially rests on financial services digitalization. An increase in the banking competition has stimulated the ecosystems development for strengthening the competitiveness. The banks have launched the Fintech (financial technologies) to reduce the costs and increase the number of customers with the target to improve the business margin. However, any innovation development thrusts new risks for market participants. In view of GEF and the geopolitical tensions, the "slippery slope" could emerge from the opposing bloc's appearance. The IMF head Kristalina Georgieva stressed in her speech in the year 2023 discussion in Davos, that "the risk is the policy intervention adopted in the name of economic or national security could have unintended consequences or they could be used deliberately for economic gains at the expense of others...Any progress we can make in rebuilding trust and boosting international cooperation will be critical" (Blog, 2023). Under GEF, the digitalization of financial sector elevates the relevance of systemic risk. Without a comprehensive regulatory coordination, financial risk management is likely to weaken. Thus, the risk of financial crises could become inevitable.

References

Aguayo, F. Z., & Slusarczyk, B. Risk of banking' digitalization: The practice of diversification and sustainable development goals. Sustainability 2020, 12, 4040. https://doi.org/10.3390/su12104040, p. 2–3. https://www.mdpi.com/2071-1050/12/10/4040. Date of access: 14 January 2022.

Bank of Russia. *Bank of Russia annual report for 2020* (p. 93). https://cbr.ru/Collection/Collection/File/39294/ar_2020.pdf. Date of access: 14 January 2022.

Bank of Russia. (2021a, April). *Ecosystems: Regulatory approaches. consultive report* (p. 20). Moscow. https://www.cbr.ru/Content/Document/File/19962/Consultation_Paper_eng_0204021.pdf. Date of access: 14 January 2022.

Bank of Russia. (2021b). *Draft of the main digitalization areas of the financial market in 2022–2024*. Moscow. https://www.cbr.ru/Content/Document/File/131360/oncfr_2022-2024.pdf. Date of access: 10 January 2022.

Berner, A. R., Cecchetti, S., & Schoenholtz, K. (2022, March 21). Russian sanctions: Some questions and answers. *VoxEU* [online]. https://voxeu.org/article/russian-sanctions-some-questions-and-answers. Date of access: 27 May 2022.

Boehm, J., Shelly Brown, J., Sabbagh, L., & Thomas, K. (2021, June 30). *Lessons from banking to improve risk and compliance and speed up digital transformation* (p. 8). McKinsey & Company. https://www.mckinsey.com/business-functions/mckinsey-digital/our-insights/lessons-from-banking-to-improve-risk-and-compliance-and-speed-up-digital-transformations. Date of access: 6 January 2022.

Gospodarchuk, G., & Amosova, N. (2020). Geo-financial stability of the global banking system. *Banks and Bank Systems, 15*(4), 164–178. https://www.researchgate.net/publication/347848054_Geo-financial_stability_of_the_global_banking_system. Date of access: 15 December 2021.

IMF. (2023, January). *Geo-economic fragmentation and the future of multilateralism*. SDN/2023/001. https://www.imf.org/issues. Date of access: 5 February 2023.

IMF Blog. (2023, January 16). *Confronting fragmentation. Where it matters most: Trade, debt, and climate action*. Kristalina Georgieva. https://www.imf.org.blog. Date of access 6 February 2023.

IMF Working Paper. (2021, February). European Department. Stay competitive in the digital age: The future of banks. Prepared by Estelle Xue Liu. Authorized for distribution by Alfredo Cuevas. Issue 046, p. 18. https://www.imf.org/-/media/Files/Publications/WP/2021/English/wpiea2021046-print-pdf.ashx. Date of access: 14 January 2022.

Institute of International Finance. (2017, October). *The future of risk management in the digital era*. McKinsey&Company Report. https://www.mckinsey.com/~/media/McKinsey/Business%20Functions/Risk/Our%20Insights/The%20future%20of%20risk%20management%20in%20the%20digital%20era/Future-of-risk-management-in-the-digital-era-IIF-and-McKinsey.ashx. Date of access: 14 January 2022.

Kaufman, G., & Scott, K. (2003, Winter). What is systemic risk, and do bank regulators retard or contribute to it? *The Independent Review*, v. VII, #3. ISSN 1086-1653, pp. 371–372. http://www.independent.org/pdf/tir/tir_07_3_scott.pdf. Date of access: 17 August 2022.

KPMG Report. (2020). Global banking fraud survey (pp. 22; 25). KPMG: Amstelveen, The Netherlands. https://assets.kpmg/content/dam/kpmg/xx/pdf/2019/05/global-banking-fraud-survey.pdf. Date of access: 6 January 2022.

OECD. (2020). *Digital disruption in banking and its impact on competition* (p. 35). http://www.oecd.org/daf/competition/digital-disruption-in-financial-markets.htm. Date of access: 2 January 2022.

Partha, S. *10 Hidden risks of digital finance services*. LinkedIn. https://www.linkedin.com/pulse/10-hidden-risks-digital-financial-services-fintech-partha-sinha. Date of access: 14 January 2022.

RSA Security. White Paper. Digital risk management in banking, p. 3. https://www.rsa.com/content/dam/en/white-paper/digital-risk-management-in-banking.pdf. Date of access: 4 January 2022.

Russia is the world's top 10 in terms of digital banking. The banks' digital maturity level. (2020). *Deloitte*. https://www2.deloitte.com/ru/ru/pages/research-center/articles/digital-banking-maturity-2020.html. Date of access: 11 January 2022.

Conclusion

Systemic financial risk is a crucial notion from the perspective of maintaining financial stability, which has turned into a genuine buzzword since the GFC. The collective monograph assesses a number of conventional and burgeoning issues related to measuring systemic risk, identifying its new forms and elaborating policies to curb it. To accomplish these research goals, the monograph is split into three complementary parts.

The chapters constituting Part 1 tackle the research questions which exert an important impact on the buildup of systemic risk, whereas in most studies, such impact is overlooked. Namely, there are chapters providing insights about the linkage between household income dynamics and the fragility of the Russian banking sector, corporate ESG performance and companies' resilience toward financial shocks, asymmetric spillovers among the BRICS stock markets. Also, this part encompasses the chapters proposing new approaches to measuring financial development as well as reviewing the developments in the international market for green finance. The latter chapters promote the idea that an unbalanced financial deepening and climate challenges are hazardous for financial stability, thereby exacerbating systemic risk.

The chapters from Part 2 are largely centered on the elaboration and practical implementation of various quantitative techniques in the realm of financial stability. These allow to create a new theoretical framework to assess catastrophic (extreme) risks, to quantify risks in the Russian

A. Karminsky and M. Stolbov (eds.), *Systemic Financial Risk*,
https://doi.org/10.1007/978-3-031-54809-3

banking sector and to measure the probability of default of European airlines during the COVID-19 pandemic.

Part 3 is devoted to the regulatory aspects of systemic risk. It contains the chapters reviewing the evolution of macroprudential policies worldwide, new approaches to the post-crisis bank resolution as well as the impact of financial sector digitalization on systemic risk in Russia.

Although the literature on systemic risk is no longer scarce, our monograph possesses the following distinctive features. First, it offers a more detailed analysis of systemic risk and risk management peculiarities in emerging market economies, with an emphasis on the BRICS. Second, our monograph goes beyond the conventional sources of systemic risk, also investigating its unconventional dimensions which often lie outside the perimeter of the financial sector and its regulation, while heavily influencing them, e.g. financial resilience/fragility of systemic non-financial industries. Third, the book examines the role of new socioeconomic trends which have had a close interaction with systemic risk, risk management and financial regulation, but have remained largely under-explored in the extant literature, e.g. ESG and digital transformation.

Overall, these distinctive features of the book would make it an important contribution, enriching the ongoing debate on financial risks and risk management in emerging market economies.

Index

A. Karminsky and M. Stolbov (eds.), *Systemic Financial Risk*,
https://doi.org/10.1007/978-3-031-54809-3

GPSR Compliance
The European Union's (EU) General Product Safety Regulation (GPSR) is a set of rules that requires consumer products to be safe and our obligations to ensure this.

If you have any concerns about our products, you can contact us on

ProductSafety@springernature.com

In case Publisher is established outside the EU, the EU authorized representative is:

Springer Nature Customer Service Center GmbH
Europaplatz 3
69115 Heidelberg, Germany

www.ingramcontent.com/pod-product-compliance
Ingram Content Group UK Ltd.
Pitfield, Milton Keynes, MK11 3LW, UK
UKHW022221051026
15624UKWH00002B/271
9783031548086